OECD Skills Studies

The Assessment Frameworks for Cycle 2 of the Programme for the International Assessment of Adult Competencies

OECD
BETTER POLICIES FOR BETTER LIVES

This work is published under the responsibility of the Secretary-General of the OECD. The opinions expressed and arguments employed herein do not necessarily reflect the official views of OECD member countries.

This document, as well as any data and map included herein, are without prejudice to the status of or sovereignty over any territory, to the delimitation of international frontiers and boundaries and to the name of any territory, city or area.

The statistical data for Israel are supplied by and under the responsibility of the relevant Israeli authorities. The use of such data by the OECD is without prejudice to the status of the Golan Heights, East Jerusalem and Israeli settlements in the West Bank under the terms of international law.

Note by Turkey
The information in this document with reference to "Cyprus" relates to the southern part of the Island. There is no single authority representing both Turkish and Greek Cypriot people on the Island. Turkey recognises the Turkish Republic of Northern Cyprus (TRNC). Until a lasting and equitable solution is found within the context of the United Nations, Turkey shall preserve its position concerning the "Cyprus issue".

Note by all the European Union Member States of the OECD and the European Union
The Republic of Cyprus is recognised by all members of the United Nations with the exception of Turkey. The information in this document relates to the area under the effective control of the Government of the Republic of Cyprus.

Please cite this publication as:
OECD (2021), *The Assessment Frameworks for Cycle 2 of the Programme for the International Assessment of Adult Competencies*, OECD Skills Studies, OECD Publishing, Paris, *https://doi.org/10.1787/4bc2342d-en*.

ISBN 978-92-64-64927-9 (print)
ISBN 978-92-64-94606-4 (pdf)

OECD Skills Studies
ISSN 2307-8723 (print)
ISSN 2307-8731 (online)

Foreword

The Programme of the International Assessment of Adult Competencies (PIAAC) is an international assessment of the literacy, numeracy and problem solving skills of adults. The first cycle of the study involved three rounds of data collection involving a total of 39 countries and regions. Preparations for Cycle 2 of PIAAC started in 2018. As part of this process, the assessments of literacy, numeracy and problem solving have been redeveloped to reflect contemporary understandings of these skills and to make use of the opportunities offered by advances in testing technologies since Cycle 1 of the study. This document contains the frameworks that define and describe the skills assessed in Cycle 2 of PIAAC.

PIAAC is a collaboration between the countries participating in the study, the international contractor (a consortium led by Education Testing Service) responsible for the development of the study instruments, survey procedures, quality control and data preparation and the Organisation for Economic Co-operation and Development (OECD) responsible for the management of the project on behalf of participating countries.

The project is steered by the PIAAC Board of Participating Countries. Over the course of the development of Cycle 2 of PIAAC, the Board has been chaired by Ted Reininga (the Netherlands), together with Aviana Bulgarelli of Italy (until September 2020) and, from October 2020, Katalin Zoltán (Hungary).

Acknowledgements

This document is the fruit of a collective effort involving the international contractor for Cycle 2 of PIAAC, the members of the expert groups guiding the development of the assessment in the domains of literacy, numeracy and adaptive problem solving and the OECD.

The literacy framework was developed by the PIAAC Cycle 2 literacy expert group (LEG) under the leadership of Jean-François Rouet (Centre national de la recherche scientifique [CNRS], University of Poitiers, France). The members of the expert group contributing to the development of the literacy framework were Mary Anne Britt (Northern Illinois University, USA), Egil Gabrielsen (University of Stavanger, Norway), Johanna Kaakinen (University of Turku, Finland) and Tobias Richter (University of Würzburg, Germany).

The numeracy framework was developed by the PIAAC Cycle 2 numeracy expert group (NEG), chaired by Dave Tout (Australian Council for Educational Research, Australia). The members of the expert group contributing to the development of the numeracy framework were Isabelle Demonty (University of Liège, Belgium), Javier Díez-Palomar (University of Barcelona, Spain), Kees Hoogland (HU University of Applied Sciences Utrecht, the Netherlands), Terry Maguire (National Forum for the Enhancement of Teaching and Learning, Ireland) and Vince Geiger (Australian Catholic University, Australia).

The adaptive problem-solving framework was developed by the PIAAC Cycle 2 adaptive problem solving expert group, chaired by Samuel Greiff (University of Luxembourg). The members of the expert group contributing to the development of the adaptive problem solving framework were Art Graesser (University of Memphis, United States), Dragos Iliescu (University of Bucharest, Romania), Jean-François Rouet (CNRS, University of Poitiers, France), Katharina Scheiter (University of Tübingen, Germany) and Ronny Scherer (University of Oslo, Norway), with assistance from Juliana Gottschling (University of Luxembourg) and Jan Dörendahl (University of Luxembourg).

William Thorn (OECD) wrote the introduction.

Marylou Lennon, Laura Halderman and Irwin Kirsch (Education Testing Service) supported the work of the expert groups and preparation of the individual framework documents.

Sabrina Leonarduzzi (OECD) prepared the document for publication.

Table of contents

FIGURES

TABLES

Follow OECD Publications on:

http://twitter.com/OECD_Pubs

http://www.facebook.com/OECDPublications

http://www.linkedin.com/groups/OECD-Publications-4645871

http://www.youtube.com/oecdilibrary

http://www.oecd.org/oecddirect/

Executive summary

This publication contains the frameworks for the assessment of literacy, numeracy and adaptive problem solving in the second cycle of the OECD's Programme for the International Assessment of Adult Competencies (PIAAC Cycle 2).

The assessment frameworks represent key documents for understanding what is measured by PIAAC and for interpreting its results.

The introductory chapter provides an overview of the PIAAC assessment and its relationship to previous international assessments of adult skills. It also describes the purpose of the assessment frameworks and the evolution of the concepts of literacy, numeracy and problem solving since the first international assessment of adult literacy was conducted in the mid-1990s as well as the relationship of PIAAC to the OECD's assessment of 15-year-old school students, PISA.

The individual frameworks are presented in separate chapters: literacy (Chapter 2), numeracy (Chapter 3) and adaptive problem solving (Chapter 4). They define the particular skills assessed, describe their salient features, outline a recommended approach to the assessment of the skill and identify other matters relevant to test development. The similarities and differences with the frameworks of previous assessments are outlined with a focus on the social, theoretical and measurement considerations that have contributed to the development of the frameworks over time.

1 The assessment frameworks for Cycle 2 of PIAAC: An introduction and overview

This chapter introduces the assessment frameworks that define and describe the skills assessed in Cycle 2 of PIAAC. It provides some background to the PIAAC assessment, outlines the purposes of the assessment frameworks and explains how the understanding and conception of the skills measured in PIAAC has evolved over time.

Introduction

This volume contains the frameworks for the assessment of literacy, numeracy and adaptive problem solving in the second cycle of the OECD's Programme for the International Assessment of Adult Competencies (PIAAC Cycle 2). This introductory chapter provides some context and background to the study as well as to the frameworks guiding the assessment. In particular, it describes:

- the main features of the PIAAC assessment and how it relates to previous international assessments of adult literacy, numeracy and problem solving
- the purposes of the assessment frameworks
- the way in which the constructs assessed in PIAAC and its predecessors have been conceived.

The PIAAC assessment

PIAAC is an international assessment of the information-processing skills of adults. It assesses three broad skills: reading and understanding written texts (literacy), understanding and using mathematical and numerical information (numeracy) and solving problems. A comprehensive background questionnaire is also administered in conjunction with the assessment.

PIAAC is the third in a series of international adult assessments conducted since the mid-1990s. It builds on the experience of the International Adult Literacy Survey (IALS) and the Adult Literacy and Life Skills Survey (ALL).[1] IALS collected data in three waves between 1994 and 1998 in 22 countries and regions. ALL collected data in two waves over the period 2002-2008 in 11 countries and regions.

The study is designed as a repeated cross-sectional study that provides comparable estimates of proficiency in literacy and numeracy over time. The first cycle of the assessment took place over the period 2008-2019 with three data collection rounds: the first in 2011-12, the second in 2014-15 and the third in 2017-18.[2] A total of 39 countries/regions took part in the first cycle of the study and 33 are currently preparing to collect data in the second cycle (see Table 1.1). Preparations for Cycle 2 of the assessment began in 2018. Data collection was originally planned for 2021-22, ten years after data collection in the first round of Cycle 1, but due to the Covid-19 crisis of 2020 which delayed the Field Trial, it has been rescheduled to 2022-23.

Data are collected in PIAAC using a combination of personal interview and a self-completed assessment. Data collection takes place in the respondent's own home[3] under the supervision of trained interviewers. The background questionnaire is administered in Computer Aided Personal Interview (CAPI) mode by the interviewer. Following completion of the background questionnaire, the respondent completes the assessment under the supervision of the interviewer. In the first cycle of the study, the assessment could be completed on a laptop computer or in paper-and-pencil format. The computer-based assessment (CBA) format constituted the default format with the paper-based assessment (PBA) option being made available to those respondents who had little or no familiarity with computers, had poor information communications technology (ICT) skills, or who did not wish to take the assessment on computer. In the second cycle of the study, the assessment will be delivered on a tablet device. The assessment interface has been designed in such a way as to ensure that most, if not all, respondents will be able to take the assessment on the tablet even if they have limited experience with such devices. It will still be possible for participating countries to provide a paper-based option to respondents who cannot or are unwilling to take the assessment on the tablet.

Table 1.1. Countries and regions participating in PIAAC

PIAAC Cycle 1			PIAAC Cycle 2
Round 1	Round 2	Round 3	
Main study 2011-12	Main study 2014-15	Main study 2017-18	Main study 2022-23
Australia	Chile	Ecuador	Australia
Austria	Greece	Hungary	Austria
Canada	Jakarta (Indonesia)[2]	Kazakhstan	Canada
Cyprus[1]	Israel	Mexico	Chile
Czech Republic	Lithuania	Peru	Croatia
Denmark	New Zealand	United States	Czech Republic
England (UK)	Singapore		Denmark
Estonia	Slovenia		England (UK)
Finland	Turkey		Estonia
Flanders (Belgium)			Finland
France			Flanders (Belgium)
Germany			France
Ireland			Germany
Italy			Hungary
Japan			Ireland
Korea			Israel
Netherlands			Italy
Northern Ireland (UK)			Japan
Norway			Korea
Poland			Latvia
Russian Federation			Lithuania
Slovak Republic			Netherlands
Spain			New Zealand
Sweden			Norway
United States[3]			Poland
			Portugal
			Russian Federation
			Singapore
			Spain
			Sweden
			Switzerland
			United States

1. Note by Turkey:
The information in this document with reference to "Cyprus" relates to the southern part of the Island. There is no single authority representing both Turkish and Greek Cypriot people on the Island. Turkey recognises the Turkish Republic of Northern Cyprus (TRNC). Until a lasting and equitable solution is found within the context of the United Nations, Turkey shall preserve its position concerning the "Cyprus issue".
Note by all the European Union Member States of the OECD and the European Union:
The Republic of Cyprus is recognised by all members of the United Nations with the exception of Turkey. The information in this document relates to the area under the effective control of the Government of the Republic of Cyprus.
2. Indonesia's data was subsequently withdrawn.
3. The United States also collected data as part of a PIAAC National Supplement in 2013-14. This included representative samples of a) unemployed adults (aged 16-65); b) young adults (aged 16-34) and c) older adults (aged 66-74). See Krenzke et al. (2019[1]) for details.

The basic specifications for the design of PIAAC (common across the two cycles of the study) are summarised in Table 1.2. More details regarding Cycle 1 of the study can be found in PIAAC (2014[2]).

Table 1.2. Key features of the PIAAC study design

Target population	Non-institutionalised adults aged 16-65 years normally resident in the national territory of the participating country.
Sample frame	The sample frame should cover the target population. Exclusions of up to 5% of the target population permitted.
Sample design	Probability-based sample with each individual in the target population having a known probability of selection.
Sample size	Minimum sample size of 5 000 completed cases per reporting language.
Data collection method	Computer-aided personal interview and self-completed assessment under the supervision of the interviewer.
Mode of assessment	Computer (Cycle 1) and tablet (Cycle 2) delivered assessment with a paper-based alternative for respondents with insufficient experience of the use of digital devices.
Quality assurance and quality control	Central review of key elements of the study such as sampling, translation and adaptation of instruments. Monitoring of data collection. Data adjudication based on indicators of data quality.

Instrumentation

As noted above, respondents complete both a background questionnaire and a skills assessment.

The background questionnaire in PIAAC Cycle 2 will consist of 11 modules collecting information on demographic characteristics, social and language background, education, labour-force participation, employment, the task composition of the respondent's job, literacy and numeracy practices and personality traits.[4]

The direct assessment involves the following components:

- a locator test
- an assessment of reading and numeracy components
- assessments of literacy, numeracy and adaptive problem solving.

The *locator test* consists of eight literacy and eight numeracy items of low difficulty. It is designed to provide an initial estimate of the proficiency of the respondent. This is used to direct the respondent to the testing pathway appropriate to his/her proficiency (see below).

The *reading and numeracy components assessment* consists of set of items assessing:

- the ability to understand the meaning of simple sentences and to read and understand short passages fluently (reading)
- understanding basic notions of quantity and magnitude (numeracy).

The *assessments of literacy, numeracy and adaptive problem solving* each consist of around 80 items. Any individual respondent is administered test items covering only two of the three domains and in each of these domains he or she is presented a subset of the test items. In all three domains, the assessments use an adaptive design. The goal is to maximise the efficiency and precision of the assessment by presenting respondents with test items that are neither too easy nor too difficult for them.

In each domain, the assessment consists of a set of units in which each unit is made up of one or more stimuli (e.g. a description of a problem situation, a text, a table – see Figure 1.2 below) and a set of questions or tasks. These units are combined into groups called 'testlets' with different average levels of difficulty. The testlets are presented to respondents in two stages. Information from the background questionnaire, the component measures and the locator are used to assign a testlet that is most appropriate for the respondent at Stage 1. The respondent's performance on the Stage 1 testlet is automatically scored. The test application then assigns a second testlet to the respondent based on his/her performance on the first. While all respondents have a small probability of being allocated any testlet, they have a greater probability of being allocated a testlet closer to their estimated proficiency. For example, at each stage in the assessment, a respondent of high estimated ability has a greater chance of being allocated a testlet of high average difficulty than does a respondent with lower estimated proficiency.

The design for the main study in PIAAC Cycle 2 is presented in Figure 1.1 below. The background questionnaire is administered in CAPI mode by the interviewer and is estimated to take 20-45 minutes to complete depending on the situation of the respondent (with an average of around 30 minutes). The direct assessment is completed by the respondent on a tablet device supplied by the interviewer. The average time for completion of the assessment is estimated to be 60 minutes. However, as PIAAC is not a timed assessment, actual completion times are expected to vary widely.

Figure 1.1. Assessment design: PIAAC Cycle 2

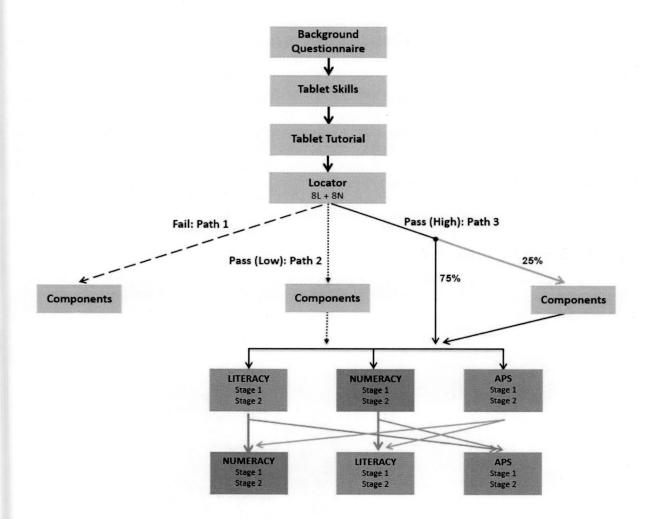

Respondents undertake the assessment in the following sequence:

- The interviewer administers the background questionnaire. The background questionnaire is answered by all respondents and includes a set of questions dealing with the familiarity of the respondent with electronic devices.

- After agreeing to continue with the survey, the respondent is handed the tablet device on which he/she completes the assessment. The interviewer demonstrates the basic skills required to complete the direct assessment tasks, e.g., tapping, using drag and drop, and highlighting.
- Respondents then complete a tutorial in which they perform each of the skills independently.
- The respondent then completes the locator test.
- Depending on their responses to relevant background items and their performance on locator tasks, respondents are directed to one of three paths:
  - Respondents who 'fail' the locator follow path 1 and receive the reading and numeracy components only.
  - Respondents who 'pass' the locator, but perform relatively poorly, follow path 2 and receive the components plus the two-stage adaptive modules of literacy, numeracy, or adaptive problem solving (APS).
  - Respondents who perform well on the locator test follow path 3. A quarter of these respondents are randomly assigned to the reading and numeracy components assessments before moving on to the two-stage adaptive modules of literacy, numeracy, or adaptive problem solving (APS), while the other 75% of respondents proceed directly to the two-stage cognitive modules.

The assessment tasks in PIAAC consist of 1) a set of instructions and a question or task statement that defines what the respondent must do to complete the task, 2) stimulus material (e.g. texts, graphic representations, simulated websites) with which the respondent must interact to complete the task and 3) a means of registering a response. All items in the assessment have the same format. The instructions to the respondent and the task question/statement together with forward and back arrows and access to help are on the left-hand side of the screen with the stimulus materials(s) on the right. Responses are recorded on the left-hand side as in the sample item below or through interaction with the stimulus material. Figure 1.2 provides an example of a PIAAC computer-based test item.

Figure 1.2. Sample PIAAC test item (Numeracy)

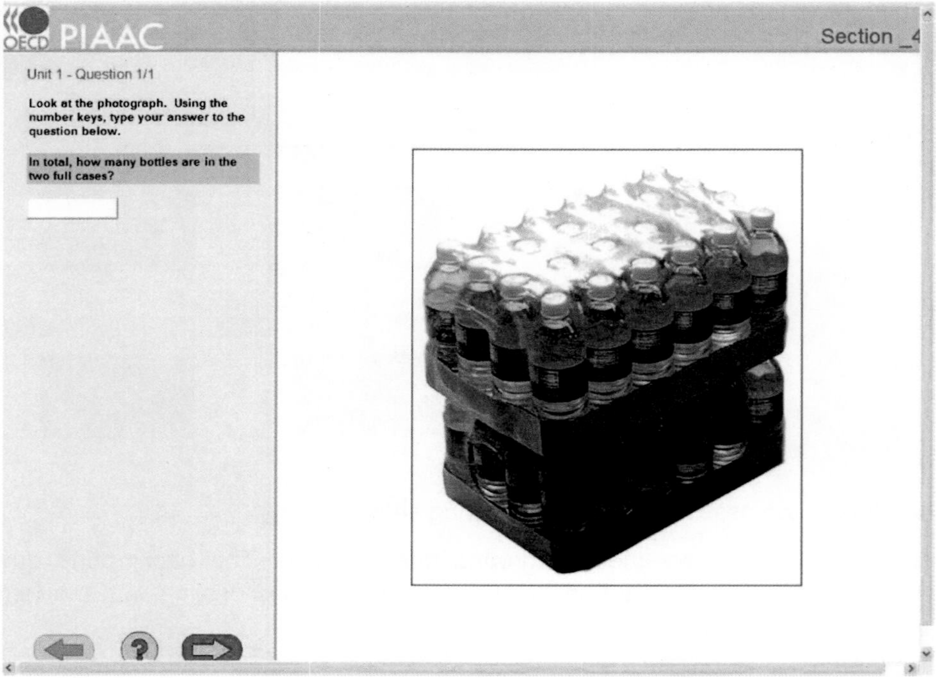

The response modes used in PIAAC Cycle 1 were numeric entry, clicking on multiple choice check boxes, radio buttons and pull-down menus (left-hand side of the screen), and highlighting or clicking on elements in the stimulus material – text, graphic element, links (in simulated we environments) and check boxes (right-hand side) [see OECD (2019[3]), Section 5.2.1)]. In PIAAC Cycle 2, similar response modes will be used with the interaction with the test application interface being via the use of a stylus or tapping with fingers. A simulated calculator will be used for numeric entry. No constructed responses are used in PIAAC.

Assessment frameworks

In large-scale international assessments, the constructs measured are usually described by an assessment framework.[5] The framework has a dual purpose: 1) to guide the development of the items (tasks) used to assess the skill in question and 2) to guide the interpretation of the results of the assessment. To this end, the framework provides a definition and detailed description of the features of the construct assessed. In addition, it outlines the recommended approach to the assessment of the skill in question and identifies (e.g. the recommended coverage of the various aspects or dimensions of the construct) and discusses other matters relevant to test development such as the factors that affect the difficulty of items.

Table 1.3. Main features of the assessment frameworks for PIAAC Cycle 2

	Literacy	Numeracy	Adaptive Problem Solving
Definition	Literacy is accessing, understanding, evaluating and reflecting on written texts in order to achieve one's goals, to develop one's knowledge and potential and to participate in society.	Numeracy is accessing, using and reasoning critically with mathematical content, information and ideas represented in multiple ways in order to engage in and manage the mathematical demands of a range of situations in adult life.	Adaptive problem solving involves the capacity to achieve one's goals in a dynamic situation, in which a method for solution is not immediately available. It requires engaging in cognitive and metacognitive processes to define the problem, search for information, and apply a solution in a variety of information environments and contexts.
Cognitive processes	• Accessing text • Understanding • Evaluating	• Access and assess situations mathematically • Act on and use mathematics • Evaluate, critically reflect, make judgements	• Definition • Searching • Application
Content	Texts characterised by their: • Type (description, narration, exposition, argumentation, instruction, transaction) • Format (continuous, non-continuous, mixed) • Organisation (the amount of information and the density of content representation and access devices) • Source (single vs. multiple texts)	Mathematical content information and ideas • Quantity and number • Space and shape • Change and relationships • Data and chance Mathematical representations • Text or symbols • Images of physical objects • Structured information • Dynamic applications	Task dimensions • Problem configuration • Dynamics of the situation • Features of the environment • Information environment
Contexts	• Work and occupation • Personal • Social and civic	• Personal • Work • Societal/community	• Personal • Work • Social/community

In PIAAC, the skills assessed are described in terms of 1) a broad definition, and 2) the dimensions of:

- Cognitive processes: the mental processes that form part of the skill in question.
- Content: the artefacts, knowledge, representations, situations that constitute the 'object(s)' to which these cognitive processes are applied.
- Contexts: the settings in which the skill is used.

The main components of the assessment frameworks for PIAAC Cycle 2 are summarised in Table 1.3.

Some of the key implications for the assessment of these skills arising from the frameworks are briefly discussed below.

Coverage of the constructs

In order for the assessment to represent the construct adequately, the set of tasks that constitute the assessment must include tasks designed to cover the range of cognitive processes, type of content and contexts identified by the framework. To this end, each of the framework documents proposes a desirable distribution of tasks across the different dimensions of the framework.

Factors affecting the difficulty of assessment tasks

The PIAAC assessment is intended to measure the entire range of proficiency in the skills of interest that exists in the adult population – from very low to very high. The adult population in participating countries includes individuals who have completed no more than primary education as well as adults who have completed post-doctoral studies. In addition, in countries with relatively high levels of immigration, a substantial proportion of the population may have limited proficiency in the language or languages in which the assessment is delivered.[6]

The frameworks identify the factors that affect task difficulty and can be manipulated to ensure that tasks covering the full spectrum from very easy to very difficult are included in the assessments. In broad terms, these can be categorised as encompassing features of:

- the task statement (e.g. the instructions provided to test-takers, the explicitness of the presentation and definition of the task to be completed)
- the stimulus material (e.g. its complexity, length, organisation)
- the interaction of task and stimulus (e.g. the presence of distracting/irrelevant material, the number of operations/steps required to be undertaken to successfully complete the task).

Authenticity of tasks

The skills assessed in PIAAC are primarily conceived as skills that enable adults to engage and function effectively in social and economic life and perform the range of tasks required in their various social roles. In line with this focus, assessment tasks are intended to represent the types of reading, mathematical and problem solving demands and situations that the generality of adults face in their everyday lives. In the words of the numeracy framework document: 'PIAAC is interested in the ability of individuals to cope with tasks that are embedded in the real world, rather than assessing decontextualised mathematical tasks'. Stimulus materials (e.g. the texts that respondents must read, the presentations and representations of numerical and mathematical information and problem situations to which they must respond) represent the kinds of texts, mathematical information and problems that adults encounter in 'real-world' situations. Regarding the stimulus material used in literacy tasks, for example:

> *Many of them are directly drawn from authentic materials with little, if any adaptation. This means that no effort is made to make these texts easier to read or to improve their organisation or presentation. Using naturalistic*

texts, sometimes even clearly suboptimal ones (for instance, poorly organised or using complex language), ensures a high level of face validity. However, no artificial difficulty or flaw is introduced at the time of test design. (see literacy framework)

Content appropriate to the entire adult population

As PIAAC is an assessment of the entire adults aged 16-65 years, the assessment tasks do not assume highly technical or occupation-specific knowledge. In addition, they do not assume knowledge or skills relevant in formal educational settings such as the use of formal mathematical notation and symbolisation. This reflects the fact that there are countries in which a significant proportion of adults (especially older adults) have very low educational attainment and, more importantly, the reality that most adults left the formal education system long ago. In the case of adults aged 55-65 years, for example, most will have completed their education between 40-50 years ago.

Assessment at low skill levels: Reading and numeracy components

One of the challenges in the assessment of the information-processing skills of adults is to gain information regarding the skills of adults with low proficiency. Low skills are manifested through the inability of a test-taker to successfully complete most tasks in the assessment. In other words, for this group, a lot is known about what they *cannot do* and little about what they *can do*.

To provide more information regarding the skills of low-skilled readers, an assessment of reading component skills was introduced in PIAAC Cycle 1 (Sabatini and Bruce, 2009[4]). This covered three skills: print vocabulary, sentence processing and passage fluency. Print vocabulary assessed basic vocabulary knowledge, sentence processing evaluated the ability to understand the semantic logic of simple sentences, and passage fluency assessed the capacity to understand passages of text. Reading components will continue to be assessed in PIAAC Cycle 2 with some modifications. Only two skills (sentence processing and passage fluency) will be assessed.

An assessment of numeracy components has been developed and will be administered as part of PIAAC Cycle 2. This involves two types of tasks designed to measure number sense: 1) identifying how many objects are displayed in photographs of real-life items, and 2) selecting the biggest number from a set of four choices.

No components measures have been developed in the domain of APS. The experience with previous assessments of problem solving has been that a reasonable level of proficiency in literacy and numeracy is a precondition for the successful completion of problem solving items. This is expected to be true also for the assessment of APS. As can be seen from the presentation of the drivers of task difficulty in APS (APS Framework, Table 4.A1.1), even simple problems have a level of complexity and difficulty far in excess of the type of tasks forming the literacy and numeracy components measures.

The evolution of assessment frameworks in international adult assessments

As noted above, PIAAC Cycle 2 is the latest in a series of related international assessments of adults. Table 1.4 presents the domains assessed in each successive study from IALS to PIAAC Cycle 2. The domains in which results are psychometrically linked and can be compared over time are indicated by shading.

The assessment frameworks in each of broad domains assessed in adult skills assessments have evolved considerably since IALS was conducted in the mid- to late-1990s. This is most obvious in the domain of problem solving where different (albeit related) constructs were measured in ALL and PIAAC Cycles 1 and 2 and that of managing numerical and mathematical information where the construct of numeracy was introduced in ALL in place of that of quantitative literacy. However, even within the domains of reading and of numeracy, there has been considerable change in the conceptualisation of the constructs between assessments. These changes are briefly described below and summarised in Tables 1.A.1-1.A.3 in Annex 1.A.

Table 1.4. Domains assessed in IALS, ALL and PIAAC

	Domains assessed						
	Reading		Managing numerical and mathematical information		Problem solving		
IALS	Prose Literacy	Document Literacy	Quantitative Literacy				
ALL	Prose Literacy	Document Literacy		Numeracy	Analytic Problem Solving		
PIAAC Cycle 1	Literacy + Literacy Components			Numeracy		Problem Solving in Technology-Rich Environment	
PIAAC Cycle 2	Literacy + Literacy Components		Numeracy + Numeracy Components				Adaptive Problem Solving

Understanding the evolution of the assessment frameworks and, therefore, of the constructs measured is important for the interpretation of the distributions of skills observed both within and between assessments. The link between the most recent and the older assessments becomes more attenuated over time as the constructs continue to evolve. While the different international adult assessments have been designed to be linked psychometrically in the domains of literacy (IALS and its successors) and numeracy (ALL and its successors), the constructs measured have undergone considerable revision and extension even if a common core remains. Literacy as it will be measured in PIAAC Cycle 2 in 2022-23 is not exactly the same as literacy as measured in PIAAC Cycle 1, ALL and IALS, and the same is true for numeracy. In particular, although IALS and ALL recognised the growing importance of electronic texts, those two earlier assessments were delivered only on paper. Starting with PIAAC Cycle 1, the assessment moved to computer delivery which provided a means to include various types of electronic texts and materials.

The evolution of the assessment frameworks in large-scale assessments (including adult assessments) is the outcome of competing demands: on the one hand, the desire for continuity in measures (to provide reliable measures of change over time) and, on the other, the need for measures to be relevant to contemporary realities and understandings of the phenomena measured. Three main factors push in the direction of change: developments in the understanding of the skills measured, technological and social developments that affect the nature and practice of these skills in everyday life, work and study and technological and methodological advances in the science and practice of measurement.[7]

The assessment of problem solving provides a particular illustration of the impact of the forces that lead to change in large-scale assessment. Of the domains assessed in PIAAC and its predecessors, it is the one in which the impact of the introduction of computer-based testing has been greatest as it opened up possibilities for its assessment that did not exist in a world of paper-based tests. In addition, the demand for measures of problem solving that speak to current understandings of the phenomenon has been evident in the changes in the points of view from which the assessment of problem solving have been approached over time.

As in any area of scientific endeavour, the understanding of the skills assessed in large-scale assessments changes over time. This is a consequence of theoretical developments as well as reflection on the outcomes of empirical research including the results of large-scale assessments themselves.

Comprehensive discussions of the theoretical and conceptual considerations that led to the development of the assessment of APS and to the substantial revision of the numeracy assessment framework in Cycle 2 of PIAAC, can be found in Greiff et al. (2017[5]) for APS and Tout et al. (2017[6]) and Tout (2020[7]) for numeracy as well as in framework documents included in this publication.

The nature of skills such as literacy, numeracy and problem solving has changed in many ways since the early 1990s. Information and communications technologies have altered what it is to read, engage with numerical and mathematical information and solve problems by changing the ways in which information is accessed, communicated and analysed and transformed. For example, print-based texts and representations constituted the source of much of the information accessed by adults in the mid-1990s. At the start of the third decade of the 21st century, electronic texts and representations accessed through digital devices (e.g. computers, tablets, and smartphones) and applications (e.g. web browsers, hypertext, pdf and html files) have become primary sources of information. This has involved the appearance of new types of texts and representations; new forms of navigation within and between texts and representations (scrolling, clicking on icons or radio buttons, hyperlinks); and new tools for the processing and communication of information and increased interlinkages between texts, documents and representations (hypertext, strings of related texts). In addition, on-line service delivery has increased the information-processing demands on adults through the reduction (or removal) of the role of intermediaries in providing access to information and assistance with decision making in many domains (e.g. health, finances and travel).

ICTs have also transformed assessment. The introduction of computer-based assessment (CBA) has had a major impact on the design, delivery and processing of assessments and on the quality, amount and complexity of the resulting data. It has made possible the assessment of proficiency in the digital dimensions of information-processing skills (e.g. the reading of electronic texts, interaction with digital tools presenting and transforming mathematical information, the use of ICT applications to access and transform information to solve problems). It has also enabled the development of more complex assessment tasks. For example, digital assessment platforms make it possible to design tasks that are iterative in nature, and in which not all information is given as part of the initial conditions, as well as tasks involving complex displays of information, modelling and exploration of variation in a range of parameters. This is particularly important in the assessment of problem solving. The introduction of CBA has also permitted the implementation of more complex and efficient test designs (e.g. adaptive testing) as well as features such as automatic scoring. It has also allowed the development of more efficient and timely quality assurance and control procedures and considerably increased the possibilities of identifying data fabrication and fraud. The availability of log-files in which interactions between test-takers and the testing application are captured and stored has provided a new and rich source of data for analysts and test developers interested in understanding test-taking behaviour.[8]

The introduction of CBA as the default assessment mode in PIAAC Cycle 1 constituted one of the major factors influencing the evolution of the assessment frameworks of adult skills assessments between IALS and PIAAC. This made it possible for PIAAC to 1) reflect the changes in the practices of reading, managing mathematical and numerical information and problem solving brought about by the diffusion of digital tools and media in the way it assessed these skills and 2) use much more efficient test designs for adults.

Box 1.1. Assessment frameworks for previous assessments of adult literacy

Presentations of the assessment frameworks for IALS, ALL and PIAAC Cycle 1 can be found in the following documents:

IALS

Murray, S., I. Kirsch and L. Jenkins (eds) (1998[8]), *Adult Literacy in OECD Countries: Technical Report on the First International Adult Literacy Survey*, National Center for Education Statistics, Office of Educational Research and Improvement, Washington, DC.

OECD/Statistics Canada (2000[9]), *Literacy in the Information Age: Final Report of the International Adult Literacy Survey*, OECD Publishing, Paris, http://dx.doi.org/10.1787/9789264181762-en.

ALL

Murray, S., Y. Clermont and M. Binkley (eds) (2005[10]), *Measuring Adult Literacy and Life Skills: New Frameworks for Assessment*, Statistics Canada, Ottawa, Catalogue No. 89-552-MIE, No. 13.

PIAAC Cycle 1

OECD (2012[11]), *Literacy, Numeracy and Problem Solving in Technology-Rich Environments: Framework for the OECD Survey of Adult Skills*, OECD Publishing, Paris, http://dx.doi.org/10.1787/9789264128859-en.

PIAAC Expert Group in Problem Solving in Technology-Rich Environments (2009[12]), "PIAAC Problem Solving in Technology-Rich Environments: A Conceptual Framework", *OECD Education Working Papers*, No. 36, OECD Publishing, Paris, http://dx.doi.org/10.1787/220262483674.

PIAAC Literacy Expert Group (2009[13]), "PIAAC Literacy: A Conceptual Framework", *OECD Education Working Papers*, No. 34, OECD Publishing, Paris, http://dx.doi.org/10.1787/220348414075.

PIAAC Numeracy Expert Group (2009[14]), "PIAAC Numeracy: A Conceptual Framework", *OECD Education Working Papers*, No. 35, OECD Publishing, Paris, http://dx.doi.org/10.1787/220337421165.

Sabatini and Bruce (2009[4]), "PIAAC Reading Component: A Conceptual Framework", *OECD Education Working Papers*, No. 33, OECD Publishing, Paris, http://dx.doi.org/10.1787/220367414132.

Developments in literacy

The evolution of the constructs of literacy from IALS to PIAAC Cycle 2 has occurred in four main areas: 1) a reduction of the number of separate domains of literacy assessed, 2) the expansion of the range of text types covered in the assessment, 3) an increasing emphasis placed on evaluation and evaluating metacognition as cognitive strategies required for effective reading and 4) the disentangling of the description and specification of cognitive strategies from questions of task difficulty.[9]

In IALS, three separate domains of literacy were assessed and represented by separate scales: prose, document and quantitative literacy (Murray, Kirsch and Jenkins, 1998[8]). Prose literacy covered the reading of continuous texts or texts organised in paragraphs. Document literacy covered the reading of written information presented in matrix formats (e.g. tables and lists). Quantitative literacy represented the knowledge and skills required to apply arithmetic operations to numbers embedded in printed materials. ALL continued to assess prose and document literacy as separate domains (Murray, Clermont and Binkley, 2005[10]). However, the assessment of quantitative literacy was dropped in ALL and replaced by the assessment of numeracy (see below). The construct of 'literacy' as a single domain was introduced in PIAAC Cycle 1.

'Literacy' as defined in PIAAC Cycle 1 represented a global construct that no longer differentiated between the reading of prose and document texts. The other major (and probably the most significant) development was the expansion of the range of texts covered by the assessment to include digital or electronic texts.[10] In PIAAC Cycle 2, the classification of texts has been revised to include the dimensions of organisation (density of content, representations and access devices) and source (single or multiple authors/publishers) to better represent the universe of texts accessible in digital environments, including the interactive texts typical of the Web 2.0.

The conceptualisation of the cognitive strategies brought into play by competent readers has also evolved between assessments. In IALS/ALL, the cognitive strategies were conceived in terms of the 'matching' of information in the question (the given information) to the information in the stimulus text to respond correctly to a question or directive. These 'matching' strategies included the identification of pieces of information in the text (locating/cycling), connecting different parts of the text (integrating), and developing some understanding of the text as a whole (generating). In PIAAC Cycle 1, 'evaluation and reflection' (the making of judgements regarding aspects of the text such as truthfulness, relevance and quality) was added as a cognitive strategy required of competent readers. The dimension of evaluation has been further emphasised in Cycle 2 where it is conceived in terms of the evaluation of the accuracy, soundness, and task relevance of a text in relation to both its source and content.

There has also been a gradual separation of the identification and description of cognitive processes involved in literacy from the description of the factors that make assessment tasks more or less difficult. In IALS/ALL, matching strategies were treated as one of the three main factors determining task difficulty, the second being the type of information requested by the question and the third, the plausibility of distractors (the presence of other information in the stimulus text that could distract the test-taker's attention from the information needed to answer the question) (Murray, Clermont and Binkley, 2005, pp. 101-103[10]). The Cycle 2 framework treats cognitive strategies and the factors affecting task difficulty independently. Task difficulty is conceived as being driven by the features of the stimulus text(s), the formulation of the question/task description and the interaction of the text and question/task description (see literacy framework, Table 2.5).

The assessment of reading components was another new element of the assessment of literacy introduced in PIAAC Cycle 1 (Sabatini and Bruce, 2009[4]) to provide more detailed information about adults with poor literacy skills. Reading components were defined as the basic set of decoding skills essential for extracting meaning from written texts: knowledge of vocabulary (word recognition), the ability to process meaning at the level of the sentence, and fluency in reading passages of text. In PIAAC Cycle 2, the assessment of reading components will be continued but cover only the sentence meaning and passage fluency dimensions. Performance on the reading components tasks will also be integrated as part of the literacy proficiency scale in Cycle 2,[11] adding precision to its lower end.

Developments in numeracy

The measurement of 'numeracy' was introduced in ALL. This replaced the assessment of 'quantitative literacy' conducted in IALS. The rationale for the development of an assessment of numeracy was that the assessments of quantitative and document literacy represented 'only a subset of the much wider range of tasks and responses that are typical of many every day and work tasks' (Murray, Clermont and Binkley, 2005, p. 148[10]) relating to the engagement with mathematical information. In particular, key aspects of mathematical information such as measurements and shapes as well as information in formats that did require comprehension of text were not covered. The construct of 'numeracy' was developed to more comprehensively cover the mathematical knowledge and skills relevant in work and the everyday life of adults.

> *[Numeracy's] key concepts relate in a broad way to situation management and to a range of effective responses (not only to application of arithmetical skills). It refers to a wide range of skills and knowledge (not only to computational operations) and to a wide range of situations that present actors with mathematical information of different types (not only those involving numbers embedded in printed materials). (Murray, Clermont and Binkley, 2005, p. 151[10])*

In contrast with the domain of literacy, only minor changes to the specification of the numeracy domain were made in PIAAC Cycle 1 compared to ALL. These concerned presentation more than content. One of the major drivers for the revision of the numeracy assessment framework for PIAAC Cycle 2 was the view that the assessment of numeracy in the 21st century had to be expanded to cover the engagement with mathematical information in digital environments as well as to increase use of the possibilities offered by CBA.[12] The revised framework reflects the importance of digital information, representations, devices and applications as realities that adults have to deal with in responding to the numerical demands of everyday life. To this end, the content dimension of the numeracy framework has been significantly updated to include representations of mathematical information in the form of 'structured information' (infographics, etc.) and also 'dynamic applications' (e.g. online interactive websites and applications alongside more standard software applications and tools). The dimension of cognitive processes has also been revised to emphasise the ability to recognise and identify how and when to use mathematics; to be able to understand, use and apply mathematical concepts and procedures; and the capacity to use strategic, reasoning and reflective skills when using and applying mathematics.

In PIAAC Cycle 2, the assessment of numeracy will be accompanied by an assessment of 'numeracy components'. As for literacy, the numeracy components assessment focuses on some of the skills essential for achieving automaticity and fluency in managing mathematical and numerical information. The focus is on 'number sense' defined as 'the sense of quantities and the sense of how numbers represent quantities' (see numeracy framework). The items to be used will be of two types: items relating to quantities (using the stem 'How many…?') and items relating to relative magnitudes ('The biggest?').

Developments in problem solving

Problem solving represents the domain in which the changes in the conceptualisation of the skill in question have been greatest.[13] This is one of the reasons why the assessments of problem solving have not been linked across assessments. An assessment of problem solving was first undertaken in ALL, based on the construct of 'analytical problem solving' (Murray, Clermont and Binkley, 2005[10]) and assessed in paper-based format. This was replaced with the assessment of 'problem solving in technology-rich environments' (PS-TRE) in PIAAC Cycle 1 which has been replaced, in its turn, by adaptive problem solving (APS) in PIAAC Cycle 2.

Analytical problem solving in ALL focused on the generic aspects of the process of problem solving understood as 'goal-directed thinking and action in situations for which no routine solution procedure is available' (Murray, Clermont and Binkley, 2005, p. 197[10]), in particular the steps of:

- identifying a problem
- searching for relevant information and integrating it into a coherent problem representation
- evaluating the problem situation with respect to given goals and criteria
- devising a plan for the solution – i.e. an ordered sequence of appropriate actions
- monitoring its execution.

The assessment of problem solving in ALL was a paper-based assessment involving static problems in which all necessary information was provided up front. The limitations of this approach were explicitly acknowledged. In particular, computer simulated tasks were seen as the only way to address the dynamic aspects of task regulation (continuous processing of incoming information, coping with processes that cannot be influenced directly, coping with feedback and critical incidents).

In Cycle 1 of PIAAC, the assessment of problem solving moved to CBA mode in the form of the assessment of PS-TRE. PS-TRE represented a hybrid construct, at the intersection of the capacity to use information and communication technologies (ICTs) on the one hand, and of the ability to solve problems on the other. This was reflected in the restriction of the domain of problems covered to that of 'information problems' – problems that involved interaction with digital devices and applications (PIAAC Expert Group in Problem Solving in Technology-Rich Environments, 2009, pp. 8-9[12]):

- The problem is primarily a consequence of the availability of new technologies.
- The solution to the problem requires the use of computer-based artefacts (applications, representational formats, computational procedures).
- The problems are related to technology-rich environments themselves (e.g. how to operate a computer, how to fix a settings problem, how to use an Internet browser).

The focus on the assessment of problems in digital environments constituted both the strength and the weakness of PS-TRE. By design, only test-takers who had some (basic) ICT skills could display proficiency in this domain. Non-response for reasons of lack of familiarity with ICT devices or poor computer skills was construct relevant and could be interpreted as lack of proficiency. The downside was that a sizeable proportion (between 8 to 57%) of respondents in all participating countries did not take the assessment at all as they either lacked familiarity with computers or did not wish to undertake PIAAC on a laptop[14] (OECD, 2019[15]). This created difficulties in comparisons of results between participating countries[15] and meant that there was a considerable gap in the knowledge regarding the problem solving skills *per se* of the adult population.

APS, as conceptualised for PIAAC Cycle 2, represents the return to a concept of general problem solving that is relevant to a range of information environments and contexts and is not limited to digitally embedded problems even though digital aspects as a mode of problem solving play an important role in APS. What differentiates it from analytical problem solving as assessed in ALL is its focus on the dynamic and adaptive aspects of problem solving – the capacity to react to unforeseen changes and new information that emerge during the process – and on metacognition – the capacity to reflect on the process of problem solving as it takes place (monitoring progress, adjusting goals and strategies in the light of new information and changes in the problem situation).

Relationship of the PIAAC and PISA assessments

In addition to PIAAC, the OECD manages the Programme of International Student Assessment (PISA), an assessment of 15-year-old school students that has been administered every three years since 2000. In each assessment cycle, PISA assesses skills in three core domains (reading literacy, mathematical literacy and scientific literacy) as well as an additional domain unique to each cycle. Assessments of problem solving were administered as the additional domain in 2003, 2012 and 2015.

While similar skills are assessed in PIAAC and PISA in the domains of literacy/reading literacy, numeracy/mathematical literacy and problem solving, the two studies have followed separate development paths and have not been designed to be linked psychometrically. The measurement scales in related domains (e.g. literacy/reading literacy) are independent and the assessments have no items in common.[16] This reflects a degree of path dependency (PIAAC is designed to be linked to IALS and ALL) as well as the fact that the two assessments have different target populations.

At the same time, PIAAC and PISA share much at a conceptual level. They belong to the same measurement tradition, share a similar approach to the conceptualisation and definition of the constructs that they measure and a similar assessment methodology. In addition, there have been many experts who have worked on both studies. Reviewing the relationship between the assessment of numeracy in PIAAC and the assessment of mathematical literacy in PISA, Gal and Tout (2014, p. 52[16]) conclude that:

> *Both assessments of numeracy in PIAAC and mathematical literacy in PISA appear to have substantial conceptual similarities and quite a few practical commonalities in the nature of their test items and their design principles, as well as the range of content areas and skills they cover. The two surveys are highly consistent in their descriptions and structures for contexts and real world content classifications, along with how they describe the types and breadth of responses and actions expected of the respondents.*

Much the same comments could be made regarding the literacy/reading literacy and problem solving frameworks in both studies [see OECD, 2019 (pp. 91-93[17])].

Over time, there has been considerable mutual influence between adult and student assessments, particularly regarding the conceptualisation and definition of skills in reading and managing mathematical and numeric information. The IALS literacy frameworks were extremely influential on the development of the first PISA reading framework (OECD, 1999[18]) at the end of the 1990s. The adoption in PISA of an approach to the assessment of reading, mathematics and science that focused on the use of these skills in settings outside school owes much to the IALS approach to the assessment of literacy with its emphasis on the role of reading for social functioning. The PISA 2000 reading framework took over the classification of text types developed in IALS, particularly the prose/document distinction. In many ways, PISA could be viewed as an IALS for school students.[17] The PISA frameworks have in their turn influenced PIAAC, particularly in the domain of reading/literacy. The single reading scale adopted by PISA prefigured the single PIAAC literacy scale, for example, and the classifications of texts and cognitive processes adopted in PIAAC Cycle 1 reflects that used in PISA.

Reflecting the conceptual links between the two studies, one of the considerations in the development of the assessment frameworks for PIAAC Cycle 2 was to maximise the conceptual and terminological consistency between the PIAAC and PISA frameworks where relevant and appropriate. At the same time frameworks continue to reflect the fact that the PIAAC represents an assessment of adults.

The framework documents

The framework documents included in this volume were each prepared by a dedicated expert group[18] over the 2018-19 with the process being managed and coordinated by the PIAAC international contractor led by Education Testing Service (ETS). Members were selected to include experts from different backgrounds and countries. In all groups, some members had also served as members of the groups responsible for the Cycle 1 frameworks, thus ensuring continuity between the cycles and others had also worked on the PISA project in various capacities. While each expert group worked independently, there was close communication between the groups, particularly between the Chairs. In addition, there was overlap in membership with the Chair of the reading group also serving a member of the problem solving group.

In both adaptive problem solving and numeracy, the work of the expert groups built on earlier exploratory work commissioned by the PIAAC Board of Participating Countries (BPC), the steering committee for the PIAAC project. An initial conceptual framework for the assessment of adaptive problem solving was prepared in 2017 (Greiff et al., 2017[5]) as was a review of the PIAAC numeracy framework (Tout et al., 2017[6]).

The framework documents represent a work in progress. They will be updated following the completion of the main study data collection. At this point, the expert groups will review and revise the descriptors for the proficiency levels used to describe the measurement scales in the case of literacy and numeracy and develop the described scale in the case of APS.

References

Gal, I. and D. Tout (2014), "Comparison of PIAAC and PISA Frameworks for Numeracy and Mathematical Literacy", *OECD Education Working Papers*, No. 102, OECD Publishing, Paris, https://dx.doi.org/10.1787/5jz3wl63cs6f-en. [16]

Greiff, S. et al. (2017), "Adaptive problem solving: Moving towards a new assessment domain in the second cycle of PIAAC", *OECD Education Working Papers*, No. 156, OECD Publishing, Paris, https://dx.doi.org/10.1787/90fde2f4-en. [5]

Keslair, F. (2018), "Interviewers, test-taking conditions and the quality of the PIAAC assessment", *OECD Education Working Papers*, No. 191, OECD Publishing, Paris, https://dx.doi.org/10.1787/5babb087-en. [19]

Krenzke, T. et al. (2019), *U.S. Program for the International Assessment of Adult Competencies (PIAAC) 2012/2014/2017: Main Study, National Supplement, and PIAAC 2017 Technical Report (NCES 2020042)*, U.S. Department of Education, National Center for Education Statistics, Washington, DC, https://nces.ed.gov/pubsearch/pubsinfo.asp?pubid=2020224. [1]

Maehler, D., S. Jakowatz and I. Konradt (2020), *PIAAC Bibliography - 2008-2019*, (GESIS Papers, 2020/04), GESIS - Leibniz-Institut für Sozialwissenschaften, Köln, https://doi.org/10.21241/ssoar.67732. [29]

Mullis, I. and M. Martin (eds.) (2015), *PIRLS 2016 Assessment Frameword, 2nd Edition*, TIMSS & PIRLS International Study Center, Lynch School of Education, Boston College and International Association for the Evaluation of Educational Achievement (IEA), https://timssandpirls.bc.edu/pirls2016/framework.html. [28]

Mullis, I. and M. Martin (eds.) (2013), *TIMSS 2015 Assessment Frameworks*, TIMSS and PIRLS International Study Center, Lynch School of Education, Boston College and International Association for the Evaluation of Educational Achievement (IEA), https://timssandpirls.bc.edu/timss2015/frameworks.html. [27]

Murray, S., Y. Clermont and M. Binkley (eds.) (2005), *Measuring Adult Literacy and Life Skills: New Frameworks for Assessment*, Catalogue No. 89-552-MIE, No. 13. Statistics Canada, Ottawa. [10]

Murray, S., I. Kirsch and L. Jenkins (eds.) (1998), *Adult Literacy in OECD Countries: Technical Report on the First International Adult Literacy Survey*, (NCES 98-053), National Center for Education Statistics, Office of Educational Research and Improvement, Washington, DC. [8]

OECD (2019), *Beyond Proficiency: Using Log Files to Understand Respondent Behaviour in the Survey of Adult Skills*, OECD Skills Studies, OECD Publishing, Paris, https://dx.doi.org/10.1787/0b1414ed-en. [24]

OECD (2019), *PISA 2018 Assessment and Analytical Framework*, PISA, OECD Publishing, Paris, https://dx.doi.org/10.1787/b25efab8-en. [23]

OECD (2019), *Skills Matter: Additional Results from the Survey of Adult Skills*, OECD Skills Studies, OECD Publishing, Paris, https://dx.doi.org/10.1787/1f029d8f-en. [15]

OECD (2019), *Technical Report of the Survey of Adult Skills, Third Edition*, http://www.oecd.org/skills/piaac/publications/PIAAC_Technical_Report_2019.pdf. [3]

OECD (2019), *The Survey of Adult Skills: Reader's Companion, Third Edition*, OECD Skills [17]
Studies, OECD Publishing, Paris, https://dx.doi.org/10.1787/f70238c7-en.

OECD (2016), *Skills Matter: Further Results from the Survey of Adult Skills*, OECD Skills [22]
Studies, OECD Publishing, Paris, https://dx.doi.org/10.1787/9789264258051-en.

OECD (2013), *OECD Skills Outlook 2013: First Results from the Survey of Adult Skills*, OECD [21]
Publishing, Paris, https://dx.doi.org/10.1787/9789264204256-en.

OECD (2012), *Literacy, Numeracy and Problem Solving in Technology-Rich* [11]
Environments: Framework for the OECD Survey of Adult Skills, OECD Publishing, Paris,
https://dx.doi.org/10.1787/9789264128859-en.

OECD (2002), *Reading for Change: Performance and Engagement across Countries: Results* [20]
from PISA 2000, PISA, OECD Publishing, Paris, https://dx.doi.org/10.1787/9789264099289-
en.

OECD (1999), *Measuring Student Knowledge and Skills: A New Framework for Assessment*, [18]
OECD Publishing, Paris, https://dx.doi.org/10.1787/9789264173125-en.

OECD/Statistics Canada (2011), *Literacy for Life: Further Results from the Adult Literacy and* [26]
Life Skills Survey, OECD Publishing, Paris, https://dx.doi.org/10.1787/9789264091269-en.

OECD/Statistics Canada (2005), *Learning a Living: First Results of the Adult Literacy and Life* [25]
Skills Survey, OECD Publishing, Paris, https://dx.doi.org/10.1787/9789264010390-en.

OECD/Statistics Canada (2000), *Literacy in the Information Age: Final Report of the International* [9]
Adult Literacy Survey, OECD Publishing, Paris, https://dx.doi.org/10.1787/9789264181762-
en.

PIAAC (2014), *PIAAC Technical Standards and Guidelines - June 2014*, OECD Publishing, [2]
http://www.oecd.org/skills/piaac/PIAAC-
NPM(2014_06)PIAAC_Technical_Standards_and_Guidelines.pdf.

PIAAC Expert Group in Problem Solving in Technology-Rich Environments (2009), "PIAAC [12]
Problem Solving in Technology-Rich Environments: A Conceptual Framework", *OECD*
Education Working Papers, No. 36, OECD Publishing, Paris,
https://dx.doi.org/10.1787/220262483674.

PIAAC Literacy Expert Group (2009), "PIAAC Literacy: A Conceptual Framework", *OECD* [13]
Education Working Papers, No. 34, OECD Publishing, Paris,
https://dx.doi.org/10.1787/220348414075.

PIAAC Numeracy Expert Group (2009), "PIAAC Numeracy: A Conceptual Framework", *OECD* [14]
Education Working Papers, No. 35, OECD Publishing, Paris,
https://dx.doi.org/10.1787/220337421165.

Sabatini, J. and K. Bruce (2009), "PIAAC Reading Component: A Conceptual Framework", [4]
OECD Education Working Papers, No. 33, OECD Publishing, Paris,
https://dx.doi.org/10.1787/220367414132.

Tout, D. (2020), "Evolution of adult numeracy from quantitative literacy to numeracy: Lessons [7]
learned from international assessments", *International Review of Education*, Vol. 66/2-3,
pp. 183-209, http://dx.doi.org/10.1007/s11159-020-09831-4.

Tout, D. et al. (2017), *Review of the PIAAC Numeracy Assessment Framework: Final Report*, Australian Council for Educational Research, Camberwell, Australia. [6]

Wallin, G. (2018), "New PIAAC study coming up – to measure abilities among adults", *Nordic Labour Journal*, http://www.nordiclabourjournal.org/nyheter/news-2018/article.2018-12-14.7343538187. [30]

Annex 1.A. Summary of the evolution of assessment frameworks – from IALS to PIAAC Cycle 2

Annex Table 1.A.1. Literacy (Reading)

Construct	IALS/ALL		PIAAC Cycle 1	PIAAC Cycle 2
	Prose Literacy	Document Literacy	Literacy	Literacy
Definition	Literacy is using printed and written information to function in society, to achieve one's goals, and to develop one's knowledge and potential. Prose literacy is the knowledge and skills needed to understand and use information from texts, including editorials, news stories, brochures and instruction manuals.	Literacy is using printed and written information to function in society, to achieve one's goals, and to develop one's knowledge and potential. Document literacy is the knowledge and skills required to locate and use information contained in various formats, including job applications, payroll forms, transportation schedules, maps, tables and charts.	Literacy is the ability to understand, evaluate, use and engage with *written texts* to participate in society, to achieve one's goals, and to develop one's knowledge and potential. Literacy encompasses a range of skills from the decoding of written words and sentences to the comprehension interpretation, and evaluation of complex texts.	Literacy is accessing, understanding, evaluating and reflecting on written texts in order to achieve one's goals, to develop one's knowledge and potential and to participate in society.
Cognitive processes	• Locating • Cycling • Integrating • Generating		• Access and identify • Integrate and interpret (relating parts of text to one another) • Evaluate and reflect	• Accessing text • Understanding • Evaluating
Content	Continuous texts: • Description • Narration • Exposition • Argumentation • Instruction • Document or record	Non-continuous texts: • Matrix documents • Graphic documents • Locative documents • Entry documents • Combination documents	Texts characterised by their medium (*print-based* or *digital*) and by format: • *Continuous or prose texts* which involve narration, argumentation or descriptions for example • *Non-continuous or document texts*, for example, tables, lists and graphs • *Mixed texts* which involve combinations of prose and document elements • *Multiple texts* which consist of the juxtaposition or linking of independently generated elements	Texts characterised by their: • Type (description, narration, exposition, argumentation, instruction, transaction) • Format (continuous, non-continuous, mixed) • Organisation (the amount of information and the density of content representation and access devices) • Source (single vs. multiple texts)

	IALS/ALL	PIAAC Cycle 1	PIAAC Cycle 2
Contexts	• Home and family • Health and safety • Community and citizenship • Consumer economics • Work • Leisure and recreation	• Personal • Work • Community • Education	• Work and occupation • Personal • Social and civic
Factors affecting task difficulty	• Type of match • Type of information requested • Plausibility of distractors	• Transparency of the information • Degree of complexity in making inferences • Semantic complexity and syntactic complexity • Amount of information needed • Prominence of the information • Text features (such as text cohesion signals)	• Text factors (length, type of text, familiarity of content, presence of content signalling devices) • Task factors (length of stem, explicitness of guidance) • Text-by-task factors (type of match, presence of distracting or irrelevant information)
Assessment mode	Paper-based	Computer-based (laptop device) + paper-based option	Computer-based (tablet device) + paper-based option in a limited number of countries

Sources: For IALS: Murray, Kirsch and Jenkins (1998[8]). For ALL: Murray, Clermont and Binkley (2005[10]). For PIAAC Cycle 1: (OECD, 2019[17]). For PIAAC Cycle 2: the frameworks included in this volume.

Annex Table 1.A.2. Managing numerical and mathematical information

	IALS	ALL	PIAAC Cycle 1	PIAAC Cycle 2
Construct	Quantitative Literacy	Numeracy	Numeracy	Numeracy
Definition	Quantitative literacy is the knowledge and skills required to apply arithmetic operations, either alone or sequentially, to numbers embedded in printed materials, such as balancing a chequebook, figuring out a tip, completing an order form or determining the amount of interest on a loan from an advertisement.	Numeracy is the knowledge and skills required to effectively manage and respond to the mathematical demands of diverse situations. Numerate behaviour is observed when people manage a situation or solve a problem in a real context; it involves responding to information about mathematical ideas that may be represented in a range of ways; it requires the activation of a range of enabling knowledge, factors and processes.	Numeracy is the ability to access, use, interpret and communicate mathematical information and ideas, in order to engage in and manage the mathematical demands of a range of situations in adult life. To this end, numeracy involves managing a situation or solving a problem in a real context, by responding to mathematical content/information/ideas represented in multiple ways.	Numeracy is accessing, using and reasoning critically with mathematical content, information and ideas represented in multiple ways in order to engage in and manage the mathematical demands of a range of situations in adult life.
Content	Non-continuous texts: • Matrix documents • Graphic documents • Locative documents • Entry documents • Combination documents	Mathematical information: • *Dimension and shape* • *Pattern, functions and relationships* • *Data and chance* • *Change* Representations of mathematical information: • *Objects* • *Pictures* • *Symbolic notation* • *Formulae* • *Visual displays* • *Texts*	Mathematical content, information and ideas: • *Quantity and number* • *Dimension and shape* • *Pattern, relationships, change* • *Data and chance* Representations of mathematical content: • *Objects and pictures* • *Numbers and symbols* • *Diagrammes, maps, graphs, tables* • *Texts* • *Technology-based displays*	Mathematical content information and ideas: • *Quantity and number* • *Space and shape* • *Change and relationships* • *Data and chance* Mathematical representations: • *Text or symbols* • *Images of physical objects* • *Structured information* • *Dynamic applications*
Cognitive processes	• Locating • Cycling • Integrating • Generating	• Identify or locate • Act upon or react • Interpret • Communicate	• Identify, locate or access • Act upon and use (order, count, estimate, compute, measure, model) • Interpret, evaluate and analyse • Communicate	• Access and assess situations mathematically • Act on and use mathematics • Evaluate, critically reflect, make judgements
Contexts	• Home and family • Health and safety • Community and citizenship • Consumer economics • Work • Leisure and recreation	• Everyday life • Work-related • Society and community • Further learning	• Everyday life • Work-related • Society and community • Further learning	• Personal • Work • Societal/community

	IALS	ALL	PIAAC Cycle 1	PIAAC Cycle 2
Factors affecting task difficulty	• Type of match • Type of information requested • Plausibility of distractors • Type of calculation • Operation specificity	• Type of match/problem • Plausibility of distractors • Complexity of mathematical information • Type of operation • Expected number of operations	• Type of match/problem • Plausibility of distractors • Complexity of mathematical information • Type of operation • Expected number of operations	• Type of match/problem • Plausibility of distractors • Complexity of mathematical information • Type of operation • Expected number of operations
Assessment mode	Paper-based	Paper-based	Computer-based (laptop device) + paper-based option	Computer-based (tablet device) + paper-based option in a limited number of countries

Sources: For IALS: Murray, Kirsch and Jenkins (1998[8]). For ALL: Murray, Clermont and Binkley (2005[10]). For PIAAC Cycle 1: (OECD, 2019[17]). For PIAAC Cycle 2: the frameworks included in this volume.

Annex Table 1.A.3. Problem solving

	ALL	PIAAC Cycle 1	PIAAC Cycle 2
Construct	Analytical Problem Solving	Problem Solving in Technology-Rich Environments	Adaptive Problem Solving
Definition	Problem solving involves goal-directed thinking and action in situations for which no routine solution procedure is available. The problem solver has a more or less well defined goal, but does not immediately know how to reach it. The incongruence of goals and admissible operators constitutes a problem. The understanding of the problem situation and its step-by-step transformation based on planning and reasoning, constitute the process of problem solving.	Problem solving in technology-rich environments involves the ability to use digital technology, communication tools and networks to acquire and evaluate information, communicate with others and perform practical tasks. The assessment focuses on the abilities to solve problems by setting up appropriate goals and plans, and accessing and making use of information through computers and computer networks.	Adaptive problem solving involves the capacity to achieve one's goals in a dynamic situation, in which a method for solution is not immediately available. It requires engaging in cognitive and metacognitive processes to define the problem, search for information, and apply a solution in a variety of information environments and contexts.
Cognitive processes	• Defining the goal • Analysing the given situation and construct a mental representation • Devising a strategy and plan the steps to be taken • Executing the plan, including control and – if necessary – modification of the strategy • Evaluating the result	• Setting goals and monitoring progress • Planning • Acquiring and evaluating information • Using information	• Definition • Searching • Application
Content	Problems	Technology: • *Hardware devices* • *Software applications* • *Commands and functions* • *Representations* (e.g. text, graphics, video) Nature of problems: • *Intrinsic complexity* which includes the number of steps required for solution, the number of alternatives, complexity of computation and/or transformation, number of constrains • *Explicitness of the problem statement*, for example largely unspecified or described in detail	Aspects of problems: • Problem configuration • Dynamics of the situation • Features of the environment • Information environment
Contexts	Not specified	• Personal • Work and occupation • Civic	• Personal • Work • Social/community

	ALL	PIAAC Cycle 1	PIAAC Cycle 2
Factors affecting task difficulty	Not specified	• Minimal number of steps required to solve the problem • Number of options or alternatives at various stages in the problem space • Diversity of operators required, complexity of computation/transformation • Likelihood of impasses or unexpected outcomes • Number of constraints to be satisfied • Amount of transformation required to communicate a solution • Ill defined (implicit, unspecified) vs. well defined (explicit, described in detail)	• Number of elements, relations, and operations • Salience and accessibility of operators • Interactions between problem elements • Number of parallel tasks and goals • Number of features that change and their relevance • Salience of change (if something changes) • Frequency of change • Degree of impasse • Wealth of information • Proportion of irrelevant information • (Lack of) Structure of the environment • Number of sources of information
Assessment mode	Paper-based	Computer-based (laptop device)	Computer-based (tablet device)

Sources: For ALL: Murray, Clermont and Binkley (2005[10]). For PIAAC Cycle 1: (OECD, 2019[17]). For PIAAC Cycle 2: the frameworks included in this volume.

Notes

[1] Results from IALS can be found in OECD/Statistics Canada (2000[9]) and results from ALL in OECD/Statistics Canada (2005[25]; 2011[26]).

[2] Results have been published in OECD (2013[21]; 2016[22]; 2019[15]). A comprehensive bibliography of publications based on PIAAC over the period 2008 to 2019 is provided in Maehler, Jakowatz and Konradt (2020[29]).

[3] The PIAAC Technical Standards and Guidelines [(PIAAC, 2014[2]), Guideline 10.4.1] provide that the interview should be completed in the respondent's home. However, if the respondent prefers, it may be conducted at a neutral location such as a library, community centre or office. On average, across all countries, around 91% of interviews took place in the respondent's home [see Keslair, 2018 (pp. 11-13[19])]. In a small number of countries, around a third of interviews took place in a location other than the respondent's residence.

[4] The background questionnaire used in Cycle 1 of PIAAC can be accessed at: http://www.oecd.org/skills/piaac/BQ_MASTER.HTM. The background questionnaire for Cycle 2 will be largely similar, although it will be improved and updated in a number of dimensions.

[5] See, for example, the frameworks for PISA (OECD, 2019[23]), TIMSS (Mullis and Martin, 2013[27]) and PIRLS (Mullis and Martin, 2015[28]).

[6] The assessment is usually delivered in the national language or languages only. In a small number of participating countries, the assessment is also made available in widely spoken minority languages [see Table 4.11 in OECD (2019[17]).

[7] Tout (2020[7]) offers a comprehensive overview of the changes in the conceptualisation of 'numeracy' between IALS and PIAAC Cycle 2. A good discussion of the factors that influence the evolution of assessment frameworks in reading in PISA which is also relevant to PIAAC can be found in OECD (2019, pp. 22-27[23]).

[8] See OECD (2019[24]) for an exploration of the log-file data derived from PIAAC.

[9] One aspect of the assessment of literacy has remained constant since IALS in adult assessments is that it has been undertaken as an assessment of *reading* (of the understanding of and engagement with written texts) and has not included the dimension of *writing* or the production of text. This represents a pragmatic choice rather than a theoretical position. It is acknowledged that writing represents an important dimension of a broad concept of literacy. However, the challenges of directly assessing proficiency are sufficiently large to make it impractical in large-scale cross-national assessments such as PIAAC.

[10] As well as text formats common in digital environments (e.g. multiple texts or texts constituted by series of juxtaposed texts).

[11] Performance in the reading components assessment was reported separately from performance in literacy in PIAAC Cycle 1.

[12] In the words of the numeracy framework, Cycle 1 numeracy test items were 'based predominantly around static images and associated responses' and were 'more like paper-based assessments transferred onto a computer' (numeracy framework).

[13] This is also true of PISA where three separate constructs have been assessed: analytical problem solving (2003), creative problem solving (2012) and collaborative problem solving (2015).

[14] Paper-based versions of the assessments of literacy and numeracy were available for respondents.

[15] As a variable proportion of the 16-65 year-old population took the assessment on computer, comparison of mean scores between countries was not possible. Presentation of country differences focusses on the proportion of the population performing at different proficiency levels.

[16] The exception is the reading assessment in PISA 2000 in which fifteen prose literacy items from IALS were included. The intention was to see whether the results of the two studies could be reported on a common scale. Chapter 8 of (OECD, 2002[20]) discusses the findings of an analysis of the performance of students on the IALS items.

[17] The description of PIAAC as a 'PISA for adults' [see, for example, Wallin (2018[30])] ignores the fact that adult assessments (in the form of IALS) predated PISA and fails to acknowledge the strong influence of IALS on PISA. It is important to note that PISA also owes a considerable debt to the International Evaluation Association (IEA) studies TIMSS and PIRLS which demonstrated the feasibility and utility of large-scale international assessments of school students.

[18] The members of the expert groups are listed in the acknowlegments.

2 PIAAC Cycle 2 assessment framework: Literacy

Jean-François Rouet (Chair), Centre national de la recherche scientifique, University of Poitiers

Mary Anne Britt, Northern Illinois University

Egil Gabrielsen, University of Stavanger

Johanna Kaakinen, University of Turku

Tobias Richter, University of Würzburg

In cooperation with Marylou Lennon, Educational Testing Service

Literacy skills play an essential part in adults' personal, social and professional life. In addition, the spread of digital technologies further emphasises the importance of reading literacy. As a set of cognitive abilities, literacy involves: accessing texts, or passages within texts, that match readers' tasks and needs; understanding the literal contents of text(s) and drawing adequate inferences both within and across texts; and evaluating texts and their sources for accuracy, soundness, and relevance, as well as reflecting on authors' purposes and strategies. The PIAAC assessment of literacy draws from a broad range of contexts and text types, from personal narratives to descriptions and arguments. It is designed as a set of scenarios involving one or several texts and a set of questions using various response formats. The main factors expected to drive item difficulty and to define proficiency levels are identified in this framework document.

Introduction

The term literacy (from the Latin "litera": letter, written sign) refers to one's ability to comprehend and use written sign systems. Literacy may be defined both as a set of generalised abilities [e.g., decoding words and comprehending sentences; (Perfetti, 1985[1])] and a set of cultural practices and values that vary across human groups and communities (Street and Street, 1984[2]). Thus, the literate individual is both a person who is able to make use of a broad diversity of written materials in the service of wide range of activities, and a person who is knowledgeable of the cultural standards of their communities of practice (Rouet and Britt, 2017[3]).

Since the invention of written sign systems some five thousand years ago, written communication has played an increasing role in societies throughout the world. The percentage of humans who can read and write has increased steadily over the past centuries, even though an estimated 750 million adults still cannot read and write fluently, with the highest rates of illiteracy matching the lowest levels of economic development (UNESCO, 2017[4]). In countries where people are given a chance to become literate, teenagers' and adults' actual levels of mastery vary to a remarkable extent. Furthermore, individual levels of literacy are usually associated with better living conditions, jobs, and health (Morrisroe, 2014[5]; OECD, 2013[6]).

One reason why literacy has become so important is that, in the modern world, written communication pervades most aspects of people's lives, whether personal, social, or professional. A study found that typical American adults read on an average of nine occasions per day, slightly more on working days than on weekends and holidays, and mostly in relation with practical tasks (White, Chen and Forsyth, 2010[7]). Depending on the context and purpose, reading may take a wide diversity of forms. Adults sometimes read extended pieces of continuous texts for the sake of enjoyment or just to comprehend an author's main points, but they more often scan pages to search for information that matches specific needs or questions. To serve these purposes, adults read a wide variety of texts ranging from e-mails to leaflets to timetables and instruction manuals. While doing so, they use a broad diversity of strategies and tactics, which all belong to the construct of literacy (Alexander and The Disciplined Reading and Learning Research Laboratory, 2012[8]; Britt, Rouet and Durik, 2018[9]; Goldman, 2004[10]).

The spread of computers and Internet access over the past two decades has further exacerbated the importance of literacy skills in contemporary societies (Leu et al., 2017[11]). There is little that an illiterate person can do with a smartphone, a tablet or a laptop. Written signs are ubiquitous in most computer applications, including the most widely used video sharing platforms. Digital reading is increasingly important for people to access jobs, services and goods, and to participate in communities.

For these reasons, acquiring valid and reliable estimates of what adults can do with printed texts has become a prominent target for public institutions. Several rounds of studies have been conducted at an international level over the past decades.

The second PIAAC study in the context of past international literacy studies

Since the early 1990s, three large-scale cross-country assessments of literacy and basic skills of the adult population have taken place. The first was the International Adult Literacy Survey (IALS) (Murray, Kirsch and Jenkins, 1998[12]), which was conducted in 22 countries and regions over the period 1994-1998. The second, known as the Adult Literacy and Life Skills Survey (ALL) (OECD/Statistics Canada, 2005[13]; 2011[14]), was undertaken over 2002-2008 in 11 countries. A successor to IALS and ALL – the Programme for the International Assessment of Adult Competencies (PIAAC Cycle 1) (OECD, 2013[6]) was administered in 39 countries and regions over the period 2011-2019 (National Center for Education Statistics (NCES), n.d.[15]).

IALS, ALL and PIAAC share a common conceptual framework and approach to the assessment of literacy skills, covering the conceptualisation of literacy, the approach to measurement, data quality and reporting of results (Kirsch and Lennon, 2017[16]).

Developments between IALS and PIAAC

One of the major areas in which there has been a change between the three assessments concerns the skill domains assessed. IALS included three separate domains of literacy: prose literacy, document literacy and quantitative literacy. The major change between IALS and ALL was that a new numeracy scale replaced the quantitative scale, while the prose and document scales were kept.

The measurement framework for literacy in PIAAC Cycle 1 was heavily based on those used in IALS and ALL, but in PIAAC literacy was assessed on a single scale rather than on two separate scales (prose and document literacy in ALL). PIAAC Cycle 1 also expanded the kinds of texts covered by including electronic texts in addition to the continuous (prose), non-continuous (document) and combined texts of the IALS and ALL frameworks. In addition, the assessment of literacy was extended to include a measure of reading component skills. This was designed for people with low levels of literacy competence and focused on assessment of the foundational skills needed to gain basic meaning from texts. The skills tested were print vocabulary, sentence processing and passage fluency.

PIAAC Cycle 1 also differed from IALS and ALL in that it mainly was an integrated computer-based assessment. The majority of respondents were assessed using a laptop computer. A pen-and-paper version of the literacy (and numeracy) assessment was available for respondents who had insufficient familiarity with computers or preferred the paper-and-pencil version for other reasons (26%).

Information technology and the changing nature of literacy

During the past 10 years, the use of internet has grown rapidly all over the world. According to a recent estimate (ITU, 2017[17]), more than half (53.6%) of the world's households has internet access – a dramatic increase from just less than 20% of the households having internet access in 2005, and just over 30% in 2010. The number of individuals using the internet has naturally grown as the internet access has become more common. It is estimated that there are 3.5 billion internet users today, representing almost half (48%) of the world's population (ITU, 2017[17]).

The rapid growth of the use of internet means that in today's world, reading often takes place in digital environments: people search and read timetables, maps and calendars online, they look for products and product reviews and purchase them on the internet, look up information in Wikipedia, read newspapers and blogs online, and participate in social media. The medium for accessing information is rapidly moving from print to screens to handheld devices, such as smartphones. As digital media affords different types of activities than traditional print media, reading in digital environments poses different cognitive demands and challenges to the reader than reading in print (Mangen and van der Weel, 2016[18]). While digital environments allow features that can support comprehension, recent evidence suggests that reading comprehension of informational texts may suffer when text material is presented in digital form in comparison to print (Delgado et al., 2018[19]).

One notable difference between print and digital media is that printed text is static and linear in nature, whereas digital texts often are hypertexts, which can include embedded hyperlinks to other sources, including multimedia. The ability to navigate within the interrelated network of documents, and the ability to locate relevant information among the potentially distracting information, are thus crucial aspects of skillful digital reading (Salmerón et al., 2018[20]).

The current framework aims at describing reading literacy in the present day context, in which digital reading is a central aspect of active participation in society. Three core sets of abilities are required for skilful reading in the complex information environments readers interact with: 1) ability to navigate within and between networked documents, 2) ability to comprehend and integrate multiple and sometimes disparate sources of information, and 3) ability to critically evaluate the information presented (Britt and Gabrys, 2001[21]; Rouet and Potocki, 2018[22]; Salmerón et al., 2018[20]).

Evolution of the PIAAC Cycle 2 Literacy domain in comparison with previous frameworks

As a consequence of the increasing uses of digital communication, there is a need to expand the construct of literacy to account for the advanced skills that enable people to interact with complex repositories of information. These include an ability to identify relevant items within sets of texts, and to scan the selected texts in order to locate information of interest. During their search for relevant information, readers use a range of criteria to discard irrelevant or inadequate information while identifying the most helpful resources. In addition, proficient readers need to comprehend information not just from one text, but also across multiple texts potentially containing fixed or animated graphs, still pictures and video segments in addition to written information. As evidenced in research studies, integrating information from multiple documents requires specific mental processes that come on top of the more traditional comprehension processes (Rouet, Britt and Potocki, 2019[23]). Finally, being literate increasingly requires readers to distance themselves from the information they are processing, questioning the accuracy, completeness, actuality of the information, as well as the competence, perspective and potential biases of the authors and publishers. These validation processes (Britt, Richter and Rouet, 2014[24]; Singer, 2013[25]) rest on specific types of knowledge and heuristics that any assessment of literacy should give due consideration.

As the domain expands to represent more sophisticated strategies, care must also be taken to describe the skills of those who only have a limited ability to comprehend and use written texts. Studies like PIAAC have found that in many countries a substantial proportion of adults still experience difficulties with the foundational processes that support any kind of literate activities: identify written words or symbols, make sense of simple sentences, draw basic inferences. There have been calls to increase the precision of the assessment at the lower end of the proficiency scale. The PIAAC framework acknowledges the role of these foundational skills and aims to provide satisfactory coverage of their distribution in the population.

Finally, an assessment of literacy must also consider people's active engagement in literate activities both at work and in their daily life. Exposure to written texts has been found to be a factor of children's acquisition of literacy skills (Stanovich and West, 1989[26]). Likewise, adults who encounter frequent opportunities to use texts are likely to develop better skills and to maintain them over time. Therefore, information about individual exposure to and engagement with texts may provide helpful information to understand the links between skill use and proficiency.

Definition of literacy

PIAAC Cycle 2 uses a parsimonious definition of literacy that aims to highlight a set of core cognitive processes involved in most, if not all literate activities. At the same time, the definition acknowledges that literate activities "do not happen in a vacuum" (Snow and the RAND reading study Group, 2002[27]). Instead, they are done in the service of one's goals, one's development and participation in society. These diverse purposes and contexts contribute to shaping the way individuals make use of written texts, hence their inclusion in the definition.

> "Literacy is accessing, understanding, evaluating and reflecting on written texts in order to achieve one's goals, to develop one's knowledge and potential and to participate in society."

We elaborate on each part of the definition below, emphasising some important theoretical advances in the domain, as well as evidence from the first PIAAC cycle and former research studies.

"Literacy..."

Although the etymology of the word literacy directly points to written language, in past decades the term has been used to refer to an increasingly broad array of domains and interests, for instance in "health literacy", "financial literacy" or "computer literacy". In some definitions, the activities denoted by these phrases have only remotely and incidentally to do with written language. In the present framework, the word is taken in its broadest but also most literal sense, to describe the proficient use of written language artefacts such as texts and documents, regardless of the type of activity or interest considered. This characterisation of literacy highlights both the universality of written language (i.e., its potential to serve an infinite number of purposes in an infinite number of domains) and the very high specificity of the core ability underlying all literate activities, that is, the ability to read written language. As demonstrated in neuroscience research, learning to read is a very special experience with consequences on the organisation of some areas of the brain (Dehaene, 2009[28]).

"is accessing..."

Proficient readers are not just able to comprehend the texts they are faced with. They can also reach out to texts that are relevant to their purposes, and search passages of interest within those texts (McCrudden and Schraw, 2007[29]; Rouet and Britt, 2011[30]). Searching text is cognitively distinct from reading for comprehension (Guthrie and Kirsch, 1987[31]). When searching, the proficient reader makes use of text organisers (such as tables of contents and headers) in order to inform relevance decisions; the proficient reader can also adjust the pace and depth of processing, alternating phases of quick skimming with phases of sustained, deep reading for comprehension. Finally, proficient readers are parsimonious: they may decide to quit a passage upon realising that it does not contain helpful information. In the PIAAC literacy framework, these processes are subsumed under the term "accessing".

"understanding..."

Most definitions of literacy acknowledge that the primary goal of reading is for the reader to make sense of the contents of the text. This can be as basic as comprehending the meaning of the words, to as complex as comprehending the dispute between two authors making opposite claims on a social-scientific issue. Whatever the context, any literate activity (including accessing a piece of text or a passage within a text) requires some level of understanding. Theories of text comprehension (Kintsch, 1998[32]) usually distinguish the literal understanding of the message from a deeper level of understanding in which the reader integrates their prior knowledge with the text contents through the production of various types of inferences (i.e., a situation model). Prior knowledge of the domain has a strong (usually positive) impact on the deeper level of understanding.

"evaluating and reflecting..."

Readers continually make judgements about a text they are approaching. They evaluate whether the text is appropriate for the task at hand and whether it will provide the information they need. Readers also make judgements about the accuracy and reliability of both the content and the source of the message (Bråten,

Strømsø and Britt, 2009[33]; Richter, 2015[34]). They attempt to detect and explain any biases and gaps in the coherence or persuasiveness of the text. And, for some texts, they must make judgements about the quality of the text, both as a craft object and as a tool for acquiring information.

"on written text…"

In the context of PIAAC Cycle 2, the phrase "written text" designates pieces of discourse primarily based on written language. Written texts may include non-verbal elements such as charts or illustrations. However, pictures, video and other visual media are not considered written texts per se.

A text typically includes two broad components: a source and a content. The source of the text is a set of parameters that identify the origin and dissemination of the text. The most typical source parameters are a description of the author (for instance, "Alfred Nobel, a Swedish chemist and businessman"), the publication medium and date of the text. But source information sometimes includes more specific details about the text, for instance "second edition", or "confidential". Although all texts have a source, source information is not always provided together with the content. In addition, emerging practices of online publishing and social media have tended to make it more challenging for the reader to identify the source of the text.

As in the first cycle of PIAAC (and in related studies such as PISA), the assessment of literacy will include a wide variety of text types, such as narrative, descriptive or argumentative. Texts in various formats, such as continuous, non-continuous or mixed will be included. Just as in the real world, some of these texts may be presented in a static way, meaning that the reader has only a limited opportunity to navigate through them,[1] whereas others, especially in digital environments, contain interactive navigation tools such as interactive tables of contents, hyperlinks and other devices. The PIAAC definition of written texts encompasses both static and interactive materials.

"in order to achieve one's goals,"

Just as written languages were created to meet the needs of emergent civilisations, at an individual level, literacy is primarily a means for one to achieve their goals. Goals relate to personal activities but also to the workplace and to interaction with others. Literacy is increasingly important in meeting those needs, whether simply finding one's way through a building, or negotiating complex bureaucracies, whose rules are commonly available only in written texts (and increasingly only in digital forms). Literacy is also important in meeting adult needs for sociability, for entertainment and leisure, for developing one's community and for work.

"to develop one's knowledge and potential and to participate in society."

Developing one's knowledge and potential highlights one of the most powerful consequences of being literate. Written texts may enable people to learn about topics of interest, but also to become skilled at doing things and to understand the rules of engagement with others.

Written communication is primarily and ultimately a consequence of humans being a sophisticated social species. Texts are communication artefacts, they serve the purpose of transmitting information but also feelings and values to others. As such, literacy contributes to building, nurturing and preserving social cohesion.

Core dimensions of the literacy domain

The PIAAC literacy assessment aims to provide a complete and accurate description of what adults can do with texts in a broad range of contexts and tasks. To that aim, the literacy domain is organised along a set of dimensions that ensure a broad coverage and a precise description of what people can do at each level of proficiency. In this section we describe the most important dimensions, which will be used to help define the proficiency levels for literacy.

Cognitive task demands

Naturalistic reading is a complex and versatile process. Proficient readers can read systematically and intensely extended passages of texts, but they can also quickly scan a page in search for a single keyword. How readers approach texts is primarily determined by their reading goals, which themselves are informed by the reader's understanding of the context and the task demands (Britt, Rouet and Durik, 2018[9]). PIAAC identifies three groups of processes that support most reading activities: accessing text, understanding, and evaluating (Figure 2.1).

Figure 2.1. Three core cognitive processes supporting literacy

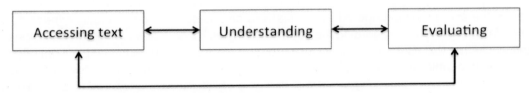

Note: These processes may unfold in any order and even in parallel.

The three processes correspond to those included in related assessments such as PIAAC Cycle 1 and PISA 2018. Table 2.1 shows the correspondence between the processes in these frameworks.

Table 2.1. Correspondence between the processes in PIAAC Cycle 2, PIAAC Cycle 1 and PISA 2018

PIAAC Cycle 2 (processes)	PIAAC Cycle 1 (aspects of tasks)	PISA 2018 (processes)
Accessing text	Access and identify information in the text	Locate information
Understanding	Integrate and interpret	Understand
Evaluating	Evaluate and reflect	Evaluate and reflect

Accessing text

Accessing text encompasses a number of literacy processes whereby readers examine the text(s) available, select the most relevant text, scan contents in search for specific pieces of information and locate these pieces through various types of cues. In addition, accessing conveys the sense of navigating across various texts or passages within texts as a function of task demands and the reader's progress towards their goal.

Ability to access information within and across texts is a core component of skilful reading in print and perhaps even more in digital environments (Salmerón et al., 2018[20]). Successful navigation means that the reader is capable of searching and locating relevant information within the texts, and this is influenced by the type of the question posed to the reader, as well as the nature of the materials. When searching, the proficient reader also calibrates their depth of processing of the information, merely scanning task-irrelevant contents while pausing and engaging in deeper processing of passages they deem relevant to the task.

The task or the question the reader has in mind has a big impact on how readers navigate within and between text documents (McCrudden and Schraw, 2007[29]). Identifying what information is relevant is only possible if the reader has formed an appropriate task model that provides specific criteria and guides the strategies utilised in searching and locating relevant information (Britt, Rouet and Durik, 2018[9]). Theories of purposeful reading suggest that when reading with specific objectives in mind, the incoming text information is constantly processed in the light of the task model (Britt, Rouet and Durik, 2018[9]). When task-relevant information is detected, attention is zoomed in to meet the task demands (Kaakinen and Hyönä, 2014[35]). The complexity of the task model depends on the question posed to the reader: simple questions may only require the search for a match between the question item and information within the text, whereas forming an appropriate task model for a more complex question may require background knowledge and inferencing. Lack of related prior knowledge may thus make it harder to search and locate relevant information (Kaakinen, Hyönä and Keenan, 2003[36]), as the reader's task model might not specify what is relevant, and reader has to scrutinise all information in order to decide whether it is relevant or not.

The nature of the text materials obviously influences how easy or hard it is to access information from a text or set of texts. The PIAAC literacy framework distinguishes two types of search processes: identifying a relevant text from a set, and locating information within a single text.

Identifying a relevant text in a set. If the available material consists of multiple texts (for instance, several documents on the same topic), readers have to first search and select the text that is expected to contain the most helpful information, disregarding the other items. Then readers need to search and locate relevant information within that text (Britt, Rouet and Durik, 2018[9]). Searching a relevant text in a set often involves using lists such as a table of contents (Dreher and Guthrie, 1990[37]) or the page showing the results of a query in a search engine. In selecting an item in this type of list, readers often use very simple heuristics such as the ranking of the items [priority given to the first items in the list, see (Fu and Pirolli, 2007[38]; Pan et al., 2007[39]; Wirth et al., 2007[40]) for evidence from search engine tasks] or the presence of highlighted information (Rouet et al., 2011[41]). However, in some tasks these simple heuristics may lead to suboptimal selections. For instance, in the Rouet et al. (2011[41]) study, 5th and 7th grade students were more likely to select irrelevant items when the items contained capitalised keywords. Moreover, if the materials contain a lot of distracting (irrelevant) information, the reader has to work harder to reject that information, which poses extra demands on their reasoning and working memory skills (Kaakinen and Hyönä, 2008[42]), and may cause them to forget the question (Rouet and Coutelet, 2008[43]).

Locating information within a text. When readers need to locate a relevant passage within a single text, signalling devices, such as headings and highlighting, can be used to facilitate the visual scanning and the identification of the relevant passage (Lemarié et al., 2008[44]). Knowing the function of text signals and using them while scanning a text are characteristics of proficient readers (Garner et al., 1986[45]; Potocki et al., 2017[46]).

Readers' search and locate processes pervade the whole reading cycle, from readers' initial decision of which text or passage they want to focus on, to their post-reading assessment of whether the passage contributes to reaching their goal (see below, "Evaluate and reflect").

Understanding

A large number of reading activities involve the parsing and integration of one or several extended passage(s) of text in order to form a complete representation of what the text is about. Cognitive theories of text comprehension usually distinguish two levels of representation (Kintsch, 1998[32]): a representation of the literal content of the text (literal comprehension), and a representation integrating the literal content with the reader's prior knowledge through mapping and inference processes [inferential comprehension or "situation model"; (McNamara and Magliano, 2009[47]; Zwaan and Singer, 2003[48])]. In addition, theories of multiple text comprehension (Perfetti, Rouet and Britt, 1999[49]; Britt and Rouet, 2012[50]) consider that text comprehension sometimes includes a representation of source features together with the respective contents.

Literal comprehension requires readers to comprehend the meaning of written words (e.g., "the kitten") and semantic propositions (i.e., small groups of words usually containing a substantive and a verb, adverb or an adjective, such as "the kitten is sleeping"). Propositions are then organised into hierarchies corresponding to one or a few sentences (Kintsch and van Dijk, 1978[51]). Literal comprehension tasks involve a direct or paraphrase type of match between the question and target information within a passage (for instance "what is the kitten doing?"). The reader may need to hierarchise or condense information at a local level in order to answer literal comprehension questions. Tasks requiring integration across entire text passages, such as identifying the main idea, summarising, or giving a title, are not considered literal, but rather inferential comprehension.

Inferential comprehension is the outcome of readers' integration of text information with their prior knowledge. The outcome is often labelled a "situation model" or "integrated text representation". Integrated text representations may be based on sentences but also on paragraphs or even on extended passages of text. As readers proceed through several sentences and paragraphs, they need to generate various types of inferences ranging from simple connecting inferences (such as the resolution of anaphora) to more complex coherence relationships (e.g. spatial, temporal, causal or claim-argument links). Sometimes the inference connects several portions of the text; in other cases, the inference is needed to connect the question and a text segment. Finally, the production of inferences is also needed in tasks requesting the reader to identify an implicit main idea, in order to produce a summary or a title for a given passage.

Multiple text inferential comprehension. When readers are faced with more than one text, integration and inference generation may be based on pieces of information located in different texts (Perfetti, Rouet and Britt, 1999[49]). Integration of information across texts poses a specific problem when the texts provide inconsistent or conflicting information. In those cases, readers must engage in evaluation processes in order to acknowledge and handle the conflict (Bråten, Strømsø and Britt, 2009[33]; Stadtler and Bromme, 2014[52]).

Evaluating

Competent readers can critically assess the quality of information in a text, even when the task does not explicitly require such an evaluation. The importance of evaluation as part of literacy has increased with the amount and heterogeneity of written information readers are faced with. Adult readers need to be able to evaluate to protect themselves from misinformation and propaganda and to make sense of conflicting information, such as political or scientific controversies. Evaluation can be based on attending to and assessing the accuracy, soundness, and task relevance of a text. The focus of these evaluations can be on the content or on the source of a text. Source evaluation plays a critical role when evaluating information from multiple texts, which sometimes provide discrepant or conflicting information (Bråten et al., 2011[53]; Leu et al., 2015[54]; Rouet and Britt, 2014[55]; Stadtler and Bromme, 2014[52]; Stadtler et al., 2013[56]). Handling conflict can require readers to assign discrepant claims to their respective sources and assess the credibility of the sources or believability of the claims (accuracy), to assess the relevance of the support or evidence provided for the discrepant claims (relevance), to evaluate the completeness of the provided perspectives and information from those possible (sufficiency), and to coordinate these outcomes to inform one's weight to make a decision about the conflict.

Evaluating accuracy. The information conveyed in written texts can be more or less accurate, ranging from agreed upon facts to intentionally false information. Even websites conveying science information often contain inaccurate or misleading information (Allen et al., 1999[57]). The evaluation of the accuracy of claims and statements can be based on the content or on the source of the text. Content evaluation includes validation against one's beliefs and knowledge (is the assertion true? Is it plausible? What information is presented to support the claim?) (Richter, Schroeder and Wöhrmann, 2009[58]). Readers can also assess accuracy indirectly, by identifying and assessing the source of the information (sourcing) (Britt and Aglinskas, 2002[59]; Wineburg, 1991[60]). For instance, the reader may ask whether the author is competent, well-informed and benevolent. When reading from web sources, readers may also check whether the information offered was submitted to any kind of editorial control prior to its publication (i.e., academic institutions, professional journalism vs. personal blogs or sites).

When dealing with conflicting information, readers have to be able to assign conflicting claims to different sources and use the credibility of the sources to assess the quality of information (Bråten, Strømsø and Britt, 2009[33]; Stadtler and Bromme, 2014[52]). Readers of multiple texts can also evaluate accuracy by comparing information across different sources (i.e., corroboration) (Britt and Aglinskas, 2002[59]; Wineburg, 1991[60]).

Evaluating soundness. The modern reader has to deal with texts that vary on a continuum of internal quality or soundness (Magliano et al., 2017[61]). In this framework, soundness encompasses two characteristics of discourse, namely completeness and internal consistency (Blair and Johnson, 1987[62]). Readers have to identify the completeness of the set of facts or evidence that is presented and to identify what is not accounted for or considered. Readers also have to identify perspectives presented in a text and assess whether all the important perspectives are represented. They may also have to account for any biases they find in the text. Evaluating bias may be based on language (does the text use neutral, factual language or rather colourful, evaluative language), or on the source of the text (i.e., interpreting, explaining or resolving different author biases that may impact sufficiency).

When evaluating internal consistency, readers must identify the structure of a text (e.g., persuade, inform) and evaluate the quality of the information in achieving that goal (e.g., warranted or sound claim-reason connections or reasonable cause-effect relationships). Does the author provide the type of information that is expected given the structural organisation of the text and what is the quality of that information for achieving the goal of the text? The evaluation of internal consistency can be especially challenging for argumentative texts (those attempt to convince the readers to accept a proposition, or claim by presenting supporting reasons; (Galotti, 1989[63]) because consistency cannot be determined by formal logic (Toulmin, 1958[64]).

When facing multiple texts that contradict each other, readers need to become aware of the conflict, understand where the conflict comes from (e.g., texts reporting discrepant facts or proposing discrepant interpretations) and to find ways to deal with the conflict (Britt and Rouet, 2012[50]; Stadtler and Bromme, 2014[52]).

Evaluating task relevance. As discussed in the section on "Accessing text" above, evaluating task relevance takes place throughout the reading process, from the reader's attempt to locate a text or passage of interest, to their post-reading assessment of whether the text or passage they have read was helpful (i.e., post-reading task relevance assessment); (Rieh, 2002[65]). When evaluating task relevance after reading a passage, readers must reconsider the task or question using an activated schema to understand what is being asked for and how to achieve that goal state (Britt, Rouet and Durik, 2018[9]; Rouet, Britt and Durik, 2017[66]). They must then assess whether a text they have just read contributes to reaching the goal state.

Research considers that there are two main routes in assessing task relevance. One consists in evaluating the content of the text, the other consists in evaluating the source (i.e., the person or the organisation responsible for authoring and disseminating the text). Both content and source evaluation can focus on accuracy, soundness or task relevance (Table 2.2). For instance, a layperson may realise that the text comes from a specialised medium (e.g., an academic journal or institution) and that the level of language and details is not suited to their prior knowledge and goals. Importantly, task relevance evaluation requires task readers to interpret the task or question using activated schema to understand what is being asked for and how to achieve that goal state (Britt, Rouet and Durik, 2018[9]).

The PIAAC literacy assessment will include tasks involving multiple, possibly discrepant texts and a series of items assessing each of the evaluate processes.

Table 2.2. Summary of different types of evaluation processes

	Accuracy	Soundness	Task relevance
Content evaluation	Plausibility Quality of evidence	Completeness of facts or perspectives; bias in explanation or interpretation Internal consistency	Contribution to reading goals
Source evaluation	Author competence, bias Editorial control	Author's explicit or covert interests	Appropriateness of text type with respect to one's goals and abilities

Reflecting on the author's intent, purpose, and effectiveness. When evaluating texts, readers need to be aware of the author's intent or purpose for writing. Author purposes include to entertain, to inform, to explain or to describe, or to persuade. Author purposes generally have to be inferred from the structure and form of the text, although they are sometimes stated explicitly, for instance in a preface, an overview, or in a separate text, for instance a publisher leaflet or an interview with a journalist. Readers can also infer authors' purposes by acquiring information about the author's opinion, beliefs, attitude, assumption, or bias.

In addition to identifying the author's purpose and viewpoint, the reader can evaluate how the author conveyed their points and whether it was effective. The structure of the text as well as tone, word choice and writing style can provide cues to author purpose and perspective. In the context of the PIAAC literacy study, "Reflect" represents tasks in which the reader is explicitly asked about authors' intentions, purposes or effectiveness.

Because handling conflict across texts includes all aspects of evaluating and reflecting, it is important to include units involving multiple, discrepant texts to assess the extent to which adults can meet the challenges involved in contemporary reading situations.

Texts

Texts are vehicles that convey the ideas, beliefs and intentions of their authors. They are communication artefacts anchored in space and time (Wineburg, 1994[67]). Every text involves a source (where the text comes from: author, date and so forth) and some content (what is said in the text). Source and content information are both important for comprehending and making use of texts (Perfetti, Rouet and Britt, 1999[49]). Moreover, with the advent of digital technology, laypersons have access to a growing diversity of textual materials. In addition to traditional genres such as a novel, a newspaper article or a cooking recipe, new genres have appeared such as blogs, forums, or instant messaging systems (e.g. Twitter). Furthermore, text genres tend to be presented in combination, such as when readers react to an online article or offer their versions of a cooking recipe. The profusion of text genres represents new opportunities, but also new challenges for contemporary readers. In addition, readers are increasingly faced with multiple texts that they may have to read in parallel in order to achieve their purpose. For instance, a person who seeks advice about a health issue may look up a web forum and read several messages posted by different people. The person may then turn to the website of a hospital to seek further information, and so on and so forth. Therefore, modern text comprehension involves an ability to make sense of multiple and sometimes heterogeneous sets of texts.

In this context, ensuring the coverage of the literacy domain is a challenge, as there is no universal categorisation of text types, genres and formats. The PIAAC literacy framework rests on a distinction between single and multiple texts (as defined by a distinct source). In addition, the framework relies on distinctions made in previous assessments, such as text types (e.g., narration, description), text format (i.e., continuous vs. non-continuous texts) and the presence of organising devices enabling readers to navigate within and across texts.

Text types

Text types describe the diversity of texts as prototypical representations of the world and communication acts. The most frequently encountered text types are description, narration, exposition, argumentation, instruction and transaction. Naturalistic texts are usually difficult to categorise, as they tend to cut across these prototypical categories. For example, a newspaper article might start with a specific story (narration), then engage in some definitions and context (explanation), and a critical analysis (argumentation). Nevertheless, it is useful to categorise texts according to the text type, based on the predominant characteristics of the text, in order to ensure that the instrument samples across a range of texts that represent different types of reading. The classification of texts used in the PIAAC literacy assessment is borrowed from that used in the previous PIAAC and PISA assessments.

Description is the type of text where the information refers to properties of objects in space. Descriptive texts are mostly meant to answer "what" or "how" type of questions. Descriptions can take several forms. Impressionistic descriptions present information from a subjective point of view reflecting the viewer's impressions of elements, relations, qualities and directions in space. Technical descriptions present information from a more objective and perspective-independent viewpoint. Frequently, technical descriptions use non-continuous text formats such as diagrams and illustrations. Typical examples of descriptions are a depiction of a particular place in a travelogue or diary, a catalogue, a geographical map, an online flight schedule or a description of a feature, function or process in a technical manual.

Narration is the type of text where the information refers to properties of characters and objects in time. Narration typically answers questions relating to "what", "when", "how" or "in what sequence". Why characters in stories behave as they do is another important question that narration typically answers. Narration can take different forms. Narratives present change from the point of view of subjective selection and emphasis, recording actions and events from the point of view of subjective impressions in time. Reports present change from the point of view of an objective situational frame, recording actions and events which can be verified by others. News stories intend to enable the readers to form their own independent opinion of facts and events based on the reporter's account. Typical examples narrations are a novel, a biography, a play, a comic strip and a newspaper report of an event.

Exposition is the type of text meant to communicate concepts, phenomena and other mental constructs involving a set of interacting elements. The text provides an explanation of how the different elements interrelate in a meaningful whole and often answers questions about "how" and "why" (referring to enabling conditions and causal relationships). Expositions can take various forms. Expository essays provide a simple explanation of concepts, mental constructs or conceptions from a subjective point of view. Definitions explain how terms or names are interrelated with mental concepts. In showing these interrelations, the definition explains the meaning of words. Explications are a form of analytic exposition used to explain how a concept can be linked with words or terms. Minutes are a record of the results of meetings or presentations. Typical examples of expositions are a scholarly essay about the metabolism of sugar, a diagram showing a model of memory, and a graph of population trends.

Argumentation is the type of text that presents factual or interpretive claims about a situation, together with supporting reasons and warrants. Argumentative texts often answer "why" (as in, for instance, "why did this happen?" or "why should we do this?"), but also "what if" questions. An important subcategory of argumentative texts is persuasive and opinionative texts, referring to opinions and points of view. A "comment" relates the concepts of events, objects and ideas to a private system of thoughts, values and beliefs. "Scientific argumentation" relates concepts of events, objects and ideas to systems of thought and knowledge so that the resulting propositions can be verified as valid or non-valid. Examples of text objects in the text type category argumentation are a poster advertisement, the posts in an online forum and a web-based review of a book or film.

Instruction (sometimes called injunction) is the type of text that provides directions on what to do. Instructions present directions for certain behaviours in order to complete a task. Rules, regulations and statutes specify requirements for certain behaviours based on impersonal authority, such as practical validity or public authority. Examples of textual instruction are a cooking recipe, a series of diagrams showing a procedure for giving first aid and guidelines for operating digital software.

Transaction represents a written text that supports interpersonal communication, such as requesting that something is done, organising a meeting or making a social engagement with a friend. Before the spread of electronic communication, this kind of text was a significant component of some kinds of letters and, as an oral exchange, the principal purpose of many phone calls. Transactional texts are often personal in nature, rather than public, and this may help to explain why they do not appear to be represented in some of the corpora used to develop many text typologies. With the extreme ease of personal communication using e-mail, text messages, blogs and social networking websites, this kind of text has become much more significant as a reading text type in recent years. Transactional texts often build on common and possibly private understandings between communicators – though clearly, this feature is difficult to explore in a large-scale assessment. Examples of text objects in the text type transaction are everyday e-mail and text message exchanges between colleagues or friends that request and confirm arrangements.

Text format: Continuous, non-continuous and mixed texts

The building blocks of texts are written words, which can be organised according to the rules of syntax, coherence and cohesion, but also according to spatial dimensions such as in lists, tables and charts. In the PIAAC literacy framework, continuous texts are defined as sequences of sentences and paragraphs. These may fit into even larger structures such as sections, chapters and books. Non-continuous texts are defined as words, sentences or passages organised in a list or matrix format (Kirsch and Mosenthal, 1990[68]).

In both print and digital environments, written texts are often associated with non-verbal representations, such as graphics and pictures. The PIAAC assessment does not focus on these representations *per se*, but some tasks may involve the use of text in combination with graphics or pictures.

The PIAAC literacy framework also considers mixed texts, which involve both continuous and non-continuous components. In well-constructed mixed texts, the components (for example, a prose explanation including a graph or table) are mutually supportive through coherence and cohesion links at the local and global level. Mixed text is a common format in magazines, reference books and reports, where authors employ a variety of presentations to communicate information. In digital texts, authored web pages are typically mixed texts, with combinations of lists, paragraphs of prose and often graphics. Message-based texts, such as online forms, e-mail messages and forums, also combine texts that are continuous and non-continuous in format.

Text organisation: Layout, content representation and access devices

Naturalistic texts vary from a few lines to several hundreds of pages. Depending on the length and purpose, texts may include a range of devices aimed at representing content and facilitate access to passages of interest.

Organisation is primarily signalled by the sequence of sentences and texts, along with the use of different font sizes, font types such as italic and boldface or borders and patterns. Various types of discourse markers also provide information about how ideas are organised in the text. For example, sequence markers (first, second, third, etc.), signal the relation of each of the units introduced to each other and indicate how the units relate to the larger surrounding text. Causal connectors (therefore, for this reason, since, etc.) signify cause-effect relationships between parts of a text.

Larger texts often come with titles and headers, paragraphs and sections. These markers also provide clues to text boundaries (with space and a new header showing section completion, for example). Yet longer texts are organised into chapters, they include a table of contents and one or several indexes. Readers' awareness and use of these devices is critical to their effectiveness when reading texts for specific purposes (Goldman and Rakestraw Jr., 2000[69]).

Digital texts also come with a number of tools that let the user access and display specific passages. Some of these tools are identical to those found in printed texts (e.g., headers), whereas others are more specific to the electronic medium. Examples include windows, scroll bars, tabs, but also embedded hyperlinks. There is growing evidence that the processes involved in reading printed and digital texts differ, partly because of differences in presentation formats and navigation tools (Delgado et al., 2018[19]; Naumann, 2015[70]; OECD, 2011[71]). Therefore, it is important to assess readers' ability to deal with texts featuring a diversity of content representation and navigation tools.

The PIAAC literacy assessment will implement texts that vary on a continuum of length (i.e., single vs. multiple pages), but also diversity and density of content representation and access devices.

Source: Single vs. multiple texts

As mentioned in the introduction to this section, a text is defined by its source and its content. The PIAAC literacy framework defines single texts as texts that originate in a single source, i.e., an author, a publication medium, and a date of publication [other dimensions of the complex construct of a "source" will not be discussed here; see (Britt et al., 1999[72]), for a more detailed analysis of the construct of a source)]. Multiple texts are defined by having different authors, or being published through different channels or at different times.

It is important to note that in this framework the distinction between single and multiple texts is in principle independent from the amount of information contained in the text(s). A single text can be as short as a single sentence and as long as a whole book or website, as long as it has a single author (or group of authors), publication medium and date. Conversely, multiple texts can take the form of a series of brief passages, for instance in a web forum where different people post messages at different times. A single text can also contain embedded sources, that is, references to various authors or texts (Rouet and Britt, 2014[55]; Strømsø et al., 2013[73]).

Items in a set of multiple texts may have different relationships to each other: some texts may corroborate, complete, support or provide evidence for other texts, whereas others may disagree, contradict or conflict with others. Readers' cognitive representation of a set of texts together with their respective sources and the network of intertext relationships has been termed a "documents model" (Perfetti, Rouet and Britt, 1999[49]).

Table 2.3 summarises the dimensions of texts that are considered in the PIAAC literacy framework.

Table 2.3. Main dimensions of texts considered in the PIAAC literacy framework

Dimension	Levels
Text type	Description, narration, exposition, argumentation, instruction, transaction
Text format	Continuous, non-continuous, mixed
Text organisation	Continuous dimension involving the amount of information (number of pages) and the density of content representation and access devices
Source	Single vs. multiple texts

Social contexts

Reading pervades all domains of an individual's life. Reading activities are normally situated in a social situation and may serve a range of purposes from personal to professional and civic. Both the motivation to read and the interpretation of the content may be influenced by the context. As a result, the PIAAC literacy framework defines three main types of contexts that will be represented in the assessment:

a) Work and occupation. Written texts play an important role in a wide range of occupations. Uses of text in an occupational context includes finding employment, finance, and being on the job (i.e., regulations, organisation, safety instructions). However, the materials used in the PIAAC literacy assessment do not include specialised job-specific texts, which obviously would pose the problem of prerequisite background knowledge.

b) Personal use. Reading is also important for personal purposes. Many adults engage in reading when dealing with interpersonal relationships, personal finance, housing, and insurance. They also increasingly make use of written materials in addressing health and safety issues (e.g., disease prevention and treatment, safety and accident prevention, first aid, and staying healthy). Adults also use texts in relation to their consuming habits: credit and banking, savings, and advertising, making purchases, and maintaining personal possessions. Finally, texts are important in organising leisure and recreation time, including travel, restaurants, and material read for leisure and recreation itself (games etc.).

c) Social and civic contexts. Finally, literacy is essential in adults' participation in social and civic life. Community and citizenship includes materials dealing with community resources, public services and staying informed. Education and training includes materials that deal with opportunities for further learning.

Assessing literacy

General organisation of literacy tasks

The construct of literacy encompasses what readers can do with texts and also what they comprehend and remember from the texts. This warrants the design of testing situations in which test-takers may be asked to complete tasks either with the text available or after they have read the text, based on their memory for text information. Research suggests that answering comprehension questions with or without text availability tap in part on distinct mental processes, and that assessment tasks without the text available might be more sensitive to the quality of the reading processes and less dependent from reader motivation and test-taking strategies (Ozuru et al., 2007[74]; Schroeder, 2011[75]). However, the PIAAC literacy assessment focuses on what adults can do with texts, and therefore it is based on scenarios involving questions and one or several texts that remain available throughout the task. This is arguably the most common scenario in adults' daily uses of text (White, Chen and Forsyth, 2010[7]).

The PIAAC assessment of literacy is based on test units in which participants are asked to make use of one or several texts in order to answer a set of questions. A short introduction usually provides some context and motivation for the unit. Each question elicits one of the core processes defined in the framework (see section on cognitive task demands). Questions are presented one by one in a blocked format in order to decrease the influence of test-taking strategies and to reduce variance in test completion time.

The texts used as stimuli reflect texts that test-takers may encounter in real life. Many of them are directly drawn from authentic materials with little, if any adaptation. This means that no effort is made to make these texts easier to read or to improve their organisation or presentation. Using naturalistic texts, sometimes even clearly suboptimal ones (for instance, poorly organised or using complex language), ensures a high level of face validity. However, no artificial difficulty or flaw is introduced at the time of test design.

Response formats

Questions can be designed using a wide range of response formats, such as constructed (open) responses, true-false judgements, multiple choice, or responses based on filling a blank or highlighting a text passage, to cite just some of the most common types. Computerised test delivery also affords additional response modes, such as "drag and drop". The form in which responses are collected – the response format – varies according to what is considered appropriate given the kind of evidence that is being collected, and also according to the pragmatic constraints of a large-scale assessment.

Response formats can involve demands on specific cognitive processes. For example, multiple-choice comprehension questions are typically dependent on decoding skills, because readers have to decode distractors or items, when compared to open constructed response items (Cain and Oakhill, 2006[76]; Ozuru et al., 2007[74]). Conversely, constructed responses tap on written production as much as on comprehension skills. Several studies suggest that the response format has a significant effect on the performance of different groups (Grisay and Monseur, 2007[77]; Schwabe, McElvany and Trendtel, 2015[78]). Finally, participants in different countries may be more or less familiar with different response formats. Consequently, the use of a diversity of response formats is recommended to ensure precision and to reduce potential biases. However, consistent with the general guidelines for PIAAC Cycle 2, the assessment of literacy will not include any constructed response. Besides removing the need for human scoring, this reduces the confounding of comprehension and written production skills.

Adaptive testing design

The deployment of computer-based assessment in PIAAC creates the opportunity to implement adaptive testing. Adaptive testing enables higher levels of measurement precision using fewer items per individual participant. This is accomplished by targeting more items that are aligned to the ability range of participants at different points in the ability distribution.

Adaptive testing has the potential to increase the resolution and sensitivity of the assessment, most particularly at the lower end of the performance distribution. For example, participants who perform low on items that assess their ease and efficiency of reading (e.g. reading fluency) will likely struggle on highly complex multiple text items. Thus, there would be benefit in providing additional lower-level texts for those participants to better assess specific aspects of their comprehension.

Recommended distribution of items

The Literacy Expert Group recommends the following distribution of items based on a typology of cognitive task demands, text size and contexts.

Recommended distribution by cognitive task demands and number of sources

The rationale for the recommended distribution per cognitive task demands is as follows: a substantial number of items (45%) should involve text understanding, both literal and inferential, as this is considered a core process present in most if not all reading activities. Due to its increased importance in digital environments, the category "access" (which involves identifying texts in a set and locating information within texts) should also be broadly represented (35%). Finally, about 20% of the tasks should involve one type of evaluation or reflection about the text.

As regards text size, most tasks (60%) will involve texts presented on a single page, with the view that some of these need to be simple enough so as to describe basic levels of literacy. Some of these short texts may involve multiple sources (such as, e.g., a series of short messages on a web forum page). However, acknowledging that readers most often face texts distributed across multiple pages (either from one or from several sources), the test will also include multi-page units. It is expected that tasks focusing on the process of "understanding" will be proportionally more represented in single page units, whereas "access" and "evaluate" tasks should be more frequent in multi-page units.

Table 2.4 presents the recommended distribution of items as a function of text size (i.e., single vs. multiple pages) and cognitive task demands.

Table 2.4. Recommended distribution of items as a function of text size and cognitive task demands

Cognitive task demands	Single page	Multiple pages	Total
Access	20%	15%	35%
Understand	30%	15%	45%
Evaluate	10%	10%	20%
Total	60%	40%	100%

It is further recommended that a majority of the test units (goal: 60%) include single source texts.

Recommended distribution by context

A broad range of tasks drawn from realistic contexts is meant to help ensure that no group of respondents will be either advantaged or disadvantaged based on their familiarity with, or interest in, a particular context. The recommended percentage of tasks for work, personal, community and education types of contexts is 15, 40, 30, and 15%, respectively.

Distribution across other relevant dimensions

No specific recommendation is made regarding a distribution of tasks across dimensions of text types or response formats, beyond the general recommendation to ensure a broad diversity and a representation of as many types as possible.

The role of fluent reading, engagement and metacognition

Reading fluency can be defined as an individual's ability to read words, sentences and connected text efficiently (Kuhn and Stahl, 2003[79]), i.e. both quickly and accurately. Fluent readers master the basic reading processes of recognising written words, assigning meaning to these words, and establishing a coherent sentence meaning by way of syntactic parsing and semantic integration. They do so without using a large amount of working memory and attentional resources (LaBerge and Samuels, 1974[80]; Perfetti, 1985[1]). Therefore, fluent readers have more cognitive resources available to invest in higher-level comprehension processes such as inferences and reading strategies (Walczyk et al., 2004[81]). The differential allocation of mental resources to low- vs. higher-level processes in struggling vs. fluent readers accounts for the strong link between fluent reading and text-level comprehension outcomes found in many studies and in all age groups ranging from primary school to adult readers (García and Cain, 2014[82]; Klauda and Guthrie, 2008[83]; Richter et al., 2013[84]).

To better assess reading fluency, the PIAAC Cycle 2 assessment will again include a measure of reading component skills. The components assessment tasks are designed to inform our understanding of the basic reading skills that underlay proficient literacy performance levels. These tasks help describe what low literate adults can do and therefore form a basis for learning, instruction, and policy with respect to helping low literate adults achieve higher literacy levels (Sabatini and Bruce, 2009[85]). In response to the OECD's requirement that the results of the components assessment be generalisable to the overall population, the components tasks will be administered to a representative subsample of all individuals who take the full literacy assessment.

The reading components assessment will include two sets of tasks, both of which were administered in the first cycle of PIAAC. The first set focuses on the ability to process meaning at the sentence level. Respondents will be shown a series of sentences, which increase in complexity, and be asked to identify if the sentence does or does not make sense in terms of properties of the real world or the internal logic of the sentence. The second set of tasks focuses on passage comprehension. For these tasks, respondents are asked to read passages where, at certain points, they must select a word from two provided alternatives so that the text makes sense [see sample tasks in (OECD, 2019[86])].

Because PIAAC Cycle 2 will be administered on tablets, it will be possible to precisely record both accuracy and response times for the component tasks. The accuracy data in the sentence verification and passage comprehension tasks will serve as indicators of the mastery of basic reading comprehension processes. They will be included in the scaling of the items in the PIAAC literacy assessment, increasing measurement precision in the lower range of the scale. The response times will serve as an indicator of fluency in basic reading processes, allowing researchers to explore its potential contribution to the mastery of the more complex literacy tasks in the PIAAC literacy assessment.

The concept of reading engagement refers to the degree of importance of reading to an individual and to the extent that reading plays a role in their daily life. Empirical studies with children and adults have shown that differences in engagement are systematically related to differences in performance on assessments. In particular, studies with different age groups provide evidence for an upward causal spiral: more proficient readers will read more and the exposure to printed texts will promote their reading development and lead to higher proficiency (Guthrie and Wigfield, 2000[87]; Mol and Bus, 2011[88]). The construct of engagement encompasses objective aspects such as the amount and diversity of reading one experiences in daily life, and also subjective aspects such as one's interest in reading, perception of control over reading, and reading efficacy. The PIAAC literacy assessments will capture core aspects of the objective aspects of reading engagement as part of the background questionnaire.

Metacognition, or one's awareness, monitoring and control of their own cognitive processes, is also considered an important aspect of reading literacy (Baker, 1989[89]). However due to methodological and practical constraints the PIAAC literacy study will not include any specific assessment of metacognition in reading. Metacognition will be indirectly assessed through its contribution to the more complex reading tasks which require strategic decisions and self-regulation to different degrees.

Factors driving task difficulty

The difficulty of literacy tasks is expected to depend on three series of factors, namely a) characteristics of the text(s); b) characteristics of the question; and c) the specific interaction between a question and a text (or set of texts).

In addition, some of these factors affect the difficulty of the task regardless of the specific cognitive demands involved, whereas other factors are specific to a certain type of task demand. Table 2.5 lists the main text, task, and text-by-task factors driving difficulty in general, and then more specifically for each type of cognitive task demand.

Table 2.5. Text, task, and text-by-task factors driving difficulty as a function of cognitive task demands

	Text factors	Task factors	Text-by-task factors
Factors affecting all tasks	Longer, multiple texts are generally more difficult because they increase processing load and require readers to sustain their attention over a longer time span. Longer texts are also more likely to contain distracting (task-irrelevant) information. Text dealing with unfamiliar contents, using unfamiliar words and/or a complex syntax or organisation are also more difficult regardless of the task. Content representation and signalling devices such as tables of contents, headers, boldface, underlining, and bullet points generally decrease the text difficulty.	Tasks involving a longer stem and/or unfamiliar words are more likely to be forgotten en route, thus requiring the reader to re-read the question. Readers with low-levels of self-monitoring may fail to realise that they need to refresh their memory. The lack of explicit guidance regarding which portion(s) of the materials should be inspected increases the difficulty of the question, compared to questions that include instructions as to where to look the answer.	Tasks involving a direct match between the question and the text are easier than tasks that require the reader to infer the link between the question and the relevant portion of the text. Texts that contain a large number of distracting information (for instance, passages sharing keywords with the question though irrelevant content wise) are more difficult than those in which a single passage is related to the question.
Difficulty drivers for "Accessing" tasks	Texts distributed across multiple pages require multiple stages of selection: selecting the right text and then the right portion of that text. Multi-page texts that are organised in non-linear ways, with several levels of links, are more difficult to search through than texts organised linearly or in the form of more shallow hierarchies.	Questions requiring the reader to gather multiple pieces of information across texts are more difficult than questions involving a single piece of information.	Texts containing content organisers (e.g., headers) that match the topic of the question are easier to access than those in which the location of information remains implicit.
Difficulty drivers for "Understanding" tasks	In addition to the general factors listed above, texts involving an implicit and/or unfamiliar structure are more difficult to understand. In sets of multiple texts, the presence of inconsistencies add the burden of identifying and resolving them.	Questions that require a large amount of information are more difficult that those that can be answered based on a single piece of information. Simple, connecting inferences are considered easier to perform than elaborative inferences, which require using one's prior knowledge.	Comprehension questions that require the test-taker to draw an inference based on text information are more difficult than questions whose answers are explicit in the text. Questions that require the test-taker to relate several pieces of information located in distant portions of the text(s) are more difficult than those for which the relevant information is grouped within a single section.
Difficulty drivers for "Evaluating" tasks	Unfamiliar, incomplete or less salient source indications make accuracy assessment more difficult. Unusual argument structures and incomplete arguments are more difficult to evaluate.	For familiar contents, factual inaccuracies are easier to detect than flaws in an argument structure (connection of claims and supporting reasons).	Texts involving low-quality sources issuing topically-matching information make it more difficult for the reader to evaluate the relevance of the information.

References

Alexander and The Disciplined Reading and Learning Research Laboratory (2012), "Reading into the future: Competence for the 21st century", *Educational Psychologist*, Vol. 47/4, pp. 259-280, http://dx.doi.org/10.1080/00461520.2012.722511. [8]

Allen, E. et al. (1999), "How reliable is science information on the web?", *Nature*, Vol. 402/6763, p. 722, http://dx.doi.org/10.1038/45370. [57]

Baker, L. (1989), "Metacognition, comprehension monitoring, and the adult reader", *Educational Psychology Review*, Vol. 1/1, pp. 3-38, http://dx.doi.org/10.1007/bf01326548. [89]

Blair, J. and R. Johnson (1987), "Argumentation as dialectical", *Argumentation*, Vol. 1/1, pp. 41-56, http://dx.doi.org/10.1007/bf00127118. [62]

Bråten, I. et al. (2011), "The role of epistemic beliefs in the comprehension of multiple expository texts: Toward an integrated model", *Educational Psychologist*, Vol. 46/1, pp. 48-70, http://dx.doi.org/10.1080/00461520.2011.538647. [53]

Bråten, I., H. Strømsø and M. Britt (2009), "Trust matters: Examining the role of source evaluation in students' construction of meaning within and across multiple texts", *Reading Research Quarterly*, Vol. 44/1, pp. 6-28, http://dx.doi.org/10.1598/rrq.44.1.1. [33]

Britt, M. and C. Aglinskas (2002), "Improving students' ability to identify and use source information", *Cognition and Instruction*, Vol. 20/4, pp. 485-522, http://dx.doi.org/10.1207/s1532690xci2004_2. [59]

Britt, M. and G. Gabrys (2001), "Teaching advanced literacy skills for the World Wide Web", in Wolfe, C. (ed.), *Webs We Weave: Learning and Teaching on the World Wide Web*, Academic Press, New York, http://dx.doi.org/10.1016/B978-012761891-3/50007-2. [21]

Britt, M. et al. (1999), "Content integration and source separation in learning from multiple texts", in Goldman, S., A. Graesser and P. van den Broek (eds.), *Narrative Comprehension, Causality, and Coherence: Essays in Honor of Tom Trabasso*, Lawrence Erlbaum Associates, Mahwah, NJ. [72]

Britt, M., T. Richter and J. Rouet (2014), "Scientific literacy: The role of goal-directed reading and evaluation in understanding scientific information", *Educational Psychologist*, Vol. 49/2, pp. 104-122, http://dx.doi.org/10.1080/00461520.2014.916217. [24]

Britt, M. and J. Rouet (2012), "Learning with multiple documents: Component skills and their acquisition", in Lawson, M. and J. Kirby (eds.), *Enhancing the Quality of Learning: Dispositions, Instruction, and Learning Processes*, Cambridge University Press. [50]

Britt, M., J. Rouet and A. Durik (2018), *Literacy beyond Text Comprehension*, Taylor and Francis, New York, http://dx.doi.org/10.4324/9781315682860. [9]

Cain, K. and J. Oakhill (2006), "Assessment matters: Issues in the measurement of reading comprehension", *British Journal of Educational Psychology*, Vol. 76/4, pp. 697-708, http://dx.doi.org/10.1348/000709905x69807. [76]

Dehaene, S. (2009), *Reading in the Brain*, Penguin Viking, New York. [28]

Delgado, P. et al. (2018), "Don't throw away your printed books: A meta-analysis on the effects of reading media on reading comprehension", *Educational Research Review*, Vol. 25, pp. 23-38, http://dx.doi.org/10.1016/j.edurev.2018.09.003. [19]

Dreher, M. and J. Guthrie (1990), "Cognitive processes in textbook chapter search tasks", *Reading Research Quarterly*, Vol. 25/4, pp. 323-339, http://dx.doi.org/10.2307/747694. [37]

Fu, W. and P. Pirolli (2007), "SNIF-ACT: A cognitive model of user navigation on the World Wide Web", *Human–Computer Interaction*, Vol. 22/4, pp. 355-412, http://dx.doi.org/10.1080/07370020701638806. [38]

Galotti, K. (1989), "Approaches to studying formal and everyday reasoning", *Psychological Bulletin*, Vol. 105/3, pp. 331-351, http://dx.doi.org/10.1037/0033-2909.105.3.331. [63]

García, J. and K. Cain (2014), "Decoding and reading comprehension: A meta-analysis to identify which reader and assessment characteristics influence the strength of the relationship in English", *Review of Educational Research*, Vol. 84/1, pp. 74-111, http://dx.doi.org/10.3102/0034654313499616. [82]

Garner, R. et al. (1986), "Children's knowledge of structural properties of expository text", *Journal of Experimental Psychology* no. 78, pp. 411-416. [45]

Goldman, S. (2004), "Cognitive aspects of constructing meaning through and across multiple texts", in Shuart-Ferris, N. and D. Bloome (eds.), *Uses of Intertextuality in Classroom and Educational Research*, Information Age Publishing, Greenwich, CT. [10]

Goldman, S. and J. Rakestraw Jr. (2000), "Structural aspects of constructing meaning from text", in Kamil, M. et al. (eds.), *Handbook of Reading Research, Volume III*, Lawrence Elrbaum Associates, Mahwah, NJ. [69]

Grisay, A. and C. Monseur (2007), "Measuring the equivalence of item difficulty in the various versions of an international test", *Studies in Educational Evaluation*, Vol. 33/1, pp. 69-86, http://dx.doi.org/10.1016/j.stueduc.2007.01.006. [77]

Guthrie, J. and I. Kirsch (1987), "Distinctions between reading comprehension and locating information in text", *Journal of Educational Psychology*, Vol. 79/3, pp. 220-227, http://dx.doi.org/10.1037/0022-0663.79.3.220. [31]

Guthrie, J. and A. Wigfield (2000), "Engagement and motivation in reading", in Kamil, M. et al. (eds.), *Handbook of Reading Research, Volume III*, Lawrence Elrbaum Associates, Mahwah, NJ. [87]

ITU (2017), *Measuring the Information Society Report 2017*, http://www.itu.int/en/ITU-D/Statistics/Pages/publications/mis2017.aspx (accessed on 9.10.2018). [17]

Kaakinen, J. and J. Hyönä (2014), "Task relevance induces momentary changes in the functional visual field during reading", *Psychological Science*, Vol. 25/2, pp. 626-632, http://dx.doi.org/10.1177/0956797613512332. [35]

Kaakinen, J. and J. Hyönä (2008), "Perspective-driven text comprehension", *Applied Cognitive Psychology*, Vol. 22/3, pp. 319-334, http://dx.doi.org/10.1002/acp.1412. [42]

Kaakinen, J., J. Hyönä and J. Keenan (2003), "How prior knowledge, WMC, and relevance of information affect eye fixations in expository text", *Journal of Experimental Psychology: Learning, Memory, and Cognition*, Vol. 29/3, pp. 447-457, http://dx.doi.org/10.1037/0278-7393.29.3.447. [36]

Kintsch, W. (1998), *Comprehension: A Paradigm for Cognition*, Cambridge University Press, Cambridge, MA. [32]

Kintsch, W. and T. van Dijk (1978), "Toward a model of text comprehension and production", *Psychological Review*, Vol. 85/5, pp. 363-394, http://dx.doi.org/10.1037/0033-295x.85.5.363. [51]

Kirsch, I. and M. Lennon (2017), "PIAAC: A new design for a new era", *Large-scale Assessments in Education*, Vol. 5/11, http://dx.doi.org/10.1186/s40536-017-0046-6. [16]

Kirsch, I. and P. Mosenthal (1990), "Exploring document literacy: Variables underlying the performance of young adults", *Reading Research Quarterly*, Vol. 25/1, pp. 5-30, http://dx.doi.org/10.2307/747985. [68]

Klauda, S. and J. Guthrie (2008), "Relationships of three components of reading fluency to reading comprehension", *Journal of Educational Psychology*, Vol. 100/2, pp. 310-321, http://dx.doi.org/10.1037/0022-0663.100.2.310. [83]

Kuhn, M. and S. Stahl (2003), "Fluency: A review of developmental and remedial practices", *Journal of Educational Psychology*, Vol. 95/1, pp. 3-21, http://dx.doi.org/10.1037/0022-0663.95.1.3. [79]

LaBerge, D. and S. Samuels (1974), "Toward a theory of automatic information processing in reading", *Cognitive Psychology*, Vol. 6/2, pp. 293-323, http://dx.doi.org/10.1016/0010-0285(74)90015-2. [80]

Lemarié, J. et al. (2008), "SARA: A text-based and reader-based theory of signaling", *Educational Psychologist*, Vol. 43/1, pp. 27-48, http://dx.doi.org/10.1080/00461520701756321. [44]

Leu, D. et al. (2015), "The new literacies of online research and comprehension: Rethinking the reading achievement gap", *Reading Research Quarterly*, Vol. 50/1, pp. 37-59, https://ila.onlinelibrary.wiley.com/doi/epdf/10.1002/rrq.85. [54]

Leu, D. et al. (2017), "New literacies: A dual-level theory of the changing nature of literacy, instruction, and assessment", *Journal of Education*, Vol. 197/2, pp. 1-18, http://dx.doi.org/10.1177/002205741719700202. [11]

Magliano, J. et al. (2017), "The modern reader: Should changes to how we read affect research and theory?", in Schober, M., D. Rapp and M. Britt (eds.), *Routledge handbooks in linguistics. The Routledge handbook of discourse processes*, Routledge/Taylor & Francis Group, https://doi.org/10.4324/9781315687384. [61]

Mangen, A. and A. van der Weel (2016), "The evolution of reading in the age of digitisation: An integrative framework for reading research", *Literacy*, Vol. 50/3, pp. 116-124, http://dx.doi.org/10.1111/lit.12086. [18]

McCrudden, M. and G. Schraw (2007), "Relevance and goal-focusing in text processing", *Educational Psychology Review*, Vol. 19/2, pp. 113-139, http://dx.doi.org/10.1007/s10648-006-9010-7. [29]

McNamara, D. and J. Magliano (2009), "Toward a comprehensive model of comprehension", in Ross, B. (ed.), *The Psychology of Learning and Motivation*, Elsevier, http://dx.doi.org/10.1016/s0079-7421(09)51009-2. [47]

Mol, S. and A. Bus (2011), "To read or not to read: A meta-analysis of print exposure from infancy to early adulthood", *Psychological Bulletin*, Vol. 137/2, pp. 267-296, http://dx.doi.org/10.1037/a0021890. [88]

Morrisroe, J. (2014), *Literacy Changes Lives: A New Perspective on Health, Employment and Crime*, National Literacy Trust, London, https://literacytrust.org.uk/documents/652/2014_09_01_free_research_-_literacy_changes_lives_2014.pdf.pdf. [5]

Murray, T., I. Kirsch and L. Jenkins (1998), *Adult Literacy in OECD Countries: Technical Report on the First International Adult Literacy Survey*, National Center for Education Statistics, Washington, DC, https://nces.ed.gov/pubs98/98053.pdf. [12]

National Center for Education Statistics (NCES) (n.d.), *PIAAC Participating Countries*, https://nces.ed.gov/surveys/piaac/countries.asp (accessed on 31.12.2018). [15]

Naumann, J. (2015), "A model of online reading engagement: Linking engagement, navigation, and performance in digital reading", *Computers in Human Behavior*, Vol. 53, pp. 263-277, http://dx.doi.org/10.1016/j.chb.2015.06.051. [70]

OECD (2019), *The Survey of Adult Skills : Reader's Companion, Third Edition*, OECD Skills Studies, OECD Publishing, Paris, https://dx.doi.org/10.1787/f70238c7-en. [86]

OECD (2013), *OECD Skills Outlook 2013: First Results from the Survey of Adult Skills*, OECD Publishing, Paris, https://dx.doi.org/10.1787/9789264204256-en. [6]

OECD (2011), *PISA 2009 Results: Students On Line: Digital Technologies and Performance (Volume VI)*, PISA, OECD Publishing, Paris, https://dx.doi.org/10.1787/9789264112995-en. [71]

OECD/Statistics Canada (2011), *Literacy for Life: Further Results from the Adult Literacy and Life Skills Survey*, OECD Publishing, Paris, https://dx.doi.org/10.1787/9789264091269-en. [14]

OECD/Statistics Canada (2005), *Learning a Living: First Results of the Adult Literacy and Life Skills Survey*, OECD Publishing, Paris, https://dx.doi.org/10.1787/9789264010390-en. [13]

Ozuru, Y. et al. (2007), "Influence of question format and text availability on the assessment of expository text comprehension", *Cognition and Instruction*, Vol. 25/4, pp. 399-438, http://dx.doi.org/10.1080/07370000701632371. [74]

Pan, B. et al. (2007), "In Google we trust: Users' decisions on rank, position, and relevance", *Journal of Computer-Mediated Communication*, Vol. 12/3, pp. 801-823, http://dx.doi.org/10.1111/j.1083-6101.2007.00351.x. [39]

Perfetti, C. (1985), *Reading Ability*, Oxford University Press, New York. [1]

Perfetti, C., J. Rouet and M. Britt (1999), "Toward a theory of documents representation", in van Oostendorp, H. and S. Goldman (eds.), *The Construction of Mental Representations During Reading*, Lawrence Erlbaum Associates Publishers, Mahwah, NJ. [49]

Potocki, A. et al. (2017), "Children's visual scanning of textual documents: Effects of document organization, search goals, and metatextual knowledge", *Scientific Studies of Reading*, Vol. 21/6, pp. 480-497, http://dx.doi.org/10.1080/10888438.2017.1334060. [46]

Richter, T. (2015), "Validation and comprehension of text information: Two sides of the same coin", *Discourse Processes*, Vol. 52/5-6, pp. 337-355, http://dx.doi.org/10.1080/0163853x.2015.1025665. [34]

Richter, T. et al. (2013), "Lexical quality and reading comprehension in primary school children", *Scientific Studies of Reading*, Vol. 17/6, pp. 415-434, http://dx.doi.org/10.1080/10888438.2013.764879. [84]

Richter, T., S. Schroeder and B. Wöhrmann (2009), "You don't have to believe everything you read: Background knowledge permits fast and efficient validation of information", *Journal of Personality and Social Psychology*, Vol. 96/3, pp. 538-558, http://dx.doi.org/10.1037/a0014038. [58]

Rieh, S. (2002), "Judgment of information quality and cognitive authority in the Web", *Journal of the American Society for Information Science and Technology*, Vol. 53/2, pp. 145-161, http://dx.doi.org/10.1002/asi.10017. [65]

Rouet, J. and M. Britt (2017), *Literacy in 2030. Report commissioned by the OECD's Education 2030 project*, OECD, Paris. [3]

Rouet, J. and M. Britt (2014), "Multimedia learning from multiple documents", in Mayer, R. (ed.), *The Cambridge Handbook of Multimedia Learning, 2nd Edition (Cambridge Handbooks in Psychology, pp. 813-841)*, Cambridge University Press, Cambridge, http://dx.doi.org/10.1017/cbo9781139547369.039. [55]

Rouet, J. and M. Britt (2011), "Relevance processes in multiple document comprehension", in McCrudden, M., J. Magliano and G. Schraw (eds.), *Text Relevance and Learning from Text*, Information Age Publishing, Greenwich, CT. [30]

Rouet, J., M. Britt and A. Durik (2017), "RESOLV: Readers' representation of reading contexts and tasks", *Educational Psychologist*, Vol. 52/3, pp. 200-215, http://dx.doi.org/10.1080/00461520.2017.1329015. [66]

Rouet, J., M. Britt and A. Potocki (2019), "Multiple-text comprehension", in Dunlosky, J. and K. Rawson (eds.), *The Cambridge Handbook of Cognition and Education (Cambridge Handbooks in Psychology, pp. 356-380)*, Cambridge University Press, Cambridge, http://dx.doi.org/10.1017/9781108235631.015. [23]

Rouet, J. and B. Coutelet (2008), "The acquisition of document search strategies in grade school students", *Applied Cognitive Psychology*, Vol. 22/3, pp. 389-406, http://dx.doi.org/10.1002/acp.1415. [43]

Rouet, J. and A. Potocki (2018), "From reading comprehension to document literacy: Learning to search for, evaluate and integrate information across texts", *Infancia y Aprendizaje*, Vol. 41/3, pp. 415-446, http://dx.doi.org/10.1080/02103702.2018.1480313. [22]

Rouet, J. et al. (2011), "The influence of surface and deep cues on primary and secondary school students' assessment of relevance in Web menus", *Learning and Instruction*, Vol. 21/2, pp. 205-219, http://dx.doi.org/10.1016/j.learninstruc.2010.02.007. [41]

Sabatini, J. and K. Bruce (2009), "PIAAC Reading Component: A Conceptual Framework", *OECD Education Working Papers*, No. 33, OECD Publishing, Paris, https://dx.doi.org/10.1787/220367414132. [85]

Salmerón, L. et al. (2018), "Chapter 4. Comprehension processes in digital reading", in Barzillai, M. et al. (eds.), *Learning to Read in a Digital World (Studies in Written Language and Literacy, 17) (pp. 91-120)*, John Benjamins Publishing Company, Amsterdam, http://dx.doi.org/10.1075/swll.17.04sal. [20]

Schroeder, S. (2011), "What readers have and do: Effects of students' verbal ability and reading time components on comprehension with and without text availability", *Journal of Educational Psychology*, Vol. 103/4, pp. 877-896, http://dx.doi.org/10.1037/a0023731. [75]

Schwabe, F., N. McElvany and M. Trendtel (2015), "The school age gender gap in reading achievement: Examining the influences of item format and intrinsic reading motivation", *Reading Research Quarterly*, Vol. 50/2, pp. 219-232, http://dx.doi.org/10.1002/rrq.92. [78]

Singer, M. (2013), "Validation in reading comprehension", *Current Directions in Psychological Science*, Vol. 22/5, pp. 361-366, http://dx.doi.org/10.1177/0963721413495236. [25]

Snow, C. and the RAND reading study Group (2002), *Reading for Understanding. Toward a R&D Program for Reading Comprehension*, RAND, Santa Monica, CA, https://www.rand.org/pubs/monograph_reports/MR1465.html. [27]

Stadtler, M. and R. Bromme (2014), "The content-source integration model: A taxonomic description of how readers comprehend conflicting scientific information", in Rapp, D. and J. Braasch (eds.), *Processing Inaccurate Information: Theoretical and Applied Perspectives from Cognitive Science and the Educational Sciences*, MIT Press, Cambridge, MA. [52]

Stadtler, M. et al. (2013), "Dealing with uncertainty: Readers' memory for and use of conflicting information from science texts as function of presentation format and source expertise", *Cognition and Instruction*, Vol. 31/2, pp. 130-150, http://dx.doi.org/10.1080/07370008.2013.769996. [56]

Stanovich, K. and R. West (1989), "Exposure to print and orthographic processing", *Reading Research Quarterly*, Vol. 24/4, pp. 402-433, http://dx.doi.org/10.2307/747605. [26]

Street, B. and B. Street (1984), *Literacy in Theory and Practice*, Cambridge University Press, New York. [2]

Strømsø, H. et al. (2013), "Spontaneous sourcing among students reading multiple documents", *Cognition and Instruction*, Vol. 31/2, pp. 176-203, http://dx.doi.org/10.1080/07370008.2013.769994. [73]

Toulmin, S. (1958), *The Uses of Argument*, Cambridge University Press, Cambridge, MA. [64]

UNESCO (2017), "Literacy rates continue to rise from one generation to the next", *UNESCO Fact Sheet No. 45*, UNESCO Institute for Statistics, Paris, http://uis.unesco.org/sites/default/files/documents/fs45-literacy-rates-continue-rise-generation-to-next-en-2017.pdf. [4]

Walczyk, J. et al. (2004), "Children's compensations for poorly automated reading skills", *Discourse Processes*, Vol. 37/1, pp. 47-66, http://dx.doi.org/10.1207/s15326950dp3701_3. [81]

White, S., J. Chen and B. Forsyth (2010), "Reading-related literacy activities of American adults: Time spent, task types, and cognitive skills used", *Journal of Literacy Research*, Vol. 42/3, pp. 276-307, http://dx.doi.org/10.1080/1086296x.2010.503552. [7]

Wineburg, S. (1994), "The cognitive representation of historical texts", in Leinhardt, G., I. Beck and C. Stainton (eds.), *Teaching and Learning in History*, Erlbaum, Hillsdale, NJ. [67]

Wineburg, S. (1991), "Historical problem solving: A study of the cognitive processes used in the evaluation of documentary and pictorial evidence", *Journal of Educational Psychology*, Vol. 83/1, pp. 73-87, http://dx.doi.org/10.1037/0022-0663.83.1.73. [60]

Wirth, W. et al. (2007), "Heuristic and systematic use of search engines", *Journal of Computer-Mediated Communication*, Vol. 12/3, pp. 778-800, http://dx.doi.org/10.1111/j.1083-6101.2007.00350.x. [40]

Zwaan, R. and M. Singer (2003), "Text comprehension", in Graesser, A., M. Gernsbacher and S. Goldman (eds.), *Handbook of Discourse Processes*, Erlbaum, Mahwah, NJ. [48]

Note

[1] Navigation in a static piece of continuous text is always possible by simply shifting one's focus of attention from one passage of the text to another, by skimming through passages, and by browsing through pages and sections in the case of long texts.

3 PIAAC Cycle 2 assessment framework: Numeracy

Dave Tout (Chair), Australian Council for Educational Research

Isabelle Demonty, University of Liège

Javier Díez-Palomar, University of Barcelona

Vince Geiger, Australian Catholic University

Kees Hoogland, HU University of Applied Sciences Utrecht

Terry Maguire, National Forum for the Enhancement of Teaching and Learning

This chapter presents the framework for conceptualising and assessing adult numeracy and developing a reporting scale for the direct assessment of numeracy as part of the OECD's Programme for the International Assessment of Adult Competencies (PIAAC Cycle 2). Numeracy as described here refers to adults' skills in accessing, using and reasoning critically with mathematical content, information and ideas represented in multiple ways in order to engage in and manage the mathematical demands of a range of situations in adult life. The framework describes the conceptual and theoretical foundations behind the adult numeracy construct and the principles applied for assessing numeracy in PIAAC and the distribution of the numeracy assessment items by a range of task characteristics.

Introduction

This chapter presents the framework for conceptualising numeracy as part of the OECD's Programme for the International Assessment of Adult Competencies (PIAAC Cycle 2). It builds on conceptual and assessment frameworks and cumulative wisdom developed in connection with prior surveys of adult skills, primarily the first cycle of the PIAAC, the Adult Literacy and Lifeskills project (ALL) and the International Adult Literacy Survey (IALS), but also surveys of school-age students e.g., the Programme for International Student Assessment (PISA).

Structure of the chapter

This chapter has six separate sections, followed by references:

- The assessment of numeracy in PIAAC
- Conceptual and theoretical foundations
- Numeracy assessment construct in PIAAC Cycle 2
- Operationalisation of the PIAAC numeracy assessment
- Relationship between PIAAC and PISA
- Numeracy components.

The first section provides a summary of the 2017 review of the PIAAC numeracy framework and assessment, gives an indication of some other conceptual issues considered, and includes a brief rationale for assessing numeracy in PIAAC. The second section addresses the conceptual construct for numeracy. The third section addresses the assessment construct, and describes the different dimensions of numeracy being assessed, including contexts, expected responses, content areas of mathematical information and ideas, and representations, as a way of operationalising the numeracy construct for scale development. It also discusses enabling processes, both cognitive and non-cognitive or dispositional, which underlie numerate behaviour. The fourth section discusses the operationalisation of the construct of numeracy in a large-scale assessment such as PIAAC and how this is affected by many factors that determine and shape the extent to which the theoretical construct can be fully addressed by the actual collection of items used in the direct assessment. It describes what can, and what cannot, be assessed in PIAAC Cycle 2. Subsequent sections comment on differences and commonalities between PIAAC's numeracy assessment and the related construct of mathematical literacy assessed in the Programme for International Student Assessment (PISA); and another section is dedicated to describing the new numeracy components assessment.

Why have an assessment framework and construct for PIAAC?

An assessment framework and construct is required for any valid assessment. The assessment framework provides a definition of the domain and the features of the construct. Such a framework usually includes:

- the background, purpose and rationale for, and description of, the assessment programme based on a theoretical and conceptual framework
- the target groups for the assessment
- a definition of the domain
- the description of any variables that are part of the description and describe its depth and breadth (e.g., contexts, processes, content)
- a blueprint for the test development against the above descriptions and variables, which might also include item types, representations, the length of the assessment, the number of items and the spread against the different variables.

Together, these aspects and content create the conceptual and assessment framework that will guide the assessment, as is the case with this document and its role for the assessment of numeracy components in PIAAC. It defines the construct of numeracy that steers the development of the test items and eventually the interpretation of results. The assessment construct provides a formal definition of the domain and the features of the construct in terms of any key parameters or dimensions of content, cognitive strategies and range of applications that need to be covered by the content of the assessment.

It is important to note that the PIAAC numeracy assessment describes the full range of numeracy capability in the adult population. This covers at one extreme, adults who have university level training and, at the other, adults who have very limited levels of education (e.g. who left school at or before the age of 15). At the same time, it covers both young adults still in education and adults who completed their formal education 30-50 years prior to undertaking the assessment.

The assessment of numeracy in the second cycle of PIAAC will link to the assessment used in the first cycle of PIAAC and also the earlier ALL study through the use of linking items. As a result, this revised conceptual framework for assessing numeracy in PIAAC will need to maintain key conceptual and pragmatic links to the numeracy framework used for the ALL study and PIAAC Cycle 1.

At the same time, it is important that the framework identifies a construct of numeracy that is relevant to the realities of the third decade of the 21st century as well as reflecting contemporary understandings of adult numeracy and that it incorporates relevant developments in testing practice and makes the best use of the available testing technologies.

The assessment of numeracy in PIAAC

This part of the report provides a summary of the 2017 review of the PIAAC Cycle 1 numeracy framework and assessment, gives an indication of some other conceptual issues to consider—identified by the new PIAAC Cycle 2 Numeracy Expert Group (NEG)—and finishes with a brief rationale for assessing numeracy in PIAAC.

Review report

The conceptual and assessment framework for the second cycle of PIAAC numeracy was expected to be updated and revised based on a review of the numeracy assessment framework used in the first cycle of PIAAC. This review was commissioned by the OECD Secretariat and published at the beginning of 2017 (Tout et al., 2017[1]). The aim of this review project was to prepare a paper reviewing the framework that guided the assessment of numeracy in the first cycle of PIAAC.

The review aimed to evaluate the extent to which the framework developed in 2009 reflected current understandings of adult numeracy and continued to be an appropriate basis for the assessment of the capacity of adults to successfully undertake the range of numeracy tasks that they will face in their everyday and working lives in the third decade of the 21st century. In particular, the review addressed the following:

- theoretical developments in the understanding and conceptualisation of adult numeracy that are relevant for the assessment of numeracy in PIAAC
- how to ensure that the assessment reflects the importance of digital information, representations, devices and applications as realities that adults have to manage in dealing with the numerical demands of everyday life
- developments in the assessment of numeracy (particularly of adults) that could be relevant for PIAAC (e.g., item types and formats, use of animation, and modelling)

- how the relationship between the PIAAC numeracy framework and the PISA mathematical literacy framework and assessment should be conceived, developed (if appropriate) and presented
- the utility and feasibility of the development and implementation of an assessment of numeracy components equivalent to the PIAAC reading components assessment.

The review recommended a range of areas for potential improvements and enhancements, including the definition and elaborations of adult numeracy used in the framework, and of the assessment content. Many of the suggestions arose out of the concern that the existing Cycle 1 framework and assessment did not reflect some of the realities of the skills and knowledge adults needed to succeed in work, life, and citizenship in the 21st century. Some of the key elements arising from the review paper included:

- addressing 21st century skills including critical thinking and reflection, reasoning and understanding of degree of accuracy
- taking on board technology/ICT advancements while keeping a balance with more traditional modes and means of communication and undertaking numeracy tasks
- making better use of technology for assessment in relation to both authenticity and making items accessible
- addressing a number of issues regarding adults' numeracy performance and understandings, including a person's disposition to use mathematics and to see mathematics in a numeracy situation
- developing an assessment of numeracy components, which would have parallel aims to the existing reading components assessment, and provide insights into the skills and knowledge of the significant number of adults with low levels of numeracy.

This report and the recommendation have been instrumental in the writing of this framework and assessment construct. The review and this document build on conceptual and assessment frameworks and cumulative wisdom developed in connection with prior surveys of adult skills, primarily the first cycle of PIAAC – see PIAAC Numeracy Expert Group (2009[2]) and Gal and Tout (2014[3]). The PIAAC Cycle 1 framework and assessment drew heavily on the numeracy assessment framework of the Adult Literacy and Life Skills Survey (ALL) (Murray, Clermont and Binkley, 2005[4]). It also built on the work in the International Adult Literacy Survey (IALS), and surveys of school-age students, especially the Programme for International Student Assessment (PISA).

Some new issues

In the process of considering the recommendations and content of the 2017 review paper by the new PIAAC Cycle 2 Numeracy Expert Group (NEG) at its first meeting in March 2018, a number of additional issues were identified which needed some further exploration. As a result, there was a literature review undertaken by the NEG exploring the following five conceptual issues: Big Ideas in mathematics, Number sense, Embeddedness, Authenticity, and Numerate behaviour and practices. While this work has been incorporated and embedded throughout this revised numeracy framework, a brief summary is included below.

Big Ideas in mathematics

Big Ideas in mathematics, is a term that is used to talk about powerful mathematical ideas (Jones, Langrall and Thornton, 2002[5]) central to the learning of mathematics, linking numerous mathematical understandings into a coherent whole [e.g., see (Charles, 2005[6]; Hurst, 2014[7]; Hurst and Hurrell, 2014[8]; Kuntze et al., 2009[9]; Kuntze et al., 2011[10]; Steen, 1990[11])]. Initially, the term "Big Ideas" referred to how mathematical information can be classified in different ways compared with the traditional school mathematics curriculum content areas. They often include the following content domains (which are elaborated in the PIAAC framework): quantity and number, space and shape, change and relationships, and data and chance. "Big Ideas" are also used as focal points to add some structure to sometimes "overcrowded curricula" (Siemon, 2017[12]; Siemon, Bleckly and Neal, 2012[13]).

Number sense

In PIAAC Cycle 2, particularly in relationship to the challenge to develop a separate, new, numeracy components assessment, number sense is seen as relating to a person's general understanding of different types of number and operations, and it involves a critical understanding in order to make decisions and solve problems using numbers in flexible ways in *Personal, Work*, and *Societal/community* contexts (Ontario Ministry of Education, 2006[14]; Peters, 2012[15]; Wagner and Davis, 2010[16]; Yang, Reys and Reys, 2009[17]). McIntosh, Reys and Reys (1992[18]) define number sense as: "It reflects an inclination and an ability to use numbers and quantitative methods as a means of communicating, processing and interpreting information" (p. 3). In addition, "using numbers is more than reasoning about number and more than skilled calculations. It is about making sense of the situation to which we apply numbers and calculations" (Thompson, 1995, p. 220[19]). Numbers, and quantitative expressions, may be presented in a range of different representational systems, including: text or symbols, images of physical objects, structured information and dynamic information. An understanding of *number sense* has been identified as a key element and is addressed throughout the framework, and has helped underpin the development of the new numeracy components assessment for PIAAC Cycle 2. This is elaborated further in the sixth section: *Numeracy components*.

Embeddedness, authenticity, numerate behaviour and practices

These four issues are all interrelated, and the NEG has attempted to address them more explicitly throughout the new framework, its elaboration, and to some extent in the content of the assessment itself, including in the background questionnaire (BQ) questions that relate to numeracy and mathematics skill use. These issues of embeddedness, authenticity, numerate behaviour and numerate practices, all relate to an understanding of the vital and underpinning connection to the real-world context in which mathematics is utilised by adults in their daily lives as individuals, citizens, family members or as workers.

The embeddedness of mathematics refers to the deep connections the mathematics has to the context in which it is utilised. This means that the way mathematics is used to operate on a task is fundamentally shaped by the context in which it is employed, which includes socio-cultural influences that afford or constrain action in civic, personal or workplace environments. In this view there is a clear separation between school mathematical knowledge, how it is taught, learned and practised, and the use of this knowledge outside of schooling. The issue of authenticity is a significant issue in the development of the test questions in PIAAC as it relates to how alike a task is in an international assessment like PIAAC to the actual real-life situation that the assessment task has been adapted from. PIAAC items are developed on the basis of finding situations and tasks that are based on authentic stimuli and then composing sets of questions that someone would want answered about, or based on, the information in the stimulus. Numerate behaviours and practices are distinct, but complementary, issues. Numerate behaviours relate to the cognitive responses by an individual to situations where mathematics is embedded in a real-world problem where a response or action is expected. Numeracy practices relate to the different uses of mathematics within a context, defined not just by the problem itself, but also by the physical and social context in which it is situated. These issues are further elaborated and discussed throughout the framework paper.

Rationale for assessing numeracy in PIAAC

As was argued in the PIAAC Cycle 1 numeracy framework (PIAAC Numeracy Expert Group, 2009[2]), this framework and description of numeracy is founded on the assumption that a direct assessment of numeracy in PIAAC is an essential and worthwhile undertaking for four separate but related reasons (PIAAC Numeracy Expert Group, 2009, pp. 8-9[2]):

- Numeracy is essential for adults and for the societies in which they live.
- Public policy in most countries includes separate investments in literacy and numeracy.
- The policy and programme responses are different for numeracy than for literacy.
- Numeracy skill levels are not measured well by literacy measures.

Basic computational and mathematical knowledge has always been considered as part of the fundamental skills that adults need to possess to function well and be able to accomplish various goals in their everyday, work, and social life. As will be demonstrated later in this framework, societies now present increasing amounts and a wider range of information of a quantitative or mathematical nature to citizens from all walks of life, in diverse contexts such as regarding health risk factors, environmental impacts, or financial planning and insurance purchasing, to name just a few. As workplaces are becoming more technology rich and concerned with involving all workers in improving efficiency and quality, the importance of numeracy and mathematical skills is growing. Numeracy-related skills have been shown to be a key factor in labour market participation, sometimes even more so than literacy skills. Adults with lower level skills in numeracy and literacy are more likely to be unemployed or require social assistance. Further, sound numeracy skills are deemed essential for post-secondary education in many areas, including but not limited to hard sciences, engineering and technology (Benn, 1997[20]; Bynner and Parsons, 2005[21]; Coben et al., 2003[22]; Coben, O'Donoghue and FitzSimons, 2000[23]; Condelli et al., 2006[24]; Coulombe, Tramblay and Marchand, 2004[25]; Forman and Steen, 1999[26]; Gal, 2000[27]; Gal et al., 2005[28]; Ginsburg, Manly and Schmitt, 2006[29]); (Hoyles et al., 2002[30]; Johnston, 1994[31]; Jonas, 2018[32]; Jones, 1995[33]; Murnane, Willett and Levy, 1995[34]; National Research and Development Centre (NRDC), 2006[35]; OECD/Statistics Canada, 2005[36]; Tout and Gal, 2015[37]; Tout and Schmitt, 2002[38]; Willis, 1990[39])

Public policy in most countries includes separate investments in literacy and numeracy. The separate acquisition of skills in these two fundamental areas is emphasised throughout both primary and secondary school systems, and in adult education or nonformal learning schemes. Countries expect that investment in literacy and numeracy will increase citizens' ability to act independently towards their own progress and income security, thereby reducing future social expenditures as well as contributing to citizens' participation in economic and social life in an information-laden society.

The policy and programme responses are different for numeracy than for literacy. Efforts to improve literacy and numeracy levels of specific population groups are not necessarily implemented via the same mechanisms—they often require different experts, resources, and learning systems because of differences in the underlying knowledge components and learning trajectories. It is vital that nations have information about their workers' and citizens' numeracy, independently of other competency areas, in order to evaluate the human capital available for advancement, to plan school-based and lifelong learning opportunities, and to better understand the factors that affect citizens' acquisition and usage of numeracy (Johnston and Maguire, 2005[40]).

It is not possible to represent the numeracy levels in a population solely via people's performance on literacy measures that examine how well people read, process, and comprehend various types of texts and documents, or communicate about such texts. As found in PIAAC and other research that compares adult's skills and performance in literacy with numeracy , there are substantial differences in the performances, outcomes and implications/consequences of lower or higher numeracy skilled adults compared to literacy skills [e.g., see (Bynner and Parsons, 2005[21]; Jonas, 2018[32]; OECD, 2017[41]; Tout and Gal, 2015[37])]. As is explained in more detail later, numeracy involves, among other things, the handling of not only arithmetical processes, but also the understanding of proportions and probabilistic ideas, the understanding of numerical, geometric, graphical and algebraic types and representations of mathematical information, and the critical interpretation of statistical or mathematical messages. Most of these elements and processes bear little relation to what is subsumed by literacy measures (Coben, O'Donoghue and FitzSimons, 2000[23]; Gal et al., 2005[28]).

It follows that a direct assessment of numeracy in PIAAC can provide policy makers and other stakeholders with a unique and sound basis for evaluating the distribution of the actual numeracy competence in the adult population.

Conceptual and theoretical foundations

The conceptualisation of *numeracy* in an international context is a challenging undertaking. Like literacy, the term numeracy has multiple meanings across countries and languages. In some countries the term numeracy relates to basic skills which school children are expected to acquire as a prerequisite to learning formal mathematics at higher grades. In other countries the term numeracy encompasses a broad range of skills, knowledge and dispositions that adults should possess but it does not necessarily relate to formal schooling. This is discussed further in the next section. Some countries do not even have a word such as numeracy; therefore, as part of educational or policy-oriented discourse in such countries, experts or translators either had to invent a special new word for it (e.g., *Numératie* in Canada, *Numeralitet* in Denmark), or use other phrases such as "mathematical literacy", "functional mathematics", or terms equivalent to "computational ability". Such diversity in terminology, or the lack of an accepted term with which policy makers feel comfortable, can complicate the communication with and among policy makers and educators interested in PIAAC.

The range of meanings attached to the term numeracy and the lack of an equivalent term across languages may create miscommunications or gaps in expectations regarding what will be measured by a numeracy scale in PIAAC. This can affect the perceived policy relevance of a numeracy scale. Thus, attention has to be given to making sure that discussions regarding numeracy assessment in PIAAC are based on a clear description and consensus about the scope of the term and recognition of its centrality in a wide range of adult life circumstances.

It must also be remembered that what will be measured by a numeracy assessment is *jointly* determined by two interrelated factors:

- the conceptual construct describing numeracy and its elements
- the assessment construct describing how the general conceptualisation of numeracy is operationalised and manifested in the nature and range of tasks used in the assessment and the mode of administration and scoring.

Developing perspectives on adult numeracy

Formulation of what numeracy encompasses has evolved since the term was first introduced in the 1959 Crowther Report in England and Wales [e.g., see (Karaali, Villafane-Hernandez and Taylor, 2016[42])], when it was defined as something "more than mere ability to manipulate the rule of three" (Crowther, 1959, p. 270[43]). Another significant milestone in the conceptualisation and description of numeracy was in the Cockcroft report of 1982, where it was defined as:

> [n]umeracy is...an 'at-homeness' with numbers and an ability to make use of mathematical skills which enables an individual to cope with the practical mathematical demands of his everyday life...[and] an ability to have some appreciation and understanding of information, which is presented in mathematical terms, for instance graphs, charts or tables or by reference to percentage increase or decrease. (Cockcroft, 1982, p. 11[44])

The use and meaning of the term *numeracy* has gained momentum in the years since the Crowther and Cockcroft Reports. Some relevant papers and research include: (Baker and Street, 1994[45]; Benn, 1997[20]; Coben, O'Donoghue and FitzSimons, 2000[23]; Coben et al., 2003[22]; Condelli et al., 2006[24]; Forman and

Steen, 1999[26]; Gal, 2000[27]; Gal et al., 2005[28]; Ginsburg, Manly and Schmitt, 2006[29]; Hoyles et al., 2002[30]); (Johnston, 1994[31]; Lindenskov and Wedege, 2001[46]; Maguire and O'Donoghue, 2003[47]; National Research and Development Centre (NRDC), 2006[35]; Tout and Gal, 2015[37]; Tout and Schmitt, 2002[38]; Willis, 1990[39]). In the United Kingdom in 2000, Coben, O'Donoghue and FitzSimons published a work titled *Perspectives on Adult Learning Mathematics*, in which they provided a review of research related to adults' learning of mathematics. At the same time, a similar volume, *Adult Numeracy Development: Theory, Research, Practice* was published in the United States (Gal, 2000[27]). A conceptualisation of adult numeracy for the Adult Literacy and Life Skills (ALL) survey, the precursor to PIAAC, was developed around the same time (1998-2000) by an international team (Gal et al., 2005[28]). This was the first time the construct of numeracy had to be defined in an international comparative assessment context and not purely in an educational context. The ALL international team defined numeracy alongside a more elaborate definition of numerate behaviour. Coben, in 2003, led a team who wrote *Adult Numeracy: Review of Research and Related Literature* and noted that numeracy was increasingly defined as "mathematics in work and mathematics in everyday adult life" (Coben et al., 2003, p. 38[22]).

Maguire and O'Donoghue (2003[47]) reviewed and organised conceptions of numeracy from several countries (Australia, Canada, Denmark, Ireland, the Netherlands, United Kingdom and United States) along a continuum of increasing levels of complexity or sophistication: *formative*, *mathematical* and *integrative*. *Formative* conceptions view numeracy as related to basic arithmetic skills. *Mathematical* conceptions consider numeracy in a contextualised way, as a broader set of mathematical knowledge and skills (beyond basic computations) of relevance in everyday life. Finally, *integrative* conceptions consider numeracy as a multifaceted, sophisticated construct incorporating not only mathematics but also communicative, cultural, social, emotional, and personal elements which interact and pertain to how different people function in their social contexts.

At this time, formative conceptions were often associated with how numeracy was viewed in connection with goals of primary schooling, and reflected in how numeracy was defined when classifying literacy/numeracy levels worldwide e.g., UNESCO (1997[48]). Most extant conceptions which adult education, workplace training, and national and international assessments have adopted fall at different points across the mathematical and integrative phases described by Maguire and O'Donoghue. The range of conceptions and definitions of adult numeracy from late last century to more recent times illustrate that conceptions evolve over time and that variability can be noticed even within the same national system.

Lindenskov and Wedege (2001[46]) offer an interesting case study of defining numeracy. Based on their work in adult and mathematics education in Denmark, they imported numeracy from English-speaking countries and introduced a new term, *Numeralitet*, with a conceptual framework that was later adopted by the Danish Ministry of Education. According to this perspective, it is essential to distinguish between what numeracy is, or ought to be, from the individual's and from society's points of view. Lindenskov and Wedege advocated a societal view, whereby numeracy is seen as a competence that involves a dynamic interaction between functional mathematical skills and conceptions and operations on the one hand, and a series of activities and various types of data and media on the other. They argued that this skill- and activity-based view should be coupled with the understanding that in principle all people need to have this competence, and that numeracy is a competence determined by society and technology and that it changes in time and space along with social change and technological development.

The definition quoted from the United Kingdom's Cockcroft Committee (1982[44]) earlier has been quite influential in that its conception of numeracy implied it is an ability to cope with various functional tasks in real-world contexts as well as interpretive tasks, but also pointed to the centrality of underlying supporting non-cognitive components. These key ideas are reflected, albeit with different terminologies and foci, in other views of numeracy, including in the definitions used in both ALL and PIAAC Cycle 1. Another important commonality is the presence of mathematical elements or ideas in real situations, and the notion that these can be used or addressed by a person in a goal-oriented way, dependent on the needs of the individual within the given context, i.e., home, community, workplace, societal action, etc.

Common use of the term numeracy in the 2000s

Looking at publishing sources, the evidence is growing that the use and concept of the term numeracy has been displacing other terms such as mathematical literacy and quantitative literacy, and has become more popular, even though in many languages it does not have a direct translation. This is illustrated in Figure 3.1 below, which is based on work by Karaali, Villafane-Hernandez and Taylor (2016[42]), but updated.

Figure 3.1. Use of the term numeracy versus other terms in the books published between 1950 and 2008, included in Google Books

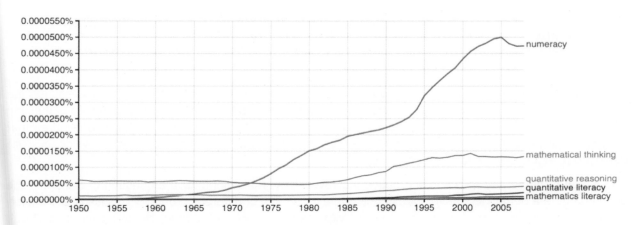

Source: Data from Google Books Ngram Viewer. Retrieved on 15th December 2018.

Competence versus skill

The two terms *Competency* and *Skill* are both used in current PIAAC documents and reports. Competencies can mean different things in different situations, and in different cultures. For example, a reductive notion of competence is used as a synonym for skill in some adult education settings within Australia. Competencies can however also mean the combination of skills and aspects of higher order thinking such as strategic planning. The latter is reflected in the OECD's Definition and Selection of Competencies project (DeSeCo) (OECD, 2005[49]), which was developed to provide a framework informing the identification of key competencies in international surveys measuring the competence level of young people and adults [see Rychen (2004, p. 321[50])].

In *The Survey of Adult Skills – Reader's Companion, Second Edition* (OECD, 2016[51]), the OECD discusses this issue of terminology and the use of these two terms (*skill* and *competency*) and concludes that there is much overlap in their understanding and use, and while acknowledging that there can be differences in the use and meaning of the two terms, concludes:

> In the context of the Survey of Adult Skills (PIAAC), however, no attempt is made to differentiate competency and skill, and the terms are used interchangeably ... Both terms refer to the ability or capacity of an agent to act appropriately in a given situation. Both involve the application of knowledge (explicit and/or tacit), the use of tools, cognitive and practical strategies and routines, and both imply beliefs, dispositions and values (e.g. attitudes). In addition, neither competency nor skill is conceived as being related to any particular context of performance, nor is a skill regarded as one of the atomic units that combine to form competency. (OECD, 2016, p. 17[51]).

This numeracy framework report similarly does not make or attach an explicit meaning or use to either term.

Numerate behaviour and practices

Establishing and extending numeracy capability requires the adoption, development or appropriation of both numerate behaviours and practices. These two constructs are distinct but complementary. Numerate behaviours are cognitive responses by an individual to particular situations where mathematics might provide advantage in addressing a real-world problem. On the other hand, numeracy practices relate to the use of mathematics within a context defined not just by the problem but also the physical and social context in which it is situated. The notion of situatedness is tied to ways of thinking, modes of reasoning and means of knowledge generation within communities that are defined by distinct social or cultural types of activity. From this perspective, numeracy is viewed as a social practice. As Yasukawa et al. (2018[52]) explain:

> A NSP [numeracy as a social practice] perspective focuses on what people do with numeracy through social interactions in particular contexts, rather than on people's performance of mathematical skills in isolation of context…Moreover, a focus on practice entails viewing numeracy activity as culturally, historically and politically situated. (p. 13)

Thus, employing numeracy behaviours to address real-world problems in different contexts requires the accommodation of unique ongoing activities, social relationships and community-based modes of thinking and reasoning (Lave, 1988[53]). This means that the use of mathematics within a practice requires that mathematical capability is nuanced by holistic strategies shaped by the specific contexts in which they are deployed (Geiger, Goos and Forgasz, 2015[54]).

The notion of numeracy as a social practice, however, has implications for the question of transfer—the use of numerate behaviours developed in one context in a new or different situation. This issue of transfer, according to Hoyles, Noss and colleagues (Hoyles, Noss and Pozzi, 2001[55]; Noss, Hoyles and Pozzi, 2002[56]), can be achieved through the abstraction of underlying invariants that are relevant across situations—a process they term situated abstraction.

> Mathematical conceptualization may be finely tuned to its constructive genesis-how it is learned, how it is discussed and communicated—and to its use in a cultural practice, yet simultaneously can retain mathematical invariants abstracted within that community of practice. (Noss, Hoyles and Pozzi, 2002, p. 205[56])

While the nature of the assessment content in PIAAC limits its primary focus to cognitive aspect of numeracy, that is, the numeracy behaviours and skills that underpin the questions, their contexts and the specific items, the notion of practices has influenced the development of the skills use questions that form part of the background questionnaire. PIAAC's background questionnaire (BQ) includes collecting a wide range of information which can help to explain differences in performance among adults, further informing our understanding of factors that affect skill acquisition and retention or motivation for further learning. The skills use questions are structured around two themes, work practices and everyday practices, where questions elicit responses about the frequency of use a different numeracy practices. The Numeracy Expert Group (NEG) worked with the OECD and the PIAAC BQ Expert Group to revise and improve the consistency and research validity and usefulness of the BQ questions on numeracy practices at work and in everyday life for the second cycle of the PIAAC. The NEG's work and recommendations helped to homogenise the set of questions, keep a sense of consistency between work/professional practices and personal uses, while also trying to preserve a continuity between the two cycles. The NEG used the descriptions of the four different content areas of the PIAAC numeracy framework to help guide them in this, alongside reviewing the existing research about numeracy practices at work and in everyday life from PIAAC Cycle 1.

Questions related to work practices and use include: the calculation of prices; counting stock; reviewing inventories; planning delivery routes; preparing budgets; undertaking measurements; interpreting charts or performing data analysis. Everyday practice questions are related to examples such as: calculations related to purchase and discounts; decisions regarding financial matters such as budgets, insurance, loans, or savings; measurements needed when you cook, garden, make clothes. Thus, while PIAAC's capacity to assess numeracy activity from a social practice perspective is necessarily limited, the role of practices in documenting and researching numeracy capability and performance is recognised as vital.

Theoretical developments and foundations

The theoretical conceptualisation of numeracy for PIAAC Cycle 2, discussed and presented below, is built on the previous review of literature and research findings reported in the two previous numeracy frameworks for ALL survey (Gal et al., 2005[28]) and PIAAC Cycle 1 (PIAAC Numeracy Expert Group, 2009[2]). As well it incorporates the review of the numeracy assessment framework used in the first cycle of PIAAC commissioned by the OECD Secretariat (Tout et al., 2017[1]), along with further research done by the Numeracy Expert Group for PIAAC Cycle 2. This is then used as the basis for the elaboration of how the assessment of numeracy in PIAAC Cycle 2 will be implemented and what the key dimensions are that will be assessed. This is described in *the third section: Numeracy assessment construct in PIAAC Cycle 2.*

This conceptualisation operates on two levels. It relates to numeracy as a construct describing a skill or competence, and to numerate behaviour and practices, which is the way a person's numeracy is manifested in the face of situations or contexts which have mathematical elements or carry information of a quantitative nature. In this way, inferences about a person's numeracy are possible through analysis of performance on assessment tasks designed to elicit numerate behaviour. In congruence with the above view of a competence, numeracy will be described as comprised both of cognitive elements (i.e., various knowledge bases and skills) as well as non-cognitive or semi-cognitive elements (i.e., attitudes, beliefs, habits of mind, and other dispositions) which together shape a person's numerate performance, behaviour and practices. This conceptualisation includes ways of knowing, the means of generating new knowledge, and using different modes of reasoning.

The following sections summarise some of the theoretical and conceptual foundations in the previous PIAAC framework document and adds more recent research and understanding about adult numeracy, mainly from the review paper. It starts with the same structure as the previous framework and first addresses the contexts and demands for numeracy, but then adds to this with a new section that adds in further research insights from the PIAAC Cycle 1 framework review and more.

But it should be noted that most recent reviews indicate that there continues to be a shortage of any empirical or theoretical developments in research on adult numeracy [see e.g., (Carpentieri, Litster and Frumkin, 2009[57]; Condelli et al., 2006[24]; Geiger, Goos and Forgasz, 2015[54]; Windisch, 2015[58])]. However, the 2017 PIAAC numeracy review team's research (Tout et al., 2017[1]) included reading and reviewing recent reports about the teaching, learning and descriptions of adult numeracy practices; e.g., (Chisman, 2011[59]; Griffiths and Stone, 2013[60]; National Institute of Adult Continuing Education (NIACE), 2011[61]). The review team found that a number of issues should be considered and addressed in the review and rewriting of the PIAAC numeracy framework for this second cycle of PIAAC. These have been incorporated into the discussions and outcomes below.

Contexts and demands for numeracy

What is encompassed by numeracy (and numerate behaviour and practices) can initially be addressed by identifying the nature of the contexts that contain quantitative and mathematical[1] elements that adults face and which pose demands with which they have to cope. This in turn provides the basis for describing the knowledge elements and supporting processes which enable adults to cope with real-world numeracy tasks (Ginsburg, Manly and Schmitt, 2006[29]), and can later help to form a road map which can guide the design and selection of tasks for inclusion in the numeracy assessment in PIAAC.

The literature pertaining to the uses of numeracy in the real world can be divided into three strands:

- the role of numeracy in adults' lives
- the mathematical demands of workplace settings
- educational perspectives on the mathematical needs of school graduates and citizens.

These three areas are certainly intertwined but also offer complementary ideas; hence, each is reviewed separately below.

Implications of 21st century skills and demands on numeracy needs

Research shows that 21st century skills requirements have changed compared with the previous century, and new ways of working, reasoning and thinking are required, and that increasingly the new skills interact with technology [e.g., see (Binkley et al., 2011[62]; Expert Group on Future Skills Needs (Ireland), 2007[63]; Foundation for Young Australians, 2017[64]; Griffin, McGaw and Care, 2012[65]; Partnership for 21st Century Skills, 2016[66]; Pellegrino and Hilton, 2012[67])]. In the literature, this is often referred to as '21st century skills' or '21st century competences' (Voogt and Roblin, 2012[68]), 'global competences' (OECD, 2019[69]) or 'the 4th industrial revolution' (Schwab, 2016[70]). Common is the acknowledgement that across education, government, and business, the skills and knowledge needed to succeed in work, life and citizenship have significantly changed in the twenty-first century. As has been argued and documented by many sources, and summarised in PIAAC planning documents, adults are presented with ever-increasing amounts of information of a quantitative or mathematical nature through Internet-based or technology-based resources. New means of communication and types of services have changed the way individuals interact with governments, institutions, services and each other, and social and economic transformations have, in turn, changed the demand for skills as well. More so than in prior decades, a wider range of quantitative and mathematical information is more readily available, but this information has to be located, selected or filtered, interpreted, at times questioned and doubted, and analysed for its relevance to the responses needed.

The implications of such 21st century skills and ICT demands on the numeracy needs for adults in their daily lives, as citizen and as workers are discussed in the following sub-sections.

The role of numeracy in adults' lives

Analysis of the purposes served by adults' numeracy skills has often focused on workplace numeracy practices or on the outcomes of school education, which are both discussed in the following two sub-sections. In the 21st century, young people and adults need to be able to cope with the aspects of the world as they encounter them, which includes the digital and technological aspects of information and society—and society already has all kinds of technological aspects that interact with numerical and mathematical information. Therefore, the focus must also be on both life as an individual, and as part of society and citizenship, and that includes with the digital aspects of information and society—the reality is that technology is now ubiquitous with all aspects of many societies. Services, interactions and communications outside the workplace have all changed in the 21st century, often driven by technological advances. This includes online processes such as banking, purchases, bookings, reviewing information (health, housing, etc.) and making decisions based on that information. It includes functioning in the bureaucratic world (applying for permits, social security applications and processes, applying for jobs, managing insurances, etc.), use of different media (e.g., the Internet, online news, Facebook, podcasts, videos, etc.), use of different aspects of communication (e-mail, SMS, apps, social media, etc.), and of a range of software and technology at home and in the community. Technology has meant greater market penetration and influence. The influences of social and mass media has implications for informed and participatory citizenship, and hence for citizens to be critical consumers of all forms of media.

Further, it has been argued that in a society in which the media constantly present information in numerical or graphical form, the ability to interpret and critically reflect on quantitative and statistical messages is vital for all adults [e.g., see (Benn, 1997[20]; Paulos, 1988[71]; Paulos, 1995[72]; Steen, 1990[11]; Utts, 2003[73]; Willis, 1990[39])]. It is seen as essential for all adults to possess the ability to critically reflect on quantitative information encountered in various media sources and documents (Frankenstein, 1989[74]), and to understand how to be a careful or critical consumer of statistical arguments of various kinds (Gal, 2002[75]; Utts, 2003[73]; Watson and Callingham, 2003[76]). This view of needing to be critical as part of being numerate was often espoused by adult education experts, focusing on the role of adults as reflective communicators and critical consumers of information in society who are involved in the exchange and interpretation of messages encountered in media or in political and community contexts (Frankenstein, 1989[74]). For example, Johnston (1994[31]) argued:

> To be numerate is more than being able to manipulate numbers, or even being able to 'succeed' in school or university mathematics. Numeracy is a critical awareness which builds bridges between mathematics and the real-world, with all its diversity. (p. 34)

Efforts to formally describe numeracy use in society more generally have been undertaken in several countries [e.g., see (McLean et al., 2012[77]; Quality and Qualifications Ireland (QQI), 2016[78]; Tertiary Education Commission, 2008[79]; U.S. Department of Education, 2013[80])]. In Australia, for example, two frameworks (Kindler et al., 1996[81]; Victorian Curriculum and Assessment Authority (VCAA), 2008[82]) proposed four broad categories regarding the uses of numeracy. The four categories are *Numeracy for practical purposes*; *Numeracy for interpreting society*; *Numeracy for personal organisation*; and *Numeracy for knowledge*. Numeracy for practical purposes addresses aspects of the physical world that involve designing, making, and measuring. Numeracy for interpreting society relates to interpreting and reflecting on numerical and graphical information in public documents and texts. Numeracy for personal organisation focuses on the numeracy requirements for personal organisational matters involving money, time and travel. Numeracy for knowledge describes the mathematical skills needed for further study in mathematics, or other subjects with mathematical underpinnings or assumptions.

Another scheme was developed by Steen (1990[11]), who outlined five dimensions of numeracy:

- practical, focused on mathematical and statistical knowledge and skills that can be put to immediate use to cope with tasks in daily life
- professional, focused on the mathematical skills required in specific jobs
- civic, focused on benefits to society
- recreational, related to the role of mathematical ideas and processes in games, puzzles, sports, lotteries, and other leisure activities
- cultural, concerned with mathematics as a universal part of human culture (and related to appreciation of mathematical aspects such as in cultural or artistic artefacts).

Overall, the purposes regarding numeracy use appear to be consistent and suggest that adults need to be able to apply their numeracy (and literacy) skills to tasks with a social or personal purpose in both informal and more formal contexts. Such perspectives supplement Bishop's (1988[83]) proposal that there are six modes of mathematical actions that are common in all cultures and pertain both to children and to adults: counting, locating, measuring, designing, playing and explaining.

Numeracy in the workplace

Mathematical and statistical skills that are important in adults' work have in part been described in large-scale efforts to define "core skills" or "key competencies" that workers should have, usually in response to the need to maintain economic competitiveness and improve employability of adults and school graduates.

In addition, several projects looked specifically at the mathematical skills of workers in a range of occupational groups or workplace clusters.

Basic computational knowledge has always been considered as part of the fundamental skills that adults need to possess, but recent research and skills framework developments claim that workers need to possess a much broader range of mathematical skills. Examples exist in many countries and the following selective description is indicative of the nature of such efforts. In the United States [see (Carnevale, Gainer and Meltzer, 1990[84]; Secretary's Commission on Achieving Necessary Skills (SCANS), 1991[85])], reviews differentiated between mastery of basic arithmetical skills and a much broader and flexible understanding of mathematical skills. The higher level skills included "choosing appropriately from a variety of mathematical techniques; uses quantitative data to construct logical explanations for real-world situations; expresses mathematical ideas and concepts orally and in writing; and understands the role of chance in the occurrence and prediction of events" (Secretary's Commission on Achieving Necessary Skills (SCANS), 1991, p. 83[85]). Forman and Steen (1999[26]) similarly argued that quantitative skills desired by employers are much broader than mere facility with the mechanics of addition, subtraction, multiplication, and division and familiarity with basic number facts. They also include some knowledge of statistics, probability, mental computation strategies, some grasp of proportional reasoning or modelling relationships, and broad problem solving and communication skills about quantitative issues.

Work in the 21st century

In relation to work in the 21st century, research is showing that there is a significant and increasingly important and underpinning role that science, technology, engineering, and mathematics (STEM) skills play [e.g., (Foundation for Young Australians, 2017[64]; PwC, 2015[86])]. In their recent 2017 review, the National Council of Teachers of Mathematics (NCTM) (2017[87]) argued that mathematics is at the heart of most innovations in the information economy. They saw mathematical and statistical literacy as needed more than ever to filter, understand, and act on the enormous amount of data and information that we encounter every day.

As well, there is a significant amount of research that has looked into specific numeracy and mathematics practices in workplaces, including in relation to 21st century skills [e.g., see (Australian Association of Mathematics Teachers (AAMT) and Australian Industry Group (AiGroup), 2014[88]; Bessot and Ridgway, 2000[89]; Buckingham, 1997[90]; Coben et al., 2010[91]; FitzSimons, 2005[92]; Geiger, Goos and Forgasz, 2015[54]; Hoyles et al., 2002[30]; Hoyles et al., 2010[93]; Kent et al., 2011[94]; Marr and Hagston, 2007[95]); (Straesser, 2015[96]; Wake, 2015[97]; Weeks et al., 2013[98]; Zevenbergen, 2004[99])]. One of the key outcomes of the research is that because of the impact of technology and digital tools and processes, the mathematics or numeracy tasks that people undertake at work involve more than basic calculation skills or 'by hand' skills and straightforward procedural competence, consistent with the above research. These practices involve more sophisticated mathematical problem solving skills and understandings, new ways of reasoning and thinking, and entail the ability to recognise and engage with the mathematics that is fully embedded within complex and "messy" workplace settings. Many 21st century workplace mathematics and numeracy practice are integrated with technology, particularly information and communications technologies (ICT), and have profoundly altered what are considered to be the key knowledge and skills that individuals need as economies and society continue to evolve.

The skills required in the 21st century include a range of mathematical capabilities such as understanding and interpreting graphical information, interpreting measures in terms of what the data are saying about a manufacturing process, making use of spreadsheets, interpreting visual, computer-generated 3D representations or virtual images, and more. Hoyles et al. (2010[93]) argue that this requirement for mathematical capabilities will be driven by the need to improve production processes and productivity; that is, there will be greater demand for what they call techno-mathematical literacies:

> *We therefore decided to introduce the term Techno-mathematical Literacies, developing from the idea of mathematical literacy that was used in our previous research ... This literacy involves a language that is not mathematical but 'techno-mathematical', where the mathematics is expressed through technological artefacts. (Hoyles et al., 2010, p. 14[93])*

In relation to technology at work, a 2014 Australian study about the use of mathematics in the workplace found similar connections and entanglements between mathematics and technology:

> *Many people in the workplace are engaged with technology, particularly in using spreadsheets and graphical outputs. There is an inter-dependency of mathematical skills and the use of technology in the workplace in ways that are not commonly reflected in current teaching practice. The perception is that technology is transforming workplace practices and the use of technology has changed the mathematical skills required – while not reducing the need for mathematics. (Australian Association of Mathematics Teachers (AAMT) and Australian Industry Group (AiGroup), 2014, p. 2[88])*

The same report (Australian Association of Mathematics Teachers (AAMT) and Australian Industry Group (AiGroup), 2014[88]) found that workers needed a blend of the following skills:

- ability to recognise and identify how and when mathematics is used in the workplace
- an understanding of mathematical concepts, procedures and skills
- an understanding of the kinds of practical tasks they need to perform
- the strategic processes they should be able to use in using and applying mathematics.

Overall, these studies complement the earlier research and studies, and suggest that employees need to possess a range of specific numeracy-related skills or knowledge, such as in the following (but not the only) areas of mathematics:

- fast and accurate computations but also estimation, and knowing when each skill is required and why
- ability to deal with proportions and percents
- understanding measurement concepts and procedures
- working with, or creating, simple formulas
- a sense for the use of models and modelling in foreseeing future needs
- understanding basic statistical concepts and interpreting data and displays.

However, it is not simply the demands of 21st century workplaces and practices that are driving the use of digital technologies in the workplace; workers themselves also use technology to support their *thinking*. That is, it is not just about the use of digital technologies and tools to replace traditional physical or cognitive skills. In particular, digital tools increasingly mediate young workers' ways of reasoning, acting, and working (Jorgensen Zevenbergen, 2010[100]; Zevenbergen, 2004[99]). At the same time, these new ways of thinking and acting are reshaping the structuring practices and deployment of skills in workplaces. Zevenbergen argues that this allows young workers to solve problems in often more inventive ways than their more experienced co-workers do.

In addition, on a broader and less technical level, these studies argue that workers need to be able to make decisions in the face of uncertainty in real situations, prioritise actions and make choices regarding the approach to handling different tasks, depending on changing external demands. As well, there is a need for workers to be able to communicate with other workers or clients or understand written documentation (e.g., through text or with tables, charts, and graphs) about issues such as quantities, schedules, variation over time, results of quantitative projections, or analysis of different courses of action in this regard. Such findings echo the earlier distinctions made by the SCANS analysis between the need to attend both to basic arithmetical skills and more elaborate and complex mathematical skills in the workplace, including ways of reasoning and thinking, making connections within and between different aspects of mathematics, and also highlight some areas where specific literacy and communication skills are intertwined with numeracy skills.

School mathematics versus everyday or workplace mathematics

Important research literature has also accumulated over the last decades regarding the ways in which people use mathematical skills or cope with mathematical tasks in both formal (i.e., school-based) and informal (i.e., everyday, workplace) contexts (e.g., (Carraher, Carraher and Schliemann, 1985[101]; Nunes, 1992[102]; Nunes, Schliemann and Carraher, 1993[103]; Presmeg, 2007[104]; Resnick, 1987[105]; Rogoff and Lave, 1984[106]; Saxe and Gearhart, 1988[107]). While too complex to discuss in detail here –see Greeno (2003[108]), for one of several reviews of this literature, among other things these studies highlight the situatedness of mathematical knowledge used in functional contexts and the need for actors in different contexts to develop situation-specific mathematical procedures and know-how.

Research suggests that, for adults as well as for children, mathematical knowledge develops both in and out of school [e.g., (Lave, 1988[53]; Saxe, 1992[109]; Saxe et al., 1996[110]; Schliemann and Acioly, 1989[111])]. Saxe and his colleagues have written about the importance of cultural practice in the development of mathematical thinking and how such practices profoundly influence an individual's cognitive constructions and mathematical ideas, depending, e.g., on the artefacts or tools they use, the nature of the measurement systems in their culture, the counting or calculating devices (abacus, calculator) they use, the distribution of work among family members, or general patterns and types of social activity.

Further, numerous researchers [e.g., (FitzSimons and Coben, 2009[112]; Kent et al., 2007[113]; Marr and Hagston, 2007[95]; Straesser, 2003[114]; Wedege, 2004[115]; Wedege, 2010[116]; Williams and Wake, 2006[117])] have argued, based on ethnographic analyses of workers' activities in diverse industries, that important portions of the mathematical activities at work are made "invisible" to occasional observers as well as to the workers themselves, or are disguised as non-mathematical. This means that mathematics can be fundamental to activities that are not obviously mathematical. This is most clearly apparent in the use of technology in the workplace where digital tools used to complete tasks often obscure underpinning mathematical activity. As Kent et al. (2007[113]) argues, within techno-mathematical situations in workplaces "there is a shift from fluency in doing explicit pen-and-paper mathematical procedures to a fluency with using and interpreting output from IT systems and software, and the mathematical models deployed within them" (p. 2-3). Building on this point, Wedege (2010[116]) defines two forms of invisible mathematics as (a) subjectively invisible mathematics where people do not recognise the mathematics that they do as mathematics and (b) objectively invisible mathematics in which mathematics is hidden in technology.

Various factors have been posited as causing this phenomenon, such as the encapsulation of many mathematical activities into routines or automated procedures; the use of tools and instruments or information technology (e.g., spreadsheets); the normative use of job-specific linguistic terms that are different than traditional school terms; or the division of labour among different workers.

Based on such and related findings, many reports have argued that mathematical skills as used in the workplace are often different and broader in scope than what is traditionally taught in school mathematics, but also take on different forms depending on the specific work context [e.g., (Australian Association of Mathematics Teachers (AAMT) and Australian Industry Group (AiGroup), 2014[88]; Marr and Hagston, 2007[95])]. The above Australian study (Australian Association of Mathematics Teachers (AAMT) and Australian Industry Group (AiGroup), 2014[88]) about the use of mathematics in the workplace summed up much of this research:

> *Although the skills observed appear to be fundamental, it is their use and application in work contexts that is not straightforward. (p. 1)*

This report went on to describe more fully the differences between school mathematics and workplace mathematics use:

> *Mathematics is applied in both routine and complex tasks requiring sophisticated use of fundamental mathematical skills and 'judgement' or 'problem-solving' procedures. Workplace mathematics is performed differently to school mathematics. Mathematical demands may be present implicitly in the workplace tasks, often through tasks that are not obviously mathematical. (Australian Association of Mathematics Teachers (AAMT) and Australian Industry Group (AiGroup), 2014, p. 2[88])*

This is consistent with earlier research by Steen in the United States:

> *"Mathematics in the workplace makes sophisticated use of elementary mathematics rather than, as in the classroom, elementary use of sophisticated mathematics. Work-related mathematics is rich in data, interspersed with conjecture, dependent on technology, and tied to useful applications. Work contexts often require multi-step solutions to open-ended problems, a high degree of accuracy, and proper regard for required tolerances. None of these features are found in typical classroom exercises." (Steen, 2004, p. 55[118])*

It needs to be emphasised that sense of number still underpins much of the mathematical thinking required—including fluency and flexibility in mental calculations and estimations.

The updated conceptualisation of numeracy for PIAAC Cycle 2 was derived with reference to the types of numeracy and mathematical demands as depicted in this sub-section. However, a working assumption has been made that it is not feasible to employ assessment items that are too workplace-specific (e.g., couched in the context of a single workplace or occupation) because mathematics or statistics as used in this context may not be visible or familiar to most other adults (Hoyles et al., 2002[30]).

School-based perspectives on numeracy and informed civic participation

A growing dialogue about the goals and impact of mathematics education in schools has intensified in recent years. This is in part due to economic pressures and industry expectations on the one hand, but also due to the realisation that mathematical knowledge and skills serve multiple and separate gateway functions on the other hand. Specifically, mathematical competencies affect chances of entry into key occupational tracks (mainly in science, technology, and economics) and may affect employability and labour-force participation, underlie some important aspects of civic participation, and may impact on the possibilities of certain population groups for social equality and mobility. While the dialogue about these issues admittedly overlaps to some extent the points raised earlier in discussing the role of numeracy in society, it is worth elaborating upon because it brings forward some additional points and broadens the understanding of contexts where demands on adults' numeracy skills exist.

Various arguments have been forwarded over the last few decades to support a broadening of the conceptions regarding the mathematical skills and knowledge that school graduates should possess, and the ways in which learned knowledge serves adults. For example, Ernest distinguishes six different types of mathematical knowledge and capabilities for the results/outcomes of mathematics education in school (Ernest, 2004, p. 317[119]). These are not intended to be seen as mutually exclusive, but as a set of different foci for mathematics education:

- utilitarian knowledge
- practical, work-related knowledge
- advanced specialist knowledge
- appreciation of mathematics
- mathematical confidence
- social empowerment through mathematics.

Apart from the third capability, 'advanced specialist knowledge', often a key focus for school mathematics, the other five categories are all compatible with and consistent with the above arguments about how adults might use mathematics in their lives and be numerate individuals, workers and citizens.

Educators working both with school students and adults increasingly aim to assist learners in developing mathematical concepts and skills in ways that are personally meaningful but also functional. Such approaches usually assume that there is often more than one right way to cope with a real-world functional task, and that adults require access to a repertoire of strategies for solving functional problems. Adults' personal methods of using mathematics are encouraged and valued. This is often a significant difference from traditional (pre-reform) school-based mathematics teaching, within which school students were often expected to solve a problem following the one correct method or algorithm, introduced by the teacher.

Several decades ago, ideas already began emerging in different countries that since mathematics is an essential aspect of society, mathematics education in schools should be derived from or prepare learners for broad real-life situations in family, work, community, and other contexts (National Council of Teachers of Mathematics (NCTM), 2000[120]; Willis, 1990[39]), beyond employers' desire to focus mostly on practical or job-specific numeracy skills. Two early influential examples are the recommendations of the Cockcroft Committee in the United Kingdom [Department of Education and Science/Welsh Office, (1982[44])], and Freudenthal's work in the Netherlands, which has led to the Realistic Mathematics Education movement (van den Heuvel-Panhuizen and Gravemeijer, 1991[121]). Over the last two or three decades, many countries have adopted adult education frameworks which give explicit attention to numeracy skills.

Indeed, the dialogue about the various demands on adults' knowledge has been reflected in part in the emphasis in PISA on the assessment of mathematical literacy and science literacy. Such constructs pertain, broadly speaking, to school students' readiness for entering adults' life contexts; it is indicative that they have been chosen to be the focus of assessment rather than more traditional notions of formal curriculum-based knowledge in mathematics or science areas which were assessed primarily in earlier studies.

A perspective on 21st century digital and technological implications

As outlined above, being numerate in the 21st century means being able to cope with the aspects of the world as we encounter it, which includes the digital and technological aspects of information and society—society generally already has all kinds of techno-mathematical aspects. The 2017 PIAAC numeracy framework review found that 21st century digital technologies provide tools and processes that mediate thinking as well as action and are not just devices that can be used to complete manual, hands-on tasks more efficiently. These tools and processes often change the numeracy task itself and so transform practices within adults' lives and within the workplace. The use and application of a range of techno-mathematical literacies underpins much of this.

This aspect of 21st century representations and tools was missing from much of the existing PIAAC Cycle 1 numeracy framework discussions, and not adequately reflected in the definition and then in the elaborations. This is explicitly addressed in the new refinements and enhancements to the numeracy framework and construct elaborated later in this paper.

However, it is important to acknowledge that in addressing this issue PIAAC is a survey of adult competencies across **all** aspects of life, not just about workplace and employment, and not just about engaging with numeracy and mathematics actions within technologically rich environments. It is essential that a balance be kept between numeracy activities in digital and technological environments and those embedded in other, non-digital media; between numeracy demands and situations met as an individual and those encountered as part of society; and between work and employment settings and home and family activities. From the PIAAC numeracy assessment perspective, this can in part be addressed by the need to keep for trend purposes some of the existing former ALL numeracy items, which were originally developed at the end of last century and are not as technologically based, along with a number of the Cycle 1 PIAAC items. The new Cycle 2 items can, hence, contain a set of new items that are more targeted at 21st century digital representations.

In addressing numeracy in adults' lives above there was reference to a set of formal based descriptions of numeracy for both adult and a youth curriculum, where numeracy use was described by four broad categories (Kindler et al., 1996[81]; Victorian Curriculum and Assessment Authority (VCAA), 2008[82]). The four categories are *Numeracy for practical purposes*; *Numeracy for interpreting society*; *Numeracy for personal organisation*; and *Numeracy for knowledge*. These categories were used to reflect on how these different purposes and uses might interact with digital information and technology. Table 3.1 below shows some possible connections between numeracy practices and 21st century digital information and technology.

Table 3.1. Four categories of numeracy use and their connections with technology

Category	Related to	Connections with digital information and technology
Numeracy for practical purposes	Aspects of the physical world that involve designing, making, and measuring	e.g., many aspects of measuring are now digital – theodolites, inclinometers, medical equipment/monitors, etc. e.g., design aspects are now available digitally, via software such as Computer-aided design (CAD) or online design software for kitchen/house planning
Numeracy for interpreting society	Interpreting and reflecting on numerical and graphical information in public documents and texts	e.g., much quantitative information is presented in digital and graphical formats, often dynamic in nature, including the use of spreadsheets for analysis. Even common software such as Word has sophisticated graphic and data options available e.g. use of data, statistics and probabilistic information through social and mass media for advertising, news and political information dissemination, etc.
Numeracy for personal organisation	Numeracy requirements for personal organisational matters involving money, time and travel	e.g., digital diaries, online banking, online shopping and planning, GPS and Google maps
Numeracy for knowledge	Mathematical skills needed for further study in mathematics, or other subjects with mathematical underpinnings or assumptions	The degree of technology inclusion is dependent on the programmes of study— some are technology intensive, others less so. But often it is expected to be able to use and work with sophisticated digital and technological tools, including calculators, software, etc.

The above reflection about numeracy use indicates a strong connection and entanglement of digital information and technology with literacy and numeracy use in adults' lives. The ubiquitous presence of social and mass media also carries implications for informed and participatory citizenship, particularly the need for citizens to be critical consumers of such media. This issue of the connection of numeracy with digital information and technology will be addressed explicitly in the later descriptions, elaborations and dimensions of numeracy in PIAAC Cycle 2.

Further research issues arising from the review paper

The research section in the review paper on the PIAAC framework (Tout et al., 2017[1]) raised a significant number of challenges, and pointed to the need for careful consideration in the revisions to the PIAAC numeracy framework and in the development of any new assessment items. The review considered not only new research but also looked at different descriptions and models for representing and describing numeracy. Some of these are considered below.

The 2017 review paper considered the PISA 2012 mathematical literacy framework and its descriptions (OECD, 2013[122]). It should be noted that the same mathematical literacy framework and assessment construct was used for the next two cycles of PISA in 2015 and 2018.

However, for PISA 2021, mathematical literacy is again the major domain for PISA, and hence the PISA framework and assessment construct is being updated and revised. This revision was happening in parallel with the development of this numeracy framework for PIAAC Cycle 2. The PIAAC Numeracy Expert Group was able to access a copy of the second draft of the PISA 2021 Mathematics Framework (OECD, 2018[123]) in November 2018. Because of the timing issues, most of the comparisons between PIAAC numeracy and PISA mathematical literacy have therefore been based on a comparison of the 2012 PISA framework and descriptions, but where possible the PIAAC NEG has also included comments and comparisons with the updated 2021 PISA mathematical literacy framework. It should be noted that it is therefore possible that information regarding 2021 PISA mathematical literacy may change from what was in the second draft of the framework paper.

The definitions of mathematical literacy in the 2012 and 2021 PISA frameworks are very similar and consistent, with some changes and updates to reflect some new perspectives. The two definitions are shown below.

Box 3.1. Definitions of mathematical literacy in PISA

PISA 2012-2018 definition of mathematical literacy

Mathematical literacy is an individual's capacity to formulate, employ, and interpret mathematics in a variety of contexts. It includes reasoning mathematically and using mathematical concepts, procedures, facts and tools to describe, explain and predict phenomena. It assists individuals to recognise the role that mathematics plays in the world and to make the well-founded judgments and decisions needed by constructive, engaged and reflective citizens. (OECD, 2013, p. 25[122])

PISA 2021 definition of mathematical literacy

Mathematical literacy is an individual's capacity to reason mathematically and to formulate, employ, and interpret mathematics to solve problems in a variety of real-world contexts. It includes concepts, procedures, facts and tools to describe, explain and predict phenomena. It assists individuals to know the role that mathematics plays in the world and to make the well-founded judgments and decisions needed by constructive, engaged and reflective 21st century citizens. (OECD, 2018, p. 8[123])

The PISA 2012 (OECD, 2013[122]) definition and description of mathematical literacy was based around a model that assumed that when individuals use mathematics and mathematical tools to solve problems set in a real-world situation, they work their way through a series of stages as depicted in Figure 3.2 (OECD, 2013, p. 26[122]).

Figure 3.2. The PISA 2012 model of mathematical literacy in practice

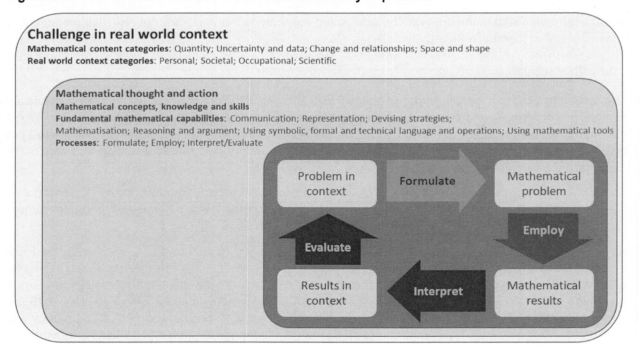

However, the PISA 2021 definition and description of mathematical literacy has extended the previous PISA 2012 model, and is based around a model that comprises two related aspects: mathematical reasoning and problem solving. When individuals use mathematics and mathematical tools to solve problems set in a real-world situation, they work their way through a series of stages as depicted in Figure 3.3 (OECD, 2018, p. 9[123]).

Figure 3.3. The PISA 2021 model of mathematical literacy: the relationship between mathematical reasoning and the problem solving (modelling) cycle

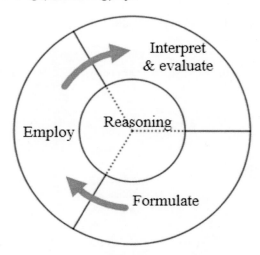

The *formulating, employing, interpreting and evaluating* processes are still key components of the mathematical modelling cycle that has underpinned the mathematical literacy construct in PISA since its beginnings. The mathematical reasoning process has been added as an explicit component in 2021 to highlight the centrality of mathematical reasoning to solving practical problems. The PISA mathematical reasoning aspect names these key understandings:

- understanding quantity, number systems and their algebraic properties
- understanding mathematics as a system based on abstraction and using symbolic representation
- seeing mathematical structure and regularities
- recognising functional relationships between quantities
- using mathematical models as a lens into the real world
- understanding variance as the heart of statistics (OECD, 2018, p. 16[123]).

As described in the draft PISA 2021 framework, these reasoning skills appear to mainly focus on reasoning skills *within* the world of mathematics, and *mathematical reasoning* is seen as a separate skill or process to the three problem solving processes of *formulating, employing, interpreting and evaluating*. As discussed further in the fifth section, this illustrates PISA's interest in the ability of 15-year-olds to use and apply curriculum-based mathematical skills and knowledge, whereas this type of more formal mathematical knowledge is not generally assessed in PIAAC.

The PIAAC description and definition of numeracy can learn from the PISA definitions, descriptions and models in relation to the need to highlight different problem solving skills and processes, including reasoning skills, and being critical (making well-founded judgements and decisions) framed around using mathematical models as a lens into the real world. The relationships between the PIAAC and PISA frameworks and their descriptions and constructs are discussed further in the fifth section: *Relationship between PIAAC and PISA*.

Another existing model for numeracy in the twenty-first century is illustrated in Figure 3.4 below, and attempts to capture the multifaceted nature, and especially the critical dimension, of using mathematics to act in the real world. This model incorporates four dimensions of settings/contexts, mathematical knowledge, tools, and dispositions that are embedded in a critical orientation to using mathematics (Goos, Geiger and Dole, 2014, p. 84[124]). These dimensions are described more fully in other publications [e.g., (Geiger, Goos and Dole, 2014[125]; Goos, Geiger and Dole, 2014[124])]. Although primarily developed for use in relation to teacher education programmes and numeracy across the curriculum, the model and its components has some consistency with both the PISA model and PIAAC's framework.

Figure 3.4. Model for numeracy in the twenty-first century

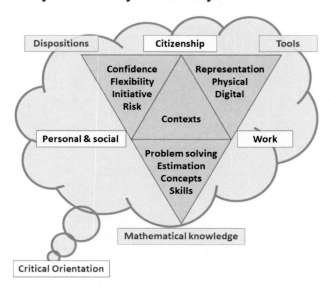

Both the PISA models and their sets of processes and this model for numeracy in the twenty-first century raise some issues to be considered in the redevelopment of the Cycle 1 definition and elaboration of numeracy for PIAAC Cycle 2.

Out of its research and review of conceptual and theoretical aspects of adult numeracy, the 2017 review recommended that there were four related issues to be explicitly addressed in updating and refining the existing PIAAC framework definition and description:

- disposition to use mathematics
- the ability to see mathematics in a numeracy situation
- critical reflection
- degree of accuracy.

Another issue that was raised in the review paper that is relevant here concerned the issue of authenticity, and this is also discussed below.

Disposition to use mathematics

The issue of a person's judgement on how to use mathematics (or not) in solving a numeracy problem is an important issue to address. The issue of choice or disposition when engaging with and solving a numeracy problem is an important factor to consider in an adult's use and application of mathematics in a real-world situation (Geiger, Goos and Dole, 2014[125]; Goos, Geiger and Dole, 2014[124]). Are individuals able to choose to use mathematics when it is relevant and appropriate? This can also relate to mathematics anxiety and individual's negative disposition to mathematics and their decision to avoid using mathematics, even when appropriate. Research about mathematics anxiety is well documented and demonstrates that it can have a significant impact on performance in mathematics [e.g., see: (Buckley, 2013[126]; Ma, 1999[127]; Tobias, 1993[128])].

There are three potentially related aspects behind this issue of disposition in relation to solving a numeracy problem where an adult is expected to use and apply some form of mathematical knowledge in a real-world situation:

- using other means than mathematics to solve a problem when mathematics should have been the obvious and most sensible approach;

- using formal mathematics when other sense-making methods would be more efficient; or

- avoiding doing anything at all and not attempting to solve the numeracy problem at hand.

This issue of disposition is addressed more explicitly in the discussions about the elaboration of numeracy and numerate behaviours and practices at the end of this section.

Seeing mathematics in a numeracy situation

Research indicates that an important aspect of a person's numeracy or numerate behaviour is their capability to "see" or notice when mathematics is embedded in a real-world situation—how to recognise the mathematics and to potentially take the next step and act on it. The ability to see the mathematics that surrounds adults in their everyday life is an important issue in relation to being numerate—to potentially link the mathematics they learned in school with mathematics embedded in a real-world situation (Maguire and Smith, 2016[129]; Roth, 2012[130]). This issue is also identified as important in research about workplace numeracy, for example in calculating medication dosage (Weeks et al., 2013[98]).

Seeing mathematics in a numeracy situation relates to aspects of two of the processes described as part of PISA's 2021 problem solving cycle for mathematical literacy: *Mathematical reasoning* and *Formulating*. In relation to *Mathematical reasoning*, before solving a problem, students need to "use their mathematics content knowledge to recognise the mathematical nature of a situation" (OECD, 2018, p. 9[123]). PISA also describes *Formulating* as: "seeing that mathematics can be applied to understand or resolve a particular problem or challenge presented" (p. 12).

As will be argued later, this aspect of being able to see and access the mathematics embedded in a numeracy situation and transposing the problem into a mathematical problem that can be solved is addressed explicitly in the revised numeracy framework and assessment construct through the new cognitive dimension.

Critical reflection and action

While the current framework mentions the notion of critical reflection under the facet *Responses* in its elaboration of numerate behaviour, having a critical orientation or reflection are aspects of numeracy that could be emphasised and described further. It is important for individuals in their lives as citizens and workers to critically review the mathematics used and the outcomes obtained to reflect on and question real-world implications, to be capable of following up with appropriate actions, and to make decisions and judgements. A critical orientation is also about supporting an argument or position with mathematical evidence or challenging the argument or position of another person or organisation.

This capability to reflect critically and to act is named and described explicitly in some other models and frameworks [e.g., (Geiger, Goos and Forgasz, 2015[54]; Goos, Geiger and Dole, 2014[124])]. The third problem solving process in the PISA mathematical literacy problem solving cycle, which is called *Interpreting and evaluating*, includes elements of critical reflection: the need to reflect and make contextual arguments, to evaluate the reasonableness of solutions, and to critique and identify the limits of any models used. As well the new *Mathematical reasoning* aspect of PISA 2021 includes evaluating and making arguments, to evaluate interpretations and inferences related to statements and problem solutions (OECD, 2013[122]; OECD, 2018[123]).

Degree of accuracy and tolerances

The Cycle 1 PIAAC numeracy framework did not explicitly address the issue of the degree of precision or accuracy that may be required in the solution of a numeracy problem. It is expected that a numerate person would use estimation and other skills to check the outcomes and decide on the appropriate degree of accuracy required when solving a problem. This is particularly true within a workplace environment, where precision, accuracy and working within specified tolerances can be critical. On the other hand in other situations and applications, there are instances in being numerate where accuracy is not a critical component (e.g., in relation to some spatial skills, in graphical/data interpretation and analysis, or in estimating quantities, where an order of magnitude estimate can often suffice).

Authenticity, embeddedness and text-related reading demands

Another issue raised in the review paper concerns the issue of authenticity, and as mentioned in the Introduction, the NEG did further research into the related issues of embeddedness, numerate behaviour and numerate practices. They relate to the connection between the real-world context in which mathematics is embedded and to their roles as individuals, citizens, family members or as workers. This can mean that the way mathematics is used to operate on a task is fundamentally shaped by the context in which it is employed (Turner et al., 2009[131]). This includes socio-cultural influences that afford or constrain action in civic, personal or workplace environments. In this view, there is a clear separation between school mathematical knowledge, how it is taught, learned and practised, and the use of this knowledge outside of schooling. As Harris (1991[132]) notes:

> In work [. . .] mathematical activity arises from within practical tasks, often from the spoken instruction of a supervisor and always for an obvious purpose which has nothing to do with the numbers working out well. Thus, students taught to react to isolated, abstract and written commands in the specialist language and carefully controlled figures of a school mathematics class, find themselves confronted with the urgent spoken, if not shouted, instructions in a completely different context and code. (p. 138)

Yasukawa, Brown and Black (2013[133]) make a clear connection between embeddedness and social practice arguing that numeracy practices cannot be understood independently of the social, cultural, historical and political contexts. They illustrate this point that make the comparison of students completing calculations individually, using paper and pen and perhaps a calculator against the use of mathematics in the supermarket, in which the same calculations completed at a checkout counter by the shop assistant using a cash register. In this situation the shopper might perform an estimation to avoid being overcharged. However, the shop assistant is equally concerned with charging the customer the correct price and recording accurate record of the items sold via the cash register. The calculations are fundamentally the same but the purpose—which is related to context—is different.

Authenticity of assessment tasks and word problems in mathematics education has been researched and documented [e.g., see (Hoogland et al., 2018[134]; Palm, 2006[135]; Palm, 2008[136]; Palm, 2009[137]; Stacey, 2015[138]; Verschaffel et al., 2009[139])]. In PIAAC it is important to have stimuli and questions that are based on authentic stimuli or scenarios with questions asked being ones that someone would want answered. While this is related to broader discussions about authentic assessment (Palm, 2008[140]) the focus in the PIAAC assessment programme is on the authenticity of the stimulus used and the questions asked. This matches what Palm describes as the "figurative context" where the context used in the assessment represents a situation taken from real life that has occurred, or might happen. PIAAC is interested in the ability of individuals to cope with tasks that are embedded in the real world, rather than assessing decontextualised mathematical tasks. This is in contrast to traditional school-based mathematical word problems which often disregard and challenge students' sense making and only continue to distance students from the real world, and the usefulness and value of mathematics. The NEG believe that the assessment of numeracy in PIAAC is about promoting the belief that the value in mathematics is about its relationship with real-world things—whereas word problems often do the opposite. Another reason for PIAAC to utilise authentic situations in its questions is to encourage a more positive disposition towards solving relevant and engaging mathematics problems, not irrelevant, nonsensical word problems as can be met in school mathematics classrooms.

Hence, the PIAAC numeracy contexts and the items are developed by finding and identifying situations and tasks from different countries that provide authentic stimuli and then writing sets of questions using the information in the stimulus. Based on the description and understanding of numeracy in PIAAC, there have been deliberate attempts to avoid what are traditionally seen as school, curriculum-based word problems that are often contrived and have little real-world relevance or authenticity.

However, a challenge is that authentic situations and scenarios that involve mathematical concepts, and their related stimuli and materials, are often complex. In relation to textual components and reading demands, there are a range of issues in relation to the intersection between literacy and numeracy skills and the role that reading literacy aspects take in solving a numeracy problem. It is clearly acknowledged in the description of numeracy and its elaborations, and then reflected in the PIAAC complexity schema (PIAAC Numeracy Expert Group, 2009[2]; Tout et al., 2020[141]), that reading literacy is an integral and important aspect of numeracy. Certainly, in society and workplaces that adults occupy, tasks and challenges do not neatly divide into, or present as, discreet 'literacy' and 'numeracy' tasks. Real-world situations and demands cross those kinds of educationally defined boundaries.

The reality is that in using authentic situations as the basis for the numeracy assessment tasks where the mathematics is embedded in a real-world setting, the associated information and data can be very complicated, unfamiliar and involve a heavy reading load. This can create challenges in trying to focus the assessment on the mathematics and numeracy skills and knowledge. Hence a key goal in the item development process is to make the wording of numeracy items as simple and direct as possible, in order to help minimise the reading literacy demands.

Recent research that systematically compares descriptive mathematical assessment tasks with more depictive representations of problem situations through using illustrations and photos and minimising the use of words (Hoogland et al., 2016[142]; 2018[134]), gives an indication that even the use of simple supporting illustrations and images could improve performance by a small margin.

Big Ideas in mathematics

As introduced in the first section, *Big Ideas in mathematics,* is about describing powerful mathematical ideas central to the learning of mathematics, linking numerous mathematical understandings into a coherent whole [e.g., see (Charles, 2005[6]; Hurst, 2014[7]; Hurst and Hurrell, 2014[8]; Kuntze et al., 2009[9]; Steen, 1990[11])]. Initially, the term "Big Ideas" referred to how mathematical information can be classified in different ways compared with the traditional school mathematics curriculum content areas. Steen (1990[11]), for example, identified six broad categories pertaining to: quantity, dimension, pattern, shape, uncertainty, and change. Rutherford and Ahlgren (1990[143]) described networks of related ideas: numbers, shapes, uncertainty, summarising data, sampling, and Reasoning. Jones and his colleagues (2002[5]) provide a summary of the main contributions of the research to what they call *powerful mathematical ideas*, which included the following domains: whole number and operations, rational numbers, geometry, probability, data exploration and algebraic thinking and other underrepresented domains. It could be argued that being numerate means using the contents of all these domains not just as procedures (instrumental understanding) but in a critical/meaningful manner.

Charles (2005[6]) defines Big Ideas as "a statement of an idea that is central to the learning of mathematics, one that links numerous mathematical understandings into a coherent whole." This view is also shared by other authors such as Hurst and Hurrell (2014[8]). In their article, they track the notion of Big Ideas in mathematics back to the work of Bruner (1960[144]), who inspired Clark's (2011[145]) definition of a Big Idea as a "cognitive file folder" that we can file with "an almost limitless amount of information" (Clark, 2011, p. 32[145]). Big Ideas became conceptual structures (or schema) that can be used to provide a numeracy framework where content might be characterised by multiple connections. As Bruner (1960[144]), Hurst and Hurrell (2014[8]), Clark (2011[145]) and other authors claim, Big Ideas may become bridges for the transfer of learning.

Big Ideas in mathematics can also refer to processes (Kuntze et al., 2009[9]) where they include processes such as: Ordering; Classifying; Dealing with variation and uncertainty; Finding arguments and proofs; Formalising; Modelling; Generating and using algorithms, among others. Big Ideas have also been seen as a potential vehicle for making mathematics education a coherent and connected study. Descriptions of effective teaching of mathematics [e.g., (Ma, 1999[146]; Sullivan, 2011[147])] and related research (Askew et al., 1997[148]; Boaler and Humphreys, 2005[149]; Clarke and Clarke, 2004[150]) also consistently refer to the need for teachers to have a sense of how mathematics is a coherent and connected whole. In the *Effective Teachers of Numeracy* study (Askew et al., 1997[148]), this view was also supported, with highly effective teachers believing that being numerate requires "having a rich network of connections between different mathematical ideas." This is in contrast to ways in which mathematical content knowledge is often reduced to lists of specific dot points in curriculum frameworks that Askew terms "death by a thousand bullet points" saying that "too much effort goes into specifying the knowledge that teachers need to know" (Askew, 2008, p. 21[151]). Hurst and Hurrell (2014[8]), quoting Charles (2005[6]), state that "Big Ideas" allow us to see mathematics as a coherent set of ideas, encouraging a deep understanding of mathematics.

These perspectives of Big Ideas in mathematics provide an overarching and integrative idea of mathematics and how mathematics is used in the world—that is, they are about framing and viewing mathematics as making connections with the real world, which is what underpins numeracy in PIAAC. It could be suggested that being *numerate* as defined within the PIAAC numeracy framework links to the idea of being able to access, use, interpret and communicate mathematical information around what the international scientific community calls Big Ideas in mathematics.

Towards a definition and description of numeracy for PIAAC Cycle 2

Reaching a consensus on a definition of numeracy that can fit an international programme of assessment is a challenging undertaking. First, as noted earlier, there are various country-specific connotations for numeracy, if such a term at all exists in a local language. Second, there are overlapping or competing constructs such as quantitative literacy, mathematical literacy, functional mathematics, and so forth [e.g., see (Gal and Tout, 2014[3]; Hagedorn et al., 2003[152]; Tout and Gal, 2015[37]; Tout and Schmitt, 2002[38])]. Third, an attempt to discuss the definition and meaning of numeracy is complicated by the fact different stakeholders already view it from within a given lens imposed by the historical and cultural aspects, whether organisational, social, economic, or linguistic, of the systems within which they operate. For example, some of the existing conceptions of numeracy were developed by educators working in delivery systems for schoolchildren, while other stakeholders link the term numeracy only to adult-related competencies.

Full range of numeracy capabilities

As stated in the Introduction it is critical to note that the PIAAC numeracy assessment aims to describe the full range of numeracy capability in the adult population. This covers at one extreme, adults who have university level training and, at the other, adults who have very low levels of education (e.g. who left school at or before the age of 15). At the same time, it covers both young adults still in education and adults who completed their formal education 30-50 years prior to undertaking the assessment. As such, it incorporates a wide range of different mathematical and quantitative skills and knowledge, and is not based on a narrow view of numeracy that sees numeracy as only dealing with numbers and arithmetical operations. This will be expanded on later in the chapter.

Numeracy assessment construct in PIAAC Cycle 2

In this section, the various aspects that are to be assessed, and eventually reported on, as part of the numeracy assessment in PIAAC are defined, described and elaborated. These aspects or characteristics of the assessment were called facets in ALL and PIAAC Cycle 1, but in PIAAC Cycle 2 they are called dimensions, which is consistent with the terminology used in literacy in PIAAC.

The initial sub-sections look at the refinement of the definition and description of numeracy from ALL through to PIAAC Cycle 1 and then to the new definition and description for this, the second cycle of PIAAC. For a backwards look at the development of numeracy definitions and developments it is best to read the PIAAC Cycle 1 framework (PIAAC Numeracy Expert Group, 2009[2]) or refer to the OECD Working Paper that compared the PISA and PIAAC frameworks (Gal and Tout, 2014[3]).

Next, an updated and refined definition of numeracy for PIAAC Cycle 2 is presented based on the research and review detailed in the second section, followed by a discussion of the dimensions of numerate behaviour and practices, including the core dimensions that comprise the numeracy assessment. This leads on to the next sub-sections, where the assessment construct is elaborated, described and defined in full.

The 2017 review report made a number of recommendations regarding the definition of the construct of numeracy and the priorities for development of the assessment framework for numeracy in the second cycle of PIAAC. Many of the suggestions arose out of the concern that the existing Cycle 1 framework and assessment did not reflect some of the realities of the skills and knowledge adults needed to succeed in work, life, and citizenship in the 21st century. These have been documented in the discussions in the previous section. The review and this document and its resulting definitions and elaborations, while building on the two previous conceptual and assessment frameworks and all the cumulative wisdom developed in connection with prior surveys of adult skills, have been able to enhance the numeracy framework and construct for PIAAC Cycle 2. The resulting framework and its associated definition, elaborations and assessment construct is contained below.

Numeracy in the ALL survey

The conceptualisation of numeracy for the first international survey of adult numeracy, the Adult Literacy and Lifeskills (ALL) survey, was developed in 1998-2000 by an international team (Gal et al., 2005[28]). This was the first time the construct of numeracy had to be defined in a comparative assessment context and not purely in an educational context.

Numeracy was conceptualised and described in ALL as a much broader construct than Quantitative Literacy that was assessed in the earlier International Adult Literacy Survey (IALS). Quantitative Literacy was described in IALS as the knowledge and skills required to apply arithmetic operations to numbers embedded in printed materials. It was argued in ALL that numeracy requires more varied responses (order, count, estimate, compute, measure, interpret, explain) to a wider range of mathematical information (quantity, dimension and shape, pattern, change and relationships, and data and chance) that may be embedded in text in varying degrees.

Cognisant of the complexity and multifaceted nature of the numeracy construct, the ALL team developed a three-tier conceptualisation which attempted to reflect key perspectives of numeracy on the one hand, but also enable operationalisation of the construct in an assessment scale on the other. The three tiers are a brief definition of numeracy, a more elaborate definition of numerate behaviour, both presented below, and a detailed listing of components of the facets of numerate behaviour (Gal et al., 2005[28]).

> *Numeracy is the knowledge and skills required to effectively manage and respond to the mathematical demands of diverse situations.*

> *Numerate behaviour is observed when people manage a situation or solve a problem in a real context; it involves responding to information about mathematical ideas that may be represented in a range of ways; it requires the activation of a range of enabling knowledge, factors, and processes.*

Both the brief and elaborate definitions shown above were seen by the ALL numeracy team to be required, given the needs of a comparative assessment. A brief definition is essential to simplify communication with various stakeholders, such as policy makers and experts. However, as with most brief definitions of complex constructs, the language used is general and abstract, hence the definition cannot be explicit about what a numerate person can do in an assessment. With this in mind, a more detailed definition of numerate behaviour was developed as a way to emphasise different facets or dimensions that were seen by the ALL numeracy team as underlying numerate behaviour.

The advantage of using a more elaborate definition of numerate behaviour was that it is more explicit about what numeracy encompasses, and thus served as a springboard for developing an actual specification for an assessment. It is important to also note that the definition of numerate behaviour points to the presence of both cognitive and non-cognitive factors that underlie or enable effective numerate behaviour and practices. Ideally, coverage of both cognitive and non-cognitive aspects of numerate behaviour is essential in order to generate a full picture regarding the competence described by this view of numeracy. However, it needs to be acknowledged that the direct assessment component of PIAAC can only assess the cognitive aspects of numerate behaviour and that the non-cognitive aspects can only be addressed in proxy via responses to questions about skills use and data collected on respondents' backgrounds.

Numeracy in PIAAC Cycle 1

The development of the conceptualisation and definition of numeracy for PIAAC went through several stages of work and consultation. An expert panel appointed to develop the overall assessment design for PIAAC presented in summer 2006 tentative recommendations regarding all competencies to be assessed in PIAAC (Gal, 2006[153]; Jones, 2006[154]; Murray, 2006[155]; Tout, 2006[156]) and then proposed to define numeracy as: *"The ability to use, apply, and communicate mathematical information".* Various perspectives on numeracy and its assessment were later examined by participants at the Canada-OECD Expert Technical Workshop on Numeracy, which met in November 2006 in Ottawa; a tentative working definition of numeracy was then proposed for PIAAC and included in a draft framework circulated for external review (Gal, 2006[153]). Further development of the numeracy framework was then undertaken by the Numeracy Expert Group for PIAAC appointed in April 2008, which released a revised framework for review by all participating countries in October 2008.

In general, work on the development of the numeracy framework for PIAAC Cycle 1, together with the assessment scale and related item pool, was conducted with two somewhat conflicting objectives in mind. One was the need to maintain compatibility with the conceptualisation of numeracy in the ALL survey, given the need for PIAAC to provide trend data related to ALL results. For this reason, PIAAC was designed with a specification that approximately 60% of the numeracy tasks that were to be employed in the final assessment would come from the item pool used in ALL. The other objective was the need to extend the ALL definition in light of PIAAC's overarching conceptualisation of "literacy competencies in the information age", and consider new or emerging uses of numeracy in the adult world.

Taking all the above into consideration, numeracy was defined for PIAAC Cycle 1 as follows:

> **Numeracy** *is the ability to access, use, interpret, and communicate mathematical information and ideas, in order to engage in and manage the mathematical demands of a range of situations in adult life.*

This definition captured essential elements in numerous conceptualisations of numeracy in the extant literature; was compatible with the definition used for ALL and provided a solid basis from which to develop an assessment for PIAAC with its emphasis on competencies in the information age. The inclusion of "engage" in the definition signalled that not only cognitive skills but also dispositional elements, i.e., beliefs and attitudes, are necessary for effective and active coping with numeracy situations.

As with ALL, the definition of numeracy developed for PIAAC Cycle 1 was not to be considered by itself, but again was to be coupled with a more detailed definition of numerate behaviour and with further specification of what were called the facets of numerate behaviour. This pairing was seen as essential in order to not only describe numeracy but to also enable operationalisation of the construct of numeracy in an actual assessment, and in order to further broaden the understanding of key terms appearing in the definition itself. Consequently, a definition of numerate behaviour similar in general terms to the one used for the ALL survey, but shorter, was adopted for PIAAC Cycle 1:

> **Numerate Behaviour** *involves managing a situation or solving a problem in a real context, by responding to mathematical content/information/ideas represented in multiple ways.*

As with ALL, each of the different facets embedded within the definition of numeracy and the elaboration of numerate behaviour were defined and described. This included the same facets as ALL: *contexts*; *responses*; *mathematical ideas/content*; and *representations*.

Definition of numeracy for PIAAC Cycle 2

Based on the discussions in the previous section: *Conceptual and theoretical foundations*, the PIAAC Cycle 2 NEG developed and agreed on a new definition for Cycle 2 of PIAAC numeracy:

> **Numeracy** *is **accessing, using and reasoning critically** with **mathematical content**, information and ideas **represented in multiple ways** in order to engage in and manage the mathematical demands of a **range of situations** in adult life.*

In this updated definition and in the elaboration below, there are four core *dimensions* (previously called facets) described and used in PIAAC Cycle 2:

- cognitive processes
- content
- representations
- contexts.

The major changes

The key words or terms that have changed or been introduced into the new definition include:

- the use of the term ability has been deleted
- access, use and reason critically has replaced access, use, interpret, and communicate
- *represented in multiple ways* has been introduced into the definition.

The use of the term ability can imply that it is an "innate" ability that some people may not possess. The NEG firmly believe that adults (and children) all have the capacity to learn mathematics successfully and apply it successfully in their lives and hence be numerate.

Based on the views and research outlined in the previous section and raised in the review report, the NEG has substantially reworked the former *Response* facet (*access, use, interpret, and communicate*), and replaced with a more comprehensive description and elaboration of what is now called the core dimension of *Cognitive Processes*. This is named and described under three classifications:

- access and assess situations mathematically (assess, identify, access and represent)
- act on and use mathematics (order, count, estimate, compute, measure, graph and draw)

- evaluate, critically reflect, make judgements (evaluate, reflect, justify and explain).

This has been done in the light of a number of the outcomes of the above research, both by the new NEG, but also from the recommendations made in the 2017 review paper. The major influences have been about the need to incorporate the aspect of being able to "see" mathematics in a real-world situation, and to include a critical aspect and the ability to reason and make judgements. This dimension has been able to be more explicitly used to drive the assessment development and the NEG believe this has greatly enhanced the item pool, helping to address a number of the concerns expressed in the review paper. It will also help develop and write the scale descriptions once the data and results are available. This dimension, along with the other core dimensions are elaborated further in the following section.

The third facet of the previous elaboration in ALL and PIAAC that has been added in and made explicit by including it in the new definition is that of *representation*. Although this was included in the previous elaborations it was not part of the definition, and did not help drive item development. Again, to address issues raised above, and specifically in relation to 21st century changes in how mathematical and quantitative information is now presented, the inclusion of *represented in multiple ways* has been introduced. This is named and described under four classifications:

- text or symbols
- images of physical objects
- structured information
- dynamic applications.

The latter two classifications have enabled the NEG, and hence the item writers, to explicitly address the issue of 21st century digitisation and technologically based materials and representations such as interactive websites, infographics, online calculators, spreadsheets and more.

The other facets in ALL and PIAAC Cycle 1, *content* and *contexts* remain, although there have been changes made to their labels and descriptions. All these core dimensions are named and elaborated below and in the following section.

Elaboration of numerate behaviour and practices

As with previous cycles, the definition leads on to an elaboration of numerate behaviour, which is included in Box 3.2 below. This box first lists the direct assessment components of the four core dimensions of the definition, and these components are explained in more detail in the next sub-section. Additionally, the bottom part of Box 3.2 also lists several non-cognitive, enabling factors and processes, whose activation underlies numerate behaviour and successful numeracy practices. Most of these enabling factors and processes appeared in the ALL conceptual framework and PIAAC Cycle 1. Overall, the definition of numeracy and the description of numerate behaviour, with the details in Box 3.2 and the further explanations of the core dimensions following in the next section, provide the structure and roadmap for the development of the numeracy assessment as part of PIAAC Cycle 2.

Box 3.2. Numerate behaviour and practices – key facets and their components

Numeracy is an individual's capacity to …

1. *access, use and reason critically*

- access and assess situations mathematically (assess, identify, access and represent)
- act on and use mathematics (order, count, estimate, compute, measure, graph and draw)
- evaluate, critically reflect, make judgements (evaluate, reflect, justify and explain)

---

2. with *mathematical content*

- quantity and number
- space and shape
- relationship and change
- data and chance

3. *represented in multiple ways*

- text or symbols
- images of physical objects
- structured information
- dynamic applications

4. in order to engage in and manage the mathematical demands of a *range of situations* in adult life:

- personal
- work
- societal/community.

An individual's numerate capacity is founded on the activation of several enabling factors and processes:

- context/world knowledge and familiarity
- literacy skills
- disposition, beliefs and attitudes
- numeracy-related practices and experience.

Enabling factors and processes

Adults' numeracy competence is revealed through their responses to the mathematical information or ideas that may be represented in a situation or that can be applied to the situation at hand. It is clear that numerate behaviour will involve an attempt to engage with a task and not delegate it to others or deal with it by intentionally ignoring its mathematical content. Numerate behaviour, however, depends not only on cognitive skills or knowledge bases, but also on several enabling factors and processes as listed in Box 3.2.

As outlined in the second section, including in the discussion about *Numerate behaviour and practices*, the PIAAC conceptualisation of numeracy operates on two levels. It relates to numeracy as a construct describing an individual's capability to solve numeracy problems, and also to numerate behaviour and practice which is the way a person's numeracy is manifested in the face of situations or contexts which have mathematical elements or carry information of a quantitative nature.

We argue therefore that numeracy as described in PIAAC is comprised both of cognitive elements (i.e., various knowledge bases and skills) as well as non-cognitive or semi-cognitive elements (i.e., attitudes, beliefs, habits of mind, and other dispositions) which together help to shape a person's numerate behaviour and practices. Based on this, there are four non-cognitive or semi-cognitive enabling factors included in the elaboration of numerate behaviour:

- context/world knowledge and familiarity
- literacy skills
- disposition, beliefs and attitudes
- numeracy-related practices and experience.

Specifically, the enabling processes involve integration of mathematical knowledge and conceptual understanding with broader reasoning, problem-solving skills, and literacy skills. Further, numerate behaviour and numerate practices and autonomous engagement with numeracy tasks depend on the dispositions (beliefs, attitudes, habits of minds, etc.), and prior experiences and practices that an adult brings to each situation. These are briefly summarised below. Most of these enabling factors and processes have also been described by Kilpatrick, Swafford and Findell (2001[157]) as part of their analysis of the construct of mathematical literacy, and further examined and deemed relevance for description of adult numeracy in the analysis by Ginsburg, Manly and Schmitt (2006[29]).

It should be noted that the direct assessment via the numeracy test component in PIAAC has, as its primary emphasis, the cognitive aspects of numerate behaviour as framed in the first part of Box 3.2, namely the numeracy and mathematical knowledge and skills that underpin answering the test questions, which are mediated by written materials, without oral support, in the context of a formal assessment. The non-cognitive aspects of numerate behaviour, are addressed indirectly through other components of the PIAAC assessment, namely through the skills use questions and the comprehensive background questionnaire.

Context/world knowledge and familiarity

Proper interpretation of mathematical information or quantitative messages by adults depends on their ability to place messages in a context and access their world knowledge, as well as rely on their personal experiences and practices. World knowledge also supports general literacy processes and is critical to enable "sense-making" of any message. For example, adults' ability to make sense of statistical claims or media-based graphs will depend on information they can glean from the message about the background of the study or data being discussed. When interpreting statistical claims made by journalists, advertisers and the like, context knowledge is the main determinant of the reader's familiarity with sources for variation and error, and helps to imagine why a difference between groups can occur (as in a medical or educational experiment), or what alternative interpretations may exist for reported findings about an association or correlation between certain variables. Likewise, world knowledge is a prerequisite for enabling critical reflection about statistical messages and for understanding the implications of the reported findings.

Different people will have very different settings and applications in which they may comfortably and more confidently use and apply their mathematical knowledge, often related to their familiarity with the actual context and the mathematics that is embedded in the situation at hand. This is related to the discussion in the previous section about numeracy practices, authenticity and the embedded nature of mathematics within a numeracy context. Finding the right problem situation or setting for each individual so that they can demonstrate their understanding of mathematics concepts will be a challenge in such an assessment as PIAAC. Hence, it is important to not have contexts, especially workplace contexts, which are too technical or so uncommon that most adults faced with that stimulus and questions will not be at all familiar with the context, and would be potentially locked out from engaging with and answering the question. This is one of the key challenges in writing items for PIAAC – to make them all relatively accessible and realistic for all the respondents, but still with a wide range of difficulty and complexity.

Literacy skills

It is clearly acknowledged in the description of numeracy and its elaborations, and then reflected in the PIAAC Complexity schema (PIAAC Numeracy Expert Group, 2009[2]; Tout et al., 2020[141]), that literacy is an integral and important aspect of numeracy. Certainly, in society and workplaces that adults occupy, tasks and challenges do not neatly divide into, or present as, discrete 'literacy' and 'numeracy' tasks. Real-world situations and demands cross those kinds of educationally defined boundaries.

The reality is that in using authentic situations as the basis for the numeracy assessment tasks where the mathematics is embedded in a real-world setting, the associated information and data can be very complicated and potentially involve a heavy reading load. In cases where "mathematical representations" involve text, one's performance on numeracy tasks will depend not only on formal mathematical or statistical knowledge but also on reading comprehension and literacy skills, reading strategies, and prior literacy experiences. For example, following a computational procedure described in text (such as the instructions for computing shipping charges or adding taxes on an order form) may require special reading strategies, as text is very concise and structured. Likewise, analysing the mathematical relationships described in words requires specific interpretive skills, as in the simple case of recognising the similarity of "the price doubled" and "the price was twice as high", but the different meanings in "production levels were constant over the last five years" and "production levels constantly increased over the last five years."

This creates challenges in trying to focus the assessment on the mathematics and numeracy skills and knowledge. Hence a key goal in the item development process is to make the wording of numeracy items as simple and direct as possible, in order to help minimise the reading literacy demands. Recent research that systematically compares descriptive assessment tasks with more depictive representations of problem situations through using illustrations and photos and minimising the use of words (Hoogland et al., 2016[142]; 2018[134]), gives an indication that even the use of simple supporting illustrations and images could make the contexts and questions more accessible. Lowrie and Diezmann (2009[158]) also researched the impact of supporting graphics and illustrations in numeracy test items, and argued that the design of mathematics assessment items is more likely to be a reliable indication of student performance if graphical, linguistic and contextual components are considered both in isolation and in integrated ways as essential elements of task design.

Disposition, beliefs and attitudes

The issue of choice or disposition when engaging with and solving a numeracy problem is an important factor to consider in an adult's use and application of mathematics in a real-world situation, and was addressed in the second section, including in the sub-section about *Numerate behaviour and practices*. Research literature suggests that the ways in which a person responds to a numeracy task, including overt actions as well as internal thought processes and the adoption of a critical stance, depend not only on their knowledge and skills but also potentially on their disposition and attitude towards mathematics. Negative attitudes towards mathematics, beliefs about one's mathematical skills, habits of mind, and prior experiences involving tasks with mathematical content are all key influencers on mathematics engagement and performance, alongside beliefs about mathematics and what it is for and who it is for (Geiger, Goos and Dole, 2014[125]; Goos, Geiger and Dole, 2014[124]; Lave, 1988[53]; Saxe, 1992[109]; Schliemann and Acioly, 1989[111]). Are individuals able to choose to use mathematics when it is relevant and appropriate?

This also relates to mathematics anxiety. In some cultures, some adults, including highly educated ones, decide that they are not "good with numbers" or have other sentiments or self-perceptions usually attributed to negative prior experiences they have had as pupils of mathematics. Such attitudes and beliefs stand in contrast to the desired sense of "at-homeness with numbers" (Cockcroft, 1982[44]) and can interfere with one's motivation to develop new mathematical skills or to tackle math-related tasks, and may also affect test performance (McLeod, 1992[159]). Research about mathematics anxiety is well documented and demonstrates that it can have a significant impact on performance in mathematics [e.g., see: (Buckley, 2013[126]; Ma, 1999[127]; Tobias, 1993[128])].

In real-world contexts, adults with a negative mathematical self-concept may elect to avoid a problem with quantitative and mathematical elements, address only a portion of it, or prefer to delegate a problem, e.g., by asking a family member or a salesperson for help. Such decisions or actions can serve to reduce both mental and emotional load (Gal, 2000[27]). Yet, such actions may fall short of autonomous engagement with the mathematical demands of real-world tasks, carrying negative consequences, e.g., not being able to fully achieve one's goals.

Numeracy-related practices and experiences

The discussion in the previous section about the research and issues about numerate behaviours and practices, and about the relationship between school mathematics and workplace mathematics, demonstrates that numerate behaviour and practices do not rely only on mathematical knowledge or related reasoning and problem-solving skills acquired as part of formal learning in a school context. Both attitudes and beliefs as well as numeracy-related practices and world knowledge are important enabling processes and may influence adults' ability to act in a numerate way. Therefore, scales assessing selected attitudes and beliefs about mathematics, and numeracy-related practices in work, everyday, and other settings, have been developed for PIAAC's background questionnaire. Information collected by such scales can help to explain differences in performance among adults, further informing our understanding of factors that affect skill acquisition and retention or motivation for further learning. They can be used to help explain the links between numeracy performance and covariates such as participation in a range of numeracy practices in their lives including at work, participation in further learning or employment/unemployment status.

Further, the frequency of engaging with mathematical tasks or of exposure to mathematical or statistical information or displays, whether at work, home, when shopping, or in other contexts, is of much interest. Engagements or practices in this regard can be both the result of a certain skill level, but also the cause of observed skill levels, or at a minimum a factor influencing observed skill level apart from prior formal schooling.

Summary

The above enabling factors address the issue of the non-cognitive aspect of numerate behaviour and practice which is the way a person's numeracy is manifested in the face of situations or contexts which have mathematical elements or carry information of a quantitative nature. They are addressed indirectly in PIAAC through the other components of the PIAAC assessment, namely the skills use questions and the comprehensive background questionnaire.

The fourth section of the framework discusses the operationalisation of the construct of numeracy in PIAAC and how this is affected by many factors which determine and shape the extent to which the theoretical construct can be fully addressed by the actual collection of test items used in the direct assessment.

The dimensions in PIAAC Cycle 2

This sub-section elaborates on the dimensions incorporated into the definition of numeracy and the elaboration of numerate capacity, as outlined in the first part of Box 3.2. Elaborations on the original facets of the previous two cycles were based on previous research and materials documented in both the ALL and PIAAC Cycle 1 framework. Key in that work was the analysis of the components of adult numeracy by Ginsburg, Manly and Schmitt (2006[29]) which was based on an integrative review of multiple numeracy frameworks from several countries. It also benefited from the positions presented in a report of the UK's National Research and Development Centre for Adult Literacy and Numeracy (NRDC) (2006[35]), background papers prepared for the OECD-Canada Expert workshop on numeracy (November 2006, Ottawa) and suggestions made by workshop participants. Input was also received from external reviews of early drafts of the PIAAC Cycle 1 framework, and professional perspectives of PIAAC's Cycle 1 Numeracy Expert Group.

For Cycle 2, these facets, or as they are now called, dimensions, have been further developed and substantially enhanced, mainly based on the 2017 review paper (Tout et al., 2017[1]). A significant factor to reworking the core dimensions was the comparison with the PISA 2012 mathematical literacy framework and its classifications. The comparison with PISA mathematical literacy is addressed explicitly and in detail in the fifth section: *Relationship between PIAAC and PISA*. Specific issues arising from this are incorporated into the discussions below.

There are four core dimensions named and described in numeracy for PIAAC Cycle 2, namely:

- cognitive processes
- content
- representations
- context.

Each of these four core dimensions are elaborated below.

Cognitive processes

This dimension is new to PIAAC Cycle 2 and replaces the previous *Response* facet of PIAAC and ALL. It also incorporates to some extent the first of the facets described under the category of *Mathematical knowledge and conceptual understanding* in the enabling processes elaboration in both ALL and PIAAC Cycle 1. This facet addressed the notion of conceptual understanding. This referred to *an integrated and functional grasp of mathematical ideas* (Kilpatrick, Swafford and Findell, 2001, p. 118[157]). Ginsburg, Manly and Schmitt (2006[29]) suggest that the two aspects of conceptual understanding, i.e., it being integrated and functional, frame the ability to think and act effectively as a numerate adult, and that across different numeracy frameworks in different countries, equivalent terms are used such as "meaning making," "relationships," "model," and "understanding." Conceptual understanding can help produce reasonable estimates that can help adults catch computational errors, or realise that an exact product is not necessary, but an estimate is enough for the purpose. Ginsburg, Manly and Schmitt (2006[29]) further explain that conceptual understanding permits one to be free from relying on memory for all methods and procedures, i.e., an adult can think about the meaning of the task and "construct or reconstruct" a representation that both illustrates what it means and suggests a method for solution.

The Cycle 1 framework described and elaborated how in different real-life situations, adults may have to react to a numeracy problem with different types of responses or actions. The Cycle 1 framework grouped those under three broad headings: *identify, locate, or access*; *act upon or use*; and *interpret, evaluate/analyse, communicate*.

The PISA 2012 to 2018 mathematical literacy framework described and used three processes—*formulating, employing, interpreting and evaluating*—as key components of their mathematical modelling cycle. The *mathematical reasoning* process has now been added as an explicit component in PISA 2021 to highlight the centrality of mathematical reasoning to solving practical problems. As described in the draft PISA 2021 framework, these reasoning skills appear to mainly focus on reasoning skills *within* the world of mathematics, and *mathematical reasoning* is seen as a separate skill or process to the three problem solving processes of *formulating, employing, interpreting and evaluating*. This highlights PISA's interest in the ability of 15-year-olds to use and apply more formal mathematical skills, knowledge and representations, whereas this type of more formal mathematical knowledge is not generally assessed in PIAAC. For PISA 2021, it is acknowledged that the assessment items will be assigned to either mathematical reasoning or one of the three mathematical processes associated with real-world based mathematical problem solving. The PISA 2021 goal "is to achieve a balance that provides approximately equal weighting between the two processes that involve making a connection between the real world and the mathematical world (formulating and interpreting/evaluating) and mathematical reasoning and employing which call for students to be able to work on a mathematically formulated problem" (OECD, 2018, p. 33[123]).

Based on the views and research outlined earlier and raised in the review report, the NEG has substantially reworked the former *Response* facet, and replaced it with a more comprehensive description and elaboration of what is now called the dimension of *Cognitive processes*. This was to more explicitly describe and address the way adults have to deal with solving a problem embedded in an authentic context. The skills adults need in the 21st century cover not only a range of specific mathematical knowledge and problem solving skills, but include the ability to recognise and identify how and when to use mathematics; to be able to understand, use and apply mathematical concepts and procedures; along with strategic, reasoning and reflective skills to use when using and applying the mathematics.

This is also derived in part from the comparison with the PISA processes as part of the PISA problem solving and modelling process. Unlike a number of the other facets of numerate behaviour in PIAAC Cycle 1 and their related descriptions, this facet of responses or actions had the least in common between PISA and PIAAC. It is the view of the NEG, that for the assessment of numeracy skills of adults the mainly intra-mathematical aspect of mathematical reasoning, as added to the PISA 2021 mathematical literacy construct, needs to be embedded within the real-world problem solving aspect for PIAAC, and not assessed as a separate part of the construct. Therefore mathematical reasoning understanding is integrated into the relevant aspects of the three cognitive processes.

The revisions and enhancements to this facet or dimension also more closely met the need to address a range of factors to do with both 21st century skills and the need to be more reflective and be able to reason and think critically, and make judgements. The NEG believes that this enhanced and more explicitly defined and described *Cognitive process* dimension has supported the test developers to write new types of items and has greatly enhanced the item pool, helping to address a number of the concerns expressed in the review paper. It will also help develop and write the scale descriptions once the data and results are available.

Table 3.2 below compares the terms used for the cognitive process or response-related descriptions in PIAAC Cycle 1 with the three processes used in PISA 2012 and the four processes used in PISA 2021 including against the new *Cognitive process* of PIAAC Cycle 2.

Table 3.2. Cognitive processes labels in PIAAC and PISA

PIAAC Cycle 1	PIAAC Cycle 2	PISA 2012	PISA 2021
Identify/locate/access	Access and assess situations mathematically	Formulating situations mathematically	Formulating situations mathematically
Act on/use (order, count, estimate, compute, measure, model)	Act on and use mathematics	Employing mathematical concepts, facts, procedures, and reasoning	Employing mathematical concepts, facts, procedures, and reasoning
Interpret/evaluate/communicate	Evaluate, critically reflect, make judgements	Interpreting, applying and evaluating mathematical outcomes	Interpreting, applying and evaluating mathematical outcomes
			Mathematical reasoning

Description

Solving problems in real-world contexts requires a range of capabilities and cognitive processes. When engaging with a real-world problem, one of the decisions to be made is whether the use of mathematics is relevant and then if it is best way to solve a problem. If the use of mathematics is deemed appropriate, the essential features of the problem will need to be identified in order to turn the real-world situation into a mathematical problem. From this point, relevant mathematical content, procedures, processes and tools needed to solve the problem must be identified and accessed by the problem solver. Once accessed, these procedures and processes will need to be employed correctly and decisions made about the appropriate degree of accuracy required to yield a mathematical solution. The solution needs to be reflected on and evaluated against the original problem situation in terms of its reasonableness and relevance to the real-world context and a decision made about whether to accept the solution or to revisit aspects that require refinement. In cases where decisions or judgements are being made on the basis of the solution, other factors might also be considered such as social or economic consequences.

So the first core dimension described in the PIAAC definition and elaboration of numeracy is about the cognitive skills and processes required to engage with and solve the task or problem at hand. These have been named as:

- access and assess situations mathematically
- act on and use mathematics
- evaluate, critically reflect, make judgements.

It is important to understand that these activities are not mutually exclusive of one another or that they take place in a rigidly linear manner. For example: the identification of a problem's essential features will have consequences for the identification of relevant mathematics to be engaged; an inability to access a particular area of mathematics may result in the selection of mathematical procedures and processes that are less effective; or the evaluation of the solution against the original problem situation may indicate those features, identified as essential, were not as relevant as first thought and so backtracking through the steps of the solution is necessary. Thus, while the cognitive processes outlined in this sub-section are described separately, the activity of addressing a real-world problem via mathematical means should be considered first and foremost as a holistic process.

It will be the combination of these three processes and their components that drive the difficulty and complexity of each numeracy problem being solved and each question asked in PIAAC numeracy units and items. After the description of each cognitive process below, there are a number of key questions outlined that describe the issues and factors that will influence the complexity of each process.

Note: for the purpose of guaranteeing a spread of types of items across PIAAC that focus on or emphasise the different aspects of these cognitive processes, each item has been prioritised against one of the three processes.

Access and assess situations mathematically (assess, identify, access and represent)

When adults encounter problems within real-world contexts they must first decide if mathematics is an appropriate means to engage with the situation. Once they deem the use of mathematics will provide advantage in addressing the problem, they need to identify the essential features to be accommodated when transforming the real-world situation into a mathematical problem. This transformation requires adults to look forward and identify and access the mathematics and mathematical representation embedded in the specifics of the situation, and make decisions about how the task can be represented and solved mathematically. The direction of the thinking and reasoning in this process is going from the real world to the mathematical world.

The actions that underpin assessing situations and accessing the mathematics in order to solve a real-world problem include:

- identifying the essential features of a real-world problem that can be represented mathematically
- identifying and describing/defining the mathematical operation(s), processes and tools needed to solve the problem
- simplifying a situation or problem in order to represent it mathematically, using appropriate representations, for example, variables, symbols, diagrams, and models
- representing a problem in a different way, including organising it according to mathematical concepts and making appropriate assumptions
- anticipating the real-world restrictions on the possible outcomes of decisions made while defining and representing the problem.

Key questions that drive the complexity of this process:

- How is the mathematics represented and embedded within the real-world situation? Through words and language? Through numbers and symbols, diagrams, pictures, graphs and charts? How informal, formal or complex are the mathematical representations and the mathematical information?

- Is a mathematical approach suitable for the presented situation – is the use of mathematics a sensible way to address the real-world problem? If so, what is the degree of transformation required of the real-world situation to move it into a mathematical problem? How implicit or explicit/obvious is it to decide on the mathematical problem solving solution? Is the question presented in an unambiguous way so that necessary mathematical processes and procedures can be identified?

- What literacy skills are required to make this transformation – what are the reading demands, how much distracting information is there?

- Will a decision need to be made about how well the solution generated by solving the mathematical representation of the problem matches the contexts of the original real-world situation? How complex is that decision?

Act on and use mathematics (order, count, estimate, compute, measure, graph and draw)

Adults utilise mathematical processes, facts and procedures in order to derive results and solve real-world problems, and will need to select and use appropriate tools, including technology. For example, they may need to perform arithmetic computations; select, create, solve equations; make logical deductions from mathematical assumptions; perform symbolic manipulations; create and extract information from mathematical tables and graphs; represent and manipulate geometrical objects in 2D and 3D; and analyse data. Mathematical processes and procedures used to solve real-world problems include:

- applying mathematical facts, rules and structures
- performing arithmetic computations and applying routine algorithms
- undertaking measurements
- looking for a pattern
- using symbolic, formal, and technical language and mathematical conventions
- using mathematical tools, including technology
- manipulating numbers, graphical, statistical and chance-based data and information, algebraic expressions and equations, geometric representations
- collecting, organising, structuring and representing information
- generating estimations and approximations
- making and extracting information from mathematical diagrams, graphs, infographics and constructions
- reviewing and reflecting upon initial or part solutions
- generalise from a more complex mathematical situation to a simpler mathematical problem/situation that can be more easily solved.

Key questions that drive the complexity of this process:

- How difficult and complex are the mathematical concepts, facts, processes and procedures that need to be used and applied?

- What level of mathematical reasoning, arguing, manipulating and computing is required for an effective response to the problem?

- How many steps and types of mathematical steps/processes are required to solve the problem? Is it one operation, action or process or does it require the integration of several steps covering more than one different operation, action or process?

Evaluate, critically reflect, make judgements (evaluate, reflect, justify and explain)

Responses to real-world tasks, including any mathematical solutions, judgements, decisions or conclusions, require reasoning and critical reflection and evaluation. Any solution of a real-world problem needs to be evaluated against the original problem situation in terms of its reasonableness and relevance to the original context and a decision made about whether to accept the solution or to revise and adjust the solution—often referred to as contextual judgement. In cases where decisions or judgements are being made on the basis of the solution, other factors might also be considered such as social or economic consequences. This will require that responses include explanations and justifications for decisions, judgements and conclusions that are reasonable and make sense within the context of the original situation. Critical reflection and evaluation within real-world contexts requires:

- evaluating the reasonableness of a solution or part solution to a problem. This includes consideration of the appropriateness of estimations and/or the degree of accuracy required
- understanding the real-world implications of solutions generated by mathematical methods, in order to critically reflect and make judgements about how the results should be adjusted or applied
- using mathematical arguments to construct, defend or challenge decisions and/or judgements
- considering social norms and influences, in addition to physical constraints, when considering the validity or effectiveness of a mathematical solution to a real-world problem
- reflecting on mathematical processes and arguments used and explaining and justifying results
- identifying and critiquing the limitations inherent in solving some real-world problems.

Key questions that drive the complexity of this process:

- How complex is it to evaluate, reflect, justify, and explain and connect the mathematical outcomes to the real-world context? Does the task require a choice from a number of provided solution options? Or does the task require an explanation to be derived or decided upon with no provided solutions?
- How complex is it to justify the validity of the mathematical outcomes and evidence with the essential elements of the original real-world problem? To what extent does the task require judgement about the quality of a mathematical argument used to defend or challenge a proposition within a real-world context?
- How complex is it to connect the mathematical evidence to the essential elements of the real-world problem? To what extent does the task require judgement about the appropriateness and reasonableness of a proposed result to the real-world context? To what extent does the mathematical result need to be adapted to fit in with the original real-world context? Does it require consideration of the appropriateness of estimations and/or the degree of accuracy required?

These three *Cognitive processes* are linked to the Numeracy Complexity Schema described further in the fourth section: *Operationalisation of the PIAAC Numeracy Assessment* and detailed in Tout et al. (2020[141]). It is believed that the cognitive processes will drive much of the item difficulty and that together with the descriptions and scores described in the Complexity Schema, these will help to describe performance when it comes to elaborating the different levels in PIAAC.

Mathematical content

Mathematical information can be classified in several ways and on different levels of abstraction. One approach is to refer to fundamental "Big Ideas in mathematics" (see discussion in the second section). Steen (1990[11]), for example, identified six broad categories: *Quantity*, *Dimension*, *Pattern*, *Shape*, *Uncertainty*, and *Change*. Rutherford and Ahlgren (1990[143]) described networks of related ideas: *Numbers*, *Shapes*, *Uncertainty*, *Summarising data*, *Sampling*, and *Reasoning*. Dossey (1997[160]) categorised the mathematical behaviours of quantitative literacy as: *Data representation and interpretation*, *Number and operation sense*, *Measurement*, *Variables and relations*, *Geometric shapes and spatial visualisation*, and *Chance*. More broadly, many curriculum frameworks around the world in one way or another refer to these key areas, albeit using somewhat different terminologies and with somewhat different groupings [e.g., National Council of Teachers of Mathematics (NCTM) (2000[120])].

This dimension remains similar to PIAAC Cycle 1 and is similar to the equivalent facet in PIAAC and ALL. There are some name changes, partly to make them more consistent with the PISA mathematical literacy descriptions and labels for *Content* (see Table 3.3).

Table 3.3. Mathematical content labels in PIAAC and PISA

PIAAC Cycle 1	PIAAC Cycle 2	PISA 2012 and 2021
Quantity and number	Quantity and number	Quantity
Dimension and shape	Space and shape	Space and shape
Pattern, relationships and change	Change and relationships	Change and relationships
Data and chance	Data and chance	Uncertainty and data

Description

Four key areas of mathematical content, information and ideas are described and used in the numeracy assessment in PIAAC:

- Quantity and number
- Space and shape
- Change and relationships
- Data and chance.

For an individual item in PIAAC numeracy, these four content areas are not mutually exclusive and any item may involve one or more of these mathematical content areas. For example, a unit and item in *Data and chance* will necessarily also include data that will be expressed as a quantity or number, and similarly a measurement item in *Space and shape* will be expressed as a quantity or number. The classification of such items is based on what content area the key conceptual understanding and skill is directed at.

Quantity and number

The notion of quantity and number is a fundamental and essential mathematical aspect of engaging with, and functioning in, our world. The *Quantity and number* content area involves understanding ordering, counts, place value, magnitudes, indicators, relative size and numerical trends. This will encompass aspects of quantitative reasoning, such as number sense, multiple representations of numbers, computation, mental calculation, estimation and judging the reasonableness of results. This content area requires knowing and applying integers, rational and irrational numbers, positive and negative numbers and equivalence. It also requires understanding and applying number operations, including order of operations, in a wide variety of settings.

Illustrative examples:

- Identify and counting the number of items shown in a photo of a set of items or object.
- Calculating the cost of one can of soup, given the cost of 4.
- Calculating the cost when buying 0.283 kg of cheese at a given price per kg.
- Another example could be deciding whether given decimal numbers are within a given range.

Space and shape

The *Space and shape* content area encompasses a wide range of phenomena that are encountered everywhere in our visual and physical world. It includes an understanding and use of: measurement (informal and standardised) systems, measurement formulas; dimensions and units; location and direction; geometric shapes and patterns; angle properties; symmetry; transformations and 2D and 3D representations and perspectives. This content area requires understanding and interpreting measurements and scales, position and orientation, plans, models, maps and diagrams, and navigation (including understanding travel distances, speeds and times, and using tools such as Global Positioning Systems).

Illustrative examples:

- The identification of a shape or matching an image of a real object to the correct plan/diagram.
- Reading the weight/mass of an object off an analogue scale.
- Interpreting an online map in relation to travel distances, speeds and times.
- Working out quantities required for a task such as wallpapering or tiling or painting given particular dimensions.

Change and relationships

The *Change and relationship* content area includes the ways to describe, model and interpret mathematical relationships, quantitative patterns, and change, where they occur in the real world. Real-world variables can be based around linear and non-linear relationships. Such relationships can be represented by descriptions, picture or images, tables, graphs or formula. In the latter case it could require the understanding and use of algebraic expressions and related methods of solution. This content area requires understanding, using and applying proportional reasoning and rates of change, including the use and application of ratios. It also requires recognising, describing, and/or using a relationship between different variables derived from a real-world situation.

Illustrative examples:

- Comparing the different proportional discounts on a shopping item in two different sales where the discounts are displayed in different ways.
- Understanding and using formulae such as for calculating interest or inflation rates, or one's BMI (Body Mass Index).
- Understanding and applying proportional reasoning to calculate values based on existing percentage or proportions of quantities/ingredients.
- Understanding and applying linear growth in order to predict future growth or decline.

Data and chance

The *Data and chance* content area encompasses topics such as data collection, data displays, charts and graphs, measures of central tendency and variance, alongside understanding appropriate approaches to data collection and sampling. The representation and interpretation of data are key concepts in this category. This content area also includes understanding and knowing about chance and probability. Chance and probability encompass subjective probability, certainty and uncertainty, likelihood and unlikelihood, prediction, and decision making. For example, attaching a numerical value to the likelihood of an instance is a ubiquitous phenomenon no matter whether it has to do with the weather, the stock market, a medical prognosis or the decision to board a plane.

Illustrative examples:

- Interpreting and identifying particular information on a simple bar graph or pie chart.
- Using an interactive online data tool and chart to interpret and analyse provided data.
- Use and understand averages (mean) to calculate required targets.
- Sort and interpret a set of data to test a number of opinions about the set of data.

Context

Context is the parameter or term used in both PISA and PIAAC for naming and classifying the settings or situations where people use and apply their mathematical knowledge to solve a realistic problem. The main purpose behind the use of the chosen context categories is to ensure a mixture or blend across the different categories to help guarantee some degree of balance in the assessment, with no particular context overwhelming the others (and therefore advantaging or disadvantaging respondents with greater or lesser daily interaction with some settings/contexts).

In PIAAC Cycle 1, the contexts used were:

- Everyday life
- Work-related
- Societal or community
- Further learning.

The sets of descriptors used in both PISA and the PIAAC Cycle 1 frameworks regarding the first three contexts (*Everyday life/Personal*; *Work-related/Occupational*; *Societal or Community/Societal*) were highly consistent with each other. One of the review team's recommendations was that the PISA label *Personal* is preferable to the PIAAC label of *Everyday*. "Everyday" suggests some "sameness" in what people do which is not particularly illuminating, whereas the term *Personal* aims to indicate that the issue at hand bears most directly just on that individual. This has been implemented.

Further Learning in PIAAC Cycle 1 was another context that the review project recommended for reconsideration. *Further learning* has some similarity and consistency with the term intra-mathematical that PISA refers to within its description of *Scientific*:

> *... Particular contexts might include (but are not limited to) such areas as weather or climate, ecology, medicine, space science, genetics, measurement and the world of mathematics itself. ... Items that are intramathematical, where all the elements involved belong in the world of mathematics, fall within the scientific context. (OECD, 2013, p. 37[122])*

This "Scientific" context of PISA has two elements to it. Some items classified as *Scientific* in PISA are in fact "intra-mathematical", that is, situations which are within the world of mathematics, explicitly related to knowing about formal aspects of mathematics, with no, or little, real-life connections. There were, in fact, no questions in PIAAC that are purely intra-mathematical, as there can be in PISA. There was a second set of questions in PISA that were classified as *Scientific*, where the situation or context related to the natural world (e.g., climate or ecology). In PIAAC Cycle 1 this context of *Further learning* was described as being related to adults needing to solve problems that may arise when participating in further study, whether for academic purposes or for vocational training, and was explicitly related to knowing about the more formal aspects of mathematics, including the conventions used to apply mathematical rules and principles. But the actual items could also be classified against the other three contexts. The sample PIAAC Cycle 1 item from this context that is discussed in the PIAAC reports was the item "Candles" (OECD, 2013, p. 77[161]). However, this item could also have been classified as *Everyday life*, *Work-related*, or even *Societal or community*.

For this, and a number of other reasons, the 2017 review paper recommended that the NEG review this fourth context of *Further learning*. The NEG considered this and decided that it was best to remove the classification named *Further Learning*. As a result, only the first three contexts continue in PIAAC Cycle 2, as these were the most relevant to adults, and that any existing *Further learning* items in PIAAC Cycle 1 should be reclassified against one of the other three contexts. The need to have items that were about knowing about the more formal aspects of mathematics, including the conventions used to apply mathematical rules and principles, would be covered through the inclusion of those requirements through the content knowledge area of *Change and Relationship*.

Hence there are some name changes, partly to make them more similar to the PISA mathematical literacy descriptions and labels for *Context*. The three versions of the *Context* labels are described in Table 3.4.

Table 3.4. Context labels in PIAAC and PISA

PIAAC Cycle 1	PIAAC Cycle 2	PISA 2012 and 2021
Everyday life	Personal	Personal
Work-related	Work	Occupational
Societal or community	Societal/community	Societal
Further learning		Scientific

Description

People try to manage or respond to a situation involving numeracy and mathematics because they want to satisfy a purpose or reach a goal. Three types of contexts that may require the use and application of numeracy skills are described below:

- Personal
- Work
- Societal/community.

These are not mutually exclusive and may involve the same underlying mathematical themes. The capability of being critically reflective about the use and application of mathematics is important in the 21st century, and adults need to be able to make decisions and judgements, and defend or support arguments. The different contexts provide the different areas of their lives where adults may encounter numeracy situations and which therefore provide the purpose for engaging in, solving and being reflective about real-world problems involving mathematics.

Personal

Numeracy tasks are often encountered in personal and family life, or revolve around hobbies, sports and games, personal development and personal interests. The personal context focuses on activities for an individual and in their interactions with immediate family. Representative tasks include (but are not limited to): handling money and personal or family finances and transactions, health and well-being, activities with family and friends, shopping, personal time management, travel and holiday planning, including reading maps, and using measurements in home situations such as cooking, gardening, administering medicines, or doing home repairs.

Work

Adults often encounter mathematical situations at work that are more specialised than those in everyday life. Today's workplaces often require increasing levels of techno-mathematical literacy. Representative tasks include (but are not limited to): completing purchase orders, maintaining inventories, totalling receipts, calculating change, managing schedules, budgets and project resources, payroll/accounting, using spreadsheets, completing and interpreting production and control charts, managing production inputs and outputs, tracking costs and expenditures, interpreting results from technological devices, and applying formulas. Work-related tasks can also include reading plans, blueprints and workplace diagrams, having spatial awareness for best storage options and organising and packing goods, and planning the most efficient delivery journey. This context can also include making and recording measurements such as lengths, weights, temperatures, dosages, areas, volumes or other work-related measurements, and using and applying measurement ratios and formulas. Occupational contexts may relate to any level of the workforce, from unskilled work to the highest levels of professional work.

Societal/community

Adults need to know about quantitative data and statistics and their representations, and be able to interpret trends and the consequences of a range of activities and actions happening in the world around them at the local, national or global level. Adults need to know about and be able to understand different mathematical relationships, such as proportional reasoning, when reading and interpreting information presented by a range of community or government authorities. Adults also may take part in a range of social events or community activities, including social and political participation, organising and participating in community-based functions and fundraising. Representative tasks include (but are not limited to) understanding and interpreting financial, statistical and numerical information and graphs about public transport, crime, health, education, politics, demographics, pollution, community events, etc. This information is increasingly being presented by the media, government services, financial institutions, utilities, and by a range of community services and organisations.

Representations

The third facet of the previous elaboration in ALL and PIAAC that has been added into the actual definition and hence made more explicit is that of *Representation*. Although this was included in the previous elaboration, it was not part of the definition, and did not help drive item development. Under *Facet 4: Representations of mathematical information*, the PIAAC Cycle 1 numeracy framework stated that mathematical content/information/ideas can be represented in multiple ways: objects and pictures; numbers and mathematical symbols; formulae; diagrams and maps, graphs, tables; texts; and finally, technology-based displays. However, none of these was expanded in much detail (PIAAC Numeracy Expert Group, 2009, p. 28[2]) and although the issue of different forms of representation of information is raised, digital or dynamic formats are not addressed.

The nature of information graphics is only now being unpacked within the field of mathematics education. Diezmann and Lowrie (2008[162]), for example, have argued for the importance of becoming proficient in interpreting information graphics (e.g., graphs, tables, maps) as these are increasingly used to manage, communicate, and analyse information. Societies are becoming increasingly reliant on representing information both diagrammatically and graphically. The new, more dynamic representation of data and information needs to be addressed. It is now no longer a matter of interpreting static images, as in the existing PIAAC Cycle 1 item pool, but also how new scenarios and different problems can be posed by interpreting and manipulating dynamic representations.

The 2017 review recommended that PIAAC Cycle 2 harness the potential of technology to support a more effective and representative 21st century assessment, through greater use of different technology, media and associated representations to make the assessment more relevant to the 21st century. This is discussed further in the fourth section.

Description

Quantitative and mathematical information in real-world situations and contexts is always represented and embedded in some format or other, whether that be in words and text, or diagrammatically or graphically, or dynamically. Mathematics, per se, does not exist in the real world by itself in its own isolated abstract form, such as 80% x €7.80 – such mathematics will be most likely embedded in an advertisement saying "20% discount" and the reader will need to read the information and decide that the solution is to take off 20% of the original price of €7.80. Hence the PIAAC framework needs to elaborate on the different ways that mathematics can be represented in the real world in a numeracy situation.

Mathematical information in a situation may be available or represented in many forms. It may appear as concrete objects to be counted (e.g., people, buildings, cars, etc.) or as pictures of such things. It may be conveyed through symbolic notation (e.g., numerals, letters, and operation or relationship signs). Sometimes, mathematical information will be conveyed by formulae, which are a model of relationships between entities or variables. Mathematical information may be encoded in visual displays such as a diagram or chart; graphs and tables may be used to display aggregate statistical or quantitative information (by displaying objects, counting data, etc.). Similarly, a map of a real entity (e.g., of a city or a project plan) may contain information that can be quantified or mathematised. Last but not least, textual elements may carry much mathematical information or affect the interpretation of mathematical (and statistical) information, as explained further below.

A person may have to extract mathematical information from various types of texts, either in prose or in documents with specific formats (such as in tax forms). Two different kinds of text may be encountered in numeracy tasks. The first involves mathematical information represented in textual form, i.e., with words or phrases that carry mathematical meaning. Examples are the use of number words (e.g., "five" instead of "5"), basic mathematical terms (e.g., fraction, multiplication, percent, average, proportion), or more complex phrases (e.g., "crime rate increased by half") which require interpretation, or coping with double meanings (or with differences in mathematical and everyday meanings of the same terms). The second involves cases where mathematical information is expressed in regular notations or symbols (e.g., numbers, plus or minus signs, symbols for units of measure, etc.), but is surrounded by text that despite its non-mathematical nature also has to be interpreted in order to provide additional information and context. An example is a bank deposit form or interactive device (e.g., on a mobile device or an *automated teller machine*, ATM) with some text and instructions in which numbers describing monetary amounts are embedded, or a parking ticket specifying an amount of money that has to be paid by a certain date due to a parking violation, but also explaining penalties and further legal steps that will be enacted if the fine is not paid by a certain date.

With the 21st century digitisation of information and processes, the types of representation now explicitly include technology-based displays and visualisations on websites, in infographics, in online calculators, spreadsheets and other software and apps on mobile devices and more.

Four classifications for the representation of real-world numeracy situations are described:

- Text or symbols
- Images of physical objects
- Structured information

- Dynamic applications.

For an individual item in PIAAC numeracy, these four descriptions of different representations are not mutually exclusive and any item may involve one or more of these dimensions.

Text or symbols

The stimulus is primarily based on running text that describes the problem situation and can include symbols and numerical information integrated into the text.

Images of physical objects

The stimulus is primarily based on photos or images of physical objects which depicts the problem situation. The image contains the crucial information to solve the problem (e.g. ruler or measuring instrument/scale, 3D objects). Sometimes some text is added to specify or narrow down the problem situation.

Structured information

The stimulus is primarily based on data or information that is represented in tables, graphs/charts, maps, plans, calendars, schedules, timetables, infographics, etc. In most cases, these are computer-generated representations of data, which are becoming more ubiquitous in all news and social media, and in information from government services, financial institutions and utilities. Text will often be used to help specify and describe the information and the problem situation.

Dynamic applications

The stimulus is primarily based on interactive applications, animations, calculation applications (for instance planning and designing software, structured spreadsheets, drawing programmes, online applications and calculators such as loan calculators, currency converters, etc.), which are designed to support users to perform calculations or plan or design activities. This category could also contain: (simulations of) handheld devices and measurement instruments. Sometimes text is used to specify or narrow down the problem situation.

Operationalisation of the PIAAC numeracy assessment

The operationalisation of the construct of numeracy in a large-scale assessment such as PIAAC is affected by many factors which shape the extent to which the theoretical construct can be fully addressed by the actual collection of items used in the direct assessment.

The 2017 review (Tout et al., 2017[1]) undertook a review of assessment developments, including in relation to numeracy and mathematics assessments. The review recommended that, because the numeracy description and construct in PIAAC is a multifaceted view and definition of numeracy, it requires a multimodal way of assessing the concept and construct, and because of the availability of new developments in technology and communication, new assessment developments could provide opportunities to enhance the assessment of numeracy in PIAAC Cycle 2.

The review also recognised and acknowledged up front that the existing PIAAC Cycle 1 items are based predominantly around static images and associated responses and are more like paper-based assessments transferred onto a computer, partly due to the transfer of many of the paper-based items from the previous ALL assessment to the computer-based assessment in PIAAC. As well, the platform used for PIAAC Cycle 1 was quite restrictive in terms of modalities and interactions that were available to house the stimulus and for the responses that could be automatically scored.

This section first begins with a general introduction about assessment developments in the 21st century, especially in relation to assessing adults' mathematical skills, followed by a sub-section outlining a possible process and structure for enhancing the assessment of numeracy in PIAAC Cycle 2. This is followed by a discussion of the constraints that affect the development of the direct assessment of numeracy in PIAAC. Based on these discussions, an outline is then presented of the principles that guide the assessment of numeracy in PIAAC, including specifying the blueprint for the proportions of items against each of the core dimensions in the construct. This discussion and the consequent blueprint specifications of the test content are critical in ensuring that the direct assessment of numeracy in PIAAC Cycle 2 meets both construct and content validity requirements.

Finally, there is a brief discussion about, and further details on, a supporting scheme regarding factors that affect task complexity (or item difficulty) which is of importance both for task design as well as interpretation of results regarding numeracy in PIAAC.

Assessment developments

There have been technologically-driven advancements in the educational measurement and assessment field in the 21st century, some of them based around the need to assess 21st century skills. There is much research about such developments [e.g., see (Bennett, 2015[163]; Geisinger, 2016[164]; Parshall et al., 2002[165]; Shute et al., 2016[166])]. Bennett (2015[163]), who has been researching and mapping educational assessment for a considerable period, describes three generations of assessment. He described first-generation technology-based testing as largely an infrastructure-building activity, laying the foundation for tests to be delivered in a new medium, where much of the testing closely resembled traditional tests. In his description of second-generation tests, he argued that qualitative change and efficiency improvement become the driving goals (Bennett, 1998[167]; 2010[168]), and where the tests use less traditional item formats, moved towards new multimodal formats and where there were attempts to measure new constructs. The driving force was often the technology. Bennett describes a third generation assessment as one of reinvention occurring on multiple fronts where these assessments were able to serve both institutional and individual-learning purposes. They are designed from both cognitive principles and theory-based domains, and where the assessments utilise "complex simulations and other interactive performance tasks that replicate important features of real environments, allow more natural interaction with computers, and assess new skills in more sophisticated ways" (Bennett, 2015, p. 372[163]). This includes the use of Augmented and Virtual Reality [e.g., see (Bower et al., 2014[169]; Sommerauer and Müller, 2014[170])].

While the review paper and the current expert group acknowledge that it is not yet possible in a large-scale international assessment such as PIAAC to implement and use the potential of Augmented and Virtual Reality, there are considerations to take on board for the future development and potential enhancements to the assessment of numeracy in PIAAC. There are many different computer-based models and options available to inform how numeracy might be more effectively assessed in future iterations of PIAAC, including in Cycle 2. The following sub-sections describe some of these possible enhancements, but also conclude with a discussion about the reality and constraints of an assessment such as PIAAC and especially the need to have all the materials and questions made available across a large number of different languages.

Computer-based assessment of mathematics and numeracy

The literature specifically on computer-based assessment of mathematics (CBAM) and multimedia learning of mathematics [e.g., (Atkinson, 2005[171])] mostly focuses on the multimodal representation of mathematical concepts: calculating, graphs, diagrams, computer algebra systems, spreadsheets, statistical programmes, etc. However, in the computer-based assessment of numeracy another focal point is also of importance, namely the role of the representation of the problem (the situations and settings in which the mathematics is embedded). More general research on representations of real-life situations in education and assessment should also be considered [e.g., see (Schnotz, 2002[172]; Schnotz, 2005[173]; Schnotz and Bannert, 2003[174]; Schnotz and Kürschner, 2007[175]; Schnotz et al., 2010[176])], as well as research on more general multimedia learning (Mayer, 2005[177]; 2009[178]), while being aware of the cognitive load discussion (Sweller, 2005[179]; 2010[180]; van Gog, Paas and Sweller, 2010[181]).

In an analysis and review of the optional computer-based assessment of mathematics items developed for PISA 2012, the Australian Council for Educational Research (ACER) test developers created a list of features that benefited and advantaged CBAM test items over traditional paper-based assessments of mathematics:

- Their appeal to students' interactive learning styles increases the engagement of students with the task.
- Items are less dependent on text and reading skills, which means students can access an item from visual cues, and then use the text to confirm the required response details.
- Response modes are more flexible and less daunting. Students can easily edit a response, so they are more inclined to "have a go".
- Relevant calculations can be automated, which means answers are correct, and less time is taken. This allows items to address higher-order mathematical reasoning.
- Items can assess spatial and visual skills using accurate simulations and manipulatives that are not readily available in pencil-and-paper formats.
- Items can test ability to use a wider range of problem solving strategies, such as observation of patterns and trends, and of the effect of manipulations and actions.
- Items can simulate computer-based processes, such as spreadsheets, drawing tools and graphing tools, and handling information in an online environment.
- Systems can collect data about what the student did within an item, such as the time taken, number of clicks, processes followed and the final state (PISA Mathematics Expert Group, 2009[182]).

These are also applicable to an adult numeracy assessment such as PIAAC. A useful classification of the CBAM item types in PISA 2012 was also developed by the ACER test development team for the set of items (PISA Mathematics Expert Group, 2009[182]; Tout and Spithill, 2015[183]). These included, for example, items that were based around automatic calculation, where calculation could be automated "behind the scenes" to support assessment of deeper mathematical skills and understanding; animations, and/or manipulations; drawing, spatial, visual cues and/or responses; simulation of computer applications (e.g., using the data sorting capability of an 'imitation' spreadsheet); interactive graphing allowing automatic mathematical function graphing and statistical graphing; and simulation of web-based applications or contexts, with or without computer-based interactivity (e.g., buying goods online).

Another advantage of computer-based (or tablet-based) assessments is that the responses and item types available and that were used and can be automatically scored is quite extensive and can include options such as: selected-response formats (e.g., multiple choice, complex multiple choice such as true/false type questions); short numeric responses; click-on and hot-spots; drag-and-drop; pull-down menus; matching and ordering; and manipulation of images to a correct, final position and solution.

Enhancing the assessment of numeracy in PIAAC Cycle 2

In the first cycle of the PIAAC assessment, there was a gap between the sophistication of the concept of numeracy used and the functionality of the assessment platform. As acknowledged above, the assessments that exist in the current item pool are relatively simple and one-dimensional. This analysis is corroborated in the literature [e.g., (Bennett, 2015[163])].

More sophisticated assessments utilising some of the possibilities outlined above are not necessarily aimed at more complex or higher order skills, but focus more on the multifaceted and multimodal nature of numeracy problem situations encountered in real life. To assess a sophisticated concept of numeracy there is the need for multimodal options to better represent reality, in which the respondents can show their competence (or not).

It is important to make a distinction and achieve a balance between the drive that stems strongly from development of technologies, that can be used in assessments (technology-driven) and the drive to design an assessment that is closely related to the concepts that are designed around the construct of numeracy (concept-driven).

Specifically, there is the need to frame any assessment development enhancements to PIAAC numeracy around two underpinning aspects of the PIAAC numeracy construct:

- That PIAAC is based on a multifaceted concept of numeracy and has an associated multimodal assessment.

- That PIAAC is an assessment of how well individuals can use their mathematical knowledge and skills to solve problems stemming from pragmatic and authentic (i.e., real-world) situations, needs or demands.

The PIAAC definition and description of numeracy falls into the category that Maguire and O'Donoghue (2002[184]) called the "integrative phase." They classified the development of definitions and ideas about numeracy into three phases: formative, mathematical, and integrative. In this "integrative" classification, as with PIAAC, numeracy is viewed as a complex, multifaceted and sophisticated construct incorporating each individual's mathematics, communication, cultural, social, emotional, and personal aspects in a real-world situation. Numeracy, as with mathematical literacy in PISA, is seen as a sophisticated capability requiring more than just arithmetic calculations and basic mathematics. These more integrative approaches to numeracy have become influential over the last few decades, as illustrated by projects that define numeracy instructional content standards and assessment frameworks such as in PISA, ALL, and PIAAC and national adult curriculum frameworks/standards [e.g., see (Department for Education (DfE), 2014[185]; McLean et al., 2012[77]; Quality and Qualifications Ireland (QQI), 2016[78]; Tertiary Education Commission, 2008[79])]. The assessment of such a multifaceted phenomenon therefore requires a multifaceted and multimodal set of assessment items that are authentic, as described above in relation to assessment developments and possibilities.

Hoogland and Tout (2018[186]) in looking at the pressures and challenges on Computer-based assessment of mathematics (CBAM) into the twenty-first century, argued that technology has the potential to support the assessment of higher-order thinking skills in mathematics, and also to represent authentic problems from the world around us to use and apply mathematical knowledge and skills. However, they also argued that the challenge is to not allow the technological capabilities, supported by psychometric analysis, to focus too much on assessment of lower order goals, such as the reproduction of procedural, calculation-based, knowledge and skills. These aims are consistent with the aims of the assessment of numeracy in PIAAC. Assessing a multifaceted concept based only on simple assessment tasks has two negative implications:

- The capabilities of individuals to cope with complex and multifaceted mathematics problems from real life are not assessed in full when the items are too straightforward and one-dimensional.

- The rollback effect of an international assessment of adult competencies on adult numeracy education practices is not to be underestimated. There is a responsibility for assessment developers such as those in PISA and PIAAC that their framework and assessment items are in sync with and reflect the complex, multifaceted constructs and concepts being assessed.

As described in the earlier sections of the framework, it is critical in the assessments of adults' numeracy to make the situations, representations and the responses authentic and make them as similar as possible to the way adults encounter mathematics in different life contexts, and not use questions such as the typical school-based word problems described earlier. Arguably the problem of authenticity and cultural appropriateness is lessened when testing pupils in schools, such as in PISA, because test designers can use conventional mathematical terminology, formulae, symbols, and so forth; this helps school-age assessments to standardise the demands from respondents by conveying the mathematical information embodied in different situations in consistent ways regardless of the cultural context. However, testing of adults' numeracy presents more challenges because many will not remember formal school-based notations or terminology. In countries where a sizeable proportion of the population are immigrants or speak multiple home-based languages, the gaps between mother tongues and school-based mathematical linguistic conventions may further affect performance on some numeracy tasks. Thus, attention has to be given to linguistic and cultural factors when adapting items for adult assessments.

21st century representation and interactivity

As developments in the 21st century impact on how mathematical and numerical information is represented, the PIAAC Cycle 1 facet, *Representations of mathematical information*, in the PIAAC framework has been significantly updated to reflect these changes. The revised framework and definition for numeracy in PIAAC Cycle 2 and the resulting new items harness the potential of technology to support a more effective and representative 21st century assessment, for example, through greater use of visual and interactive media, such as the use of infographics, interactive websites and online calculators, spreadsheet processes, graphing and measurement tools, etc. in assessment items. However, a balance has been kept between numeracy and mathematics tasks and actions embedded in 21st century digital and technological environments with those embedded in modes that are more traditional. This balance can partly be maintained by the necessary use of the existing PIAAC Cycle 1 numeracy item pool as linking items as these were based mainly around static images and the items are more like paper-based assessments transferred onto a computer.

A dimension for reviewing assessment possibilities

In order to facilitate the development of newer assessment content and delivery mechanisms, the review team developed a dimension of assessment possibilities – see Figure 3 in Tout et al. (2017, p. 31[1]), that could form a starting point for monitoring and balancing the range of PIAAC numeracy item formats and types. Hoogland and Tout (2018[186]) further developed this dimension of assessment possibilities, and argued that it could be used to reflect on, discuss and research the relevance, usefulness and effectiveness of mathematical assessment tasks, especially in relation to twenty-first century skills. Having a spread of stimuli and items developed and selected from across this spectrum would enable PIAAC numeracy to be better representative of the framework and construct, add to the issue of authenticity, and hence better assess adults' capabilities and competencies around numeracy practices in the 21st century.

The existing PIAAC Cycle 1 numeracy items which will continue to be used as link items tend to be at the left hand, more traditional, end of the dimension of assessment possibilities as described. Therefore, the focus on new item development has been to complement the existing pool by taking on board the potential enhancements and innovations due to 21st century capabilities as described in the dimension of assessment possibilities spectrum. This has provided the ability to create a balance across the spectrum of assessment possibilities.

Based on the above, the Numeracy Expert Group set the item writing teams the task of requesting that the new item development for Cycle 2 of the PIAAC numeracy assessment build on some of the assessment developments described above and to introduce new assessment content, representations and item formats that better reflect 21st century related digital representations, stimuli and numeracy tasks and assessment responses.

Outcomes

Fortunately, the PIAAC Cycle 2 platform and delivery system has been able to support many such types of stimuli, items and response types, and the items are in the process of being created and implemented for use on a tablet ready for the Field Trial. For PIAAC Cycle 2 these item types, responses, representations and interactive stimuli have included:

- illustrations and photos of authentic contexts/items/objects
- interactive calculators and online tools
- tap on area or multiple areas of the screen/image
- drag-and-drop responses
- drawing a graph
- use of a keypad to enter responses
- single and multiple selection multiple choice questions
- access to an online calculator
- interactive online charts and data
- online map
- online ruler
- simple spreadsheets.

Constraints and challenges to enhancing the assessment of numeracy in PIAAC Cycle 2

Despite the advances incorporated into the Cycle 2 assessment, there are constraints and challenges to what can be achieved in such an international assessment like PIAAC, and these need to be acknowledged. These include constraints related to the capabilities of adults aged 16-64 who will be undertaking the assessment, the practicalities and costs of developing an assessment across such a wide range of cultures and languages, and the limitations of the available computer platform.

First, the results from the Problem Solving in Technology-Rich Environments (PS-TRE) assessment in PIAAC Cycle 1 need to be considered in relation to the review and implementation of the PIAAC numeracy construct. The first cycle of the PIAAC survey provided two different pieces of information regarding the capacity of adults to manage information in technology-rich environments: the proportion of adults who had sufficient familiarity with computers to use them for PIAAC tasks, and the ability of adults with at least some basic ICT skills to solve the PS-TRE tasks.

The PIAAC Cycle 1 PS-TRE assessment results showed that there were adults with no, or extremely limited, ICT skills in all of the participating countries. The assessment found that:

> From around 7% to 27% of the adult population reported having no experience in the use of computers or lacked the most elementary computer skills, such as the ability to use a mouse. In addition, there are also adults who appear to lack confidence in their ability to use computers, primarily because they use them infrequently. Of the adults undertaking the assessment, most were proficient at Level 1, which involves the use of familiar applications to solve problems that involved few steps and explicit criteria, such as sorting e-mails into pre-existing folders. (OECD, 2013, p. 98[161])

These results from the Problem Solving in Technology-Rich Environments component of PIAAC Cycle 1 with its warnings regarding the high proportion of adults with no or extremely limited ICT skills needed to be taken into account in deciding on the balance of items incorporating the new technological and digital aspects of the PIAAC numeracy framework and its associated assessment.

Second, on a pragmatic level, some of the innovations and developments arising from technologically-driven advancements in educational measurement and assessment in the 21st century needed to be carefully reviewed and considered as to the feasibility of their use and practical implementation for PIAAC Cycle 2. Some issues that needed to be considered include:

- The costs—some technologies, media and tools would potentially be expensive to use and implement—both from a content development point of view (the production of videos/animations/etc.) and from a delivery and implementation perspective (conducting such assessments in people's homes).

- The time available for testing—would the use of such innovations in assessment take substantially more time for the delivery of the PIAAC assessment?

- The feasibility of producing and using any animations, simulations, video or audio support in potentially 30 different languages, which would be challenging, costly and require substantial quality assurance processes of translations.

- The performance of the use of any such innovations, especially the use of simulations (e.g., the use of games is highly unlikely to be relevant in such an adult assessment at this point in time), and hence the cost of the mandatory trialling and psychometric checking for performance, reliability and validity.

The aim has been to have a pragmatic and balanced set of items that meet as many of the demands as possible for the enhancement of the numeracy assessment in PIAAC Cycle 2 while taking into account the constraints outlined above, including the ICT-related capabilities of adults across the PIAAC age-range. However, it needs to be remembered that there will always be a substantial set of link items from the previous assessments and that the Field Trial can be utilised to check how any new items work compared with existing items.

It should also be noted that the change in platform for the delivery of Cycle 2—from a laptop computer requiring the use a mouse, to a tablet where respondents can use a stylus or finger—and the fact that 10 years have elapsed since Cycle 1 suggest that more participants will be able to use the platform. The Field Trial will allow the opportunity to test whether this is the case or not.

Constraints of the assessment design, platform and certain response types

One also needs to distinguish between the conceptual framework (second section) and the assessment construct (third and fourth sections). Not all real-life numeracy tasks can necessarily be simulated well in a specific assessment. Further, the ability of an assessment to actually *capture, evaluate, and score* responses associated with the full spectrum of numeracy as defined in PIAAC ultimately depends on the technical aspects of that assessment. While the computer-based assessment platform chosen for PIAAC Cycle 2 offers many advantages over Cycle 1, there are still restrictions and limitations, and this has constrained the ability to develop many sophisticated interactive items or use audio or video that required translation, for example.

Firstly, the overall testing time per respondent does not allow inclusion of extended problems or lengthy simulations of complex authentic numeracy tasks, although it is recognised that ability to solve complex or extended numeracy problems is an inherent part of the numeracy competency. In order to cover all facets of the numeracy construct in the limited time available, the use of a larger number of short tasks is prescribed.

Secondly, the need to score all responses automatically limits the type of assessment tasks that can be used. The traditional divide in item format is between selected-response (sometimes called forced-choice or multiple choice) format versus a constructed-response format. Selected-response items require the choice of one or more responses from a number of response options. Responses to such questions can usually be automatically processed and scored when presented on a computer/tablet, and can include a range of interactive responses, such as tap-on, drag and drop, etc. Within constructed response items there are closed constructed-response or open constructed-response items. Closed constructed-response items provide a more structured setting for answering, and they aim to produce a response that can be automatically scored, against a scoring rubric, to be either correct or incorrect. Open constructed-response items require respondents to communicate in their own words the answers to tasks or questions, and such items require trained experts to manually code responses.

While the platform allows respondents to provide an answer in several different modes (e.g., numeric entry, tapping on an area of the screen, choosing from different options, etc.), in its present stage of development it cannot accept most types of open constructed-response or free-form items because of the huge possible diversity in how respondents may enter their answers. The limitations stem from the difficulty to automatically code (i.e., designate an answer as correct or incorrect) free-form responses in dozens of languages while accommodating various grammatical and syntactical structures, as well as overcoming typing mistakes which are naturally expected when people type text into a computer. Examples are when respondents:

- write number ranges or estimates which have multiple mathematically equivalent representations, such as "a quarter", "0.25", "1/4", "1 in 4", or "around five to six", "1.00 to 6.00"
- describe their interpretation of given information such as in a simulated media statement
- write justifications for their answers, or list arguments supporting their conclusions.

Specifically, tasks requiring communication-based responses, such as when adults have to explain interpretations of given information, or describe their evaluation or analysis of a situation *or their thinking about that situation*, are difficult to implement in the direct assessment of the skills targeted by PIAAC. Such tasks do comprise an important, inseparable part of the landscape of adult numeracy situations and are an inherent part of the conceptual framework of adult numeracy, yet few could be included in the item pool for the second cycle of PIAAC.

Money/currency issues

Consumer and shopping issues are important components of numeracy and are represented in the numeracy tasks. Since the currencies of the participating countries vary greatly, consumer-related items present a challenge to item developers and translators. It is crucial to try to keep any questions relating to money at the same time realistic and mathematically comparable. Hence, PIAAC specifies strict guidelines about how countries can change the magnitude of any monetary amounts in order to maintain comparability. These are published as part of the *Translation and Adaptation Guidelines*, and will be based on current exchange rates for currencies.

PISA copes with this by having all its monetary-related items set in a fictional country, Zedland, with a fictional currency of zeds and zedcents. This approach has been deemed as not suitable to be applied to PIAAC due to its need to apply to adults across a wide age and educational range, where it is believed that some adults may not relate to a very unfamiliar currency nor to fictional prices and costs.

PIAAC's tasks are therefore designed to allow countries whose currencies are somewhat similar in value to the dollar to keep exactly the same number and change only the currency sign.

As a general practice, when we refer to a monetary value that can be written in different currencies, we note it as _45, for example. It signifies that 45 can be considered as a number of dollars, Euro, krona, guilders, pesos, or whatever the local currency is.

The following options for making changes to monetary values are listed in order, from the least to the greatest impact on the equivalence of the cognitive demand of the item.

- Option 1: Change the currency sign only. Keep the numbers the same and change only the currency sign to the local currency sign. (e.g. change the US Dollar sign, $, to Euro, € or GBP, £) This will be the option of choice for the European Community countries, since the Euro and the Dollar are close in value.

- Option 2: Change the numbers by multiplying or dividing them by powers of 10. When changing the currency sign does not seem to work and the object's value seems unrealistic, the translator will have to change the numbers or amounts in the item.

> **The rule:** *If numerical values must be changed to retain the realism of an item, they can only be multiplied or divided by powers of 10 (i.e., by 10, 100, 1000, etc.). This restriction aims to keep the cognitive demands of the item (such as the nature of the mathematical steps and mental operations) similar in all countries. Consider, for example, the Raincoat item (PIAAC unit 603), priced at _80. If this price is unreasonable for any type of raincoat, the translator can choose to multiply the number 80 by 100 to be 8000, if this is a reasonable price for a raincoat in the currency of the country where this change is seen to be unavoidable. [In Hungary, for example, 1 US dollar is now equivalent to 250 HUF (Hungarian Forint). The raincoat could be priced at 8000 HUF. Yet, a change to 20000 HUF (80 x 250) is <u>not</u> permitted, even though it is the "true" value of the raincoat in HUF, since it significantly changes the mental operations required by the task.]*

Different measurement units

Another challenge with an international assessment such as PIAAC relates to the fact that countries can also have different measurement systems, although most countries are now solely metric, with the exception of the US, which still (mainly) use the imperial measurement system.

The following is the approach taken to creating mathematically equivalent items for metric and imperial-based measurement units. There were different solutions that could be applied, depending on how dependent the question was on understanding the measure system embedded in the context/task.

The first issue was to decide whether a conceptual understanding of the measurement system is critical to answering the question. If not, then it is possible to leave the measurement units in their original, authentic units that fitted the context. However, if a question requires "intimate" knowledge of the metric system to answer it then parallel metric and imperial units are required. For example, when an estimation of a length or height is required, as in the existing PIAAC *Tree* and *Path* questions where the respondent is expected to have sense of size in familiar contexts–the height of a tree relative to a person, and the length of a path– all shown in photographs). In these situations you could not consider using a metric unit in the US, nor an imperial unit in a metric country. People need to have a feeling for the measurement units.

Similarly, a US version of a question that included doing a conversion between metric units as part of the solution, would **not** work—knowledge of conversion factors could be very unfamiliar to an older generation American. The other point here is that the conversions between the various measurements in the US are not consistent and all based around powers of ten like in metrics, and many people routinely need to look them up – like how many ounces in a pound, inches in a foot, yards in a mile, fluid ounces in a pint, pints in a gallon and more.

A starting point was to research and see what is common and authentic in the US—the US **does** use metric units now for a number of common commodities, such as for popular soft drinks, medication doses, etc. In some cases it was therefore possible to select particular situations/objects that are measured in metric units and hence were suitable and compatible for use in questions in the US.

If a unit needed to be created in both metric and imperial, the best solution was to maintain the same dimensions and just change the units – from meters to yards, for example, or kilometers to miles. This was more easily able to occur where the units have some similarity—like cm to inches, or meters to yards. This approach has been used in link items such as the *Path* and the *Tree*.

However in some cases there was no alternative but to change the dimensions/measurements to make them both authentic. For example, this was done in the existing link items, such as the BMI formula item in ALL survey and then PIAAC. The necessity is to then keep the degree of difficulty of any arithmetical calculations as similar as possible, so the difficulty level is maintained. For example, in a possible item based on photos—in metric it was possible to have the dimensions of 8 x 12 cm, and in inches have it as 4 x 6 inches—they are authentic, similar small photo sizes and the dimensions are in the same ratio.

The PIAAC approach to assessment

The PIAAC assessment design involves using a household survey methodology which assumes that overall testing time per respondent is around 60-80 minutes. In that time, study participants will be asked to complete:

- A background questionnaire, which collects information on possible outcomes and antecedents of key skills, as well as on demographic and structural indicators that are needed to describe the distribution of such skills within participating countries.
- A tablet tutorial and orientation to the assessment.
- A short locator test, which will be used to direct respondents to the appropriate section of the direct assessment and will also provide information about the literacy and numeracy skills of adults who may not be able to continue on to the direct assessment.
- A brief measure of component skills in reading and numeracy.
- The direct assessment, where each respondent will take two of three domains of literacy, numeracy and adaptive problem solving.

The direct assessment will utilise an adaptive design that will optimise the match between respondent ability and the difficulty of administered items. Such a design provides more reliable information about respondents' skills within the available testing time.

Item pools and scale scores

The items for the assessment are expected to enable reporting of respondents' performance in a manner similar to the one used in ALL and PIAAC Cycle 1, which scaled raw scores in the range 0-500, but focused on reporting performance on six ability levels with the following (tentative) boundaries:

- Below Level 1: below 176 (lowest level)
- Level 1: raw score 176 – 225
- Level 2: raw score 226 – 275
- Level 3: raw score 276 – 325
- Level 4: raw score 326 – 375
- Level 5: raw score 376 – 500 (highest level).

Usage of calculators and other tools or objects

The assessment of numeracy, whether by paper-and-pencil tasks or computer-based, has to take into account that the practice of numeracy in everyday or work situations also involves the use of certain objects and artefacts. First is the use of calculators, either handheld or now also available on smartphones and tablets, which are now widely available to adults from all walks of life in many countries. Thus, calculators are tools which are part of the fabric of numeracy life in many cultures. Increasingly, respondents in large-scale tests are allowed, sometimes even expected, to use calculators. It follows that adults in PIAAC should be given access to a calculator as part of an assessment of numeracy skills, and they can then choose if and how to use it. An online, basic calculator will be available on the tablet-based delivery of PIAAC, and as well a handheld basic calculator will be made available and can be used if requested. There are no numeracy questions that require the use of a more sophisticated type of calculator than a basic, four function calculator.

The use of an online ruler is also presented in one unit, in both a metric and imperial (inches) system, as rulers/measuring instruments are part of contexts where adult numeracy competence is manifested. The use of other technologies, such as a computer spreadsheet, also fit the assessment of numeracy, and in PIAAC Cycle 2 some items assess this skill.

It should also be noted that it is intended that the interviewer will provide access to a pen and paper in order for respondents to make notes, write down and undertake calculations, etc.

Basis for assessing numeracy in PIAAC Cycle 2

The development of the numeracy assessment for PIAAC has been based on a number of general principles or guidelines listed below. These principles reflect the cumulative literature on large-scale assessment of mathematical skills and adult numeracy (Gal et al., 2005[28]; Gillespie, 2004[187]; Murat, 2005[188]), and various background documents and positions prepared as part of the planning of PIAAC [e.g., (Gal, 2006[153]; Gal and Tout, 2014[3]; Jones, 2006[154]; Murray, 2006[155]; PIAAC Numeracy Expert Group, 2009[2]; Tout, 2006[156]; Tout et al., 2017[1])]. This also incorporates the general ideas discussed earlier, as well as any known technical limitations in the delivery of PIAAC Cycle 2.

Some general approaches include:

- *Items should cover as many aspects as possible within each of the four core dimensions of the numeracy definition and elaboration*. Items should require the activation of a broad range of skills and knowledge included in the construct of numeracy, as portrayed in the conceptual framework depicted in Box 3.2. The specifications and targets for the item development and spread against each of the core dimensions are spelt out in the next sub-section.

- *Items should aspire to maximal authenticity and cultural appropriateness*. Tasks should be derived from real-life stimuli and pertain to the full range of contexts or situations (i.e., everyday life, work, societal) that can be expected to be of importance or relevant in the countries participating in PIAAC. Item content and questions should appear purposeful to respondents across cultures, although it must be acknowledged that in a large-scale assessment such as PIAAC, not all items and contexts can be personally familiar to all adults within any one country, let alone across all countries.

- *Items should have different response formats*, to the extent feasible by the computer platform used for administering the direct assessments in PIAAC. Items should be structured to include a stimulus (e.g., a picture, drawing, visual display) and one or more questions, the answers to which the respondent communicates via the modes available within the platform. Numeric entry is limited to the set of 10 digits and common separators (, and .) or other mathematical symbols where relevant.

- *Items should spread over different levels of ability*. Items should span the range of ability levels anticipated within PIAAC participants, from low-skilled individuals (who are of particular interest in countries where policies and educational programmes may be earmarked for low-skill populations), all the way to those with advanced competencies. The ALL and PIAAC Complexity Schema (Tout et al., 2020[141]) was used to provide an initial estimate of the spread of item difficulties in order to assist in the selection of the items for the Field Trial.

- *Items should vary in the degree to which the task is embedded in text*. Some items should be embedded in or include relatively rich texts, while others should use little or no text. This distribution aims to reflect the different levels of text involvement in real-world numeracy tasks, as well as reduce overlap with the literacy scale.

- *Items should be efficient*. To allow for coverage of many key facets of the numeracy competency, the inclusion of a large number of diverse stimuli and questions will be needed. However, in light of testing time constraints, the use of short tasks is necessitated, precluding items that can simulate extended problem-solving processes or that require a lengthy open-ended response.

- *Items should be adaptable to unit systems across participating countries.* Items should be designed so that their underlying mathematical demands are as consistent as possible across countries, regarding language and mathematical conventions. For example, items should be designed so that different currency systems or different systems of measurement (metric or imperial) could be applied to the numbers or figures used. Items should retain equivalency with respect to their mathematical or cognitive demands after being translated.

Blueprint for assessing numeracy in PIAAC Cycle 2

Based on the definition and elaboration of numeracy described in previous sections and on the above discussions on assessment enhancements and constraints attached to delivering PIAAC Cycle 2, this sub-section specifies the blueprint for the proportions of items against each of the core dimensions in the construct. For a comparison, the specifications for each dimension is compared with the previous targets for Cycle 1 and for PISA 2012 and 2021 too.

This blueprint specifies the test content for the direct assessment of the cognitive aspects of numeracy as defined for PIAAC Cycle 2, taking on board the above constraints and limitations, and the enhanced opportunities provided for Cycle 2 compared with Cycle 1 of PIAAC. These help establish the construct and content validity requirements for the cognitive assessment aspects of numeracy, with this being confirmed and refined through the quality assurance (QA) processes and psychometric item analysis and review following the Field Trial. The QA processes include feedback from participating countries and a formal translation and review process with language experts. These QA processes pick up issues to do with the language structure and meaning of items, and also content and cultural issues. A Field Trial is undertaken with a sample of the target population in each participating country before the final assessment is implemented. Field trial data is collected and analysed psychometrically and from these detailed analyses, 'misbehaving' items are rejected on a number of levels including for reliability, fairness and validity. Then for the remaining successful items, any fine-tuning is undertaken, and a representative set of items are chosen based on the blueprint and placed into final forms.

This blueprint is specified against the four dimensions incorporated into the definition of numeracy and the elaboration of numerate capacity, as outlined earlier:

> Numeracy is **accessing, using and reasoning critically** with **mathematical content**, information and ideas **represented in multiple ways** in order to engage in and manage the mathematical demands of a **range of situations** in adult life.

The four core dimensions named and described in numeracy for PIAAC Cycle 2, namely:

- cognitive processes
- content
- representations
- context.

Cognitive processes

For the three new *Cognitive processes* the spread across the dimension is very similar to PISA 2012 processes which have a similar structure, but quite different from PIAAC Cycle 1 due to the revised and different structure of this response classification. There is also an attempt to be less focused on the traditional process of doing the mathematics (*Act on and use mathematics*), and have a good representation in the two other processes too, which are seen by the Numeracy Expert Group as significant aspects of how adults engage with and solve a numeracy problem where mathematics is embedded in an authentic situation. This target might be difficult to achieve, but these were the aspirational targets set by the NEG.

Table 3.5. Representation of cognitive processes in PIAAC and PISA

PIAAC Cycle 1	PIAAC Cycle 2	PISA 2012	PISA 2021
Identify/locate/access (10%)	Access and assess situations mathematically (25-35%)	Formulating situations mathematically (25%)	Formulating situations mathematically (25%)
Act on/use (order, count, estimate, compute, measure, model) (50%)	Act on and use mathematics (30-40%)	Employing mathematical concepts, facts, procedures, and reasoning (50%)	Employing mathematical concepts, facts, procedures, and reasoning (25%)
Interpret/evaluate/communicate (40%)	Evaluate, critically reflect, make judgements (25-35%)	Interpreting, applying and evaluating mathematical outcomes (25%)	Interpreting, applying and evaluating mathematical outcomes (25%)
			Mathematical reasoning (25%)

Content

For the four content areas the spread across the dimension was similar to Cycle 1 and similar to PISA. One difference is that PIAAC does not aim to have as many items in the more formal mathematics area of *Change and relationships*, which includes algebraic thinking, which is more of an interest to 15-year-olds in a school-based assessment such as PISA. For PIAAC Cycle 2 there has been a slightly higher focus placed on *Data and chance*. This is seen as a more common and important area that adults now have to negotiate with in the 21st century, and it is higher use and reliance on presenting numerical, quantitative and other data and related analyses in a range of ways and often in ways that are critical to people's lives.

Table 3.6. Representation of content areas in PIAAC and PISA

PIAAC Cycle 1	PIAAC Cycle 2	PISA 2012 and 2021
Quantity and number (30%)	Quantity and number (20-30%)	Quantity (25%)
Dimension and shape (25%)	Space and shape (20-30%)	Space and shape (25%)
Pattern, relationships and change (20%)	Change and relationships (15-25%)	Change and relationships (25%)
Data and chance (25%)	Data and chance (25-35%)	Uncertainty and data (25%)

Representations

For the four new *Representation* classifications, again the NEG was aspirational in its targets and aimed to set relatively high goals for 21st century type representations, which are covered under both *Structured information* types of materials (infographics etc.) and also *Dynamic applications* which includes online interactive websites and applications alongside more standard software applications and tools. This will in the end be balanced by the existing link items from PIAAC Cycle 1 and ALL, where the representation may be more traditional and less 21st century in their style and format. It should be noted that in the previous cycle, the type of representations was not explicitly monitored in terms of its proportion across the pool of items, and it is felt that incorporating representation into the definition and the dimensions will enhance the quality of items across PIAAC numeracy.

Table 3.7. The representation classifications in PIAAC

PIAAC Cycle 1	PIAAC Cycle 2
Objects and pictures (not specified)	Text or symbols (15-25%)
Numbers and mathematical symbols (not specified)	Images of physical objects (15-25%)
Formulae (not specified)	Structured information (35-45%)
Diagrams and maps, graphs, tables (not specified)	Dynamic applications (15-25%)
Texts (not specified)	
Technology-based displays (not specified)	

Context

For the three remaining contexts in PIAAC Cycle 2, the aim is to have an equal spread as per previous cycles, as also occurs in PISA.

Table 3.8. Representation of context in PIAAC and PISA

PIAAC Cycle 1	PIAAC Cycle 2	PISA 2012 and 2021
Everyday life (25%)	Personal (30-35%)	Personal (25%)
Work-related (25%)	Work (30-35%)	Occupational (25%)
Societal or community (25%)	Societal/community (30-35%)	Societal (25%)
Further learning (25%)		Scientific (25%)

Factors explaining item/task complexity

In planning an assessment, it is of course important to be able to understand what it measures. Assessment designers assume that when engaged with the assessment items (including tasks, questions, stimuli, etc.), respondents activate cognitive processes and rely on stored knowledge and learned skills which are part of the construct being measured. Thus, differential performance levels can be accounted for by the underlying cognitive knowledge bases and other enabling processes. It follows that it is useful to have a theoretical model or set of assumptions regarding what factors cause certain tasks to be harder or more complex than others, so that the assessment results can be correctly interpreted. A model or scheme of factors affecting task complexity can also help when linking the assessment results to possible social (or educational) interventions, i.e., point to the skills that are lacking and have to be further developed in the population (Brooks, Heath and Pollard, 2005[189]).

Prior seminal work by Kirsch and Mosenthal [e.g., (Kirsch and Mosenthal, 1990[190]; Kirsch, Jungblut and Mosenthal, 1998[191])] and earlier projects have pointed to several key factors which account for task difficulty when considering arithmetic items or items involving text comprehension. These include readability, type of match, plausibility of distractors, operation specificity ('transparency'), and type of calculation and number of steps. The Kirsch and Mosenthal work has informed the design of assessment tasks for IALS and other surveys, and the interpretation of their results. In designing the ALL numeracy scale, the ALL Numeracy team attempted to advance the Kirsch and Mosenthal complexity scheme and develop tentative assumptions regarding factors which affect difficulty of multiple types of new tasks introduced to measure the numeracy construct which were beyond those encompassed by the more focused construct of *quantitative literacy* in IALS. Examples are items involving percents, knowledge of measurement and spatial reasoning, statistical concepts, and so forth.

The developers of the *mathematical literacy* scale for PISA (2006) also recognised multiple factors affecting item difficulty, such as the kind and degree of interpretation and reflection required by the problem, the kind of representation skills required, or the kind and level of mathematical skill required, e.g., single-step vs. multi-step problems, or more advanced mathematical knowledge, complex decision-making, and problem solving and modelling skills, or the kind and degree of mathematical argumentation required. Further factors that are assumed to affect difficulty both in PISA, ALL and other surveys relate to the degree of familiarity with the context, and the extent to which tasks require reproduction of known procedures and steps or present novel situations requiring non-routine and perhaps more creative responses. It should be noted that the PISA description of complexity factors seems quite compatible with that of ALL, although some of the terminology is different, and published PISA reports do not explain in detail how it was used to guide the design of specific items.

The complexity scheme for numeracy used in ALL (Gal et al., 2005[28]) has been instrumental for the item development and scale construction stages of that study, especially in that it helped to evaluate in advance if items will span different difficulty levels. Given that PIAAC's numeracy assessment is founded on the principles developed for ALL and that the PIAAC numeracy assessment scale uses linking items used in ALL, the ALL complexity scheme has been adopted and updated as an analytic tool for item development and interpretation for PIAAC as well. The details about this updated PIAAC numeracy complexity schema are provided in Tout et al. (2020[141]).

Relationship between PIAAC and PISA

This section discusses the relationship between the PIAAC numeracy framework and the PISA mathematical literacy framework and assessment. Many of these aspects have been discussed earlier when considering the framework construct and its parameters, and the assessment blueprint. This section summarises the similarities and differences.

Note: in this section the references used are as those written and documented in the original, full PIAAC Cycle 1 numeracy framework (PIAAC Numeracy Expert Group, 2009[2]). Similarly, the references to PISA are mainly to the PISA 2012 mathematical literacy framework and its descriptions (OECD, 2013[122]). This is because in 2012, mathematical literacy was the major domain for PISA, when the relevant framework was revised and updated. The same mathematical literacy framework and assessment construct was used for the next two cycles of PISA in 2015 and 2018. For PISA 2021, mathematical literacy is again the major domain for PISA, and hence the framework and assessment construct is being updated and revised. This was happening in parallel with the development of the numeracy framework for PIAAC Cycle 2. The PIAAC Numeracy Expert Group was able to access a copy of the second draft of the PISA 2021 mathematics framework (OECD, 2018[123]) in November 2018. It was prepared by the Expert group for mathematics under the guidance of RTI International as the international contractor who led this work for the OECD. Most of the comparisons between PIAAC numeracy and PISA mathematical literacy have therefore been based on a comparison of the 2012 PISA framework and descriptions, but where possible the PIAAC NEG has also included comments and comparisons with the updated 2021 PISA mathematical literacy framework.

The commonalities between PIAAC and PISA

The following sub-sections look at the commonalities and links between PISA and PIAAC across the features and parameters of PIAAC.

Mathematical content

Both numeracy in PIAAC and mathematical literacy in PISA use a non-school-curriculum focused approach to naming and describing the content areas covered in their assessments. The purpose behind both frameworks is describing mathematics for use and application outside of the classroom, and so the organisational structure for mathematical content knowledge is based on how mathematical phenomena are encountered in situations in the outside world. While the PISA and PIAAC frameworks were developed by independent teams, they use very similar descriptors for their content classifications, introducing and describing these in terms of the *Big Ideas* behind mathematics.

The two frameworks are highly consistent in terms of their descriptions and structures of the mathematical content covered in their assessments. There are very similar spreads across each content area. As discussed earlier, PIAAC has less interest in the more formal mathematics area of *Change and relationships*, which is more of an interest to 15-year-olds in a school-based assessment such as PISA.

Contexts

The sets of context descriptors used in both frameworks regarding the first three contexts (*Personal*; *Work/Occupational*; *Societal* or *Societal/community*) are highly consistent with each other, with a similar spread of items.

The NEG reviewed the fourth context, *Further learning* in PIAAC Cycle 1 and after comparing it with *Scientific* in PISA, decided that it was best to remove the classification named *Further learning* which in PISA incorporated items that are considered intra-mathematical. The need to have such items in PIAAC that were about knowing about the more formal aspects of mathematics, including the conventions used to apply mathematical rules and principles, are to be covered through the inclusion of those requirements through the content knowledge area of *Change and relationships*.

The difference here with the PISA context classifications reflects the different interests in the more formal mathematical understandings of 15-year-olds within a school setting with those of adults out-of-school. Any other differences in the item coverage here are due to the age of the two target groups, with some of the PIAAC situations described being more relevant to adults, and some of the PISA situations being more appropriate for 15-year-olds.

Responses/actions

This facet of the original PIAAC Cycle 1 numeracy structure was an aspect of the numeracy framework that was recommended as needing major review by the 2017 review paper, which recommended that PIAAC could potentially learn from the processes described in the PISA 2012 mathematical literacy framework. Hence for the three new *Cognitive processes* developed for PIAAC Cycle 2 there is a significant amount of similarity and consistency with the PISA processes of *Formulate, Employ and Interpret/Evaluate*. This is because the NEG took on board the intent and structure for the three PISA 2012 process cycles in their development of the new cognitive process dimension for PIAAC Cycle 2. In relation to the new mathematical reasoning process included in PISA 2021, it is the view of the NEG, that for the assessment of numeracy skills of adults the mainly intra-mathematical aspect of mathematical reasoning needs to be embedded within the real-world problem solving aspect for PIAAC, and not assessed as a separate part of the construct. Therefore mathematical reasoning and its understanding and application is integrated across the relevant aspects of the three other cognitive processes.

Item formats

In their review and comparison of the two numeracy frameworks for PISA and PIAAC, Gal and Tout (2014[3]) concluded in relation to the issue of item formats that:

> PISA 2012, with its more comprehensive range of item types and more interactive computer-based assessment, will enable richer and extended descriptions of sub-components of mathematical literacy compared to the information that can be generated by the numeracy assessment in PIAAC. (Gal and Tout, 2014, p. 52[3])

Furthermore, the review paper commented that much of the existing PIAAC Cycle 1 and ALL item pool was based around static images and was more like paper-based assessments transferred onto a computer, and that this also does not now seem to reflect the way numeracy tasks and actions are now situated and practised in the 21st century.

As stated earlier, the next delivery of the PIAAC Cycle 2 numeracy assessment is much more capable than Cycle 1 was in terms of allowing the use of new and more interactive, 21st century style item formats. Such items have been developed and will be trialled in the Field Trial.

General comments

Based on detailed comparisons of the two numeracy frameworks for PISA and PIAAC by the review team, by Gal and Tout (2014[3]), and from two of the 2017 review team who were familiar with both the full sets of PISA 2012 and PIAAC items and not just the publicly released items, it is apparent that both assessments describe and cover very similar territories.

On the conceptual level, numeracy and mathematical literacy are closely related constructs in terms of their core, underlying ideas. In relation to the definitions and descriptions of the constructs and what they are assessing, Gal and Tout, in their comparison of the two programmes, summarised the similarities:

> Both constructs refer to the ability of individuals to cope with tasks that are likely to appear in the real world, and that contain mathematical or quantitative information, or that require mathematical or statistical skills and knowhow.
>
> Both constructs focus on how well individuals can use their mathematical knowledge and skill to solve problems stemming from pragmatic (i.e., real-world) needs or demands, and to 'engage', manage, and understand various tasks in the world around them—rather than addressing decontextualised mathematical tasks.
>
> Both PISA and PIAAC describe mathematical literacy or numeracy as not synonymous with a minimal or low level of mathematical knowledge and skills. That is, both assessments view the constructs as describing competencies lying on a continuum, i.e., individuals could be placed on a scale from low levels to high levels. (Gal and Tout, 2014, pp. 47-48[3])

They concluded that both the PIAAC and PISA frameworks, definitions and assessments have substantial conceptual similarities and also practical commonalities in their test items and design principles, as well as in the range of content areas and skills they cover (Gal and Tout, 2014[3]). However, there are some differences between the two assessments, related to the diversity in the experiential backgrounds and the distances from schooling for adults compared to children. As Gal and Tout wrote:

> Because many adults may not remember more formal school-based representations or technical language, the design of PIAAC items has taken into account from the outset the need to establish authenticity while reducing the use of formal notations and 'school-like' appearance. (Gal and Tout, 2014, p. 39[3])

An examination of the item sets of both PISA and PIAAC shows that PISA is more interested in the ability of 15-year-olds to use and apply curriculum-based mathematical skills and knowledge embedded in a real-world situation. On the other hand, PIAAC is somewhat less focused on how respondents use formal mathematical skills when solving a real-life-type mathematical problem. For example, in some of the PISA mathematical literacy items 15-year-olds are asked to use information from a real-life situation to calculate and identify specific formal characteristics of linear equation graphs, such as the gradient and the y-intercept. This type of more formal mathematical knowledge is not assessed in PIAAC, as generally PIAAC respondents are not required to show evidence of their knowledge of the use and understanding of formal school-based mathematical notations, which are often forgotten from not having been in current or recent use.

Drivers/indicators of mathematical proficiency

One of the important features of both the PISA and PIAAC frameworks is the way that each has independently developed a schema that describes aspects of test items that drive item difficulty, and which indicate the mathematical proficiency of tested individuals and populations.

PIAAC does this in considerable detail in the Appendix to the framework (PIAAC Numeracy Expert Group, 2009, pp. 44-56[2]). As well as classifying test items according to the mathematical content knowledge required to complete each item, the Annex presents a detailed scheme designed to show the complexity of test items. Five 'complexity factors' are defined, and a scheme is presented for rating mathematical tasks according to the extent each factor is present in the test items. Examples are given to show how the rating scheme would be applied, and the assumption is that a total score across the factors for an individual item (20 score points could be generated) would be strongly related to item difficulty; and by implication, successful completion of particular items can be used as indicators of levels of mathematical proficiency.

The PISA 2012 framework specifies a set of 'fundamental mathematical capabilities', the activation of which is assumed to collectively provide indicators of mathematical literacy. A scheme designed to rate individual items based on the extent to which each of those capabilities is needed to respond to PISA questions has been developed as part of research activities documented by Turner, Blum and Niss (2015[192]). This research has shown that the scheme predicts the difficulty of PISA test items. Evidence of activation of the capabilities is fundamental to PISA's descriptions of growing mathematical literacy.

Alignment of the two scales

The 2017 review team agreed that given the general consistency in what is being assessed by both PIAAC and PISA, and based on their review and knowledge of the two frameworks and item pools, there could be much to gain from making significant and more explicit connections and links between the PIAAC numeracy framework and the PISA mathematical literacy framework and assessment. The best way to do this would be by establishing an empirical relationship between the two scales through a mapping/linking study where adults and 15-year-olds would sit common items from across both assessments. This would make analysis and comparison across the two assessments stronger and more useful for research purposes, both within countries and internationally. It would also enable research into how items are approached differently by those in school versus those that are not, and support provision of stronger data to enable research into progress from school into adult life.

Numeracy components

The implementation of an equivalent to the PIAAC reading components assessment in PIAAC's numeracy assessment is outlined in this section.

Introduction

The second cycle of PIAAC will include a new set of low-level items, called numeracy components, that are aiming to shed more light on the numeracy competencies of low-scoring adults (below Level 1). In analysing the first cycle of PIAAC results it was felt that information was missing to make valid inferences on what numeracy skills adults below Level 1 possessed or lacked. It should be noted that the NEG and the 2017 review recognised that there were two solutions to achieve this. The first was to write some new easier items to complement the existing three below Level 1 items, along with this second solution of developing the numeracy components.

In the review of the PIAAC Cycle 1 numeracy framework, possible building blocks for the components were investigated and arising issues and constraints were discussed (Tout et al., 2017[1]).

During the development of this numeracy framework for PIAAC Cycle 2 and the design of the second cycle numeracy items, a further investigation was undertaken to establish which kind of numeracy assessment items would be suitable for assessing some of the identified numeracy components, given the constraints of the delivery modalities.

Reading component skills

In its first cycle, PIAAC included for the first time an assessment of 'reading component skills' often abbreviated to 'reading components' to evaluate how well individuals with low levels of proficiency master the basic building blocks of reading (Sabatini and Bruce, 2009[193]). Three types of tasks were included in Cycle 1:[2]

- Print vocabulary, where respondents were asked to identify which one of four words matched a picture.
- Sentence processing, where a single sentence was presented and respondents were asked to identify if it made sense or not by selecting "Yes" or "No".
- Paragraph comprehension, which were cloze tasks where respondents selected one of several words to make sentences within a paragraph make sense.

The delivery of the reading components assessment in the first cycle of PIAAC included a level of oral support by the test interviewer, and this is under consideration for Cycle 2. Both accuracy and timing information were captured for these items, allowing the analysis of both skill and fluency.

In Cycle 2, the reading components measure will include sentence and paragraph comprehension items and will be administered on the tablet. This will make an automated presentation of items possible, allowing respondents to better demonstrate fluency, and will also allow the collection of comparable timing information.

Rationale for the numeracy components assessment

The overall performance in PIAAC Cycle 1 showed that 5% of adults surveyed in the first round of 24 countries were at below Level 1. When including the second round of countries, the results showed 6.7% were at below Level 1 across 33 countries. This compares with a performance in reading literacy of 3.3% across the original 24 countries, and 4.5% for the second round of 33 countries. Hence, the percentages of adults performing at the lowest level in numeracy are significantly higher when compared with literacy (OECD, 2013[161]; OECD, 2016[194]). Therefore, there is a very strong argument from the empirical data for developing an equivalent to the reading components assessment in the PIAAC numeracy assessment based on the higher numbers of adults performing at that level compared with reading.

Numeracy component skills – conceptual issues

The purpose of defining, constructing, and administering items for a numeracy components assessment have the same aims: to develop a set of "fine-grained tasks" so that "at least some of these adults would demonstrate some level of **numeracy** knowledge and skills".

In numeracy, such component skills for adults have been much less researched, theorised, and examined quantitatively compared with component skills for literacy [e.g., see (Grotlüschen et al., 2016[195]; Sabatini and Bruce, 2009[193])]. Therefore, conceptualising and developing the numeracy components assessment in the second cycle of PIAAC was a challenging task. There was recognition that much more research and discussion needed to be undertaken to establish the sensible and meaningful content of such numeracy skills component for adults, the scope of those skills, and how they relate to the existing PIAAC below Level 1 items and their descriptions. However, time constraints related to the need to develop the test items within 6 months of the NEG's first meeting in March 2018, meant that the NEG had to proceed in the best way it could.

The NEG was aware, however, that it had a unique opportunity to create an assessment that had not been developed or administered before and that would potentially provide valuable research data and insights into adults with low levels of numeracy and mathematical skills. The opportunity to utilise the PIAAC Field Trial to test how such a numeracy components assessment would work was taken on board and work proceeded to research what would work best and to develop some trial items.

A range of potential sources of content were investigated by the review team (Tout et al., 2017[1]) and consequently by the NEG, but their research time was limited. In the following years, it is the NEG's recommendation this issue should be researched and trialled more thoroughly.

Numeracy component skills - prerequisites or fundamentals?

The reading components are described as fine-grained foundational reading skills which precede more complex reading skills. In numeracy, such fine-grained foundation skills are not yet clearly defined. The numeracy development of individuals starts 'in the crib', where newborns have their first experiences with numbers, shapes and sizes of objects and spatial orientation. The exact nature of these numeracy and mathematical foundation skills is still under-researched.

To complicate things further, in research literature, the term 'components of numeracy' is also used for the fundamental elements which constitute the concept of numeracy. This is a different perspective from thinking of them as the foundations or prerequisites for the development of more complex numerate skills. For instance, Ginsburg, Manly and Schmitt (2006[29]) did a comprehensive investigation in existing numeracy frameworks to discern any reoccurring aspects in a range of existing numeracy frameworks. They labelled these elements as the 'components of numeracy' and called them "those fundamental elements that are inherent in proficient numeracy practice" (p. 2). They listed the components as: *Content*, *Context* and *Cognitive and affective*. This is clearly another definition of a 'component of numeracy' compared with the perspective of describing and defining some assessable foundational aspects of low-level adult numeracy skills.

Another clarification is also necessary. Components of numeracy are not, as sometimes assumed in laymen's opinions, the "basics"—knowing by rote the arithmetical operations like addition and subtraction up to 20 and multiplication and division with 1-digit numbers. The NEG views these as basic arithmetical facts in the domain of operations with decontextualised numbers, which only covers a minute part of the PIAAC content dimension. These "basic" skills are in no way basic or elementary to many of the low level performing adults in PIAAC, as these skills make use of abstract, school-based notations and conventions and lacks the key dimension of "meaningfulness", which is an essential fundamental pillar of the numeracy framework as a whole.

So, there are two major challenges to consider in the development of a numeracy components assessment for the second cycle of PIAAC. One is the breadth and the level of the mathematical content that should be included as some of the foundational skills. Second is how the meaningfulness of the items could be maintained, for instance whether the use of real-world problems embedded in authentic situations is feasible in an assessment of the components of numeracy, or at least what considerations need to be accommodated in order for the components assessment to work and be relevant to the adult respondents undertaking the assessment.

Delivery and other constraints

Another major challenge for the NEG is that the items must fit within the delivery options of the whole PIAAC assessment, including issues to do with the time available and the uncertainty about the level of oral support available for respondents undertaking the Components Assessment.

The constraints imposed by the practicalities of delivering such an assessment internationally in multiple languages need to be considered, and will impact on what can be achieved. Furthermore, given the likelihood of an interaction between low numeracy and low literacy skill levels, delivery of a numeracy components assessment should take special account of the reading demands of the assessment. Other factors to consider include: the time available, which will impact on the number and range of items that can be utilised in terms of content areas and difficulty levels; the delivery and item types (oral instructions and support by administrator; online delivery; interactive or not) and more. A number of these factors are discussed below.

The NEG therefore believes that this second cycle of the PIAAC numeracy framework is only taking the first steps into gaining insights into the nature of low-level adult numerate behaviour and performance. However, these are important and very valuable first steps.

Representations and reading demands

It will be essential to make the reading demands as minimal as possible for this assessment of numeracy components, while maintaining the connection to real life. The review team (Tout et al., 2017[1]) suggested to offer oral/spoken support in some form or other, either from the administrator, or if conducted on a laptop or tablet, through audio or video support. Consideration could also be given to the administrator recording oral answers for the respondent.

Another recommendation is that the stimuli should be based on photos or videos of realistic representations of real-life objects, which would help to make them accessible, more familiar and more realistic and authentic, while potentially helping to reduce reading load. Another suggestion was to use real items or objects for some test items. These could be used for tasks such as comparing, sorting, or classifying. This would make the numeracy components assessment more accessible, practical and hands-on. Additionally, or alternatively, technology could be used so that similar actions could be done on screen, such as using drag-and-drop items on a laptop or tablet using touch screen capabilities. For example, respondents could be asked to order objects representing quantities by dragging and dropping rather than writing down an ordered list.

The conclusion of the NEG is that the use of the tablet allows the use of photos and realistic representations of real-life objects, which can help make them accessible and more familiar. The existing below Level 1 item on counting the number of bottles is a good example of how this can be done using a photo and little text; in fact, even without being able to read the question text it is highly likely that respondents would be able to assume what the question was asking. If some level of oral guidance or support was also made available, then this would make such questions even more accessible.

Time

Given the overall time constraints for the assessment, the NEG was informed that there would be a restriction in time to a maximum of approximately 3 minutes for the duration of the numeracy components assessment, as is the case for the reading components assessment. This obviously presents significant restrictions on what can be included in the components. However, it needs to be noted that this restriction in time will not be revealed to the participants to avoid unwarranted stress and failure anxiety. The NEG has argued that for the Field Trial, more time be allowed (up to a total of 5 minutes) in order to trial and test the new items. This then will provide the necessary empirical data and information for a more informed decision about how to best implement the numeracy components assessment in the Main Study.

The time restriction for the delivery means that after that time has expired the set of items will be terminated and no more new items will disappear. The respondent will not be told how many items are to be presented—they will continue until either all the items have been presented, or until the time limit expires. The interviewers will be instructed to ask the participant to keep working on during the set.

Oral instructions and support

As mentioned above, the Review paper suggested to offer oral/spoken support in some form or other, either from the interviewer, or if conducted on a laptop or tablet, through audio or video support. However, the constraints on the delivery of PIAAC and the need for approved translations of any spoken texts in any video or audio files, made it unfeasible to build in any oral directions into the assessment itself. However, as mentioned earlier, consideration is being given to the possibility of some level of oral support or instructions by the test interviewer.

Hence, it was very important to address the issue of minimising the use of text, and the best way to do this was through the use of photos and realistic representations of real-life objects, which can help make items more accessible and more familiar.

Using money

One other issue is that it would seem obvious that some of these numeracy components assessment items should be based around recognising and working with money, which appears to have the advantage of being a) number-based, and b) important in most adults' lives, and also relatively familiar. Money is, however, highly country-dependent: its very familiarity is grounded in its localisation in a particular set of relationships, financial and otherwise, and these are not necessarily consistent across countries. Monetary systems across participating countries vary significantly, and although PIAAC specifies strict guidelines about changing the magnitude of monetary amounts in order to try to keep them at the same time realistic and mathematically comparable, at this lowest level of mathematical complexity this may be difficult to achieve. The NEG believes that the number sense construct underpins an understanding of currency and working with money.

Item formats

Based on the delivery constraints for the components, some of the recommended item type options which were seen to best support a numeracy components assessment, would include:

- use of photos and realistic representations of real-life objects
- minimise the need to read written instructions – use a simple, single stem to introduce the sets of questions/items (note that this approach will also contribute to the fluency measure as respondents will not need to spend time reading changing item instructions)
- not expecting any written responses – so use "tap-on" style of responses.

Numeracy component skills – possible content

As with the PIAAC reading components assessment, the aim is to better understand the numeracy and mathematical skills of adults scoring below Level 1. These will be the individuals who in previous surveys essentially could not answer any, or many, of the numeracy items correctly.

The current, lowest level in PIAAC is below Level 1, and the description of this level of numeracy performance in PIAAC is:

> Tasks at this level require the respondents to carry out simple processes such as counting, sorting, performing basic arithmetic operations with whole numbers or money, or recognising common spatial representations in concrete, familiar contexts where the mathematical content is explicit with little or no text or distractors. (OECD, 2013, p. 76[161])

The existing three below Level 1 PIAAC numeracy items are:

- the counting or estimating of the number of objects shown in a photo where the objects are in layers and therefore not all visible (total is under 100)
- adding up three whole numbers listed in a short text (total is just over 200)
- identifying the item that was packed first from four supermarket price tags, each of which includes the date packed.

Therefore, the skills that need to be assessed in a numeracy components assessment would preferably need to be at a lower level than those three questions.

In a recent review of options for developing a low level assessment of numeracy for adults in low- and middle-income countries (UNESCO, 2016[196]), the authors said:

> It is therefore necessary to distinguish between people with no formal skills (those who have relatively few mental calculation skills beyond counting simple quantities and who cannot understand the meaning of written digits) and with low formal skills (those who can engage in some mental calculations using indigenous number systems or measurement techniques but know few print-based or formal numeracy symbols and systems, even if they may be able to complete very simply written math problems). (UNESCO, 2016, p. 284[196])

These issues are at the heart of the development of a numeracy components assessment.

National and international frameworks

There are existing adult numeracy standards and frameworks in different countries that have described relatively low levels of numeracy competence, and these could be used as starting points for descriptions of possible numeracy components questions and tasks. One challenge is that many such frameworks, as with PIAAC numeracy Cycle 1, do not detail or describe a level below PIAAC's existing below Level 1.

What is common at the lowest levels of existing adult numeracy frameworks is that they describe mathematical content across a number of content areas, as with PIAAC's four content areas of *Quantity and number*; *Dimension and shape*; *Change and relationships*; and *Data and chance*.

For example, Ireland has five areas described: *Quantity and number*; *Data handling*; *pattern and relationship*; *Problem solving*; and *Shape and space* (Quality and Qualifications Ireland (QQI), 2016[78]). New Zealand has three areas described: *Make sense of number to solve problems*; *Reason statistically*; and *Measure and interpret shape and space* (Tertiary Education Commission, 2008[79]). The Netherlands has described an entrance level for adults around four domains: *Numbers*, *Proportions*, *Measurement and geometry*, and *Relations*, stressing the concrete nature of the content with a few data, a minimum of text, rounded numbers and problems taken directly from everyday life and the work environment (Centre for Innovation of Education and Training (CINOP), 2013[197]).

As examples of what is described at the lower levels approximating below Level 1 of PIAAC or lower, Box 3.3 below includes some sample statements from a number of different national **adult** curriculum frameworks/standards, organised against the PIAAC content areas [excerpts from: Quality and Qualifications Ireland (QQI), (2016[78]); McLean et al. (2012[77]); Tertiary Education Commission, (2008[79])].

Box 3.3. Sample statements from national adult curriculum frameworks/standards, organised against the PIAAC content areas

Quantity and number

- Recognise the relationship between numerical value and groups of objects, up to and including 10.
- Recognise the language of mathematics in everyday situations using elementary language, e.g., greater than, less than, bigger than, farther than.
- Solve addition and subtraction problems by counting all of the objects.
- Solve addition and subtraction problems by counting on or counting back, using ones and tens.
- Solve multiplication problems by skip-counting, often in conjunction with one-to-one counting and often keeping track of the repeated counts by using materials (e.g., fingers) or mental images.
- Read and write personally relevant numbers, e.g., street number.

- Recognise and write money as symbols (e.g., $12.50) up to $100.
- Recognise and use ordinal numbers from first to tenth.

Dimension and shape

- Identify key characteristics of shapes and forms, e.g., number of sides, corners and curves.
- Use the language of measurement in relation to shape and form, e.g., longer, shorter, wider, narrower.
- Sort and describe objects by their shape attributes.
- Describe, name and interpret relative positions in space.
- Compare and order objects directly, using attributes of length, area, volume and capacity, weight, angle, temperature and time intervals in order to understand the attributes.
- Read digital time (not including concept of am/pm).
- Identify dates in a calendar.
- Recognise common time sequences; e.g., the order of the days of the week.
- Identifies differences and similarities between common 2 dimensional (2D) shapes.

Pattern, relationships and change

- Make a pattern; e.g., a sequence of images, symbols or sounds with two variables (different colour, same shape, etc.).
- Data and chance.
- Identify the use of data in everyday life; e.g., the numbers of people who want tea/coffee.
- Sort objects according to their attributes, organise data about the objects and represent data, using concrete objects or pictures.
- Identify all possible outcomes in situations involving simple (single-stage) chance.
- Compare information and data within highly familiar simple texts, lists, charts, diagrams and tables.

In the review of the PIAAC Cycle 1 numeracy framework (Tout et al., 2017[1]), the review team acknowledged that there is a potential issue with using national **adult** curriculum frameworks/standards directly, because some national adult numeracy frameworks and standards have been either developed formally to align with established, hierarchical levels in child-focused curricula or are at least built on notions of children's learning. This can be illustrated in a number of ways, for example, by the inclusion in adult curriculum frameworks of simplistic, bounded statements such as 'can count to 20'; by specific, school-based terminology such as the 'place values of digits in whole numbers up to 100'; or where percentages are not named and included until higher levels of performance. Such statements do not acknowledge the empirical data that exists from PIAAC or other empirical data, as it does not match the knowledge of adults nor represent the day-to-day tasks that many adults can in fact successfully undertake, but who may nonetheless be performing at below Level 1 numeracy in PIAAC (Tout et al., 2017[1]).

Another perspective on possible content for the numeracy components is the growing body of research on number sense.

Number sense

Number sense appears increasingly in literature as one of the main components of "numeracy." Being numerate means having a certain sense of quantities and numbers and how we use numbers—orally, vocally and in writing—to represent, inform, predict, and estimate phenomenon from real life.

The term number sense was coined in the 1930s by Dantzig: "Man, even in the lower stages of development, possesses a faculty which, for want of a better name, I shall call Number Sense. This faculty permits him to recognise that something has changed in a small collection when, without his direct knowledge, an object has been removed from or added to the collection." (Dantzig, 1934, p. 1[198]). In the

1990s the concept became more visible [e.g., (Greeno, 1991[199]; Mcintosh, Reys and Reys, 1992[18])]. McIntosh, Reys and Reys developed a framework for number sense including three components: *Numbers, Operations* and *Computational settings*, which are interconnected. According to them, number sense involves being able to use numbers, operations and their applications in different computational settings. They talk about the meaningful understanding of the Hindu-Arabic number system, the development of a sense of orderliness of the number, the multiple representations for numbers (including the idea of composition / decomposition), the understanding of mathematical properties, and the relationship between operations. For them, having "number sense" means being able to solve problems in the real world, providing suitable answers, using (or creating) effective strategies to compute, count, etc. It is not just reproducing instrumentally a certain algorithm, but being able to use the mathematical knowledge and components in a flexible manner. At the same time Dehaene (1997[200]) published his best-selling book *Number Sense – How the Mind Creates Mathematics*, which made a connection of number sense with the structure of our brains.

Yang, Reys and Reys (2009[17]) defined number sense as "a person's general understanding of numbers and operations and the ability to handle daily life situations that include numbers. This ability is used to develop flexible and efficient strategies (including mental computation and estimation) to handle numerical problems" (2009, p. 384[17]). Regarding the components of number sense, these authors argue "Number sense is a complex process involving many different components of numbers, operations, and their relationships" (Yang, Reys and Reys, 2009, p. 384[17]). Among these processes, they highlight two aspects, 1) the use of benchmarks in recognising the magnitude of numbers, and 2) the knowledge on the relative effects of an operation on various numbers.

Faulkner and Cain (2009[201]) claim that "the characteristics of good number sense include: a) fluency in estimating and judging magnitude, b) ability to recognise unreasonable results, c) flexibility when mentally computing, d) ability to move among different representations and to use the most appropriate representations" (Faulkner and Cain, 2009, p. 25[201]). Cain et al. (2007[202]) described a set of components of number sense as shown in Figure 3.5, where the different components of number sense all relate to and are underpinned by language:

Figure 3.5. Components of number sense

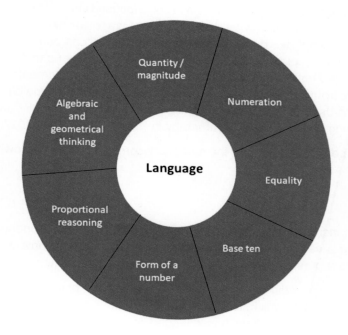

As stated by Thompson (1995[19]), using numbers is more than reasoning about number and more than skilled calculations. It is about making sense of the situation to which we apply numbers and calculations" (Thompson, 1995, p. 220[19]). It also involves a critical way to make decisions and solve problems in *Personal*, *Work*, and *Societal/community* contexts (Peters, 2012[15]).

Summary and where to next?

Based on the above research about the potential content of a new numeracy components assessment, the NEG also considered the possibility of developing a spatial sense components assessment, as spatial sense was also seen as a key foundational skill for the target cohort of adults. However, mainly due to a number of the constraints on the delivery of the numeracy components discussed below, especially in relation to the time available for administering the components, alongside the greater difficulty of reducing the literacy/reading demands of items based around an assessment of spatial sense, the NEG decided to move forward with using number sense as the content base for the new numeracy components assessment.

In its broadest definition, 'number sense' overlaps to a great extent the 'big ideas' and the domains of the (inter)national frameworks mentioned before. In a smaller and more fundamental interpretation, number sense relates to the sense of quantities and the sense of how numbers represent quantities. This latter interpretation turned out to be the most suitable basis for the further development of the items that must operationalise the numeracy components.

Numeracy component skills – the scope

Another significant issue that needs to be addressed in developing a numeracy components assessment is that of the embedded nature of the mathematics in real-world settings and situations and the role that this plays. This is often called context-based in contrast to non-context-based tasks or contextualised in contrast to decontextualised. Individuals acquire mathematical knowledge through both formal and informal learning, and informal learning is as valuable as formal, school-based learning. The field of ethnomathematics richly documents this issue of "street maths versus school maths" and as this components assessment will often target adults with little formal schooling but who are functioning as adults in society, this issue needs to be taken on board and addressed. For example, D'Ambrosio (1985[203]) theorised the concept of ethnomathematics. Carraher, Carraher and Schliemann's (1985[101]) research with street children in Brazil found they could operate in quite sophisticated ways when using mathematics to survive in a commercial sense, although they had been previously adjudged as being incapable of doing mathematics in schools. This was discussed in more detail in the second section under the topic *School mathematics versus everyday or workplace mathematics*.

Matthijsse (2000[204]) specifically addressed the issue of how adults cope with mathematical knowledge in practical daily situations and the gap between school mathematics and its formal algorithms and the mathematics that adults use in their daily lives. He looked at the informal methods adults used in daily life, and found they were often anchored and embedded in familiar knowledge and real-life settings and situations. Although his focus was on instructional methods to use with learners, his research, like the other ethnomathematical research, indicates that this proposed PIAAC numeracy components assessment cannot be constrained by only offering non-context-based tasks with the mathematics being like formal, school-based questions. However, a significant risk, and challenge, exists with regard to cultural and the possible national specificity of particular rule of thumb or informal methods, and how these differences could be overcome in an international assessment. Given this, a low-level components assessment could aim to find out about adults' informal/common sense ways of doing mathematics—what mental models and processes do adults use when solving a numeracy problem? In addition, can data and information be collected about the connections (or non-connections) between the school ways of doing mathematics (and the use of algorithms) versus the way adults solve such problems in everyday life?

Different people will have very different settings and applications in which they may comfortably and more confidently use their mathematical knowledge. Finding the right problem situation or setting for an individual so that they can demonstrate their understanding of mathematics concepts will be a challenge. At this more basic level of mathematical knowledge, the familiarity of the setting and situation could be critical. A potential solution could be to use a form of adaptive delivery to allow respondents to be able to select from a range of settings and situations where the same content and level of mathematics content is embedded.

In relation to the three named PIAAC numeracy contexts (*Personal, Work, Societal/community*), it would make sense for the numeracy components assessment to focus on the more common, generic and familiar settings and contexts which would appear to be *Personal, Work, Societal/community*. The three existing below Level 1 numeracy items are located within those contexts. Again, a challenge exists in how to use work-related situations, given that research shows that adults with poor formal skills are often able to function 'perfectly well' in particular jobs where they have learned rule of thumb or other methods that enable them to get by.

One challenge with context-based items is that where the mathematics is embedded within texts and stimuli, some of the targeted cohort will not be easily able to read, interpret and hence engage with and understand the mathematics required to be used due to their potential low level of literacy skills.

These considerations strengthen the idea of keeping items for assessing numeracy components in line with the fundamental definition of number sense, focusing on the connection with quantities in real life and the way numbers are used to represent quantities. This seems feasible without necessarily using long or complex verbal descriptions to present contexts of items or to ask the questions.

The proposed numeracy components for PIAAC Cycle 2

Given the constraints of level, reading demands, time, and the available representation of tasks, the NEG decided to implement a modest set of number sense items that would be the main ingredients in the landscape of relevant numeracy components. These items will ask the participants to estimate quantities from real-life pictures and furthermore estimate the relative magnitude of several numerical representations of quantities.

It was intended that the respondent would be able to quickly view the stimulus without needing to read much text at all, tap on a response and immediately be sent to the following question that would be based on the same stem, requiring no need to read anything further.

The content is limited to a fundamental perspective on number sense and more specifically to:

- A set of 12 items where the respondent must select the quantity (<20) of a number of objects displayed. The representations are limited to pictures of real-life objects.
- A second set of 15 items on the relative magnitude of quantities or phenomena, partly from real life and partly more decontextualised.

Based on the above decisions, the NEG:

- Consulted the translating partner for PIAAC, cApStAn, to assist in identifying the best question wording that could be used that would utilise a simple, single stem and reduce the need to read each question separately.
- Developed a draft of the components assessment and ran two brief pilots.
- Revised the draft prior to release to countries for feedback and comment.
- Reviewed and revised the draft again at the NEG meeting held in October 2018.

Linguistic issues

In discussions with cApStAn it was soon realised that when translated into other languages, what seemed simple solutions and wording in English often become complicated when translated into a range of other languages. This often depended on what the objects or images were that would be presented to respondents.

After a period of discussion with cApStAn about what wording, and what content and images would work best without creating the need to change the stem throughout, it was decided that the best solution was fourfold:

- To have an introduction up front that would foreground the assessment items to follow.
- Include some simple practice questions that would model what was required.
- To have the two sets of items – the first using the stem **How many ...?** for identifying a quantity.
- The second set was using the stem **The biggest?** for identifying the relative magnitude of different quantities/values.

It did mean that some of the NEG's ideas *re* items and their images or stimuli to include could not be used, such as temperatures, charts, people etc. Some items and images were gender-sensitive and this restricted some of the options.

Feedback from pilots

Two pilots of the first drafts of the Numeracy Components assessment were held, utilising access to adults participating in adult literacy and numeracy classes, and who were known to be low-performing adults. One pilot was in Belgium with 10 adults, and the other in Spain with 29 adults. The main outcomes from the pilots included:

- The participating adults were positive about the experience—they were normally used to not getting mathematics/numeracy questions correct.
- They liked the real-life images to quantify/count.
- They could all answer all of the **How Many?** questions correctly, but some took a long time.
- Some of the adults took up to 30 minutes to answer the sets of questions.
- There were clear boundaries in knowledge with **The biggest?** set of questions. Difficulty started with the understanding and comparing of decimal numbers and fractions.

The results from the pilots indicated that the assessment, for the most part, worked successfully. A number of issues resulted that enabled the NEG to make further decisions and refinements to the draft assessment. These included the following:

- For the most part, the content was appropriate for the target group, and the wording and presentation seemed to be accessible—some questions were able to be refined based on the observations made as the adults undertook the assessment.
- The items that assessed the ability to recognise and answer some decontextualised basic sums where the adults needed to recognise the meaning of some standard arithmetical operations were confusing and not appropriate for these learners—this reinforced the beliefs of the NEG about the relevance and meaning of such types of test items for adults. They have been removed for the Field Trial.
- Given the length and range of times taken, the timing and the estimate of fluency will be crucial to measure.

- The number of items to be included in the Field Trial have been reduced, both due to the time taken, but also because it was felt that the extra number of items was not collecting extra data or information.

The NEG has refined the sets of questions and have developed two different forms for the Field Trial, with linking items. The NEG will select best performing items from the Field Trial for the Main Study.

The questions and items being asked—How many ...?

For the Field Trial there will be 12 questions of this type, with a maximum time allowance of 2 minutes. Here is a mock-up of an example of the sort of item asked in this set of questions. The respondent is to tap on the matching number.

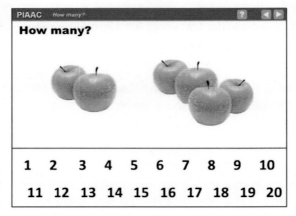

The questions and items being asked—The biggest?

For the Field Trial there will be 15 questions of this type, with a maximum time allowance of 3 minutes. Here is a mock-up of the sort of item asked in this set of questions. The respondent is to tap on the biggest item/number of the set shown.

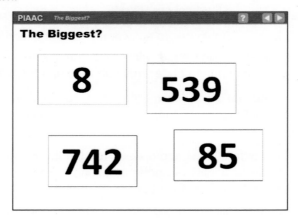

Timing

There will be a restriction in time for the Field Trial to a maximum of 5 minutes – 2 minutes for the set of *How many?* items; and 3 minutes for the set of *The biggest?* items. However, this restriction in time will not be revealed to the participants to avoid unwarranted stress and potential anxiety about failure. Respondents will just be told to do their best to work both accurately and quickly. The timeframe for the delivery will be limited to the number of minutes and after that time has expired the set will be terminated and no more new items will appear. The respondent will not be aware that there were unanswered items in the set, if that is the case. The time parameter will be recorded for each participant and will be analysed in relation to a measure of fluency. However, a decision how to incorporate the time issue and the estimate of fluency in the reporting will only be decided after the Field Trial data is analysed.

Automaticity/fluency

Given that in the delivery of the reading components assessment each part was timed in order to be able to get an estimate of speed and automaticity, this should also be made available for the numeracy components assessment. Collecting the timing information and the ability to create measures of fluency in number sense will provide the capability to look for any correlates of interest, such as with the respondent's performance in numeracy overall and/or with particular dimensions of the numeracy assessment.

References

Askew, M. (2008), "Mathematical discipline knowledge requirements for prospective primary teachers, and the structure and teaching approaches of programs designed to develop that knowledge", in Sullivan, P. and T. Woods (eds.), *Knowledge and Beliefs in Mathematics Teaching and Teaching Development*, Sense Publishers. [151]

Askew, M. et al. (1997), *Effective teachers of numeracy in primary schools: Teachers' beliefs, practices and pupils' learning*, Paper presented at the British Educational Research Association Annual Conference, September 1997, University of York. [148]

Atkinson, R. (2005), "Multimedia Learning of Mathematics", in *The Cambridge Handbook of Multimedia Learning*, Cambridge University Press, http://dx.doi.org/10.1017/cbo9780511816819.026. [171]

Australian Association of Mathematics Teachers (AAMT) and Australian Industry Group (AiGroup) (2014), *Tackling the School–Industry Mathematics Divide*, Commonwealth of Australia. [88]

Baker, D. and B. Street (1994), "Literacy and numeracy: Concepts and definitions", in Husen, T. and E. Postlethwaite (eds.), *Encyclopedia of Education*, Pergamon Press, New York. [45]

Bennett, R. (2015), "The changing nature of educational assessment", *Review of Research in Education*, Vol. 39/1, pp. 370-407, http://dx.doi.org/10.3102/0091732x14554179. [163]

Bennett, R. (2010), "Technology for large-scale assessment", in Peterson, P., E. Baker and B. McGaw (eds.), *International Encyclopedia of Education, 3rd edition*, Elsevier, Oxford. [168]

Bennett, R. (1998), *Reinventing assessment: Speculations on the future of large-scale educational testing*, Policy Information Center, Educational Testing Service, Princeton, NJ, https://www.ets.org/research/policy_research_reports/publications/report/1998/cgln. [167]

Benn, R. (1997), *Adults Count Too: Mathematics for Empowerment*, National Institute of Adult Continuing Education (NIACE), Leicester. [20]

Bessot, A. and L. Ridgway (eds.) (2000), *Education for Mathematics in the Workplace*, Springer, New York. [89]

Binkley, M. et al. (2011), "Defining twenty-first century skills", in Griffin, P., B. McGaw and E. Care (eds.), *Assessment and Teaching of 21st Century Skills*, Springer, Dordrecht, http://dx.doi.org/10.1007/978-94-007-2324-5_2. [62]

Bishop, A. (1988), *Mathematical Enculturation: A Cultural Perspective in Mathematics Education*, D. Reidel Publishing Co., Dordrecht. [83]

Boaler, J. and C. Humphreys (2005), *Connecting Mathematical Ideas: Middle School Video Cases to Support Teaching and Learning*, Heinemann, Portsmouth, NH. [149]

Bower, M. et al. (2014), "Augmented reality in education – cases, places and potentials", *Educational Media International*, Vol. 51/1, pp. 1-15, http://dx.doi.org/10.1080/09523987.2014.889400. [169]

Brooks, G., K. Heath and A. Pollard (2005), *Assessing adult literacy and numeracy: A review of assessment instruments*, National Research and Development Centre for Adult Literacy and Numeracy, London. [189]

Bruner, J. (1960), *The Process of Education*, Harvard University Press, Cambridge, MA. [144]

Buckingham, E. (1997), *Specific and Generic Numeracies of the Workplace*, Deakin University, Melbourne. [90]

Buckley, S. (2013), *Deconstructing maths anxiety: Helping students to develop a positive attitude towards learning maths (ACER Occasional Essays)*, Australian Council for Educational Research (ACER), Melbourne, Victoria, https://research.acer.edu.au/learning_processes/16. [126]

Bynner, J. and S. Parsons (2005), *Does numeracy matter more?*, National Research and Development Centre for Adult Literacy and Numeracy (NRDC), London, http://www.nrdc.org.uk/wp-content/uploads/2005/01/Does-numeracy-matter-more.pdf. [21]

Cain, C. et al. (2007), *The Components of Number Sense*, NC Math Foundations Training, Exceptional Children's Division of the North Carolina Department of Public Instruction (NCDPI), Raleigh, NC. [202]

Carnevale, A., L. Gainer and A. Meltzer (1990), *Workplace Basics: The Essential Skills Employers Want*, Jossey Bass, San Francisco. [84]

Carpentieri, J., J. Litster and L. Frumkin (2009), *Adult numeracy: A review of research*, National Research and Development Centre for Adult Literacy and Numeracy (NRDC), London, England, https://www.nationalnumeracy.org.uk/sites/default/files/documents/Adult_numeracy_a_review_of_research/carpentieri_et_al_2009_bbc_adult_numeracy_a_review_of_research.pdf. [57]

Carraher, T., D. Carraher and A. Schliemann (1985), "Mathematics in the streets and in schools", *British Journal of Developmental Psychology*, Vol. 3/1, pp. 21-29, http://dx.doi.org/10.1111/j.2044-835x.1985.tb00951.x. [101]

Centre for Innovation of Education and Training (CINOP) (2013), *Standaarden en Eindtermen VE [Standards and Attainment Goals Adult Education]*, Den Bosch, https://taalenrekenenmbo.nl/app/uploads/nieuw-2.-Standaarden-en-eindtermen-ve.pdf. [197]

Charles, R. (2005), "Big ideas and understandings as the foundation for elementary and middle school mathematics", *Journal of Mathematics Education*, Vol. 7/3, pp. 9-24. [6]

Chisman, F. (2011), *Facing the Challenge of Numeracy in Adult Education*, Council for Advancement of Adult Literacy, New York, http://www.caalusa.org/NumeracyChallenge.pdf. [59]

Clark, E. (2011), "Concepts as organizing frameworks", *Encounter*, Vol. 24/3, pp. 32-44, http://www.ojs.great-ideas.org/Encounter/Clark243.pdf. [145]

Clarke, B. and D. Clarke (2004), "Using questioning to elicit and develop children's mathematical thinking", in Bright, G. and R. Rubenstein (eds.), *Professional Development Guidebook for Perspectives on the Teaching of Mathematics*, National Council of Teachers of Mathematics, Reston, VA. [150]

Coben, D. et al. (2003), *Adult Numeracy: Review of Research and Related Literature*, National Research and Development Centre for Adult Literacy and Numeracy (NRDC), London. [22]

Coben, D. et al. (2010), *Benchmark Assessment of Numeracy for Nursing: Medication Dosage Calculation at Point of Registration*, NHS Education for Scotland, Edinburgh. [91]

Coben, D., J. O'Donoghue and G. FitzSimons (eds.) (2000), *Perspectives on Adults Learning Mathematics*, Kluwer Academic Publishers, London. [23]

Cockcroft, W. (1982), *Mathematics Counts*, Her Majesty's Stationery Office (HMSO), London, http://www.educationengland.org.uk/documents/cockcroft/cockcroft1982.html. [44]

Condelli, L. et al. (2006), *A Review of the Literature in Adult Numeracy: Research and Conceptual Issues*, American Institutes for Research, Washington D.C. [24]

Coulombe, S., J. Tramblay and S. Marchand (2004), *Literacy scores, human capital and growth across fourteen OECD countries*, Statistics Canada, Ottawa, https://www150.statcan.gc.ca/n1/pub/89-552-m/89-552-m2004011-eng.pdf. [25]

Crowther (1959), *15 to 18: A report of the Central Advisory Council of Education (England), Volume 1*, Her Majesty's Stationery Office (HSMO), London, http://www.educationengland.org.uk/documents/crowther/crowther1959-1.html. [43]

D'Ambrosio, U. (1985), "Ethnomathematics and its place in the history and pedagogy of mathematics", *For the Learning of Mathematics*, Vol. 5/1, pp. 44-48. [203]

Dantzig, T. (1934), *Number - The Language of Science*, Macmillan Company, New York. [198]

Dehaene, S. (1997), *Number Sense – How the Mind Creates Mathematics*, Penguin Books, London. [200]

Department for Education (DfE) (2014), *Statutory framework for the early years foundation stage: Setting the standards for learning, development and care for children from birth to five*, Department for Education, London. [185]

Diezmann, C. and T. Lowrie (2008), "The role of information graphics in mathematical proficiency", in Goos, M., R. Brown and K. Makar (eds.), *Navigating Currents and Charting Directions. Proceedings of the 31st annual conference of the Mathematics Education Research Group of Australasia*, Mathematics Education Research Group of Australasia Inc., Brisbane, https://merga.net.au/Public/Publications/Annual_Conference_Proceedings/2008_MERGA_CP.aspx. [162]

Dossey, J. (1997), "Defining and measuring quantitative literacy", in Steen, L. (ed.), *Why Numbers Count: Quantitative Literacy for Tomorrow's America*, College Entrance Examination Board, New York. [160]

Ernest, P. (2004), "Relevance versus utility: Some ideas on what it means to know mathematics", in Clarke, B. et al. (eds.), *International Perspectives on Learning and Teaching Mathematics*, National Centre for Mathematics Education, Göteborg University. [119]

Expert Group on Future Skills Needs (Ireland) (2007), *Tomorrow's Skills: Towards a National Skills Strategy: 5th Report*, Expert Group on Future Skills Needs, Dublin. [63]

Faulkner, V. and C. Cain (2009), "The components of number sense: An instructional model for teachers", *Teaching Exceptional Children*, Vol. 41/5, pp. 24-30, http://dx.doi.org/10.1177/004005990904100503. [201]

FitzSimons, G. (2005), "Numeracy and Australian workplaces: Findings and implications", *Australian Senior Mathematics Journal*, Vol. 19/2, pp. 27-42. [92]

FitzSimons, G. and D. Coben (2009), "Adult numeracy for work and life: Curriculum and teaching implications of recent research", in *International Handbook of Education for the Changing World of Work*, Springer, Dordrecht, http://dx.doi.org/10.1007/978-1-4020-5281-1_179. [112]

Forman, S. and L. Steen (1999), *Beyond Eighth Grade: Functional Mathematics for Life and Work*, National Center for Research in Vocational Education, University of California, Berkeley. [26]

Foundation for Young Australians (2017), *The New Basics: Big data reveals the skills young people need for the New Work Order*, https://www.fya.org.au/wp-content/uploads/2016/04/The-New-Basics_Update_Web.pdf. [64]

Frankenstein, M. (1989), *Relearning mathematics: A different third 'R' – Radical maths*, Free Association Books, London. [74]

Gal, I. (2006), *Assessment of adult numeracy in PIAAC: A conceptual and development framework (Unpublished manuscript prepared for OECD)*, University of Haifa, Haifa. [153]

Gal, I. (2002), "Adults' Statistical Literacy: Meanings, Components, Responsibilities", *International Statistical Review / Revue Internationale de Statistique*, Vol. 70/1, p. 1, http://dx.doi.org/10.2307/1403713. [75]

Gal, I. (2000), *Adult numeracy development: Theory, research, practice*, Hampton Press, Cresskill, N.J. [27]

Gal, I. and D. Tout (2014), "Comparison of PIAAC and PISA Frameworks for Numeracy and Mathematical Literacy", *OECD Education Working Papers*, No. 102, OECD Publishing, Paris, https://dx.doi.org/10.1787/5jz3wl63cs6f-en. [3]

Gal, I. et al. (2005), "Adult numeracy and its assessment in the ALL survey: A conceptual framework and pilot results", in Murray, S., Y. Clermont and M. Binkley (eds.), *Measuring Adult Literacy and Life Skills: New Frameworks for Assessment*, Ottawa: Statistics Canada.   [28]

Geiger, V., M. Goos and S. Dole (2014), "Students' perspectives on their numeracy development across the learning areas", in Li, Y. and G. Lappan (eds.), *Mathematics Curriculum in School Education*, Springer, New York.   [125]

Geiger, V., M. Goos and H. Forgasz (2015), "A rich interpretation of numeracy for the 21st century: A survey of the state of the field", *ZDM: The International Journal on Mathematics Education*, Vol. 47/4, pp. 531-548, http://dx.doi.org/10.1007/s11858-015-0708-1.   [54]

Geisinger, K. (2016), "21st century skills: What are they and how do we assess them?", *Applied Measurement in Education*, Vol. 29/4, pp. 245-249, http://dx.doi.org/10.1080/08957347.2016.1209207.   [164]

Gillespie, J. (2004), *The "Skills for Life" national survey of adult numeracy in England. What does it tell us? What further questions does it prompt?*, paper presented at ICME-10, the 10th International Congress on Mathematics Education, Copenhagen, Denmark.   [187]

Ginsburg, L., M. Manly and M. Schmitt (2006), *The Components of Numeracy (NCSALL Occasional Paper)*, Harvard Graduate School of Education, National Center for the Study of Adult Learning and Literacy, Cambridge, MA.   [29]

Goos, M., V. Geiger and S. Dole (2014), "Transforming professional practice in numeracy teaching", in Li, Y., E. Silver and S. Li (eds.), *Transforming Mathematics Instruction: Multiple Approaches and Practices*, Springer, Cham, http://dx.doi.org/10.1007/978-3-319-04993-9_6.   [124]

Greeno, J. (2003), "Situative research relevant to standards for school mathematics", in Kilpatrick, J., W. Martin and D. Schifter (eds.), *A Research Companion to Principles and Standards for School Mathematics*, National Council of Teachers of Mathematics, Reston, VA.   [108]

Greeno, J. (1991), "Number sense as situated knowing in a conceptual domain", *Journal for Research in Mathematics Education*, Vol. 22/3, pp. 170-218, http://dx.doi.org/10.2307/749074.   [199]

Griffin, P., B. McGaw and E. Care (eds.) (2012), *Assessment and Teaching of 21st Century Skills*, Springer, New York.   [65]

Griffiths, G. and R. Stone (2013), *Teaching Adult Numeracy: Principles and Practice*, Open University Press, Maidenhead.   [60]

Grotlüschen, A. et al. (2016), "Adults with Low Proficiency in Literacy or Numeracy", *OECD Education Working Papers*, No. 131, OECD Publishing, Paris, https://dx.doi.org/10.1787/5jm0v44bnmnx-en.   [195]

Hagedorn, L. et al. (2003), *Frameworks for adult numeracy education: A survey and discussion*, National Literacy Secretariat, Ontario.   [152]

Harris, M. (1991), *Schools, Mathematics and Work*, Falmer Press, London.   [132]

Hoogland, K. et al. (2018), "Changing representation in contextual mathematical problems from descriptive to depictive: The effect on students' performance", *Studies in Educational Evaluation*, Vol. 58, pp. 122-131, http://dx.doi.org/10.1016/j.stueduc.2018.06.004. [134]

Hoogland, K. et al. (2016), "Representing contextual mathematical problems in descriptive or depictive form: Design of an instrument and validation of its uses", *Studies in Educational Evaluation*, Vol. 50, pp. 22-32, http://dx.doi.org/10.1016/j.stueduc.2016.06.005. [142]

Hoogland, K. and D. Tout (2018), "Computer-based assessment of mathematics into the twenty-first century: pressures and tensions", *ZDM*, Vol. 50/4, pp. 675-686, http://dx.doi.org/10.1007/s11858-018-0944-2. [186]

Hoyles, C. et al. (2010), *Improving Mathematics at Work: The Need for Techno-Mathematical Literacies*, Routledge, London and New York. [93]

Hoyles, C., R. Noss and S. Pozzi (2001), "Proportional reasoning in nursing practice", *Journal for Research in Mathematics Education*, Vol. 32/1, p. 4, http://dx.doi.org/10.2307/749619. [55]

Hoyles, C. et al. (2002), *Mathematical Skills in the Workplace: Final Report to the Science Technology and Mathematics Council*, Institute of Education, University of London, Science, Technology and Mathematics Council, London, https://discovery.ucl.ac.uk/id/eprint/1515581/1/Hoyles2002MathematicalSkills.pdf. [30]

Hurst, C. (2014), "Big challenges and big opportunities: The power of 'Big Ideas' to change curriculum and the culture of teacher planning", in Anderson, J., M. Cavanagh and A. Prescott (eds.), *Curriculum in Focus: Research Guided Practice. Proceedings of the 37th annual conference of the Mathematics Education Research Group of Australasia (MERGA)*, MERGA, Sydney, https://www.merga.net.au/Public/Public/Publications/Annual_Conference_Proceedings/2014_MERGA_CP.aspx. [7]

Hurst, C. and D. Hurrell (2014), "Developing the big ideas of number", *International Journal of Educational Studies in Mathematics*, Vol. 1/2, pp. 1-18. [8]

Johnston, B. (1994), "Critical numeracy?", *Fine Print*, Vol. 16/4, pp. 7-12. [31]

Johnston, B. and T. Maguire (2005), "Adult numeracy: Policy and practice in global contexts of lifelong learning", Adult Literacy and Numeracy Australian Research Consortium (ALNARC), School of Education, Victoria University, Melbourne. [40]

Jonas, N. (2018), "Numeracy practices and numeracy skills among adults", *OECD Education Working Papers*, No. 177, OECD Publishing, Paris, https://dx.doi.org/10.1787/8f19fc9f-en. [32]

Jones, G., C. Langrall and C. Thornton (2002), "Elementary students' access to powerful mathematical ideas", in English, L. (ed.), *Handbook of International Research in Mathematics Education*, Lawrence Erlbaum Associate, Mahwah, New Jersey. [5]

Jones, S. (2006), *Designing Numeracy in PIAAC (Background paper prepared for the OECD-Canada Expert Technical Workshop on Numeracy, Ottawa, November 10, 2006)*, Ottawa. [154]

Jones, S. (1995), "The distribution of literacy", in *Literacy, Economy and Society: Results of the First International Adult Literacy Survey*, OECD and Statistics Canada, OECD Publishing, Paris. [33]

Jorgensen Zevenbergen, R. (2010), "Young workers and their dispositions towards mathematics: Tensions of a mathematical habitus in the retail industry", *Educational Studies in Mathematics*, Vol. 76/1, pp. 87-100, http://dx.doi.org/10.1007/s10649-010-9267-0. [100]

Karaali, G., E. Villafane-Hernandez and J. Taylor (2016), "What's in a name? A critical review of definitions of quantitative literacy, numeracy, and quantitative reasoning", *Numeracy*, Vol. 9/1, pp. 1-34, http://dx.doi.org/10.5038/1936-4660.9.1.2. [42]

Kent, P. et al. (2011), "Measurement in the workplace: The case of process improvement in manufacturing industry", *ZDM*, Vol. 43/5, pp. 747-758, http://dx.doi.org/10.1007/s11858-011-0359-9. [94]

Kent, P. et al. (2007), "Characterizing the use of mathematical knowledge in boundary-crossing situations at work", *Mind, Culture, and Activity*, Vol. 14/1-2, pp. 64-82, http://dx.doi.org/10.1080/10749030701307747. [113]

Kilpatrick, J., J. Swafford and B. Findell (eds.) (2001), "Mathematics Learning Study Committee, National Research Council: Conclusions and recommendations", in *Adding It Up: Helping Children Learn Mathematics*, National Academies, Washington, DC. [157]

Kindler, J. et al. (1996), *Certificates in General Education for Adults*, Adult, Community and Further Education Board, Melbourne, Victoria. [81]

Kirsch, I., A. Jungblut and P. Mosenthal (1998), "The measurement of adult literacy", in Murray, S., I. Kirsch and L. Jenkins (eds.), *Adult Literacy in OECD Countries: Technical Report on the First International Adult Literacy Survey*, National Center for Education Statistics, U.S. Department of Education, Washington, DC. [191]

Kirsch, I. and P. Mosenthal (1990), "Exploring document literacy: Variables underlying the performance of young adults", *Reading Research Quarterly*, Vol. 25/1, p. 5, http://dx.doi.org/10.2307/747985. [190]

Kuntze, S. et al. (2009), *Awareness of Big Ideas in Mathematics Classrooms (ABCmaths). Final report to the European Union about the EU-funded project "ABCmaths"*, European Union, https://www.researchgate.net/publication/301298435_Awareness_of_Big_Ideas_in_Mathematics_Classrooms_ABCmaths_Progress_report_Fortschrittsbericht_an_die_Europaische_Union_zum_EU-geforderten_Projekt_ABCmaths. [9]

Kuntze, S. et al. (2011), "Professional knowledge related to Big Ideas in Mathematics–an empirical study with pre-service teachers", in Pytlak, M., T. Rowland and E. Swoboda (eds.), *A Study of Teaching Practices to Issues in Teacher Education. Proceedings of the 7th Congress of the European Society for Research in Mathematics Education (pp. 2717-2726)*, ERME, Rzeszów, http://www.cerme7.univ.rzeszow.pl/WG/17a/CERME7_WG17A_Kuntze_et_al..pdf. [10]

Lave, J. (1988), *Cognition in Practice: Mind, Mathematics and Culture in Everyday Life*, Cambridge University Press, New York, http://dx.doi.org/10.1017/cbo9780511609268. [53]

Lindenskov, L. and T. Wedege (2001), *Numeracy as an Analytical Tool in Mathematics Education and Research*, Centre for Research in Learning Mathematics, Roskilde. [46]

Lowrie, T. and C. Diezmann (2009), "National numeracy tests: A graphic tells a thousand words", *Australian Journal of Education*, Vol. 53/2, pp. 141–158, https://research.acer.edu.au/aje/vol53/iss2/3. [158]

Maguire, T. and J. O'Donoghue (2002), "A grounded approach to practitioner training in Ireland: Some findings from a national survey of practitioners in adult basic education", in Johansen, L. and T. Wedege (eds.), *Numeracy for Empowerment and Democracy? Proceedings of the 8th International Conference of Adult Learning Mathematics*, Roskilde University, Centre for Research in Learning Mathematics, Roskilde. [184]

Maguire, T. and J. O'Donoghue (2003), "Numeracy concept sophistication - an organizing framework, a useful thinking tool", in Maass, J. and W. Schlöglmann (eds.), *Learning Mathematics to Live and Work in our World. Proceedings of the 10th international conference on Adults Learning Mathematics (ALM-10), Strobl, Austria*, ALM and Johannes Kepler Universität, Linz. [47]

Maguire, T. and A. Smith (2016), *Maths Eyes- A Concept with Potential*, Invited paper presented at TSG 6, ICME 13 (13th International Congress on Mathematical Education, Hamburg, 24-31 July 2016). [129]

Ma, L. (1999), *Knowing and teaching elementary mathematics: Teachers' understanding of fundamental mathematics in China and the United States*, Lawrence Erlbaum, Mahwah, N.J. [146]

Marr, B. and J. Hagston (2007), *Thinking Beyond Numbers: Learning Numeracy for the Future Workplace*, NCVER, Adelaide, https://www.ncver.edu.au/__data/assets/file/0017/5426/nl05002.pdf. [95]

Matthijsse, W. (2000), "Adult numeracy at the elementary level: Addition and subtraction up to 100", in Gal, I. (ed.), *Adult Numeracy Development: Theory, Research, Practice. Series on Literacy: Research, Policy, and Practice*, Hampton Press, Cresskill, NJ. [204]

Ma, X. (1999), "A meta-analysis of the relationship between anxiety toward mathematics and achievement in mathematics", *Journal for Research in Mathematics Education*, Vol. 30/5, pp. 520-540, http://dx.doi.org/10.2307/749772. [127]

Mayer, R. (2009), *Multimedia Learning (2nd edition)*, Cambridge University Press, New York. [178]

Mayer, R. (ed.) (2005), *The Cambridge Handbook of Multimedia Learning*, Cambridge University Press, http://dx.doi.org/10.1017/cbo9780511816819. [177]

Mcintosh, A., B. Reys and R. Reys (1992), "A proposed framework for examining basic number sense", *For the Learning of Mathematics*, Vol. 12/3, pp. 2-8. [18]

McLean, P. et al. (2012), *Australian Core Skills Framework: 5 Core Skills, 5 Levels of Performance, 3 Domains of Communication*, Australian Government, Canberra. [77]

McLeod, D. (1992), "Research on affect in mathematics education: A reconceptualization", in Grows, D. (ed.), *Handbook of Research on Mathematics Teaching and Learning*, Macmillan Publishing Company, New York. [159]

Moore, D. and G. Cobb (2000), "Statistics and mathematics: Tension and cooperation", *The American Mathematical Monthly*, Vol. 107/7, pp. 615-630, http://dx.doi.org/10.1080/00029890.2000.12005247. [205]

Murat, F. (2005), *Les compétences des adultes à l'écrit, en calcul et en compréhension orale (Report No.1044)*, INSEE, Paris, https://www.epsilon.insee.fr/jspui/bitstream/1/224/1/ip1044.pdf. [188]

Murnane, R., J. Willett and F. Levy (1995), "The Growing Importance of Cognitive Skills in Wage Determination", No. 5076, National Bureau of Economic Research, Cambridge, MA, http://www.nber.org/papers/w5076.pdf. [34]

Murray, S. (2006), *Reflections on the Rationale for, and Measurement of, Numeracy in PIAAC*, (Background paper prepared for the OECD-Canada Expert Technical Workshop on Numeracy, Ottawa, November 10, 2006), Statistics Canada, Ottawa. [155]

Murray, S., Y. Clermont and M. Binkley (eds.) (2005), *Measuring Adult Literacy and Life Skills: New frameworks for Assessment*, Catalogue No. 89-552-MIE, No. 13, Statistics Canada, Ottawa. [4]

National Council of Teachers of Mathematics (NCTM) (2017), *Catalyzing Change in High School Mathematics*, NCTM, Reston, VA, https://www.nctm.org/uploadedFiles/Standards_and_Positions/CatalyzingChangePublicReview.pdf. [87]

National Council of Teachers of Mathematics (NCTM) (2000), *Principles and Standards for School Mathematics*, NCTM, Reston, VA. [120]

National Institute of Adult Continuing Education (NIACE) (2011), *Numeracy Counts*, NIACE Committee of Inquiry on Adult Numeracy Learning. NIACE, Leicester, https://learningandwork.org.uk/wp-content/uploads/2020/02/Numeracy-Counts.pdf. [61]

National Research and Development Centre (NRDC) (2006), *Programme for the International Assessment of Adult Competencies: An Adult Numeracy Assessment Instrument for the UK*, (Background paper prepared for the OECD-Canada Expert Technical Workshop on Numeracy, November 10, 2006, Ottawa). National Research and Development Centre for Adult Literacy and Numeracy, London. [35]

Noss, R., C. Hoyles and S. Pozzi (2002), "Abstraction in Expertise: A Study of Nurses' Conceptions of Concentration", *Journal for Research in Mathematics Education*, Vol. 33/3, p. 204, http://dx.doi.org/10.2307/749725. [56]

Nunes, T. (1992), "Ethnomathematics and everyday cognition", in Grouws, D. (ed.), *Handbook of Research on Mathematics Teaching and Learning*, Macmillan, New York. [102]

Nunes, T., A. Schliemann and D. Carraher (1993), *Street Mathematics and School Mathematics*, Cambridge University Press, Cambridge. [103]

OECD (2019), "PISA 2018 Global Competence Framework", in *PISA 2018 Assessment and Analytical Framework*, OECD Publishing, Paris, https://dx.doi.org/10.1787/043fc3b0-en. [69]

OECD (2018), *PISA 2021 Mathematics Framework (Second Draft) EDU/PISA/GB(2018)19*, Directorate for Education and Skills, Programme For International Student Assessment. [123]

OECD (2017), *Building Skills for All in Australia: Policy Insights from the Survey of Adult Skills*, OECD Skills Studies, OECD Publishing, Paris, https://dx.doi.org/10.1787/9789264281110-en. [41]

OECD (2016), *Skills Matter: Further Results from the Survey of Adult Skills*, OECD Skills Studies, OECD Publishing, Paris, https://dx.doi.org/10.1787/9789264258051-en. [194]

OECD (2016), *The Survey of Adult Skills: Reader's Companion, Second Edition*, OECD Skills Studies, OECD Publishing, Paris, https://dx.doi.org/10.1787/9789264258075-en. [51]

OECD (2013), "Mathematics Framework", in *PISA 2012 Assessment and Analytical Framework: Mathematics, Reading, Science, Problem Solving and Financial Literacy*, OECD Publishing, Paris, https://dx.doi.org/10.1787/9789264190511-3-en. [122]

OECD (2013), *OECD Skills Outlook 2013: First Results from the Survey of Adult Skills*, OECD Publishing, Paris, https://dx.doi.org/10.1787/9789264204256-en. [161]

OECD (2005), *The Definition and Selection of Key Competencies. Executive Summary.*, https://www.oecd.org/pisa/35070367.pdf (accessed on 31st October 2016). [49]

OECD/Statistics Canada (2005), *Learning a Living: First Results of the Adult Literacy and Life Skills Survey*, OECD Publishing, Paris, https://dx.doi.org/10.1787/9789264010390-en. [36]

Ontario Ministry of Education (2006), *Number Sense and Numeration, Grades 4 to 6*, Ontario Department of Education, Toronto, http://www.eworkshop.on.ca/edu/resources/guides/NSN_vol_1_Big_Ideas.pdf. [14]

Palm, T. (2009), "Theory of authentic task situations", in Verschaffel, L. et al. (eds.), *Words and Worlds: Modelling Verbal Descriptions of Situations*, Sense Publishers, Rotterdam. [137]

Palm, T. (2008), "Impact of authenticity on sense making in word problem solving", *Educational Studies in Mathematics*, Vol. 67/1, pp. 37-58, http://dx.doi.org/10.1007/s10649-007-9083-3. [136]

Palm, T. (2008), "Performance assessment and authentic assessment: A conceptual analysis of the literature", *Practical Assessment, Research, and Evaluation*, Article 4, https://doi.org/10.7275/0qpc-ws45. [140]

Palm, T. (2006), "Word problems as simulations of real-world situations: a proposed framework", *For the Learning of Mathematics*, Vol. 26/1, pp. 42–47. [135]

Parshall, C. et al. (2002), *Practical Considerations in Computer-based Testing*, Springer-Verlag, New York. [165]

Partnership for 21st Century Skills (2016), *Framework for 21st Century Learning*, http://www.p21.org/storage/documents/docs/P21_framework_0816.pdf. [66]

Paulos, J. (1995), *A Mathematician Reads the Newspaper*, BasicBooks, New York. [72]

Paulos, J. (1988), *Innumeracy: Mathematical Illiteracy and its Consequences*, Hill and Wang, New York. [71]

Pellegrino, J. and M. Hilton (eds.) (2012), *Education for Life and Work: Developing Transferable Knowledge and Skills in the 21st Century*, The National Academies Press, Washington, DC, http://dx.doi.org/10.17226/13398. [67]

Peters, E. (2012), "Beyond comprehension: The role of numeracy in judgments and decisions", *Current Directions in Psychological Science*, Vol. 21/1, pp. 31-35, http://dx.doi.org/10.1177/0963721411429960. [15]

PIAAC Numeracy Expert Group (2009), "PIAAC Numeracy: A Conceptual Framework", *OECD Education Working Papers*, No. 35, OECD Publishing, Paris, https://dx.doi.org/10.1787/220337421165. [2]

PISA Mathematics Expert Group (2009), *PISA CBAM Item Types*, Australian Council for Educational research, Melbourne. (Unpublished manuscript). [182]

Presmeg, N. (2007), "The role of culture in teaching and learning mathematics", in Lester, F. (ed.), *Second Handbook of Research on Mathematics Teaching and Learning*, Information Age Publishers, New York. [104]

PwC (2015), *A Smart Move: Future-proofing Australia's Workforce by Growing Skills in Science, Technology, Engineering and Maths (STEM)*, https://www.pwc.com.au/pdf/a-smart-move-pwc-stem-report-april-2015.pdf. [86]

Quality and Qualifications Ireland (QQI) (2016), *General Learning P1GL0*, http://qsearch.qqi.ie/WebPart/AwardDetails?awardCode=P1GL0. [78]

Resnick, L. (1987), "The 1987 Presidential Address: Learning in school and out", *Educational Researcher*, Vol. 16/9, pp. 13-20, http://dx.doi.org/10.2307/1175725. [105]

Rogoff, B. and J. Lave (eds.) (1984), *Everyday Cognition: Its Development in Social Context*, Harvard University Press, Cambridge, MA. [106]

Roth, W. (2012), "The Work of Seeing Mathematically", in *Alternative Forms of Knowing (in) Mathematics*, SensePublishers, Rotterdam, http://dx.doi.org/10.1007/978-94-6091-921-3_11. [130]

Rutherford, F. and A. Ahlgren (1990), *Science for all Americans*, Oxford University Press, New York. [143]

Rychen, D. (2004), "An overarching conceptual framework for assessing key competences in an international context. Lessons from an interdisciplinary and policy-oriented approach", in Descy, P. and M. Tessaring (eds.), *The Foundations of Evaluation and Impact Research. Third report on vocational training research in Europe: Background report*, Office for Official Publications of the European Communities, Luxembourg, http://www.cedefop.europa.eu/files/BgR1_Rychen.pdf. [50]

Sabatini, J. and K. Bruce (2009), "PIAAC Reading Component: A Conceptual Framework", *OECD Education Working Papers*, No. 33, OECD Publishing, Paris, https://dx.doi.org/10.1787/220367414132. [193]

Saxe, G. (1992), *Culture and Cognitive Development: Studies in Mathematical Understanding*, Lawrence Erlbaum Associates, Hillsdale, NJ. [109]

Saxe, G. et al. (1996), "Culture and children's mathematical thinking", in Sternberg, R. and T. Ben-Zeev (eds.), *The Nature of Mathematical Thinking*, Lawrence Erlbaum Associates, Hillsdale, NJ. [110]

Saxe, G. and M. Gearhart (eds.) (1988), *Children's Mathematics (pp. 71-88)*, Jossey-Bass, San Francisco. [107]

Schliemann, A. and N. Acioly (1989), "Mathematical knowledge developed at work: The contribution of practice versus the contribution of schooling", *Cognition and Instruction*, Vol. 6/3, pp. 185-221, http://dx.doi.org/10.1207/s1532690xci0603_1. [111]

Schnotz, W. (2005), "An Integrated Model of Text and Picture Comprehension", in *The Cambridge Handbook of Multimedia Learning*, Cambridge University Press, http://dx.doi.org/10.1017/cbo9780511816819.005. [173]

Schnotz, W. (2002), "Commentary: Towards an integrated view of learning from text and visual displays", *Educational Psychology Review*, Vol. 14/1, pp. 101-120, http://dx.doi.org/10.1023/a:1013136727916. [172]

Schnotz, W. et al. (2010), "Creative thinking and problem solving with depictive and descriptive representations", in Verschaffel, L. et al. (eds.), *Use of Representations in Reasoning and Problem Solving - Analysis and Improvement*, Routledge, London. [176]

Schnotz, W. and M. Bannert (2003), "Construction and interference in learning from multiple representation", *Learning and Instruction*, Vol. 13/2, pp. 141-156, http://dx.doi.org/10.1016/s0959-4752(02)00017-8. [174]

Schnotz, W. and C. Kürschner (2007), "External and internal representations in the acquisition and use of knowledge: visualization effects on mental model construction", *Instructional Science*, Vol. 36/3, pp. 175-190, http://dx.doi.org/10.1007/s11251-007-9029-2. [175]

Schwab, K. (2016), *The Fourth Industrial Revolution: What it Means, How to Respond*, http://www.weforum.org/agenda/2016/01/the-fourth-industrial-revolution-what-it-means-and-how-to-respond/. [70]

Secretary's Commission on Achieving Necessary Skills (SCANS) (1991), *What Work Requires of Schools: A SCANS Report for America 2000*, U.S. Department. of Labor, Washington, DC. [85]

Shute, V. et al. (2016), "Advances in the science of assessment", *Educational Assessment*, Vol. 21/1, pp. 34-59, http://dx.doi.org/10.1080/10627197.2015.1127752. [166]

Siemon, D. (2017), "Targeting 'big ideas' in mathematics", *Teacher Magazine*, http://www.teachermagazine.com.au/articles/targeting-big-ideas-in-mathematics. [12]

Siemon, D., J. Bleckly and D. Neal (2012), "Working with the Big Ideas in number and the Australian curriculum: Mathematics", in Atweh, B. et al. (eds.), *Engaging the Australian National Curriculum: Mathematics – Perspectives from the Field*, http://www2.merga.net.au/sites/default/files/editor/books/1/Chapter%202%20Siemon.pdf. [13]

Sommerauer, P. and O. Müller (2014), "Augmented reality in informal learning environments: A field experiment in a mathematics exhibition", *Computers & Education*, Vol. 79, pp. 59-68, http://dx.doi.org/10.1016/j.compedu.2014.07.013. [170]

Stacey, K. (2015), "The real world and the mathematical world", in Stacey, K. and R. Turner (eds.), *Assessing Mathematical Literacy: The PISA Experience*, Springer, New York. [138]

Steen, L. (2004), "Data, shapes, symbols: Achieving balance in school mathematics", in Madison, B. and L. Steen (eds.), *Quantitative Literacy: Why Numeracy Matters for Schools and Colleges*, Mathematical Association of America, Washington, DC, http://www.statlit.org/pdf/2003-Steen-QL-Data-Shapes-Symbols.pdf. [118]

Steen, L. (ed.) (1990), *On the Shoulders of Giants: New Approaches to Numeracy*, The National Academies Press, Washington, DC, http://www.nap.edu/openbook.php?isbn=0309042348. [11]

Straesser, R. (2015), "'Numeracy at work': a discussion of terms and results from empirical studies", *ZDM Mathematics Education*, Vol. 47/4, pp. 665-674, http://dx.doi.org/10.1007/s11858-015-0689-0. [96]

Straesser, R. (2003), "Mathematics at work: Adults and artefacts", in Maasz, J. and W. Schloeglmann (eds.), *Learning Mathematics to Live and Work in our World: Proceedings of the 10th International Conference on Adults Learning Mathematics (pp. 30-37)*, Johannes Kepler Universitat, Linz, https://www.alm-online.net/images/ALM/conferences/ALM10/proceedings/alm-03-proceedingsalm10.pdf. [114]

Sullivan, P. (2011), "Teaching mathematics: Using research-informed strategies", *Australian Education Review*, Vol. 59, http://research.acer.edu.au/cgi/viewcontent.cgi?article=1022&context=aer. [147]

Sweller, J. (2010), "Element interactivity and intrinsic, extraneous, and germane cognitive load", *Educational Psychology Review*, Vol. 22/2, pp. 123-138, http://dx.doi.org/10.1007/s10648-010-9128-5. [180]

Sweller, J. (2005), "Implications of cognitive load theory for multimedia learning", in Mayer, R. (ed.), *The Cambridge Handbook of Multimedia Learning*, Cambridge University Press, http://dx.doi.org/10.1017/cbo9780511816819.003. [179]

Tertiary Education Commission (2008), *Learning Progressions for Adult Numeracy*, Wellington, https://ako.ac.nz/knowledge-centre/learning-progressions-for-adult-numeracy/. [79]

Thompson, P. (1995), "Notation, convention, and quantity in elementary mathematics", in Sowder, J. and B. Schappelle (eds.), *Providing a Foundation of Teaching Mathematics in the Middle Grades*, Suny Press, Albany, NY. [19]

Tobias, S. (1993), *Overcoming Math Anxiety*, W. W. Norton & Company, New York. [128]

Tout, D. (2006), *Review of Numeracy Component of PIAAC (Background paper prepared for the OECD Canada Expert Technical Workshop on Numeracy, Ottawa, November 10, 2006)*, Centre for Adult Education, Melbourne. [156]

Tout, D. et al. (2017), *Review of the PIAAC Numeracy Assessment Framework: Final Report*, Australian Council for Educational Research, Camberwell, https://research.acer.edu.au/transitions_misc/29. [1]

Tout, D. and I. Gal (2015), "Perspectives on numeracy: Reflections from international assessments", *ZDM*, Vol. 47/4, pp. 691-706, http://dx.doi.org/10.1007/s11858-015-0672-9. [37]

Tout, D. et al. (2020), *PIAAC Numeracy Task Complexity Schema: Factors that impact on item difficulty*, Australian Council for Educational Research, Camberwell, http://dx.doi.org/10.37517/978-1-74286-609-3. [141]

Tout, D. and M. Schmitt (2002), "The inclusion of numeracy in adult basic education", in Comings, J., B. Garner and C. Smith (eds.), *The Annual Review of Adult Learning and Literacy: Volume 3*, Jossey-Bass, San Francisco. [38]

Tout, D. and J. Spithill (2015), "The challenges and complexities of writing items to test mathematical literacy", in Stacey, K. and R. Turner (eds.), *Assessing Mathematical Literacy: The PISA Experience*, Springer, New York. [183]

Turner, E. et al. (2009), "'Everything is math in the whole world': Integrating critical and community knowledge in authentic mathematical investigations with elementary Latina/o students", *Mathematical Thinking and Learning*, Vol. 11/3, pp. 136-157, http://dx.doi.org/10.1080/10986060903013382. [131]

Turner, R., W. Blum and M. Niss (2015), "Using competencies to explain mathematical item demand: A work in progress", in Stacey, K. and R. Turner (eds.), *Assessing Mathematical Literacy: The PISA Experience*, Springer, New York. [192]

U.S. Department of Education (2013), *College and Career Readiness Standards for Adult Education*, Office of Vocational and Adult Education, US Department of Education, Washington, DC, https://lincs.ed.gov/publications/pdf/CCRStandardsAdultEd.pdf. [80]

UNESCO (2016), "Chapter 15: Literacy and Numeracy", in *Global Education Monitoring Report 2016. Education for People and Planet: Creating Sustainable Futures for All*, United Nations Educational, Scientific and Cultural Organization, Paris, http://unesdoc.unesco.org/images/0024/002457/245752e.pdf. [196]

UNESCO (1997), *International Standard Classification of Education: ISCED*, United Nations Educational, Scientific and Cultural Organization, Paris, https://unesdoc.unesco.org/ark:/48223/pf0000146967. [48]

Utts, J. (2003), "What educated citizens should know about statistics and probability", *The American Statistician*, Vol. 57/2, pp. 74-79, http://dx.doi.org/10.1198/0003130031630. [73]

van den Heuvel-Panhuizen, M. and K. Gravemeijer (1991), "Tests are not all that bad: An attempt to change the appearance of written tests in mathematics instruction at the primary school level", in Streefland, L. (ed.), *Realistic Mathematics Education in Primary School*, Utrecht. [121]

van Gog, T., F. Paas and J. Sweller (2010), "Cognitive load theory: Advances in research on worked examples, animations, and cognitive load measurement", *Educational Psychology Review*, Vol. 22/4, pp. 375-378, http://dx.doi.org/10.1007/s10648-010-9145-4. [181]

Verschaffel, L. et al. (2009), *Words and Worlds: Modeling Verbal Descriptions of Situations*, Brill | Sense, http://dx.doi.org/10.1163/9789087909383. [139]

Victorian Curriculum and Assessment Authority (VCAA) (2008), *Curriculum Planning Guide: Literacy and Numeracy Skills Strand Numeracy Skills Units. First Edition*, Victorian Curriculum and Assessment Authority, Victoria. [82]

Voogt, J. and N. Roblin (2012), "A comparative analysis of international frameworks for 21st century competences: Implications for national curriculum policies", *Journal of Curriculum Studies*, Vol. 44/3, pp. 299-321, http://dx.doi.org/10.1080/00220272.2012.668938. [68]

Wagner, D. and B. Davis (2010), "Feeling number: Grounding number sense in a sense of quantity", *Educational studies in Mathematics*, Vol. 74/1, pp. 39-51. [16]

Wake, G. (2015), "Preparing for workplace numeracy: A modelling perspective", *ZDM Mathematics Education*, Vol. 47/4, pp. 675-689, http://dx.doi.org/10.1007/s11858-015-0704-5. [97]

Watson, J. and R. Callingham (2003), "Statistical literacy: A complex hierarchical construct", *Statistics Education Research Journal*, Vol. 2/2, pp. 3-46. [76]

Wedege, T. (2010), "People's mathematics in working life: Why is it invisible?", *Adults Learning Mathematics*, Vol. 5/1, pp. 89-97. [116]

Wedege, T. (2004), "Sociomathematics: Researching adults' mathematics at work", in Maasz, J. [115]
and W. Schloeglmann (eds.), *Learning Mathematics to Live and Work in our World: Proceedings of the 10th International Conference on Adults Learning Mathematics in Strobl (Austria), 29th June to 2nd July 2003 (pp. 38-48)*, Johannes Kepler Universitat Linz.

Weeks, K. et al. (2013), "Safety in Numbers 7: veni, vidi, duci: A grounded theory evaluation of [98]
nursing students' medication dosage calculation problem-solving schemata construction", *Nurse Education in Practice*, Vol. 13/2, pp. e78-e87, http://dx.doi.org/10.1016/j.nepr.2012.10.014.

Williams, J. and G. Wake (2006), "Black boxes in workplace mathematics", *Educational Studies* [117]
in Mathematics, Vol. 64/3, pp. 317-343, http://dx.doi.org/10.1007/s10649-006-9039-z.

Willis, S. (1990), *Being numerate: What counts?*, Australian Council for Educational Research, [39]
Victoria.

Windisch, H. (2015), "Adults with low literacy and numeracy skills: A literature review on policy [58]
intervention", *OECD Education Working Papers*, No. 123, OECD Publishing, Paris, https://dx.doi.org/10.1787/5jrxnjdd3r5k-en.

Yang, D., R. Reys and B. Reys (2009), "Number sense strategies used by pre-service teachers [17]
in Taiwan", *International Journal of Science and Mathematics Education*, Vol. 7/2, pp. 383-403.

Yasukawa, K., T. Brown and S. Black (2013), "Production workers' literacy and numeracy [133]
practices: Using cultural-historical activity theory (CHAT) as an analytical tool", *Journal of Vocational Education & Training*, Vol. 65/3, pp. 369-384, http://dx.doi.org/10.1080/13636820.2013.820214.

Yasukawa, K. et al. (eds.) (2018), *Numeracy as Social Practice: Global and Local Perspectives*, [52]
Routledge, New York and London, http://dx.doi.org/10.4324/9781315269474.

Zevenbergen, R. (2004), "Technologizing numeracy: Intergenerational differences in working [99]
mathematically in new times", *Educational Studies in Mathematics*, Vol. 56/1, pp. 97-117.

Notes

[1] The term "mathematical" is used here as inclusive of situations where *statistical* or *probabilistic* information may appear or where statistical thinking or statistical literacy are required as well. Such usage is made for brevity and convenience only. It is acknowledged that statistics is not a branch of mathematics, and that statistical reasoning and statistical literacy have unique elements, concepts and processes which are not mathematical in nature (Moore and Cobb, 2000[205]).

[2] For more discussion and examples of the reading components tasks see OECD (2016[51]), *The Survey of Adult Skills: Reader's Companion, Second Edition.*

4 PIAAC Cycle 2 assessment framework: Adaptive problem solving

Samuel Greiff (Chair), University of Luxembourg

Art Graesser, University of Memphis

Dragos Iliescu, University of Bucharest

Jean-François Rouet, Centre national de la recherche scientifique, University of Poitiers

Katharina Scheiter, University of Tübingen

Ronny Scherer, University of Oslo

With assistance from Juliana Gottschling and Jan Dörendal, University of Luxembourg

This chapter defines the concept of adaptive problem solving (APS) in the second cycle of PIAAC. The concept of APS accounts for the fact that we need to be vigilant, adaptive, and willing to modify our plans when interacting with the social, physical, and technological world of the 21st century. In this framework chapter, the cognitive and metacognitive processes that successful people engage into when solving problems and when adapting to changing conditions are described. In this, the PIAAC assessment of APS draws from a large set of information contexts and task dimensions that drive overall APS performance and individual proficiency levels. Several example items, considerations on item scoring and data capturing as well as a thorough discussion of the relation between APS and other competencies provide a comprehensive overview of the APS measurement framework for PIAAC.

Introduction

Rapid changes in the social, physical, and technological world require individuals to be more vigilant to changes, more adaptive, and more willing to modify their plans in pursuit of their goals. It is therefore indisputable that the competence to solve problems and to adapt to changing conditions is of crucial importance in the 21st century, where citizens are faced with increasingly complex technologies, social systems and subject matters (Levy and Murnane, 2006[1]; National Research Council, 2012[2]). The need for problem solving is ubiquitous in the workplace, as well as everyday life, for most adults. For instance, Felstead et al. (2013[3]) conclude that problem solving skills are more important than numerical or communication skills for a worker to be successful, a finding that is likely to generally apply to economies that are service-oriented. Problem solving is therefore generally important to assess as an overarching construct.

The Programme for the International Assessment of Adult Competencies (PIAAC) included a measure of problem-solving proficiency in its first cycle in 2011. In addition to core dimensions of adult skills, i.e., reading component skills, literacy, and numeracy, the survey assessed problem solving in technology-rich environments (PS-TRE) for individuals aged 16 to 65. PS-TRE focused on goal setting, monitoring, and planning in technology-rich environments (OECD, 2012[4]) and assessed proficiency in the use of specific digital applications to access, search, manage, interpret, and evaluate information. The second cycle of PIAAC in 2022 will focus on adaptive problem solving (APS). "Adaptive" underlines that problem solving is a process that takes place in complex environments and that this process is not a static sequence of a number of pre-set steps but rather a constant attempt to solve a problem. Hence, while problems themselves can either be static (i.e., with no changes in the given states or the goal states) or dynamic (i.e., with changes occurring in the problem situation), the process of problem solving when confronted with dynamic problems is adaptive (i.e., problem solvers need to adapt to the dynamic nature of such problems).

There are three important core aspects that distinguish APS from previous large-scale assessments of problem solving, such as PS-TRE or as implemented in the assessment of the Programme for International Student Assessment (PISA):

- First, the competence to handle dynamic and changing problem situations has become increasingly important in today's society, and therefore the need for skills that enable adults to adjust their thinking and reasoning to novel and changing information has grown crucially. The assessment of APS will therefore focus on dynamic problems that require problem solvers to monitor their problem solving and to adapt their initial solution to new information or circumstances.

- Second, the characteristics of the typical problems that individuals encounter at work and everyday life have been changing over the last five decades, in part because of radical changes in digital technologies and communication media (Autor, Levy and Murnane, 2003[5]). The solutions to particular problems are also more distributed over time as people take advantage of social and digital resources that have particular constraints in access and timetables. This new wealth of information, and the shift in the information environment that people are confronted with, will be reflected in the characteristics of the tasks included in the APS assessment, i.e., the information environments (physical, social, and digital) and problem contexts (personal, work, and social community) in which tasks will be situated.

- Finally, cognitive processes are inherently bound to the problem-solving process and have always been an important aspect of the problem-solving assessment. However, especially in highly adaptive and higher difficulty problems, problem solvers also need to strongly engage in metacognitive processes (i.e., the ability to calibrate one's comprehension of the problem, evaluate potential solutions, and monitor progress towards the goals). Consequently, the assessment of APS in the second cycle of PIAAC will put emphasis also on metacognitive processes.

The purpose of this document is to provide an assessment framework following the conceptual framework paper for APS (Greiff et al., 2017[6]) to guide the construction of APS items to be used in the second cycle of PIAAC as well as the definition of the proficiency scale for APS.

Adapting to dynamically changing situations: The importance of adaptive problem solving

The ability to quickly and flexibly adapt to new circumstances, learn throughout life, and turn knowledge into action has always been important for full participation in labour markets and society (National Research Council, 2012[2]). However, in a world that has become increasingly and dynamically changing, and which provides a plethora of information from different resources, the need to flexibly adapt to unexpected changes has become more and more important. Over the course of a single day, an individual can be a purchaser of consumer goods, an organiser of local transportation, a holiday planner (searching for flights and accommodation arrangements in hotels or house swaps), a financial planner, and a home decorator. These various activities address multiple goals in non-routine ways that require APS skills. People need to adjust, for example, to prices of commodities that change overnight, a strike of transportation workers, internet sites that go down, and people who cancel appointments. Adapting to these unexpected changes in these various environments requires problem solvers to consider different resources in the physical, social, and digital environments, in addition to their own mental activities. Therefore, APS is particularly important to assess as problems often dynamically change during the course of problem solving, which then requires constant monitoring and, if necessary, adaptation of the original problem solution. These changes occur because of unexpected physical and/or social events in the environment and because of unintended consequences of the problem solver's actions.

It is important to emphasise that the assessment of APS in the second cycle of PIAAC goes beyond what was assessed in previous OECD international assessments of problem solving. For one, the problems assessing individual problem solving in PISA 2009 were entirely static (i.e., the given states and goal states did not change) and preceded the collection of data on computers. In PISA 2012, the assessment of problem-solving competency was computer-based and allowed the implementation of interactive problem situations in addition to static ones (OECD, 2014[7]). The items became dynamic in the sense that the problem solver needed to interact with the problem environment in order to find all the relevant information to solve the problem. PISA 2015 then focused on collaborative problem solving with computer agents that interacted with a problem solver through chat facilities and actions performed in shared workspaces (OECD, 2017[8]). It is important to stress that the term *dynamic* is broadened in the assessment of APS as it refers not only to the exploration of the environment, i.e. the interaction between the problem solver and the information context, but also to changes in the problem situation to which the initial solution needs to be adapted to. When we refer to "dynamic" in the following, we always use the term in this broadened manner.

As mentioned before, problem solving was already assessed in the first cycle of PIAAC. The PS-TRE assessment was conceived to monitor the problem solver's information-processing skills when operating in technology-rich environments using information and communications technology (ICT) skills. Core to the PS-TRE assessment therefore was the understanding and evaluation of meaningful information available in technology-rich environments, including simulated websites, e-mail and spreadsheet environments (OECD, 2012[4]). The assessment of APS will also use technology-rich environments. However, these environments will rather form the context in which the problem unfolds dynamically and to which the problem solvers need to adapt their initial problem solution.

The cognitive and metacognitive components of adaptive problem solving

As mentioned before, successful problem solving requires the problem solver to engage in cognitive as well as metacognitive processes. Previous assessments of problem solving have incorporated core cognitive theories of problem solving (Funke, 2010[9]; Mayer and Wittrock, 2006[10]). They start with the definition of a problem as having a given state, a goal state, a set of legal operators to get from the given to the goal state, and plans for solutions to subtasks. The PISA 2012 and 2015 assessments identified the problem-solving components as 1) exploring, understanding, and representing the problem, 2) searching, planning, and executing potential solutions, and 3) monitoring and reflecting on the progress towards solving the problem. The assessment of APS in the second cycle of PIAAC will have the following *cognitive* problem-solving components that are similar but not exactly the same: *defining the problem* – the same as 1) –; *searching for information*, and *applying a solution* – these latter two components mapping onto 2) –, whereas the explicit assessment of metacognition will incorporate 3).

The cognitive processes become more complicated in APS where the problem solution might need to be adapted in reaction to dynamically changing situations. That is, physical, social, and digital worlds are frequently undergoing changes that an adaptive problem solver must accommodate. The problem solver faces the additional challenge of having to continuously monitor, often through conscious effort, whether the current problem state remains the same or changes throughout the course of problem solving, whether operators that are already known from similar problem-solving attempts are still available or whether new ones need to be identified, and which plans can be executed using the available resources at a given point in time. The second cycle of PIAAC will contain items that measure metacognitive processes in addition to cognitive processes. The role of metacognitive processes becomes more important to the extent that problems are more complex and difficult to comprehend (requiring comprehension calibration), the problems change dynamically (requiring evaluation and re-evaluation of the suitability of operators and plans), and progress towards the solution becomes more difficult to discern (requiring monitoring and reflecting on progress towards the goals).

Both cognitive and metacognitive processes will be assessed at three stages of problem solving: defining the problem, searching for a solution, and applying a solution. There are cognitive processes and metacognitive processes required at each stage, with some items tapping both processes and others focusing on either cognition or metacognition.

In a nutshell, in the second cycle of PIAAC, the APS assessment will put greater emphasis on individuals' capacity to a) flexibly and dynamically adapt their problem-solving strategies to a dynamically changing environment, b) identify and select among a range of available physical, social, and digital resources, and c) monitor and reflect on their progress in solving problems through metacognitive processes. The assessment tasks will therefore reflect the fact that solutions to problems in the modern world require a reflexive, flexible, and adaptive mind.

In the following, we will first define APS and introduce two tasks to exemplify how APS can be assessed. We then detail the task dimensions that define each APS tasks and describe the required cognitive and metacognitive processes. The next section describes the factors that may be used to describe the APS proficiency levels and is followed by a summary of the assessment of APS. We close with a comparison of APS with other core competencies, i.e., literacy, numeracy, and digital competency.

Definition of adaptive problem solving

Explanation of the definition of adaptive problem solving

As mentioned above, there are three core aspects that are represented in the conceptual framework (Greiff et al., 2017[6]) and in the assessment framework of APS. First of all, in a dynamically changing world, it is essential to react to unforeseen changes and new information in a flexible and adaptive way. This is represented in the term "adaptive" in APS. Second, as the amount of information available in the world of the 21st century is ever increasing, we are faced with a wealth of information from different sources. This expansion of information environments needs to be taken in account and will be reflected in the tasks developed for APS, which will be situated in a range of information environments and contexts. Finally, whereas cognitive aspects have always been an important part of problem solving, the necessary change of plans and approaches to a problem and the adaptability and flexibility coming along with this require a stronger focus on metacognition in addition to the existing focus on cognition. Thus, APS puts a strong focus on metacognitive aspects throughout the process of problem solving.

The definition of adaptive problem solving in the second cycle of PIAAC is as follows:

> "Adaptive problem solving involves the capacity to achieve one's goals in a dynamic situation, in which a method for solution is not immediately available. It requires engaging in cognitive and metacognitive processes to define the problem, search for information, and apply a solution in a variety of information environments and contexts". (Greiff et al., 2017[6])

Each part of this definition is explained in more detail below.

Adaptive problem solving…

The term "adaptive" stresses the adaptive nature of problem solving irrespective of the environment or the context in which the problem solving takes place. This underlines that problem solving is a process that takes place in complex environments and that this process is not a static sequence of a number of pre-set steps. Rather there could be an adaptive nature to the problem-solving process in each step. Put differently, problem solvers need to remain open and pay attention to changes in the situation and adapt their problem-solving approach accordingly. The term "adaptive" readily connects to notions such as cognitive flexibility or plasticity, but is broader in its meaning and encompasses the entire set of cognitive and non-cognitive components involved in APS.

"Problem solving" was chosen as a core term for the focus on situations that require non-routine solutions (as opposed to tasks, see below) independent of the specific content domain. Problem solving is generally regarded as one of the most ubiquitous activities that is necessary to successfully master challenges in unforeseen situations, be it in educational contexts, on the job, or in private life. Because problems can occur in a number of settings, the process of problem solving, including its different components, can be applied across different domains. In fact, a transversal understanding of problem solving has recently been included in several large-scale assessments, such as PIAAC and PISA, but those assessments differed in that they did not focus on the "adaptive" nature of problem solving in the 21st century.

…involves the capacity to achieve one's goals in a dynamic situation…

The broad term of "capacity" is meant to convey that APS is a complex proficiency that is composed of a number of more specific sets of skills, most notably cognitive and metacognitive aspects that are explicitly targeted in the assessment. APS also includes the motivation to deal with the problem situation and to face the challenges of the problem situation and its unforeseen changes. Through this, the motivational aspect is implicitly part of the assessment, but it is not an explicit part of the core APS assessment.

Problem solving is a goal-directed activity, in which the problem solver is embedded into a situation that needs to be mastered successfully and this situation may be dynamic. That is, as opposed to static problem solving that takes place exclusively in situations that have no dynamic component, which implies that all relevant information is available at the outset and that there is no change in the problem setup, the constraints, or the goals have to be foreseen. When engaging into APS, problem solvers need to anticipate, incorporate, and deal with the many types of dynamic changes that might happen while moving from an initial state to a desired goal state. APS therefore refers to the process of problem solving in dynamically changing situations. More precisely, the dynamic aspect of the problem situation implies on the one hand that relevant information from different sources might need to be acquired throughout the process, something that has been considered relevant in previous assessments of problem solving (cf. the assessment of problem solving in PISA 2012). However, in addition to the capacity of exploring a problem situation, the problem solver also needs to deal with various types of changes in the situation and needs to react to these changes. Put differently, problem solvers need to monitor their progress, the problem state, and the environment and context in an attempt to pay tribute to the dynamic nature of the overall problem situation that might exhibit constant change or hardly any change at all. From an assessment perspective, the inclusion of the dynamic component relies on the use of technologically based assessments that allow for the type of items in which such dynamic changes can be implemented. In this, the second cycle of PIAAC is a technology-based assessment that allows a broadening of the scope of the proficiencies through the technical means and, through this, new item formats available to test developers.

…in which a method for solution is not immediately available.

This part of the definition alludes to a core component of virtually any problem-solving definition: at the outset, the path to the solution and the solution itself are not immediately clear and require that the problem solver initiates a process that, ultimately, leads to the goal state. This distinguishes problem solving from a mere task, in which a solution usually is readily available. It also shows that, even in specific domains such as mathematics or science not all items are problem solving items as some of them could be solved merely by knowing the correct answer, and it also stresses the non-routine aspect of the problems in this domain. In this, there is a direct link between existing frameworks of problem solving (e.g., problem solving in PISA 2012 or collaborative problem solving in PISA 2015), but the notion of a solution that is not immediately accessible is even more central to APS because changes in the problem setup or the problem situation require a re-examination of initial solutions and, in some cases, new approaches to solve the presented problem.

…It requires engaging in cognitive and metacognitive processes…

Cognitive and metacognitive components are both critical aspects of APS. Problem solving always requires some cognition such as organising and integrating information into a mental model or evaluating operators as to whether they are relevant for reaching the desired goal state. But metacognition, such as setting a goal or reflecting on progress, is equally important. In fact, both components are often intertwined in a way that makes it difficult to separate them and it will be a challenge in the assessment to do so. While the role of metacognition has been acknowledged in previous assessment frameworks, it has often not been targeted explicitly but rather been considered as a part implicitly included into the assessment. Here, APS differs in the sense that dealing with a dynamic situation in an adaptive way always requires a certain level of metacognition. For instance, if the situation changes, without a sufficient level of metacognitive awareness, this change will go by unnoticed and will not lead to a solution of the problem. Thus, the conceptual framework (Greiff et al., 2017[6]) stresses that the world of the 21st century cannot be successfully mastered without a certain level of metacognition. The assessment of APS will be designed in a way that it clearly reflects the need for metacognition and will also develop items that primarily target the problem solver's metacognitive proficiency.

…to define the problem, search for information, and apply a solution…

The APS framework defines three broad problem-solving stages that are logically ordered from first defining the problem, second searching for information, and, finally, applying a solution. However, this is a schematic description and any problem-solving activity switches between the different stages or might even employ them simultaneously. The description here is meant to convey that usually one of those activities prevails. The assessment will aim to elicit problem solvers' cognitive and metacognitive proficiencies along these three stages in a comprehensive way.

In each of the three stages, both cognitive and metacognitive processes are relevant and while there is some overlap, many of the processes are distinct for a specific stage. In fact, the delineation of the problem-solving process into different stages is ubiquitously found in the problem-solving literature even though there is some disagreement as to the number and the nature of the stages. In APS, the problem solver is faced with the challenge that a change in the setup might occur at any time, requiring constant monitoring and a readiness to react throughout these stages. That is, as compared to other problem-solving approaches, a once derived definition, a set of information, or a chosen path towards solution might become obsolete, but instead, a new definition, new information, or a new path towards the solution needs to be derived.

…in a variety of information environments and contexts.

This final part of the definition stresses that in information-rich environments – and virtually all of today's problems are embedded into such – the different sources from which the information originates and the different contexts are of high relevance. Information can be gathered from physical, social, or digital environments, which is meant to cover the ubiquitous nature from which the problem solver derives the knowledge about a problem in today's world. In this, APS differs from previous problem-solving assessments that focused on specific sources of information such as the social environment in collaborative problem solving in PISA 2015 or on knowledge gathered on websites in the assessment of problem solving in technology-rich environments in the first cycle of PIAAC. In addition, as situations that require APS may occur throughout different contexts, there can be problems that are embedded into a personal, a work, or a social community context because good adaptive problem solvers must be able to apply their proficiency across contexts and derive their information from a comprehensive set of sources.

The next section outlines two example tasks, "Dinner Preparation" and "Stock Market", to give an exemplary understanding of what is meant by APS in terms of real-world situations. We then proceed with a more detailed description of the problem characteristics underlying APS tasks, the associated difficulty drivers, the cognitive and metacognitive processes involved, and define the assumed proficiency levels that determine the quality of the derived solution. We will link this formal description to both of the example tasks throughout this framework document to illustrate the process of APS.

Example tasks "Dinner Preparation" and "Stock Market"

The APS assessment in the second cycle of PIAAC will contain scenario-based tasks, that describe every day and working-life problems. In the following, we describe two examples of APS tasks, in order to illustrate how the principles of APS are transposed into practice. It is important to note that participants will learn how to interact with the provided environments before starting with the assessment. Also, the two units listed below are examples of how APS tasks can look like. None of the examples will be part of the final APS assessment.

- The first example, *Dinner Preparation*, covers an everyday life scenario in which the problem solver has to plan and accomplish different goals over the course of a day. Because of the often encountered need to adapt initial plans by reacting flexibly to changing circumstances and upcoming impasses, and by incorporating and dealing with new information, navigating through everyday life might be seen as the prototype of an APS task.

- The second example, *Stock Market*, describes a financial simulation in which the problem solver has to make buying and selling decisions for a number of companies, depending on their market evolution, in order to maximise profits. The problem is highly dynamic as the problem setup constantly changes and the problem solvers have to continuously adapt their solutions to the latest evolution of the problem environment.

Example task: Dinner Preparation

In the example unit *Dinner Preparation* (see Box 4.1), the problem solver is asked to use an interactive map to accomplish a set of pre-defined goals. The initially static situation becomes dynamic through obstacles that present a change in the presented problem and the available solutions.

Box 4.1 shows two example items for *Dinner Preparation*. The unit starts with a static planning task. In the first item, the problem solver needs to use an interactive map to find the fastest route to accomplish three goals, keeping a set of time constraints in mind. The problem solver needs to: take a child to school by a designated time, purchase ingredients for dinner, and return home by a designated time. This could be considered a standard problem-solving task, in which a solution needs to be found given some constraints that need to be satisfied. In the second item, the situation becomes dynamic as the problem solver has to deal with new circumstances that interfere with the initial problem solution. Impasses must be overcome and additional constraints need to be taken into consideration when adapting the initial problem solution.

Box 4.1. Example unit "Dinner Preparation"

General description of the problem background:

Planning and coordinating different, sometimes contradicting, goals are elementary parts of our everyday lives. This ranges from activities that involve single and multiple goals that have to be planned daily, to long-term goals, and they can arise in a variety of contexts, be it personal, work, or social. However, plans are also repeatedly thwarted by unforeseeable events, or changes in the initial situation. Successfully dealing with such dynamically changing situations, in which the solution is often not directly available requires everybody to engage into APS. More specifically, the emerging problem situation needs to be defined, information about how to approach the situation has to be considered, and the (new) solution has to be applied.

How the unit unfolds:

Imagine that you need to accomplish one single or even multiple goals over the course of the day, such as picking up the child from school, and getting the groceries for dinner. In order to accomplish both goals, you would plan the best route for the car trip, look up the driving times, and make a shopping list. At first, the situation seems to be manageable and quite predictable.

Example Item 1

Problem solvers are provided with a map that shows different locations and a sticky note that summarises the goals to be accomplished and the time constraints to be met. A clock shows the time of the day, information on the driving time can be viewed by clicking on the locations. In this first item, problem solvers need to navigate through the map by drawing lines in order to find the fastest way to a) take the child to school by 8.30 and to b) get to a market to buy the ingredients for dinner.

However, just as in real life, while on your way, you suddenly find that one of the local shops is closed and you need to come up with a different plan – you could for example go to a different store, call someone to get the missing ingredient, or change the dinner plans.

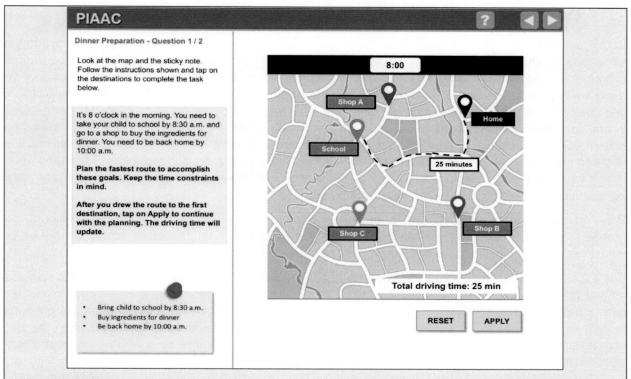

Example Item 2

When the problem solvers have planned their route, they get informed that their chosen market got closed due to a water leakage. Problem solvers need to adjust their route while keeping in mind the time constraints.

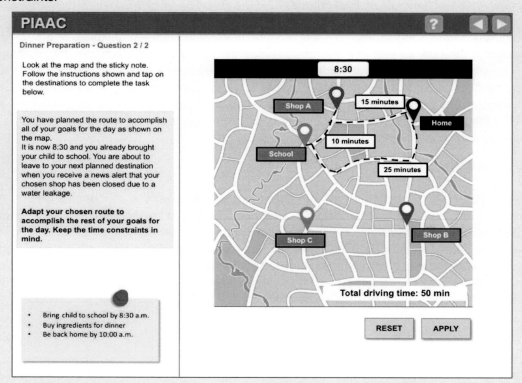

Example task: "Stock Market"

In the example unit *Stock Market* (see Box 4.2), problem solvers are provided with a stock market simulation, in which they begin with initial stock holdings in five companies, and a small disposable sum of cash that they can invest. They can sell stock for cash, or buy new stock with cash. Stock prices vary on a day-by-day basis. The situation describes a "continuous drip" problem, i.e., the problem is not turn-based, and does not progress to a new stage only after the problem solver commits to an action. It rather evolves in real-time, even if the problem solver does not perform an action – in this case, a new "day" comes on screen every 60 seconds. By judging the history of each company, problem solvers have to make a decision regarding the investment solution that will most likely yield a profit in the future. They then need to sell the undesirable investments that they hold in their portfolio and buy stock in the more promising companies, in order to maximise the value of their portfolio.

While the unit architecture may appear to be quite specialised (i.e., stock market, financial operations), the problem is, in fact, a knowledge-lean task. It does not contain any references to actual companies or industries, and the solution does not depend on specialised knowledge.

Box 4.2 shows two example items for *Stock Market*. In the first item, the problem solver needs to optimise an investment portfolio, while considering the current status and the performance of the five companies over a defined period of time. In the second item, the situation becomes complicated, as the previous pattern of performance for the five companies changes. An impasse is generated by having the two companies with a previous positive evolution turning to negative; this interferes with the initial problem solution and requires problem solvers to rethink their problem-solving strategy.

Box 4.2. Example unit "Stock Market"

General description of the problem background:

Most financially complex situations have a few characteristics in common: a limited number of options are assessed on the go, as part of a dynamically changing situation, in which the optimal state of the system, i.e., when to commit to a decision, is uncertain. Interestingly, financial transactions are typical in a large number of contexts, and are not limited to work, social, or community contexts. Complex financial transactions are now part of everyday life in virtually every culture and are consonant with the demands of the modern world. Throughout their lives, most people will have to solve problems having a complex financial component.

How the unit unfolds:

Imagine that you have to make a number of financial decisions over the course of a week or month, decisions that involve selling uncompetitive assets and buying more competitive ones. In order to accomplish the goal of maximising your money, you will have to consider the evolution of each of your assets each day and decide which ones have become less desirable and should to be sold, and which ones have become more attractive and should be bought to benefit you. The situation is complex from the start, and the problem unfolds day by day – not reacting in a meaningful way may already diminish your investments, as the worth of each share changes day by day.

Example Item 1

Problem solvers are provided with a stock market simulation, in which they begin with initial stock in five companies, and a small disposable sum of cash that they can invest. They can sell stock for cash, or buy new stock with cash. Stock prices vary on a day-by-day basis. A new "day" comes on screen every 60 seconds, with new information about the evolution of the five companies. A short history, i.e., the last few days in each company's evolution are displayed on the screen. The pattern of change for some of the companies is transparent, i.e., future change is predictable.

In this first item, problem solvers need to decide, based on the past evolution history of each company, where to invest their money. They need to sell the stock they do not need, and buy stock in the more promising companies, in order to maximise the value of their portfolio.

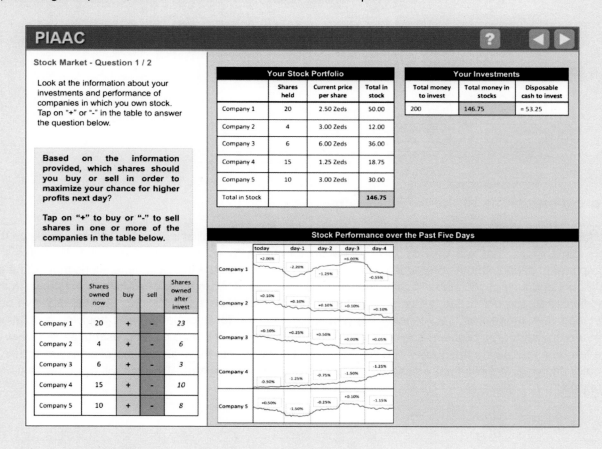

Example Item 2

After the problem solvers have committed their portfolio to one or both of the more promising and predictable companies (Companies 2 and 3), the behaviour of these companies changes, and they begin to have negative yield. Problem solvers need to adjust their investment while keeping in mind the ultimate goal to generate as much money as possible.

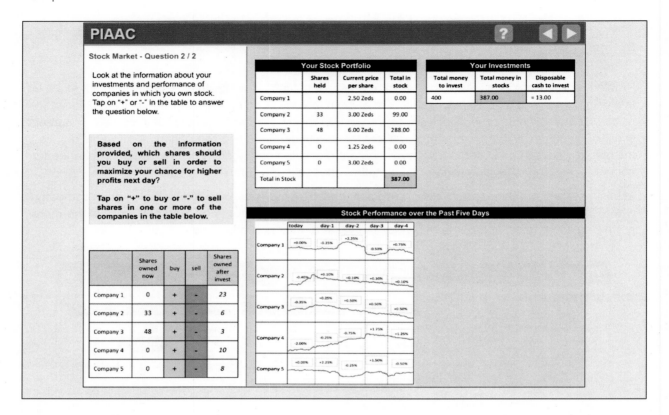

Core dimensions of the APS domain

So far, we have outlined the theoretical underpinnings of APS. This following section will now focus on the core dimensions that will provide the foundation for the APS assessment. Figure 4.1 illustrates the components of each of the core dimensions. The first panel shows the five task dimensions that define an APS task and their associated difficulty drivers. These are described in more detail below. As shown in the middle panel, and discussed in the next section, a second set of core components are the cognitive and metacognitive processes (i.e., defining the problem, searching for information, and applying a solution) that are crucial for the problem-solving process in greater detail. The third panel presents an overview of the features that define the quality of a solution, as associated with three levels of proficiency in adaptive problem solving. We will then outline the assumed proficiency levels of APS that will form the basis for analysis.

Figure 4.1. The nexus of task dimensions, metacognitive and cognitive processes, and proficiency levels

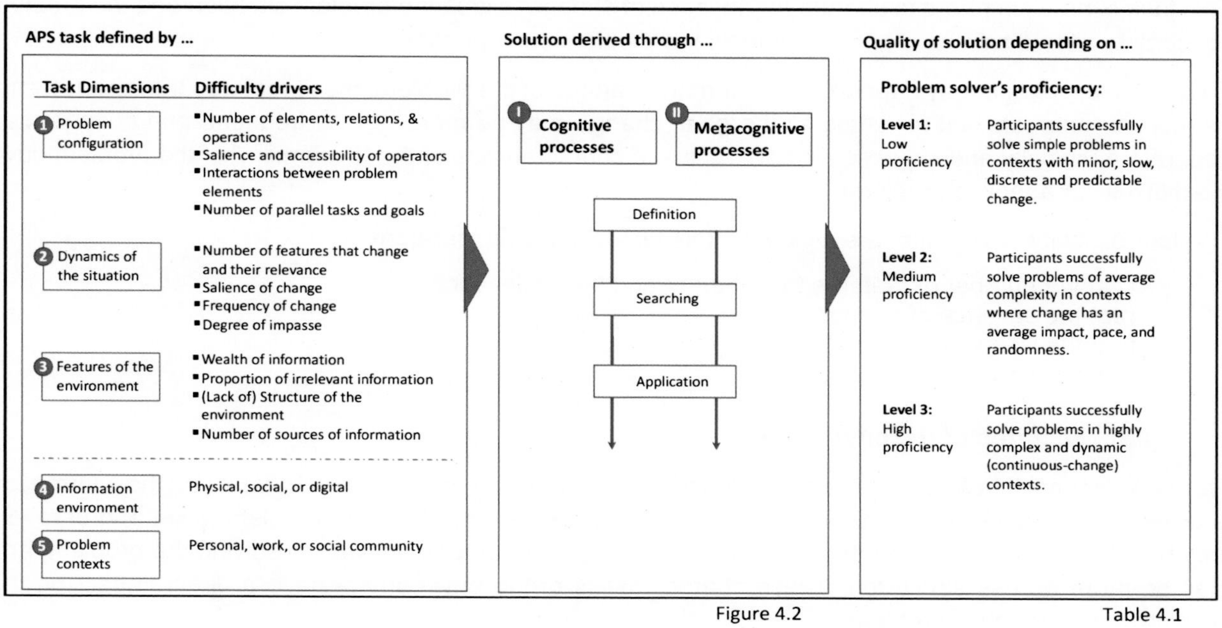

Figure 4.2   Table 4.1

Task dimensions

To really understand what forms an adaptive problem, it is crucial to identify specific characteristics that make a problem adaptive, and to ask whether there are any qualitative and/or quantitative differences between various adaptive problems. When decomposing a problem, it becomes apparent that each adaptive problem can be described by five problem characteristics, or "task dimensions": (1) the problem configuration, (2) the dynamics of the situation, (3) the features of the environment, (4) the information environment, and (5) the problem context (see left panel of Figure 4.1). These five task dimensions are descriptive of any adaptive problem (see Box 4.3) and will guide the development of the APS assessment in the second cycle of PIAAC.

The first three of these five task dimensions permit changes in *quantity*, and thus can drive the difficulty of the problem. Each of these three task dimensions has four even more specific difficulty drivers and by tweaking these, a problem can become easier or more difficult, requiring different abilities from problem solvers. More specifically, these three dimensions, along with the respective difficulty drivers, can be characterised as follows:

1) Problem configuration:

This task dimension refers to the initial problem setup and the goal state(s) including the problem elements, the relations, and the resources/operators. A problem may have more or fewer elements, and these elements may interact with each other or be relatively independent. The different elements may be accessible with ease or with difficulty, and may be more or less salient. The various elements may interact with each other or be relatively independent. And the problem requirement may include the accomplishment of only one or of several goals. All these characteristics of the initial problem configuration drive difficulty in adaptive problems.

The four difficulty drivers that are typical for this task dimension, therefore, are:

> (1a) the number of elements, relations, and operations
> (1b) the salience and accessibility of operators
> (1c) the interactions between problem elements
> (1d) the number of parallel tasks and goals

2) Dynamics of the situation:

This task dimension refers to change (or absence of change) within the problem situation and the problem constraints across time, and how this affects the problem configuration.

For example, change may happen in one or more features of the problem, these features that change may be more or less relevant for attaining the goal, change may be more or less frequent, and change may generate a difficulty and impasse (or not). All these characteristics of the "dynamism" of the problem drive the difficulty of adaptive problems.

The four difficulty drivers that are typical for this task dimension therefore are:

(2a) the number of features that change and their relevance
(2b) the salience of change
(2c) the frequency of change
(2d) the degree of impasse

3) Features of the environment:

This task dimension refers to various features that are characteristic of the environment and the information and resources available from it. For example, the environment in which the problem is set and unravels may be rich in information, and that information may be more or less relevant to solving the problem, and may be more or less structured. These characteristics of the environment have a direct impact on the difficulty of the adaptive problem.

The four difficulty drivers that are typical for this task dimensions therefore are:

(3a) the wealth of information
(3b) the proportion of irrelevant information
(3c) the (lack of) structure of the environment
(3d) the number of sources of information

Task dimensions (1) to (3) and their respective difficulty drivers are the building blocks through which a purposeful construction of the units and items of the test is able to elicit the relevant cognitive and metacognitive processes in problem solvers. It is indispensable to understand their structure and role in the architecture of adaptive problems. It is also important to mention that we do not consider these difficulty drivers to be exhaustive in any way. The ones used here reflect important aspects of APS and can be manipulated with relative ease when constructing the test items. We have therefore settled on them, while explicitly acknowledging the possibility to also describe the problem configuration, the dynamics of the situation, and the features of the environment under other, different parameters. Annex 4.A. more specifically defines the respective difficulty drivers and relate them to how simple and difficult problems would look like.

The last two task dimensions only permit changes in the *quality* of the context in which the problem is set and therefore these two task dimensions do not drive the difficulty of the problem. Task dimensions (4), i.e., information environment, and (5), i.e., problem contexts, give context to the problems featured in the items. Contextualisation is important for any problem-solving effort: no actual problem that people encounter in their lives is free of context. Any problem occurs (and is solved in) an environment with its specific information that may not be directly part of the problem, but that may shape both, the "flavour" of the problem, and the resources that are available for a meaningful solution. More specifically, any problem occurs in a context that is related to people's lives: some problems are personal, other occur in work settings, or in community and social contexts. The goal in specifying these two dimensions is to ensure that the item pool reflects a range of information environments and contexts.

4) Information environment:

This task dimension refers to the sources for the resources that are available for solving the problem. The nature of the information environment can be physical, social, or digital. Of course, all these resources appear more or less simultaneously in a digital problem-solving effort, but the problem imposes the need to handle (at least mentally) a specific kind of resource. These resources will be simulated in the assessment tasks.

(4a) Physical resources are those that require hands-on handling: driving a car, operating a machine by pressing buttons and pulling levers, connecting pipes, and others.

(4b) Social resources are those that require the problem solver to engage in interpersonal and social interactions with other people, such as leading a group, planning an activity with friends or family, or presenting a speech to an audience.

(4c) Digital resources are those that require the problem solver to interact with digital features or devices and make use of digital knowledge and skills, such as sorting a table, sending an e-mail, searching the web, formatting a text and others.

5) Problem contexts:

This task dimension refers to the situational embedding of the problem, whereby people encounter problems in their personal life, at work or in social and community contexts.

(5a) Contexts that are personal may refer to one's home, family, career, education, hobbies, or financial investments; these problems will therefore require problem solvers to solve a problem that occurs in the context of their personal life.

(5b) Contexts that are work-related may require problem solvers to solve a work-related task, or place them in a work-related context, in which they work under supervision or with co-workers.

(5c) Contexts that are social and community related may refer to interaction with other people in leisure activities (e.g., going to a party or hiking in the mountains) or with community resources (e.g., police, firefighters, or administrative institutions).

Box 4.3. Task dimensions in the example units

The *Dinner Preparation* unit has a specific problem configuration: it asks test-takers to accomplish two goals at the same time, the problem elements are accessible and salient and presented in a visually ordered fashion. The information environment of this example is not rich, and not much information, relevant or irrelevant, is provided beyond the problem itself. The dynamic of the situation is average: when change is induced, test-takers are prompted to the change, and the specifics are explained; still, changes can produce an impasse. The problem is placed in a personal problem context and a mixed digital and physical information environment.

The *Stock Market* example also has a specific mix of these characteristics. The problem configuration requires solving of only one goal, and is based on a high number of elements, that are salient and easily accessible to problem solvers. The problem environment is not very rich and does not offer much information, relevant or irrelevant, beyond the problem itself. The dynamic of the situation is high, with frequent but salient change, that does not create an explicit impasse. The information environment is digital, and the problem context is personal.

The various task dimensions are critical in the description of any given adaptive problem, and the difficulty drivers are the operational building blocks through which task dimensions are implemented in the units and items of the test (right panel of Figure 4.1). However, the task dimensions only reflect the *adaptive problem*, and they do not directly describe in any relevant manner the cognitive and metacognitive processes underlying adaptive problem *solving*.

For the cognitive and metacognitive processes, it is assumed that three distinctive cognitive and metacognitive stages, i.e., definition of the problem, search for a solution, and apply the solution (second panel of Figure 4.1), are involved to differing degrees in the process of solving the respective problem tasks. These cognitive processes are inherently bound to the problem-solving process.

Purposeful construction of the units and items of the test uses the task dimensions and their respective difficulty drivers as building blocks with which to elicit the relevant cognitive and metacognitive processes in problem solvers. The next section will focus directly on these important, and often intertwined processes that are key to any APS task.

Cognitive and metacognitive processes in adaptive problem solving

As stated in the definition of APS, there are multiple cognitive and metacognitive processes a problem solver has to accomplish in order to arrive at a problem's solution. These processes can be organised with respect to three stages of problem solving, namely, *defining the problem*, *searching for information* relevant to its solution, and *applying a solution*. Figure 4.2 illustrates how APS is conceptualised according to these stages (shown as boxes organised from left to right to reflect the overall process of adaptive problem solving) and the processes embedded within each stage.

Figure 4.2. Adaptive problem solving

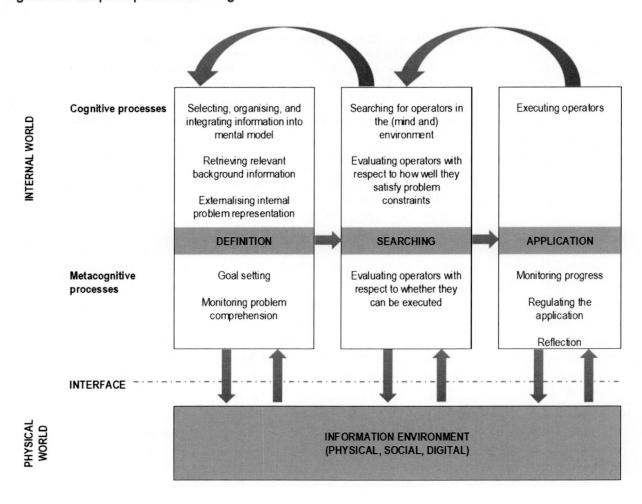

Source: Adapted from Greiff et al. (2017, p. 19[6]).

In the following, we will define the cognitive and metacognitive processes within each stage of APS from an assessment perspective and illustrate them by referring back to the example tasks provided in Boxes 4.1 and 4.2. For each process, we will make connections to the previous section on task dimensions to exemplify how they elicit cognitive and metacognitive processes and render them more or less challenging for problem solvers. Only few references will be made to task dimensions (4) and (5) since they refer to the contextual embedding of the problem and its solution-relevant information only; it is assumed that these task dimensions have no systematic influence on the quality of the cognitive and metacognitive processes that need to be conducted to solve a problem (e.g., constructing a mental model of the problem is not inherently different for problems embedded in either a physical or digital information environment nor do personal problems require different processes than social ones).

The present section ends with some general remarks regarding the relationship between the conceptual framework of APS (Greiff et al., 2017[6]) and the way the cognitive and metacognitive processes are considered when conceptualising them from an assessment perspective. While the present description is grounded in the conceptual framework (Greiff et al., 2017[6]), some amendments are necessary to take into account the specific requirements and constraints of the assessment context.

The remainder of this section will start with the definition of cognitive processes (shown in the upper part of Figure 4.2) and then turn to metacognitive processes (shown in the lower part of Figure 4.2). This is done because cognitive processes, which refer to reasoning about the problem and its solution, are involved in any kind of problem solving irrespective of how the task dimensions are implemented in the problem. In easy problems, cognitive processes may be conducted without considerable effort. Especially in more complex problems, however, these cognitive processes may require effortful monitoring and control to ensure that they are correctly executed. For instance, any change of information about the problem (as introduced in example item 2 of the *Dinner Preparation* example) will make it necessary for a problem solver to verify the understanding of what the problem is about and whether the initially derived solution plan still matches the current problem configuration. As a consequence, problem solvers also need to apply metacognitive processes by reasoning about the quality of their own thinking. Box 4.4 illustrates the cognitive and metacognitive processes necessary for the two example units.

In general, more complex problems are more likely to require metacognitive processes in order to be solved effectively. That is, the more (interacting) elements and relations are involved in the problem configuration (task dimension 1), the more dynamic a problem is (task dimension 2), and the richer, the more unstructured and less salient the information environment is (task dimension 3), the higher the likelihood that metacognitive processes will be involved. Of all these task dimensions with their respective difficulty drivers, task dimension 2 (dynamics of the situation) is likely to contribute most strongly to metacognitive requirements in APS, since any change in the problem configuration or the information environment always requires monitoring whether one's reasoning is still aligned with the newly evolving situation and possibly modifying one's cognitive structures (i.e., the mental model of the problem and/or the solution plan).

Box 4.4. Cognitive and metacognitive processes in the example units

First of all, the problem would need to be defined on a cognitive and a metacognitive level. From a cognitive point of view, the *Dinner Preparation* example requires problem solvers to search for the relevant information about the goals by browsing the map, the problem requirements and by selecting, organising and integrating the information to plan the fastest route. The *Stock Market* example requires problem solvers to mentally organise and integrate the information about the companies and their histories in order to plan the most promising investment strategy. From a metacognitive point of view, the *Dinner Preparation* example requires problem solvers to set subgoals – for example, to first drive

---

to school, then to the store. Both problems require problem solvers to monitor their problem comprehension.

On a cognitive level, the second stage of the adaptive problem-solving process, searching for solution, would involve the search for relevant information on the map and the sticky note in the *Dinner Preparation* example. For the *Stock Market* example, it would involve a continuous search of changes in the problem statement and the environment, and an analysis of these continuous changes. On a metacognitive level, problem solvers would need to evaluate different alternatives to accomplish both goals in time in the *Dinner Preparation* example. In the *Stock Market* example, problem solvers would need to constantly look at the most promising investment alternatives continuously opening up as a function of the "daily" changes in company prices.

In the apply the solution stage, in both of the examples, the plans would then be applied to solve the problem on a cognitive level, while, on a metacognitive level the progress would be monitored.

Cognitive processes

In the following we will describe the different cognitive processes as specified in Figure 4.2.

Problem definition: Mental model construction

In order to define a problem, a person needs to construct a mental model of the state of affairs described in the problem (Mayer and Wittrock, 2006[10]; Nathan, Kintsch and Young, 1992[11]). This mental model comprises information on the initial state (i.e., the problem configuration, cf. task dimensions), the goal state to be achieved, the legal operators, and the set of intervening states that are required in order to move from the initial state to the goal state; together these various states make up the problem space (Klahr, 2002[12]; Klahr and Dunbar, 1988[13]; Newell and Simon, 1972[14]; Vollmeyer, Burns and Holyoak, 1996[15]). Accordingly, items assessing mental model construction need to provide an account of the accuracy and comprehensiveness regarding the problem solver's understanding of what the problem is about. Three cognitive sub-processes were identified in the conceptual framework (Greiff et al., 2017[6]) as contributing to mental model construction (cf. lower left corner of Figure 4.2). In the following, these will be re-introduced and discussed from an assessment perspective.

1) Selecting, organising, and integrating problem information into mental model

To define the problem, one first needs to *select relevant information* about the initial problem state. This means that a problem solver will need to decide for every piece of available information whether it is necessary in order to understand the current problem configuration. The exploration of information will be rather broad and involve the use and evaluation of multiple sources of information as resources with respect to their reliability, relevance, adequacy, and comprehensibility. The selected information will then need to be *organised and integrated into a coherent mental representation* that comprises all information that is known about the problem configuration.

The more (interacting) elements and relations a problem contains, the less salient the problem information is (e.g., because problem-irrelevant information is also included in the problem statement, task dimension 1), and the more the problem information is subject to change over time (task dimension 2), the more difficult will it be for a problem solver to select, organise, and integrate problem information into an accurate mental model. Accordingly, items can be varied along these dimensions to make this cognitive process more or less challenging for problem solvers. Items assessing mental model construction need to reflect whether a problem solver considered all relevant information for defining the problem, while ignoring irrelevant information also embedded in the storyline.

Box 4.5. Selecting, organising, and integrating problem information into mental model in the example units

For instance, in the *Dinner Preparation* example, an example item could consist of a list of options describing which information is available for solving the problem (e.g., driving times to reach a grocery store, its opening hours, availability of organic food). The problem solver is then asked to tick all information categories that s/he wants more details on. In example item 1, only driving time matters for the problem definition; hence, none of the other options should be ticked. Such an item provides information on a problem solver's accuracy in solving the problem, while at the same time delivering information on the underlying cause of problem-solving failure, namely, a problem solver's inability to construct an adequate mental model of the problem.

---

2) Retrieving relevant background information

In real-world problem solving, relevant background knowledge will help an individual to distinguish between relevant and irrelevant information as well as building a coherent mental model. Memories from past problem-solving activities are one important source of background knowledge. Thus, a problem solver has to activate these memories from past problem-solving activities, which has been shown to be difficult for many problem solvers who fail to recall these past activities and do not recognise that they possess potentially helpful past experiences (Ross, 1989[16]). Moreover, many problem solvers will fail to distinguish between a problem's structural features, which will affect how the problem can be solved and superficial or contextual features that are irrelevant to its solution (Braithwaite and Goldstone, 2015[17]; Ross, 1989[18]). Therefore, they will activate memories of past problems that are only superficially similar to the problem at hand or construct a situation model that is heavily based on irrelevant information, which will misguide the subsequent problem-solving steps.

Accordingly, a problem solver's ability to make effective use of his or her past experiences and knowledge is likely to have a profound impact on performance in real-world problem solving. However, assessing this sub-process in the second cycle of PIAAC is problematic for various reasons. It is not known what kind of prior or expert knowledge problem solvers already possess nor can it be comprehensively assessed; moreover, expert knowledge is likely to vary between individuals and countries. The goal in the assessment is to include problems that are accessible to most people, thereby also not confounding availability of expert knowledge with a person's ability to solve problems. Accordingly, while problems cannot be totally free of background knowledge, problems in which expert knowledge is required or where those with expert knowledge will find that the scenario conflicts with what they know should be avoided.

3) Externalising internal problem representation

Even though problem solving itself is mostly an internal process (Mayer and Wittrock, 2006[10]), it can largely benefit from externalising one's thoughts. With respect to the construction of a situation model, problem solving will benefit from *forming an external representation of a problem's main features* [e.g., in a drawing or table; (Ainsworth, Prain and Tytler, 2011[19]; Fischer, Greiff and Funke, 2012[20]; Zhang, 1997[21])].

From an assessment perspective, these externalisations can provide important insights into the way a person conceptualises a problem and into his or her misconceptions or gaps in the mental model (Lee, Jonassen and Teo, 2011[22]). Hence, it is suggested to include externalising tasks in the assessment that ask problem solvers to make a drawing or create a table, where they would need to include all the relevant features and show the relationships among those features. Because problem solvers are explicitly instructed to create externalisations, such tasks do not assess spontaneous use and hence the cognitive process underlying it. Rather, such tasks are recommended because they are instrumental to the assessment of yet another, albeit pivotal process contributing to mental model construction, namely, selecting organising, and integrating problem-relevant information in a specific format. In consequence, the same task dimensions as for selecting, organising, and integrating problem information affect the difficulty by which a mental problem representation can be externalised.

Search solution: Identifying effective operators

This second stage heavily relies on the mental model that was built when defining the problem (cf. middle box in Figure 4.2). The solution of the problem can be described as the sequence of steps necessary to get from the initial state of the problem to the goal state. The process of searching for a solution marks the distinction between a task and a problem. A task is present if a solution can be directly retrieved from memory and applied to the situation at hand effortlessly and without modification. A problem, on the other hand, requires that a person breaks down a problem into parts, searches for a solution among different alternatives, plans a sequence of actions, and possibly tries out different ways of reaching the goal state (Gick, 1986[23]). The search for a solution thus requires cognitive strategy knowledge on different solution methods and the metacognitive skills to handle this knowledge (Fischer, Greiff and Funke, 2012[20]; Mayer and Wittrock, 2006[10]).

Two cognitive sub-processes were identified in the conceptual framework (Greiff et al., 2017[6]) as contributing to solution search. In the following, these will be re-introduced and discussed from an assessment perspective.

1) Searching for operators in the (mind and) environment

Whereas information search aimed at defining the problem is tailored towards understanding the problem with the goal of acquiring as much knowledge as possible about the problem, the search during this stage aims at identifying possible operators that will help to make the transition from the initial state to the goal state [cf. dual space theory (Klahr and Dunbar, 1988[13]); see also (Greiff, Wüstenberg and Avvisati, 2015[24])]. Operators may be in the mind of the problem solver (i.e., cognitive actions such as adding two numbers) or they may be located in the information environment. In general, the more complex the problem configuration and the features of the information environment (task dimension 3) are, the more difficult searching for operators will become.

Box 4.6. Searching for operators in the example units (1)

For instance, in the *Dinner Preparation* example there is one overarching operator that refers to taking the car to go grocery shopping and that has different instantiations in that the stores are differentially suited to fulfill the problem's constraints given the driving times to them. In the *Stock Market* example, on the other hand, there are two operators (i.e., buying and selling stocks) with various stock options, making this problem harder than the *Dinner Preparation* example (cf. task dimension 1). As for the complexity of the problem configuration, the map used in the *Dinner Preparation* example might not be as clean as the one presented above, but might be very cluttered with unnecessary information and occlude the relevant information on driving times, in which case searching for operators would be far more difficult.

Sequences of operators that are determined prior to executing solution steps make up problem-solving plans. In the remainder, we will always talk about operators only, even though in a specific problem they might be composed into a problem-solving plan.

Searching for operators involves using appropriate devices, tools or information as well as communicating and coordinating one's activities with other parties [cf. collaborative problem solving (OECD, 2017[8])]. Resources for locating operators may hence be located in the social, physical, or digital environment. Due to the digital assessment to be implemented in the second cycle of PIAAC, access to resources is always embedded in a digital interface for the sake of representing the problem, but this does not mean that the resources would be necessarily digital in the real world as well.

> ### Box 4.7. Searching for operators in the example units (2)
>
> For instance, in the *Dinner Preparation* example, the map to read off driving times to different grocery stores might as well be a physical map; on the other hand, the diagrams illustrating the dynamics of the stock market are likely to be digital even in the real world since they need to be updated in real time.

Because the situations in which 21st century citizens solve problems often undergo change over time (cf. task dimension 2), APS requires that they constantly update their knowledge about operators.

> ### Box 4.8. Searching for operators in the example units (3)
>
> For instance, in the second, dynamic example item of the *Dinner Preparation* problem the problem solver receives a message while being on the road that there has been a water leak in the designated grocery store, thereby requiring a change of plans. Similarly, in the second example item of the *Stock Market* problem there is constant change in the performance of the different companies that needs to be considered when buying or selling stocks.

2) Evaluating operators with respect to how well they satisfy problem constraints

There may be many operators that come up during the aforementioned search for operators, but not all of them may be legal. That is, they may fail to satisfy the constraints as expressed in the problem configuration.

> ### Box 4.9. Evaluating operators in the example units (1)
>
> For instance, while grocery store A and B may both offer the required food choices, store A may have opening hours that conflict with the requirement of being home before 10 a.m. Hence, for every potential operator it has to be determined whether it is effective in principle (i.e., enables the transition from initial to goal state) and whether it satisfies all constraints.

Evaluation of operators becomes harder for problem solvers, if there are many potential operators and many constraints to be considered (cf. task dimension 1) as well as if information on these operators is embedded in a rich and unstructured environment (cf. task dimension 3). Moreover, whereas in static problems a problem solver can rely on the operators' (un-) suitability for problem solving once it has been evaluated, in dynamic problems, a problem solver has to continuously re-evaluate whether either the operators or the constraints have changed, thereby affecting the effectiveness of the solution.

Box 4.10. Evaluating operators in the example units (2)

For instance, a grocery store is no longer available due to a water leakage or a formerly well-performing company does no longer make any profit, which is why its stocks should potentially be sold rather than bought (cf. the dynamic example items of the two sample problems).

In real-world problem solving, the sub-process of evaluating operators typically includes two aspects: evaluating whether the operator is in line with the options that have been provided (e.g., is store A better suited than store B?) and evaluating whether the problem solver is capable of using the operator. The prior evaluation refers to a cognitive process since it requires reasoning about the problem. The latter requires problem solvers to consider their own or the fictitious problem solver's resources that they could invest into applying the solution, thereby addressing metacognitive aspects. From an assessment perspective, these two aspects are difficult to disentangle in an artificial problem-solving context. For this reason, it is recommended that items in this category might be coded on both dimensions for analysis purposes (see section on assessing APS below).

Apply solution: Applying plans and executing operators

During this third stage, a problem solver *applies plans to solve a problem* and *executes the specified operators* (cf. right box in Figure 4.2). This stage relies on having procedural knowledge available (Mayer and Wittrock, 2006[10]). The nature of this procedural knowledge will depend on the requirements of the problem and may, for instance, comprise algebra skills to solve equations, logical reasoning skills or other domain-specific operators. In the context of simulating problem solving for the purpose of assessing problem-solving skills, this process must be confined to selecting an operator, as problem solvers do not actually perform any actions (i.e., they do not actually go grocery shopping).

Note that the conceptual framework (Greiff et al., 2017[6]) mentioned 'predicting the environment' as yet another cognitive sub-process relevant to applying a solution. However, the expert group agreed that this aspect was not well defined and could not be measured so it will be dropped as a process to be included in the assessment.

A summary of the cognitive processes of APS together with a brief definition is provided in Box 4.11.

Box 4.11. Cognitive processes in adaptive problem solving in a nutshell

Defining

(1) *Selecting, organising, and integrating information into mental model*: Constructing a mental representation of the problem space (initial state, goal state, legal operators).

(2) *Retrieving relevant background information*: Accessing memory to retrieve background knowledge (note: assessment tasks should be designed to avoid necessity of this process).

(3) *Externalising internal problem representation*: Creating an external representation (e.g., drawing, table) that illustrates the problem solver's mental model of the problem.

Searching

(1) *Searching for operators in the mind and environment*: Locating information about available action options that might be suited to solve the problem.

> (2) *Evaluating operators with respect to how well they satisfy problem constraints*: Determining which of the action options will be best to reach the goal while considering all possible constraints.
>
> ### Application
>
> (1) *Applying plans and executing operators*: Implementing the selected operator(s) to solve the problem.

Metacognitive processes

As already mentioned, metacognitive processes are also inherently bound to the process of problem solving. However, metacognitive processes become more important to the extent that problems are more complex and difficult to comprehend, that the problems change, and that progress towards the solution becomes more difficult.

Problem definition: Setting goals and monitoring problem comprehension

Problem-solving situations in real life may differ in whether the goal (i.e., what is to be achieved) is clear and whether only the way to get there is not yet known. In particular, there may be ambiguous problems where the goal and hence the direction to take in order to solve the problem needs to be figured out first. Moreover, especially in complex problems, that is, problems whose solutions are composed of multiple steps (cf. task dimension 1) or that require adaptation to changing circumstances due to their dynamic nature (cf. task dimension 2), the problem solver has to constantly evaluate whether the current understanding of what the problem is about still matches the current state of affairs. Thus, s/he must monitor the quality of the cognitive processes regarding the definition of the problem. Due to the fact that goal setting and monitoring problem comprehension require thinking about one's own state ('what do I want to achieve?') and mental representations rather than contemplating about the problem, these processes are metacognitive in nature.

Accordingly, the conceptual framework mentioned 'goal setting' and 'monitoring problem comprehension' as two important metacognitive sub-processes (Greiff et al., 2017[6]), which are shown in the lower left part of Figure 4.2. For reasons mentioned below, the assessment framework will consider only the latter process.

1) Goal setting

Goal setting refers to defining dimensions of the problem that require a change and identifying features that characterise the state one wants to achieve. Different from the initial problem state, the definition of the goal state crucially depends on the problem solver, his/her motives, and the resources that s/he has available, and also willing to invest these, for a favourable outcome. Hence, setting goals requires reflection about one's own cognition and motivation, thereby making it a metacognitive process.

In real life, goal setting is an important metacognitive process when solving a problem for one's own purpose, since it gives direction and is the motivational driving force behind many actions taken towards solving the problem. However, from an assessment perspective, letting problem solvers chose among different goals would impose immense challenges in terms of scoring their performance, since problem solvers would differ in their goals, which in turn determine which solution steps would be appropriate. Hence, every goal would require its own scoring rules; moreover, problem solvers might even set goals whose achievement is not supported by the information environment made available in the assessment. For these reasons, goal setting will not be assessed in the APS tasks as the goals will be given to the problem solver in the description of the units.

Box 4.12. Goal setting in the example units

For instance, in a real-world situation, a problem solver faced with the *Dinner Preparation* problem might actually decide to give up the initial goal of preparing a healthy dinner and get take-out food instead; in the *Stock Market* problem s/he might contemplate between making a quick, but potentially risky bargain versus optimising profit in the long run at a medium level, but with less risk involved.

---

2) Monitoring problem comprehension

An accurate understanding of the problems' initial and goal state (i.e., "where am I and where do I need to be?") is crucial for all subsequent problem-solving steps. Hence, problem solvers need to monitor whether their understanding of the problem is sufficient in order to find a solution to it. An accurate comprehension monitoring is especially important, since it will determine whether the process of defining the problem is adequately regulated (Nelson and Narens, 1990[25]). For instance, overconfidence in one's understanding of the problem may lead to a premature termination of the search for problem-relevant information, whereas underconfidence may yield an inefficient construction process, where information search is continued even after all relevant information has been identified. Research on metacognitive judgements has shown that many people, especially those with little prior knowledge, make rather inaccurate judgements of their level of comprehension and rely on invalid cues when making these judgements (Bjork, Dunlosky and Kornell, 2013[26]). Notably, monitoring becomes more difficult the more information needs to be considered when constructing a mental model of the problem (task dimension 1). Moreover, dynamic problems require constant monitoring of problem comprehension, since the problem configuration may be affected by the dynamics (task dimension 2).

In contrast to some of the other metacognitive processes, monitoring problem comprehension can be assessed relatively easily by administering items in which problem solvers have to indicate whether they would require additional information on the problem before they can start solving it.

Box 4.13. Monitoring problem comprehension in the example units

For instance, in the *Dinner Preparation* example, only upon taking an action (e.g., activating an additional display option by clicking on it) would the map display not only the locations of the grocery stores but also the problem solver's location, which is necessary to infer the driving distances. Problem solvers who take this action are aware of the fact that their understanding of the problem's initial state is incomplete and that further information is necessary. Similarly, items could ask problem solvers whether they have understood the problem and relate their answers to their actual comprehension performance. Ideally, corresponding questions should be asked by an agent or problem-solving partner, thereby embedding the assessment into the story line and making the assessment of metacognition less evident. In the *Dinner Preparation* example, for instance, a problem solver may respond to a friend's question that s/he has looked up the opening hours to grocery store A, so that s/he is ready to go – thereby not accounting for the fact that driving there would take far too much time in order to be back home at 10 a.m.

Search for solution: Evaluating operators with respect to whether they can be executed

Operators need to be eventually selected based on an integrated evaluation of their effectiveness and their ability to satisfy problem constraints as well as internal constraints such as the problem solver's ability to apply an operator (cf. middle box in Figure 4.2). Because these two evaluation criteria are difficult to disentangle in an artificial problem-solving context, it is suggested to code items in this category as reflecting both, cognitive and metacognitive processes for analysis purposes. Accordingly, metacognitive evaluation is affected by the same task dimensions, in that it becomes more difficult if there are many potential operators and many constraints (cf. task dimension 1) as well as if relevant information is embedded in a rich and unstructured environment (cf. task dimension 3). Moreover, the need to constantly update the evaluation process makes dynamic problems more challenging (task dimension 2).

Box 4.14. Search for solution in the example units

For instance, to assess metacognitive evaluation processes, in the *Stock Market* example, the problem solver could be involved in a discussion with another broker who suggests two (or more) different plans that fulfill the problem constraints to different degrees. The problem solver could be asked to continue the discussion by making a decision regarding the suggested options and also providing a reason for this decision (e.g., possible answer options: 'both options sound good to me. I will decide spontaneously which stocks to buy'; 'I will go for option A, because …[right/wrong reason]'; 'I do not think that either option will work, because …[right/wrong reason]'). Such a task requires that the problem solver reflects upon the adequacy of the cognition (solution plan) rather than about the problem, which is why such a task is assumed to mainly trigger metacognitive reasoning processes. Again, an agent is introduced to not make the need for metacognitive evaluation less evident and to not trigger processes that, in the real world, would have to be carried out spontaneously.

Apply solution: Monitoring progress and regulating the problem-solving process

When applying a solution, problem solvers need to evaluate whether they are making progress towards the goal and/or take actions if this is not the case (cf. right box in Figure 4.2). Especially in dynamic problems (task dimension 2) there may be changes in the problem configuration or obstacles that may affect the availability of operators, thereby making it necessary to regulate the problem-solving process and to modify existing plans in order to steer towards goal achievement.

1. Monitoring progress

When executing a problem-solving strategy, a problem solver needs to constantly monitor the degree to which progress towards solving the goal has been made. To do so, it is important that the goal has been defined in a way that clear criteria for goal achievement exist against which the current problem state can be evaluated. In the case the goal state has been achieved, the problem-solving process can be terminated. However, monitoring will often lead to the detection and interpretation of unexpected events, impasses, or breakdowns. If there is no or too little progress towards the goal state, problem solvers will need to identify possible reasons for this in order to regulate their future efforts accordingly (see below). Importantly, again test items need to be designed in a way that they do not trigger monitoring.

Box 4.15. Monitoring progress in the example units

For instance, a variant of the *Dinner Preparation* example could involve a more complex task where the problem-solving process is interrupted at a point where two subgoals (e.g., doing part A of the grocery shopping and picking up the child) have already been achieved. The problem solver could be asked what next options would be. If s/he decides to drive home to prepare dinner – thereby forgetting that part B of the shopping in a different store has not yet been accomplished – this suggests poor progress monitoring. Similarly, in the *Stock Market* problem the goal could be to buy and sell stocks so that at a given point in time the custody account is of a certain value. If a problem solver stops interacting with the simulation prior to having reached this value, this would denote poor progress monitoring.

2. Regulating the application of operators

The process of regulating the application of operators heavily depends on progress monitoring (Bjork, Dunlosky and Kornell, 2013[26]; Nelson and Narens, 1990[25]). When progress monitoring implies that the goal has been reached, the application process can be terminated. When a problem-solving failure due to an inadequate plan has occurred, the problem solver needs to devise a modified or entirely novel plan, thereby backtracking to earlier stages of the problem-solving process. Alternatively, the plan may have been adequate, but a problem solver may have failed to carry out the involved operators, because s/he lacked the procedural knowledge. In this case, the formerly devised plan can still be used to solve the problem, but its execution needs to be optimised. Finally, modifications might be necessary because of changes in the problem configuration and its constraints (cf. task dimension 2), which would be noticed by a problem solver if s/he was good at monitoring problem comprehension.

Box 4.16. Regulating the application of operators in the example units

For instance, in a variant of the *Dinner Preparation* example impasses may occur during execution of the plan such as that the problem solver notices that store A actually ran out of fish, which is, however, a necessary ingredient for dinner. In contrast, there could also be other things on the shopping list that are not available at this moment as well, but that are not necessary for dinner on that day. Items can assess whether problem solvers in the first scenario will plan to go to a different store instead to fetch the missing ingredient there (correct option) or drive home instead; for problem solvers in the second scenario driving home without making a detour to a second store is the correct option. In the *Stock Market* problem, the change from example item 1 to 2 where suddenly formerly well-performing companies now show a dip in their performance requires that the problem solver notices that these companies should no longer be considering in buying stocks.

As can be seen, regulation also requires the comparison of different solutions, which is why the latter process that had been mentioned separately in the conceptual framework is subsumed here.

3. Reflection

People who are good at solving problems have been shown to reflect upon their problem-solving experiences and abstract strategy knowledge from it that can be put to use in future problem-solving situations. Thus, problem solving is assumed to leave memory traces, which can be used in the future. This sub-process involves the development of a principal or set of principals related to general problem solving. While being an important aspect for the development of problem-solving expertise, it is unlikely that this can be assessed in the context of a large-scale assessment.

A summary of the metacognitive processes in APS together with a brief definition is provided in Box 4.17.

Box 4.17. Metacognitive processes in adaptive problem solving in a nutshell

Defining

(1) *Goal setting*: Deciding upon what the to-be-achieved state is about (cannot be considered in large-scale assessments because allowing problem solvers to set their own goals would yield too many degrees of freedom).

(2) *Monitoring problem comprehension*: Supervising whether one's mental model of the problem matches the current state of affairs.

Searching

(1) *Evaluating operators with respect to whether they can be executed*: Determining which of the action options will be best to reach the goal while considering all possible constraints.

Application

(1) *Monitoring progress*: Determining whether executing operators achieves the desired outcome.

(2) *Regulating application of operators*: Modifying selection of operators in case the problem configuration has changed (cf. monitoring problem comprehension) or impasses have been noted (cf. monitoring progress).

(3) *Reflection*: Deliberating about one's own capabilities to solve problems with the goal of abstracting knowledge from it that can be applied in the future (cannot be considered in a large-scale assessment context because it requires repeated confrontation with similar problem-solving instances).

Conclusions

In the previous section we have attempted to illustrate the cognitive and metacognitive processes that constitute APS referring back to the example items provided in Boxes 4.1 and 4.2, to describe how they are affected by the different problem characteristics, i.e. task dimensions, described previously, and commented on their relevance and how well they can be assessed in a large-scale context. General principles regarding the design and scoring of items for the assessment of APS will be addressed in the next section; however, here we would like to point out some important issues that arise when attempting to consider cognitive and metacognitive processes underlying APS in a large-scale assessment such as PIAAC.

(1) Not all processes are equally important to APS. For instance, once a comprehensive mental model of a problem has been constructed and the correct operators identified, applying operators from a cognitive perspective may just be a technicality. On the other hand, metacognitive processes during the latter stage can play a major role for problem-solving success, especially if the problem solver faces impasses or the problem configuration changes. Hence, it is unlikely that processes will be equally distributed across problem-solving assessment scenarios without distorting their naturally occurring distribution in real-world problem solving.

(2) Not all processes can be considered in a large-scale assessment context. Some processes such as setting a problem-solving goal and managing this goal during problem solving (i.e., making sure it is maintained and shielded against distractions) are highly relevant from a metacognitive perspective in that they can provide substantial barriers for problem solvers; however, the test-taking situation requires that the goal is already pre-defined so that its accomplishment can be unambiguously scored as correct or

incorrect. As a consequence, some processes, albeit important from a conceptual perspective are not considered in the assessment framework discussed here.

(3) Not all processes can be unambiguously disentangled in a large-scale assessment context. Some processes are difficult to tease apart in an assessment situation where no "real action" is required. For instance, selection of a set of problem-solving operators and its application appear to be the same in a test, where, for example, a problem solver does not actually need to drive the route to get to a shop. As a consequence, in some cases it is suggested to merge processes into one, where no separation in an assessment context seems possible. Moreover, in real life, cognitive and metacognitive processes can usually not directly be observed and they are tightly intertwined with each other. For this reason, in some cases it is suggested to devise items that can be scored both ways, as being evidence for cognitive and metacognitive processes.

(4) An explicit assessment of processes is likely to alter their occurrence. Especially metacognitive processes may often be implicit only. Thus, they may often be better reflected in the ease of problem solving (e.g., in response times, choices NOT made, or feelings of confidence in one's decisions) than in a ratable response to an explicit question. Moreover, explicit questions tailored towards metacognitive processes may serve as trigger for these processes, which would otherwise not have been conducted spontaneously by the problem solver. For instance, explicitly asking a problem solver whether s/he has fully comprehended the problem will most likely make him or her monitor comprehension in that situation; however, the response will not be a good indicator of spontaneous monitoring. This problem pervades research on metacognition and a lot of effort is invested into identifying more implicit measures of metacognition. For the assessment context, it is suggested to embed tasks targeting the problem solver's metacognition as much as possible into the storyline of the problem, so that their true purpose remains concealed.

Reporting proficiency in adaptive problem solving

So far, we have described the different task dimensions that define an APS task and specified the various cognitive and metacognitive processes that form the basis of the problem-solving process. We also outlined how these processes translate into the actual assessment of APS. In a next step we describe the way in which the quality of the solution of an adaptive problem depends on the problem solver's proficiency to deal with the various demands. These demands are inherent in the *quantitative* task dimensions (1) to (3) and their respective difficulty drivers (see right panel of Figure 4.1 and previous section). Task dimensions (4) and (5) however, are only of *qualitative* nature and do not contribute to the actual process of problem solving.

More specifically, whether a problem solver scores high or low in APS will depend on how s/he deals with different problem configurations (task dimension 1), the dynamics of the situation (task dimension 2), and features of the environment (task dimension 3), whose respective difficulty is determined by the assumed difficulty drivers (see Annex 4.A. for a detailed description of the difficulty drivers and how they shape the difficulty of a problem). In the following, we differentiate high from low scorers in the three relevant task dimensions to build the ground for the specification of the assumed APS proficiency levels (see right panel of Figure 4.1).

Problem solvers may score low or high when confronted with different <u>problem configurations</u> (cf. task dimension 1). Low and high scorers will exhibit different levels of cognitive and metacognitive processes. In any possible adaptive problem,

A low scorer:

- integrates in his/her mental model only a small number of elements, relations and operations;
- accesses only that extra information that is readily available and that does not require the problem solver to take extra steps (such as pushing a button in the interface);

- understands only simple, clear, direct and straightforward effects and understands incompletely or incorrectly those problems that contain indirect effects, or effects generated by interactions between various elements;

- identifies operators that are not salient, i.e., resources that are not readily available and identifiable as such;

- handles only one task at a time, has difficulties in handling several tasks in parallel;

- considers only one of several goals (end states) at the same time for a problem; only focuses on a single goal at a time; if several goals are given for the problem, needs to accomplish them one after the other (consecutively).

A high scorer:

- mentally manipulates and integrates in his/her mental model a large number of elements and the relations between them;

- accesses information that is not immediately and readily available by taking the extra steps needed;

- understands complicated effects based on non-linear relationships, and on interaction effects between operators;

- identifies resources and relationships that are not salient, i.e., are not straightforwardly defined as such, but are "hidden" in the context;

- handles multiple tasks at the same time, such as controlling multiple effects towards an end goal; considers several goals at the same time, as end states of the problem-solving process, and works towards their accomplishment in parallel (not consecutively).

Box 4.18. Task dimension 1 low and high scorers in the example units

For instance, low scorers in the *Dinner Preparation* example will have difficulty in keeping in mind the various elements of the problem, and will need to continuously check on the routes and on the sticky note. They will try to only handle one task at a time and will have difficulties in handling potentially competing goals. They will use the resources that are on screen, but in case the problem will permit invoking a calculator to aid in planning the route, they may not press the button that is needed in order to make use of this resource. In the same example, high scorers will handle various goals at the same time, will use the resources available on screen while also identifying those resources that are not readily available (such as the calculator), and will keep in mind all the various elements of the problem.

Problem solvers may also score low or high when confronted with different <u>dynamics in a situation</u> (cf. task dimension 2). Low and high scorers will have different abilities to cope with dynamic changes during the problem-solving process. In any possible adaptive problem,

A low scorer:

- identifies only some of the features that change;

- identifies only the most salient features, and may miss those that are less salient;

- reacts only to change that is transparent, for example when s/he is prompted that something changed;

- is based in reasoning on the current situation, has difficulties in predicting future change based on past changes (or prior information);

- builds incomplete or incorrect mental models of the change process (to understand how and why "things" change);

- adjusts the mental model to change incompletely or incorrectly (e.g., has difficulties in making adequate changes to resolution strategy).

A high scorer:

- identifies all relevant features that change, irrespective of their number, salience, transparency;
- predicts likely future changes based on past changes (prior information);
- constructs a mental model of the actual change (not only of the problem) (i.e., understands how and why things change);
- adjusts the mental model to changes (e.g., changes resolution strategy if needed).

Box 4.19. Task dimension 2 low and high scorers in the example units

For instance, low scorers in the *Stock Market* example might not identify that the prices for all stocks have changed. They will have difficulty predicting future changes in any of the stocks, and may only be able to predict how stocks will vary in the case of those that have a very transparent and univocal past evolution. They may build incomplete or incorrect mental models of the problem and its dynamics. In the same example, high scorers will quickly identify that change takes place in all the stocks, on a "daily" basis, will correctly predict future changes based on prior evolutions of these stocks, will build a correct mental model of the problem and its dynamics. Based on these abilities to constantly monitor the problem solution and to react to changes, they will easily adjust this mental model to any supplementary change, if induced, i.e., they will adapt to the new circumstances.

Finally, problem solvers may score low or high when confronted with <u>different features of the environment</u> (cf. task dimension 3). Low and high scorers will have different abilities. In any possible adaptive problem,

A low scorer:

- works with only one or a small number of variables about the state of the environment;
- integrates only one or a small number of variables from the environment in the conceptualisation of the problem;
- filters out distractors with difficulty and incompletely; is distracted by irrelevant information; continuously manipulates variables that have no effect on anything;
- is distracted by background material; does not recognise distractors; continues to consider all material, even if not relevant (e.g., reads through all the update notes);
- interacts with structured environments, but interacts in an inefficient (and sometimes not meaningful) way with environments that are not structured.

A high scorer:

- mentally manipulates and integrates in mental models a large number of variables about/from the environment;
- integrates "the environment" (and its variables) in the conceptualisation of the problem;
- filters out distractors (irrelevant information);
- focuses on relevant variables from the environment, is not distracted by stimuli that are external to the task or are irrelevant for the task;
- recognises the distracting background material;
- interacts efficiently with unstructured environments (i.e., structures environment, constructs mental model of environment).

Box 4.20. Task dimension 3 low and high scorers in the example units

For instance, low scorers in the *Dinner Preparation* example will only integrate a small amount of the available information in their conceptualisation of the problem. They will be distracted by irrelevant background information and will operate the map in an inefficient way. In the same example, high scorers will integrate a large number of only relevant information into their mental model of the problem. They will recognise changes in the environment and will interact with the map efficiently even if the map would be cluttered with irrelevant information.

The described core task characteristics and their difficulty drivers form the basis upon which the high and low scorers of APS can be described. However, the final score of problem solvers is not directly interpretable, unless related to their proficiency level. Using the task characteristics and difficulty drivers identified in the framework, the expert group will define levels of proficiency and explain what each level means. In other words, what are the specific components of APS that can be performed with proficiency by a high scorer, but cannot be performed by an average scorer, and what are those components that are performed by average scorers and cannot be performed by low scorers? Further, what are the specific components that are expected to be performed even by low scorers?

The proficiency levels will define the scale and will provide a useful way to understand the progression of APS skills. These proficiency levels are associated with the competency of problem solvers, but are also associated with the complexity of items, i.e., the specific components of APS skills that are required by each progressively more difficult items. In Table 4.1, we present a preliminary proposal for APS skills, divided into three proficiency levels. This proposal is based on theoretical considerations about how proficiency may be distributed in the population with the task dimensions as well as the cognitive and metacognitive processes outlined in this framework in mind. This proposal is not based on actual data, and analysis of the main study data will require changes in the number of levels as well as the specific descriptions of those levels of the proficiency scale. The table contains four descriptions for each proficiency level:

a) a general statement of that proficiency level, that can help readers to quickly understand each level;

b) a description of how problem solvers at that specific proficiency level deal with (i.e., adapt to) dynamically changing problems – which is, after all, the basis of adaptive problem solving;

c) a description of the various cognitive processes that are typical for that proficiency level;

d) a description of the various metacognitive processes that are typical for that proficiency level.

Table 4.1. Descriptions of the three APS proficiency levels proposed

	General statement	Dealing with dynamics	Cognitive processes	Metacognitive processes
1	At Level 1, problem solvers successfully solve simple problems in contexts with minor, slow, discrete, and predictable change. They may also be able to solve static (and not dynamic) problems, or only tasks that are part of a static or dynamic problem.	• Problem solvers at Level 1 deal well with infrequent, discrete, or slow changes. They also deal well with changes to which they have been prompted, if these are slow, explicit, discrete, and predictable. • They may perceive THAT changes in the problem environment have occurred, but may need to be prompted towards HOW specifically these changes occurred. • They integrate relevant changes into their problem-solving approach, if prompted to them.	• They define problems with low complexity and low dynamics, especially if prompted towards them, and later identify the relevant changes in the problem statement or the problem environment. They integrate them in a mental model. • They devise partial or complete solutions to static problems and react to changes that are presented in small and visible increments. They adapt their approach in order to retrieve goal-relevant information when they are prompted to them. • They adapt their resolution strategies to changes in the problem statement and the environment, if these changes are of small complexity, and especially if the changes are visible or if they are prompted towards the relevant changes.	• They may successfully evaluate their comprehension of the problem for simple problems, especially when prompted to do so. • They may be able to monitor their progress towards simple goals. • If asked to, they may be able to set subgoals for their progress, and evaluate simple alternatives in order to choose among them. • They may be able to search for solutions to the problem, yet without evaluating alternative solutions.
2	At Level 2, problem solvers successfully solve problems of average complexity in contexts where change has an average impact, pace, and randomness.	• Problem solvers at Level 2 deal well with changes of average frequency and pace. • They usually have good awareness for change, that is, they identify both THAT something has changed and HOW specifically it has changed, but may need to be prompted to specific aspects of the change. • They discriminate between changes that are relevant or trivial to the problem situation. • They predict correctly the general future behaviour of a system based on information that they have about its past behaviour.	• They successfully define problems with average complexity and dynamics (i.e., average pace or frequency) and can later identify the relevant changes in the problem statement or environment. They integrate them in a working mental model. • They devise solutions to a given problem and react to changes that are presented in visible increments. They adapt their approach in order to retrieve goal-relevant information, i.e. information that they consider relevant. • They adapt their resolution strategies to changes in the problem statement and the environment, if these changes are of small or average complexity.	• They monitor their progress towards a goal. • They search for solutions by evaluating alternative solutions to the problem. • They reflect on their solution strategy only when an impasse occurs and when forced to adapt.

	General statement	Dealing with dynamics	Cognitive processes	Metacognitive processes
3	At Level 3, problem solvers successfully solve problems in highly complex and dynamic (continuous-change) problem contexts. They solve complex problems with multiple constraints in the problem configuration and with complex features of the problem environment, and adapt their problem-solving process well to highly dynamic changes in these problems.	• Problem solvers at Level 3 deal well with frequent and even continuous changes. • They have a good awareness for change, that is, they are successful in identifying both THAT changes in the problem environment occurred and HOW these changes occurred. • They discriminate well between changes that are relevant and less relevant or even trivial to the problem situation. • They predict correctly the future behaviour of a system based on information that they have about its past behaviour. They adapt their behaviour according to the expected change.	• They can successfully define highly dynamic problems by selecting relevant information about both the problem and the change. They generate a corresponding mental model that adequately describes the problem situation. • They actively search for solutions by continuously evaluating the information provided by the environment. They adapt their approach in order to continuously retrieve goal-relevant information. • They continuously adapt their solution strategies to changes in the problem statement and the environment; this adaptation is also proactive, as they predict likely changes in their environment.	• They successfully monitor their comprehension of the problem and the changes, as well as of their progress towards their goal. • They search for solutions by setting subgoals and evaluating alternative solutions to the problem. • They continuously reflect on their approach to solving the problem and can successfully get over an impasse by revising their strategy. • They cope well with frequent and unpredictable change and adapt their solution strategy in order to advance their goals.

Assessing adaptive problem solving

The previous section presented the domain of APS and outlined the task dimensions, difficulty drivers, the cognitive and metacognitive processes involved in APS, and the proposed proficiency levels. These elements define the overall, conceptual framework of APS and form the basis for the development of test units and their corresponding items. Ensuring a sufficient match between the conceptual framework and what the APS units and items assess is critical to the crafting of a validity argument. Hence, achieving the greatest possible coverage of the task dimensions and APS processes is the key goal for the test development. The assessment of APS in the second cycle of PIAAC will emphasise the dynamic nature of problem-solving situations as defined earlier and will present problem solvers with newly developed test units that will be suited in information-rich environments.

This section provides an overview of the anchoring of the APS units in the task dimensions outlined in the previous section (see also Figure 4.1), describes overarching test design principles, and explains the scoring and capturing of data beyond item responses that will form the basis of the different proficiency levels.

Anchoring the APS assessment in the task dimensions

The APS units will represent tasks that are comprised of multiple items (i.e., questions). In this sense, an APS unit contains the following key elements: a task stimulus (e.g., introduction to the task, description of functionalities of interactive elements) and multiple items that require the problem solver to adapt to changing situations. The design of the items within a unit will be guided by (1) the task dimensions, and (2) the cognitive and metacognitive processes, as described in previous sections.

Concerning (1), the following five task dimensions formed the development of APS items: problem configuration (i.e., the initial problem setup and goal states), dynamics of the problem situation (i.e., the degree to which the problem situations and its constraints change over time), the features of the environment (i.e., construct-relevant features of information and resources), the types of information sources (i.e., physical, social, and digital), and the contexts (i.e., personal, social community, and work; as defined in the first PIAAC cycle (OECD, 2012[4]). Each and every unit will be mapped onto these five dimensions. However, as we assume information environments and problem contexts in real life to be not equally distributed (cf. section defining APS), we propose to target slightly different proportions of all the problems to be placed in the various environments and contexts as displayed in Table 4.2.

Table 4.2. Proposed distribution of the information environments and problem contexts

Task dimension 4: Information environment	Task dimension 5: Problem context
• Physical: 30%	• Personal: 30%
• Social: 35%	• Work: 30%
• Digital: 35%	• Social community: 40%

Concerning (2), all items within the APS units are located within the framework of cognitive and metacognitive processes. These processes comprise defining the problem, searching for a solution, and applying the solution (see section on cognitive and metacognitive processes in APS and Figure 4.2). For a specific item, these three processes may be required, both on the cognitive and metacognitive side. Given that the cognitive and metacognitive processes are intertwined, a clear separation of these processes – for instance, in the form of empirically distinct indicators or scores – is hardly possible. As a consequence, the APS items may require problem solvers to engage in multiple processes rather than a single process within the APS framework. Besides, to successfully solve a problem that is subject to change over time, problem solvers have to understand the problem situation and develop a mental model about it (Ericsson and Pool, 2016[27]). Ultimately, the processes of understanding the problem form the basis for all subsequent processes of search and applying a solution. This dependence between the three processes of APS results in the anchoring of the APS items in multiple cognitive or metacognitive processes. However, for a given item, some processes may be more pronounced than others and these items will be assigned to the respective, dominant processes.

The proposed distribution of the three main processes in the APS item pool is shown in Table 4.3.

Table 4.3. Proposed distribution of the three main cognitive and metacognitive processes

Processes	Cognition	Metacognition
(1) Defining the problem	Constructing a mental model (30-40%)	Monitoring the comprehension of a problem (30-40%)
(2) Searching for a solution	Searching for operators in the problem environment (40-50%)	Evaluating operators/plans (40-50%)
(3) Applying the solution	Applying plan and executing operators (20-30%)	Monitoring/regulating progress (20-30%)

As stated earlier, for reasons of test fairness and validity, reference to expert knowledge should be avoided from an assessment perspective. Accordingly, items should be designed so that information on operators should be provided through them. In this regard, the *Stock Market* example is potentially a borderline case, since experience with buying and selling stocks may be very limited in some populations. To make this scenario accessible to problem solvers, it has to be simplified compared with its real-world counterpart.

Test design

Test administration

The APS units will be administered on tablets and allow problem solvers to interact with the problem and information environments directly. The technology-based test administration further enables the implementation of problem situations that change over time or make new sources of information available to the problem solver during the problem-solving process. Moreover, in selected items and units, log-file data of specified actions may be used to inform the development of the described APS proficiency levels.

For the main study, the APS assessment will be administered together with the assessments of numeracy and literacy. Participants will be randomly assigned to two of the three domains. For these assessments, an adaptive test design is anticipated so that each participant does not work on all items within the respective domains. The adaptive testing procedure will be based on units, depending on the dependencies between items within a task. At the beginning of the assessment, participants will be assigned to one of three pathways based on their initial performance on a locator test of their literacy and numeracy skills. This design combines adaptive testing with multi-stage testing and is aimed at maximising the information about the participants gained from the assessments (OECD, 2013[28]).

Design elements

The design of the APS units and items contains several elements that facilitate the assessment of *adaptive* problem solving and ensure the fairness of the test:

a) *Explicitness of change*: In some APS tasks, change in the problem situation is not made explicit so that problem solvers will have to recognise these changes. This design element is construct-relevant as it stimulates metacognitive processes of reflecting on the problem situation and initial mental models given the changes in the environment. This element, however, increases the difficulty of the items and is thus used sparsely. In fact, most APS items make explicit the changes in the problem environment.

b) *Rescue elements*: The design of APS units as a sequence of items that gradually introduce changes to the problem environment may create dependencies between items. In other words, if a problem solver does not succeed in one item, s/he may have a disadvantage in solving subsequent items. To circumvent this problem and to ensure the comparability of items among problem solvers, the APS units will contain rescue elements. These elements represent a certain decision or problem solution to the problem solver that are based on a previous item. However, these elements do not evaluate the problem solvers actual responses on previous items but are entirely independent from the correctness of these responses. In this sense, all problem solvers receive the items with these rescue elements to ensure test fairness.

c) *Gradual introduction of changes*: At the outset of an APS task, problem solvers will be presented with a static problem. The subsequent items will gradually unfold and introduce the dynamics of the problem situation. These changes are mostly made explicit (see above) and may be of discrete or continuous nature. The initial, static tasks will ensure that a measure can be established that forms the baseline for problem solvers' performance on subsequent items.

Demands on literacy and ICT skills

The APS units and items will be designed in a way that the level of literacy required to successfully solve the problem is kept minimal [see Greiff et al. (2017[6])]. To accomplish this, the stimulus material and item statements will be formulated briefly and as clearly as possible, except when the complexity of the materials is construct-relevant (e.g., amount of distracting information for information-rich problems). Furthermore, APS units will not present problem solvers solely with written text but will also provide information in tables, schemes, diagrams, and interactive simulations to reduce the reading load and exploit the advantages of multiple representations of testing material. At the same time, a certain level of literacy will be required to successfully solve the problems, especially in order to understand the problem situation and the information material. How APS distinguishes from other core abilities, namely literacy, numeracy and ICT, will be described in detail in the following section.

Along similar lines, the technology-based administration of the APS assessment in the second cycle of PIAAC will require basic skills to deal with ICT. Whether problem solvers are likely to have these skills will be determined in the tablet training. It must be noted that the required level of ICT skills will be kept low, and APS units will mainly demand the navigation through items, switching between two to three information pages, selecting response options, inserting short responses into text boxes, and manipulating well-defined variables by operating a small number of buttons or sliders. In fact, participants will only need to tap on a selection with a stylus or finger, use drag and drop, and highlight (underline) text. To further assist problem solvers in maneuvering through the APS units, a tablet tutorial will be provided at the outset of the PIAAC test administration. This tutorial supports participants in familiarising themselves with the tools to navigate through the tests. Moreover, PIAAC Cycle 2 chose to administer the performance tests on tablets to facilitate an intuitive handling of the test environment (OECD, 2018[29]).

Drivers of item difficulty

The main purpose of the APS assessment is to assess problem solvers' capacity to successfully solve dynamic problems. To capture the broad variation of proficiency in the PIAAC population of 16- to 65-years old participants, APS units and items will need to vary with respect to their item difficulty. To achieve this, the items will be distributed along the difficulty drivers as described in detail earlier in this chapter (see also Table 4.A.1. in the Annex).

As the second cycle of PIAAC focuses on the adaptive component of problem solving, the manipulation of the dynamics of the problem situation is key to the item development. At the same time, the elements a problem situation is comprised of (i.e., its configuration and the characteristics of the information sources) also play an important role in driving item difficulty. Furthermore, in some instances, the instructions to solve a problem are not fully provided, for instance, when problem solvers interact with a simulation and thereby acquire knowledge about its functionalities. This design feature is relevant to the measurement of APS, as it presents problem solvers with an actual problem situation and triggers metacognitive processes to develop and refine a mental model about the problem situation (i.e., in this case, the functionalities of the simulation).

Assessing metacognitive processes

As noted earlier, metacognition plays an important role in the APS processes, especially as problem solvers monitor their comprehension of the problem, evaluate operators and solution plans, and monitor their progress towards the goal. As these metacognitive processes interact directly with the cognitive processes during problem solving, disentangling them from the measurements of cognition poses a challenge. For example, evaluating one's personal resources and capabilities is an aspect of metacognition that cannot be addressed in a survey such as PIAAC that does not report individual results. Moreover, test questions that are aimed at making problem solver's understanding of a problem explicit by asking them "How well do you think you understood the problem?" seem artificial (and may lack face validity) and could prompt problem solvers' responses in following items or even units.

To obtain some measures of metacognition, the APS assessment provides implicit and explicit indicators that can be derived from item scores or log-file data. For instance, in some APS items, log-file data can provide information whether a problem solver accessed certain information sources (i.e., navigation behaviour). This information may serve as an indicator of metacognitive processes to evaluate certain information sources during "searching for a solution" – in some instances, it may also indicate whether problem solvers reconsider certain pieces of information during the "applying the solution" stage. In general, the navigation behaviour may indicate certain metacognitive strategies to solving the problem.

Next to these implicit measures, some APS items explicitly assess metacognition. For instance, at the end of a problem-solving process, problem solvers may be asked to evaluate a given solution to the problem according to pre-defined criteria. Additionally, problem solvers may be asked to evaluate certain problem-solving strategies according to their efficiency and applicability. Mastering the latter is indicative of problem solvers' metacognitive strategy knowledge [e.g., (Antonietti, Ignazi and Perego, 2000[30]; Efklides and Vlachopoulos, 2012[31])]. Overall, the APS assessment will contain both explicit and implicit measures of metacognition. However, given the nature of metacognitive processes and the challenges inherent in their assessment, metacognitive processes, albeit essential to APS, will not form the major focus of the assessment itself.

For the two example units, metacognitive processes could be traced using several measurement approaches. These approaches are described below (Box 4.21).

Box 4.21. Assessment of metacognition in the example units

Metacognition in the *Dinner Preparation* example is implicitly assessed in item 2 only. It can be assessed whether problem solvers adapt their initial solution according to the new information. Metacognition in the *Stock Market* example is not assessed explicitly in this unit, but implicitly. Item 2 requires the problem solvers to understand that the previously employed and efficient solution is not working any more, due to changes in the environment. They will need to detect the impasse, to understand the reason, and to adapt decisions accordingly.

Item scoring and data capturing

General scoring principles

Each APS item will be scored according to criteria that define the correctness of the responses. For most items, the answers provided by problem solvers (e.g., by selecting a response among given response options, or by selecting certain sets of values for a set of variables) are scored dichotomously as either correct (code: 1) or incorrect (code: 0). Missing responses are also coded (code: 9). For some items, the solution must fulfill multiple criteria so that partial credits may be given. Nevertheless, the item scoring is aimed at providing scores that allow the application of parsimonious item response models – hence, a dichotomous scoring is preferred.

To exemplify the item scoring, Box 4.22 describes how problem solvers' responses are scored in the two sample units.

While the preferred scoring method is to dichotomise problem solvers' performance in items (correct vs. incorrect), in some instances, the scoring may allow for partial credits. Partial credits will be used only if the different scores represent qualitatively different responses or processes. Field trial data will be used to evaluate the appropriateness of partial credit scoring for the main study. The key criterion for considering partial credit scores is therefore their construct-relevance.

As noted earlier, the cognitive and metacognitive processes stimulated by the APS items are intertwined, and, in most APS units, their indicators cannot be separated clearly. As a consequence, the scaling of problem solvers' APS performance will not result in two distinct APS dimensions representing the two types of processes. Along the same lines, the APS assessment in the second cycle of PIAAC does not aim for distinguishing the three processes, define the problem, search for a solution, and apply the solution empirically into three correlated APS dimensions. The reporting of the APS performance scale will therefore most likely not be along these processes, and will most likely result in a single APS scale.

Given the variation of APS items and units across the task dimensions, a possible distinction between dimensions may be based on the dynamics of the situation (e.g., static vs. dynamic items) or the inclusion of metacognitive processes (e.g., items requiring metacognition vs. items not requiring metacognition to a substantial degree). These possible dimensions will, however, not be made psychometrically explicit, for instance, in the form of separate APS scores - they may be used to craft a validity argument for the APS assessment.

Box 4.22. Scoring in the example units

Dinner Preparation

Item 1: "Plan the fastest route to accomplish these goals. Keep the time constraints in mind"
Code 1: Route from Home to School to Shop A selected
Code 0: *Other responses*
Code 9: *Missing*

Item 2: "Adapt your chosen route to accomplish the rest of the goals for the day. Keep the time constraints in mind"
Code 1: Route correctly adapted School to Shop A to Home OR School to Shop C to Home
Code 0: *Other responses*
Code 9: *Missing*

Stock Market

Item 1: "Based on the information provided, which shares should you buy or sell in order to maximise your chance for higher profits next day"
Code 1: The problem solver uses the correct investment pattern to maximise profit
Code 0: *Other responses*
Code 9: *Missing*

Item 2: "Based on the information provided, which shares should you buy or sell in order to maximise your chance for higher profits next day"
Code 1: The problem solver uses the correct investment pattern to maximise profit
Code 0: *Other responses*
Code 9: *Missing*

Log-file data

Next to the scoring of problem solvers' item responses that they submitted directly after completing an item, log-file data are used to retrieve and evaluate certain behaviours while solving a problem. These data may include the sequence of actions, whether or not certain elements in the problem environment were selected or accessed, and the time spent on the tasks. Whereas the latter may be useful to identify test-taking effort or aberrant responses (Goldhammer, Martens and Lüdtke, 2017[32]; Marianti et al., 2014[33]), the former can provide insights into metacognition. Some of these behaviours may even be scored.

For instance, whether or not a problem solver makes use of a certain information source (e.g., a hyperlink to a text that contains relevant information) may be an indicator of both cognitive and metacognitive processes of search for information and understanding the problem. If, indeed, a problem solver does not access this information, the problem-solving success may only be limited due to missing information or a resultant solution that does not fully meet all criteria. For instance, considering the information about time restrictions in the *Dinner Preparation* example is essential to the APS performance. In this sense, log-file data aid the analysis or the description of problem-solving performance within the task. Overall, log-file data may provide data beyond the mere correctness of an item response to indicate test-taking behaviour and, in some cases, metacognitive processes.

Adaptive problem solving in the nexus of related constructs and implications for PIAAC Cycle 2

Up on this point we have described the importance of APS in today's changing world, defined and explained what is meant by APS and have introduced the core dimensions that form an adaptive problem before concretising how APS can be assessed. It is, however, also crucial to theoretically describe what differentiates APS from other core competencies, since APS addresses a set of higher-order cognitive skills that are related to other domains, such as literacy, numeracy, or digital competencies. For example, APS often relies on verbal and pictorial representations that the person has to be able to parse in order to acquire information that is needed to solve the problem. The *Dinner Preparation* example presented in Box 4.1 involves written instructions, a map and a sticky note; and the *Stock Market* example (Box 4.2) has a set of tables and graphs. Regardless of their ability to adaptively solve the problem, problem solvers need to be able to parse and make sense of the information in these representations, which is arguably related to their literacy skills.

In the present section we discuss the status of APS in relation to some of these overlapping domains. We review the similarities and differences between the domains and we list a number of distinctive features that differentiate APS as a construct. We also explain how the design of APS task intends to reduce the potential influence of these related domains.

Adaptive problem solving and literacy

The word literacy is sometimes used in the restricted sense of "knowing to read and write". However, over the past 20 years, the definition has been expanded to reflect abilities related to the functional use of documents, which reflects the growing pervasiveness of reading and writing in post-industrial societies (Rouet and Britt, 2017[34]). In turn, the functional use of a document often entails forms of reasoning that amount to problem solving (for instance, making a decision about which product to purchase based on two descriptions of competing products). Therefore, it is important to clarify the boundaries between APS and literacy.

Literacy is bound to overlap with most areas of assessment because most assessment procedures rely on natural language communication. Put in a concrete way, whatever the testing domain, participants always have to read and comprehend written instructions, questions, and stimuli in order to demonstrate their ability in the respective domains. Completing APS tasks is no exception to this rule as a minimum level of literacy is required to solve an adaptive problem. However, several dimensions contribute to making APS a distinct domain. Some of the main dimensions are the types of representations used in the testing materials, the level of problem specification, and the dynamics of the environment (Table 4.4).

Table 4.4. PIAAC Cycle 2 APS and literacy assessments

	PIAAC Cycle 2 APS assessment	Reading literacy assessment
Types of representations	Materials include verbal and non-verbal representations, including interactive graphs and simulated devices	Materials include texts possibly together with static graphs
Task definition	Tasks may be well defined or ill defined	Tasks are generally well defined
Characteristics of the task environment	Environment may change with time as a function of problem solvers actions or other factors (i.e., a dynamic environment)	Environment is static

Note: Other dimensions that are specific to literacy are not represented here.

In a reading literacy assessment, materials include by definition written texts sometimes with other, adjunct representations such as a graph or a picture. Materials included in the APS assessment will encompass a range of stimuli, some of them almost entirely non-verbal. In addition, reading literacy tasks are meant to be well defined, whereas some problem-solving tasks are intentionally left partially implicit. Finally, a reading literacy environment involves one or several passages of text that are provided at the onset and remain the same throughout the task. APS environments may change with time as a function of a range of factors including the problem solvers actions.

In order to maximise the specificity of APS assessment, care will be taken to develop tasks that do not pose significant challenges from a reading literacy perspective. For example, for those APS tasks that include written texts, these will be limited to short and simple passages in combination with non-verbal representations. For instance, the *Dinner Preparation* example involves a simple narrative and a short list of things to do. The *Stock Market* example contains no extended text passage. Difficulty in this unit clearly comes from the need to handle multiple dynamic sources of mostly non-verbal information, which arguably makes it distinct from a reading literacy task.

Adaptive problem solving and proficient use of information and communications technology (ICT)

Throughout the second half of the 20th century, digital devices (e.g., mainframes, computers, laptops, iPads and smartphones) have spread rapidly and profoundly in developed societies. People's ability to handle these devices has had an increasingly important impact on their access to employment, civic participation and their personal life in general. Numerous calls have been made for governments and other organisations to assess people's ability to use computers and related devices, under various constructs ranging from "ICT literacy" (Eshet-Alkalai, 2004[35]), to "digital competence" [Ferrari (2013[36]), to cite just a few].

Proficient use of digital devices involves knowing how to perform basic operations such as opening a folder, naming a file or updating a piece of software, but also to perform more complex tasks such as managing a photo or e-mail archive, addressing issues with system or application compatibility, or contacting a customer service in order to obtain information. Surveys and assessments addressing people's use of computers have typically included tasks at various levels of difficulty.

Digital devices are used to perform an ever-increasing range of tasks, including non-routine ones. In addition, these devices are typically dynamic and interactive, offering numerous opportunities for adaptation. Therefore, it is relevant to ask how APS differs from an assessment of digital competence. Table 4.5 highlights two of these dimensions.

Table 4.5. PIAAC Cycle 2 APS and digital competence

	PIAAC Cycle 2 APS	"Digital competence" [1]
Role of digital devices in task environment	Variable from none to central	Typically large
Status of tasks	Tasks involve non-trivial goals	Range of tasks from routine to complex

1. Here the phrase "Digital competence" subsumes the various constructs and frameworks that have addressed people's knowledge of and proficiency at using digital devices.
Source: Adapted from Greiff et al. (2017[6]).

Firstly, some APS tasks will require the use of digital devices and applications whereas others do not. For instance, the *Dinner Preparation* task uses a static map even though it could be set in the context of embarked information systems such as a GPS editor. The *Stock Market* example also uses simple representations although a spreadsheet application could be of some use to people with a high level of digital competence. Ideally, prerequisites in terms of digital competence should remain minimal in an assessment of APS.

Secondly, APS tasks involve non-trivial goals whereas assessments of digital competence may involve routine as well as non-routine uses. For instance, in the *Stock Market* example, information about two companies changes during the completion of the task, requiring the problem solver to adjust their investment decisions accordingly. The demand on ICT use is minimal, although the complexity in terms of goal management is expected to be moderate to high.

Adaptive problem solving and problem solving in technology-rich environments

The prevalence of problem solving in ICT use has prompted efforts to understand what participants can or cannot do when faced with tasks involving non-routine uses of technology. Therefore, the assessment of traditional competencies, namely literacy and numeracy, was augmented by an assessment of individuals' ability to effectively use information and communications technology to solve problems [i.e. PS-TRE; (OECD, 2012[4])]. The domain was defined as:

> "using digital technology, communication tools and networks to acquire and evaluate information, communicate with others and perform practical tasks." (OECD, 2012, p. 47[4])

Since the assessment of APS will also use technology-rich environments in which the problem is embedded, it is important to also compare the APS with the assessment of problem solving in the first cycle of PIAAC.

PS-TRE focused on "non-routine" uses of technology, i.e., those in which individuals have to set up *ad hoc* goals and plans, and to access and use information presented on the computer. Thus, the assessment of PS-TRE in the first cycle of PIAAC was an assessment of problem-solving skills as they apply to technology-rich environments. The stimuli were presented in the context of simulated web browser, e-mail, and spreadsheet environments. The tasks required the participants to access information relevant to their needs by using the tools available in the computer applications(s). Depending on the task, one or several applications were available. For example, a task might require respondents to use a web-based reservation system to manage requests to reserve a meeting room and send e-mails to decline requests if reservations could not be accommodated. The environment typically included more information than was needed to solve the task.

In contrast, the assessment of APS in the second cycle of PIAAC will not systematically assess the proficiency of problem solvers to interact with technology-rich environments. Instead, APS focuses on problem solvers' ability to adapt to changing conditions, such as a change in the problem definition, unexpected difficulties when taking a path towards a solution, or simply a dynamic environment that changes in more or less predictable ways as a function of time (see section defining APS). Proficient problem solvers are expected to be able to detect and manage those changing conditions. This may include giving up an initial path towards a solution, backtracking to previous stages in the problem-solving process, and/or incorporating the new conditions into one's strategy to solve the problem.

In summary (Table 4.6), APS tasks will involve a variable amount of information, and most tasks will implement a constraint to adapt to changing conditions.

Table 4.6. PIAAC Cycle 2 APS and PIAAC Cycle 1 PS-TRE

	PIAAC Cycle 2 APS	PIAAC Cycle 1 PS-TRE
Amount of information presented and/or required to solve the problem	Variable	Typically large
Use of computer applications[1]	Required in some tasks, proficient use not part of the assessment	Required in all tasks
Need to adapt to changing conditions	Required in most tasks	Required in a few tasks

1. Both PIAAC Cycle 1 and 2 use simulations of mainstream computer applications such as a spreadsheet or a web browser. The simulations typically feature a limited set of functions (for instance, a sort function on the spreadsheet), which are presented in standard ways so as to maximise transfer from real-life applications.

Summary and conclusion

In this section we have examined the relationship of APS with three related constructs and domains: literacy, digital competence and PS-TRE. Because of their breadth and the universal use of written language to convey instructions and stimuli, the domains are bound to overlap. However, we have listed a few aspects that make APS distinct from the other domains. One aspect is the diversity of the representations used in the problem-solving environment; another is the non-trivial and sometimes partly implicit nature of tasks. Finally, APS uniquely implements environments that are dynamic and interactive.

The domain of competencies that is implemented in APS reflects current demands on individuals, both at the workplace and in society in general. In particular, it addresses the need for individuals to adjust to conditions that may change at a rapid pace and sometimes in unpredictable ways.

References

Ainsworth, S., V. Prain and R. Tytler (2011), "Drawing to learn in science", *Science*, Vol. 333/6046, pp. 1096-1097, http://dx.doi.org/10.1126/science.1204153. [19]

Antonietti, A., S. Ignazi and P. Perego (2000), "Metacognitive knowledge about problem-solving methods", *British Journal of Educational Psychology*, Vol. 70/1, pp. 1-16, http://dx.doi.org/10.1348/000709900157921. [30]

Autor, D., F. Levy and R. Murnane (2003), "The skill content of recent technological change: An empirical exploration", *Quarterly Journal of Economics*, Vol. 118/4, pp. 1279-1334, https://doi.org/10.1162/003355303322552801. [5]

Bjork, R., J. Dunlosky and N. Kornell (2013), "Self-regulated learning: Beliefs, techniques, and illusions", *Annual Review of Psychology*, Vol. 64/1, pp. 417-444, http://dx.doi.org/10.1146/annurev-psych-113011-143823. [26]

Braithwaite, D. and R. Goldstone (2015), "Effects of variation and prior knowledge on abstract concept learning", *Cognition and Instruction*, Vol. 33/3, pp. 226-256, http://dx.doi.org/10.1080/07370008.2015.1067215. [17]

Efklides, A. and S. Vlachopoulos (2012), "Measurement of metacognitive knowledge of self, task, and strategies in mathematics", *European Journal of Psychological Assessment*, Vol. 28/3, pp. 227-239, https://doi.org/10.1027/1015-5759/a000145. [31]

Ericsson, K. and R. Pool (2016), *Peak: Secrets from the New Science of Expertise*, Eamon Dolan/Houghton Mifflin Harcourt, New York. [27]

Eshet-Alkalai, Y. (2004), "Digital literacy. A conceptual framework for survival skills in the digital era", *Journal of Educational Multimedia and Hypermedia*, Vol. 13/1, pp. 93-106. [35]

Felstead, A. et al. (2013), *Skills at Work in Britain: First Findings from the Skills and Employment Survey 2012*, Centre for Learning and Life Chances in Knowledge Economies and Societies, Institute of Education, London. [3]

Ferrari, A. (2013), *DIGCOMP: A Framework for Developing and Understanding Digital Competence in Europe*, European Commission, Joint Research Center, Institute for Prospective Technological Studies, Seville, http://publications.jrc.ec.europa.eu/repository/handle/JRC83167. [36]

Fischer, A., S. Greiff and J. Funke (2012), "The process of solving complex problems", *The Journal of Problem Solving*, Vol. 4/1, pp. 19-42, http://dx.doi.org/10.7771/1932-6246.1118. [20]

Funke, J. (2010), "Complex problem solving: A case for complex cognition?", *Cognitive Processing*, Vol. 11/2, pp. 133-142, http://dx.doi.org/10.1007/s10339-009-0345-0. [9]

Gick, M. (1986), "Problem-solving strategies", *Educational Psychologist*, Vol. 21/1-2, pp. 99-120, http://dx.doi.org/10.1080/00461520.1986.9653026. [23]

Goldhammer, F., T. Martens and O. Lüdtke (2017), "Conditioning factors of test-taking engagement in PIAAC: An exploratory IRT modelling approach considering person and item characteristics", *Large-scale Assessments in Education*, Vol. 5/18, http://dx.doi.org/10.1186/s40536-017-0051-9. [32]

Greiff, S. et al. (2017), "Adaptive problem solving: Moving towards a new assessment domain in the second cycle of PIAAC", *OECD Education Working Papers*, No. 156, OECD Publishing, Paris, https://dx.doi.org/10.1787/90fde2f4-en. [6]

Greiff, S., S. Wüstenberg and F. Avvisati (2015), "Computer-generated log-file analyses as a window into students' minds? A showcase study based on the PISA 2012 assessment of problem solving", *Computers & Education*, Vol. 91, pp. 92-105, http://dx.doi.org/10.1016/j.compedu.2015.10.018. [24]

Klahr, D. (2002), *Exploring Science: The Cognition and Development of Discovery Processes*, MIT press, Cambridge. [12]

Klahr, D. and K. Dunbar (1988), "Dual space search during scientific reasoning", *Cognitive Science*, Vol. 12/1, pp. 1-48, http://dx.doi.org/10.1207/s15516709cog1201_1. [13]

Lee, C., D. Jonassen and T. Teo (2011), "The role of model building in problem solving and conceptual change", *Interactive Learning Environments*, Vol. 19/3, pp. 247-265, http://dx.doi.org/10.1080/10494820902850158.   [22]

Levy, F. and R. Murnane (2006), "Why the changing American economy calls for twenty-first century learning: Answers to educators' questions", *New Directions for Youth Development*, Vol. 2006/110, pp. 53-62, http://dx.doi.org/10.1002/yd.167.   [1]

Marianti, S. et al. (2014), "Testing for aberrant behavior in response time modeling", *Journal of Educational and Behavioral Statistics*, Vol. 39/6, pp. 426-451, http://dx.doi.org/10.3102/1076998614559412.   [33]

Mayer, R. and R. Wittrock (2006), "Problem solving", in Alexander, P. and P. Winne (eds.), *Handbook of Educational Psychology, 2nd edition (pp. 287-304)*, Erlbaum, Mahwah, NJ.   [10]

Nathan, M., W. Kintsch and E. Young (1992), "A theory of algebra-word-problem comprehension and its implications for the design of learning environments", *Cognition and Instruction*, Vol. 9/4, pp. 329-389, http://dx.doi.org/10.1207/s1532690xci0904_2.   [11]

National Research Council (2012), *Education for Life and Work: Developing Transferable Knowledge and Skills in the 21st Century*, National Academies Press, Washington, DC, http://dx.doi.org/10.17226/13398.   [2]

Nelson, T. and L. Narens (1990), "Metamemory: A theoretical framework and new findings", in Bower, G. (ed.), *The Psychology of Learning and Motivation: Advances in Research and Theory, Vol. 26*, Academic Press, San Diego, http://dx.doi.org/10.1016/s0079-7421(08)60053-5.   [25]

Newell, A. and H. Simon (1972), *Human Problem Solving*, Prentice-Hall, Englewood Cliffs, NJ.   [14]

OECD (2018), *The use of tablets for collecting data in the 2nd cycle of PIAAC. 20th Meeting of the PIAAC Board of Participating Countries, 16-17 April 2018, OECD Headquarters*, OECD, Paris.   [29]

OECD (2017), "PISA 2015 collaborative problem-solving framework", in *PISA 2015 Assessment and Analytical Framework: Science, Reading, Mathematic, Financial Literacy and Collaborative Problem Solving*, OECD Publishing, Paris, https://dx.doi.org/10.1787/9789264281820-8-en.   [8]

OECD (2014), *PISA 2012 Results: Creative Problem Solving (Volume V): Students' Skills in Tackling Real-Life Problems*, PISA, OECD Publishing, Paris, https://dx.doi.org/10.1787/9789264208070-en.   [7]

OECD (2013), *Technical Report of the Survey of Adult Skills (PIAAC)*, https://www.oecd.org/skills/piaac/_Technical%20Report_17OCT13.pdf.   [28]

OECD (2012), *Literacy, Numeracy and Problem Solving in Technology-Rich Environments: Framework for the OECD Survey of Adult Skills*, OECD Publishing, Paris, https://dx.doi.org/10.1787/9789264128859-en.   [4]

Ross, B. (1989), "Distinguishing types of superficial similarities: Different effects on the access and use of earlier problems", *Journal of Experimental Psychology: Learning, Memory, and Cognition*, Vol. 15/3, pp. 456-468, http://dx.doi.org/10.1037/0278-7393.15.3.456. [16]

Ross, B. (1989), "Remindings in learning and instruction", in Vosniadou, S. and A. Ortony (eds.), *Similarity and Analogical Reasoning*, Cambridge University Press, Cambridge, CA. [18]

Rouet, J. and M. Britt (2017), *Literacy in 2030. Report commissioned by the OECD's Education 2030 project*, OECD, Paris. [34]

Vollmeyer, R., B. Burns and K. Holyoak (1996), "The Impact of Goal Specificity on Strategy Use and the Acquisition of Problem Structure", *Cognitive Science*, Vol. 20/1, pp. 75-100, http://dx.doi.org/10.1207/s15516709cog2001_3. [15]

Zhang, J. (1997), "The nature of external representations in problem solving", *Cognitive Science*, Vol. 21/2, pp. 179-217, http://dx.doi.org/10.1207/s15516709cog2102_3. [21]

Annex 4.A. Description of difficulty drivers

Annex Table 4.A.1. Description of difficulty drivers

(1) Problem configuration

Difficulty drivers		Problem description
1a: Number of elements, relations, and operations	How many elements does the problem solver need to consider in the context of the problem. This refers not only to elements that are relevant to solving the problem, but also to "clutter".	A **simple problem** will only have very few elements, and all will be relevant to the task. For example: only one dial, and one readout. A **difficult problem** will have a larger number of elements, with relations among them, and some not relevant for the task. For example, four dials and six readout panels, four of the panels react normally to dials, and two of the panels react to interaction effects between dials. Only one dial and one interaction effect are needed to solve the problem, the rest is irrelevant clutter.
1b: Salience and accessibility of operators	How visible are the resources needed to solve the problem? How accessible are they on screen and more generally in the problem environment?	A **simple problem** will have operators that are readily available from the start, arranged in a visible and logical manner on the interface. In such a problem, the problem solver will have no need to take extra actions in order to access these elements. For example, if needed to solve the problem, an extra window showing progress towards the solutions (in percent's) could show up automatically or be available in a corner of the screen all the time. A **difficult problem** will force the problem solver to take extra steps in order to access information or other resource. Such a problem will not have the resources arranged in a visible manner (they may need to be picked up from a larger number of resources, available in a "basket", or will need to be "invoked" on screen by pressing a button), or the resources will not be readily available at the beginning, but will need to be created during the problem-solving process (e.g., in a chemistry simulation, mixing base substances in order to obtain a higher level element, and some of these higher level elements can be then used to solve the problem).
1c: Interactions between problem elements	Do the manipulable elements of the interface interact in creating an effect?	A **simple problem** will have each button or dial create a clear and unique effect on a readout panel. A **difficult problem** will have the manipulable elements (e.g., buttons, dials, levers) creating effects by interaction. For example, while each of two buttons generates a readout on a dedicated panel, a third readout shows the outcome produced by the interaction of those two dials (e.g., dials for temperature and humidity, with a third readout showing the estimated time to completion of a biological culture). Or, the readout of each of the dials is dependent on the other dial (e.g., when the temperature increases, pressure also increases automatically on the pressure readout, even if the dial is not operated).
1d: Number of parallel tasks and goals	How many goals does the problem prescribe? How many tasks need to be processed in parallel in order to reach these goals?	A **simple problem** may require the problem solver to reach one goal (e.g., set the temperature of an incubator). If several goals are given, the problem solver is not required to solve them in parallel, but one after the other (one at a time, consecutively). For example, it will require the problem solver only to operate one dial in order to observe change in the readout panel. A **difficult problem** may require the problem solver to reach two or more separate goals (e.g., set the temperature and the humidity of an incubator would require the problem solver to push two buttons, or operate two dials at the same time, in order to observe a change in readout), or to reach one or several goals in a maximum number of steps (parsimony on problem solving, i.e., keeping under that threshold of steps, is a goal in itself). The problem solver would also need to work towards these goals at the same time (not one after the other).

The "Dinner Preparation" example is of average-to-high difficulty from this point of view. It asks the test-taker to accomplish two goals at the same time (shop for groceries and take the child to school, respectively pick the child up from school again) – this raises the cognitive and metacognitive demands on the test-taker. But the problem only has a low number of locations to visit, the routes that can be used are very salient and accessible to the problem solver on the interface, as well as are all of the other needed information.

The "Stock Market" example is of high difficulty in terms of problem configuration. While it asks the test-taker to accomplish only one goal (reach a certain level of cash), it has a high number of elements in the initial problem statement: the different portfolios each have a history of variation that need to be considered. On the other hand, all these elements are salient and readily available to the test-taker.

(2) Dynamics of the situation

Difficulty drivers		Problem description
2a: Number of features that change and their relevance	How many features change from one iteration to another? How relevant is change in these features for the problem-solving process? Change may be induced in critical elements or in less critical or even trivial issues.	A **simple problem** may have only one feature that changes from one step to the other. For example, one element of the interface changes position, or one dial changes function, or one parameter (e.g., temperature) changes from one iteration to another. Also, a simple problem has changes induced in trivial aspects of the problem, aspects that are not critical to the problem-solving process. Change is rather a distractor in this case, i.e., the outside temperature has changed, but the outside temperature is not relevant for solving a problem that requires the problem solver to set the luminosity of a lightbulb.
		A **difficult problem** has a larger number of elements that change. For example, the whole interface is re-arranged, and buttons change position. Or a larger number of buttons (all?) change functionality: they begin to interact now, or their effect on the readouts is no longer linear but exponential etc. Also, a difficult problem changes elements that are critical to the problem being solved and that need to be understood by the problem solver and factored into the problem-solving process in order to be successful. For example, if the problem solvers do not understand the new non-linear effect of a dial they will not be able to solve the problem.
2b: Salience of change (if something changes)	Is the problem solver prompted to the change? Is the change announced or in other way obvious, or is it hidden and needs to be discovered by the problem solver? This refers to the IF of the change (if something has changed). When the problem solver is prompted to change in an element, the particular manner in which it has changed may also be explained (or not). This refers to the HOW of the change (in what way has something changed).	A **simple problem** will announce the change to the problem solver, e.g. state that a change was made. A simple problem will also explain to the problem solver exactly what has changed and in what way.
		A **difficult problem** will not announce the change - it simply introduces a new element in the problem, that may be visible from the start, but appearance of change is not prompted for the problem solver. Or it may change the functionality of an element of the interface (e.g., button), but the fact that this has changed is not prompted. A difficult problem will also not explain to the problem solver how things have changed. For example, the function of an element of the interface may have changed, and its effect on the readout may no longer be linear, but curvilinear.
2c: Frequency of change	How frequent is the change? It could be iterative, i.e. not very frequent, or "continuous drop" change, i.e., constant.	A **simple problem** may have a low-frequency change: from one item to the other, or even every 2-3 items, there is some change in the problem statement. Throughout a whole problem with 10 items, maybe there are 2-3 changes. There is no change inside the item, but only from one item to another.
		A **difficult problem** has elements changing constantly, even inside a specific item. For example, temperature fluctuates constantly and the problem solver has to adjust dials while taking account these fluctuations in temperature.
2d: Degree of impasse	Is the change likely to induce an impasse? i.e., does the change actually create another problem that needs to be solved first, or complicates the solving of the initial problem? How likely is it that the induced change will close one avenue of solving the problem that was obvious before the change, i.e., will it require the problem solver to rethink the problem from zero?	A **simple problem** will introduce change that, while bringing with its supplementary information, will not induce impasse - the obvious avenues for solving the problem before the change remain the same after the change. For example, if the problem solver has to regulate the temperature of a room by working a dial, even if the dial no longer has a linear but an exponential effect, the effect remains positive if the dial is turned to the right.
		A **difficult problem** will induce impasse, i.e., it will throw the problem solver off the course that was obvious for problem solving until the introduction of change. It will either go against how the problem was previously solved (e.g., the same button that the problem solver knew from the previous interaction was doing something, is doing now something else), or interact with how the problem solver thought he/she would solve the problem (e.g., the problem solver works towards the goal in a predictable way with current resources, and some of those resources disappear after the change, so he/she has to rethink the problem).

The "Dinner Preparation" example is of low difficulty from this point of view. The problem configuration does not change at all, and only one element, i.e. one route, is manipulated. More impasse could be engineered in the problem, for example by having one store go out of one ingredient. But change is certainly explicit, transparent and infrequent in this example.

The "Stock Market" example is of average-to-high difficulty in terms of the dynamics of the situation. The change is continuous and frequent, and happens in a large number of elements (in all the stocks the problem solver has investments in). Change is however salient and explicit. Impasse could be engineered into items by changing the pattern with which the various stocks vary from one iteration to another.

(3) Features of the environment

Difficulty drivers		Problem description
3a: Wealth of information	How much information is in the problem statement? This includes both elements that are relevant and those that are not relevant for solving the problem.	A **simple problem** has a very limited set of elements - the barely minimum to define the problem, not much context around it, no extra irrelevant information. For example, a dial is given, a readout, and a basic description of the phenomenon (say, temperature of an oven).
		A **difficult problem** contains a large number of elements, some of which are needed to define the problem (for example, a larger number of dials and readouts, a description of the entire interface, a description of the context and the motives why the problem needs to be solved, a description of the larger story the problem is set in etc.), the functionality of the interface and the task, some of which are irrelevant to the problem, but enrich the problem environment (e.g., details could be given about how other tasks are performed with the same basic resources, or about the status of other resources that are not needed for the problem at hand).
3b: Proportion of irrelevant information	How much "clutter", i.e. irrelevant information is there in the problem environment?	A **simple problem** does not have irrelevant information: all information given is relevant for solving the problem, every single piece is critical: taking that piece away will make the problem unsolvable.
		A **difficult problem** has a larger quantity of information that is not relevant for solving the problem. If such a piece of information would be taken away, the problem would be just as easily solvable. Such information does not contribute to solving the problem, but is a distractor and challenges the problem solver to also discern what is relevant and critical from what is not.
3c: (Lack of) Structure of the environment	How structured is the environment?	A **simple problem** is constructed in a well-structured environment. Well-structured environments will have both an intuitive and a simple structure with a small number of categories that are clearly labelled and defined. Data may be presented in clear tables or charts, well grouped and structured.
		A **difficult problem** is constructed in an unstructured environment. The environment may be "structurable" by the problem solver, i.e. the problem solver could structure the available information in logical categories, but the information is not presented in such a structured manner. Unstructured environments have in principle several categories (e.g. data from several sources, regarding several phenomena) and data from these categories is provided in a narrative form and intercalated with one another, so that no structure is visible on a first glance. Structuring the information is one of the tasks the problem solver would be challenged with in order to solve the problem.
3d: Number of sources of information	How many sources does information come from? These could be the actual problem statement (introduction), the solving process itself, the system through its various buttons, help panels etc.	A **simple problem** has only one source of information: the problem description. No other information is available to the problem solver.
		A **difficult problem** has a larger number of sources of information. Basic information will come from the problem statement, but a number of other sources of information will be available. These could be extra buttons (e.g., help button, a "read the history" button, a simulated "Google search" of "Wikipedia button" etc.). The problem-solving process itself could provide continuous information and feedback on the task, especially for more complex tasks. A narrator could come up to give extra information, or maybe even several narrators, giving information from other areas.

The "Dinner Preparation" example is of low-to-average difficulty from this point of view. The environment is not extremely wealthy, it does not offer much information beyond what is absolutely necessary to solve the problem (the routes, the shops, the shopping list). No irrelevant information is presented, no separate sources of information are present and the environment, such as it is, is structured.

The "Stock Market" example is also of low difficulty in terms of features of the environment: no extra information beyond the actual problem is presented in the environment.

CANDLEWICK
The Crystal Line
Revised 3rd Edition

MYRNA & BOB GARRISON

Schiffer Publishing Ltd

4880 Lower Valley Road • Atglen, PA 19310

Dedication
In Memory of Bob Garrison, 1927-2006

The book is dedicated to the memory of a wonderful husband and father. For fifty-eight years, we had a great time doing things we enjoyed: being with family, having company, sharing our glass collecting, traveling, and enjoying our home together. To quote our favorite song, "Too Young," "This love will last though years may go."

Without hesitation, Bob put his family first. The times our children joined us at NIGCS conventions were special for us. They were proud of their father, and they made him proud of them. There was mutual admiration with his grandchildren. He enjoyed building things for us and our family. When asked for one word that described what they had learned from their dad, Janna and Robert both answered, "integrity."

Bob loved everything about our glass collecting; the trips, seminars, displays, research, books, and most of all the friends we made.

The dedication of this book would be incomplete without including our special family: our son Robert and his wife Jenny; our daughter Janna and her husband Kirkby, and our four grandchildren: Kendra, Nathan, Matthew, and Scott. Bob and I shared many holidays and special occasions with them. Before they married, we had church events, scouts, band trips, camping trips, and automobile adventures. After they married, they continued to include us in all phases of their lives. We gathered on ski slopes, cruise ships, and in foreign lands in addition to the usual family gatherings. They continue to be there for me and plan things for me to do with them.

Parts of this book appeared in a slightly different version in *Milk Glass, Imperial Glass Corporation, Plus Opaque, Slag and More* ©2001 by Myrna and Bob Garrison and *Imperial's Candlewick, Little Known Facts* ©1999 by Myrna and Bob Garrison.
The authors wish to extend appreciation to Lancaster Colony Corporation for permission to publish photographs and documents of the former Imperial Glass Corporation.
The authors wish to extend appreciation to Oneida Ltd., Oneida, New York, for permission to use its advertisement c. 1960s.

All photographs in this book were taken by the Myrna & Bob Garrison.
www.mgimperial.com

Title page: Five of the Tri-Stem items. Front: 400/221 Lemon Tray; 400/223 Cake Tray; Back: 400/220 Compote; 400/424 Candleholder; 400/264 Hurricane. In this photo, the Cake Tray and the Hurricane are the most rare of the Tri-Stem items. More information on the Tri-Stem information is included with other captions in the appropriate categories.

3rd Edition Designed by Mark David Bowyer
Originally Designed by Bonnie M. Hensley
Cover design by Bruce M. Waters

Type set in Mona Lisa Solid / Aldine 721 Lt Bt / Souvenir Lt BT

ISBN: 978-0-7643-4173-1
Printed in China

Published by Schiffer Publishing, Ltd.
4880 Lower Valley Road
Atglen, PA 19310
Phone: (610) 593-1777; Fax: (610) 593-2002
E-mail: Info@schifferbooks.com

For the largest selection of fine reference books on this and related s
please visit our website at **www.schifferbooks.com.**
You may also write for a free catalog.

This book may be purchased from the publisher.
Please try your bookstore first.

We are always looking for people to write books on new and related
If you have an idea for a book,
please contact us at *proposals@schifferbooks.com*

Schiffer Books are available at special discounts for bulk purchases for sales promotions or premiums. Special editions, including personalized covers, corporate imprints, and excerpts can be created in large quantities for special needs. For more information contact the publisher.

In Europe, Schiffer books are distributed by
Bushwood Books
6 Marksbury Ave.
Kew Gardens
Surrey TW9 4JF England
Phone: 44 (0) 20 8392 8585; Fax: 44 (0) 20 8392 9876
E-mail: info@bushwoodbooks.co.uk
Website: www.bushwoodbooks.co.uk

Contents

Electro No. 2-C

Acknowledgments

To the Imperial Glass Corporation, which made the wonderful glass that continues to please people long after the factory ceased.

To Helen and Bill Clark for so generously sharing Imperial records without which this book would not be possible. Without their friendship and contributions, our research might have stalled.

To Lucile Kennedy for helping with the beginning of our research twenty-two years ago. It was that first meeting that started us thinking about sharing facts that we were finding.

To Kathy Burch, our long standing friend, who, although miles and states away, is always nearby. She has mailed glass, exchanged items at annual conventions, and toted glass on airplanes to add to the story of Imperial Glass. She was just an e-mail away when we needed to discuss ideas and observations.

To Ruth Adkisson and Bev Harris for encouraging us to attempt the project that we have always wanted to do. Without their constant urging to "put your discoveries into a book," we would not have done this. Their help in many aspects has made a tremendous task more manageable.

To Ruth and David Adkisson, Bev and Jim Harris, Linda and Don O'Mealia, and Kathy Burch for bringing and shipping glass to be photographed for the book.

To Max Miller for sharing his expertise on glass in general and Imperial Glass in particular. His additions to our collections are treasures that we are fortunate enough to share with others. His friendship and help are additional treasures. Max has been a helpful listener in this task.

To Max Miller, Tom and Mary Stevenson, Jim and Bev Harris, David and Ruth Adkisson, Bob and Judy Schmidgall, Bill and Helen Clark, Jack and Jean Fry, Lois Quale, Kathy Burch, Marjorie Rudig, Art and Shirley Moore, Kelly O'Kane, Keith Burkart, Paul Gould, Earl and Peggy Thornton, Donald Leininger, and Dorothy and Paul Klosterman for adding to our Candlewick collection through thoughtful gifts and special deeds.

To the following dealers and friends who have shown and alerted us to exceptional items to make our collection more complete: Kevin Kiley, Mark Church, Ron Dalton, Dan Tucker, Lori Kitchen, Constance Crow, Steve Dowell, Eric and Jay Fralick, Benny and Nelda Brewer, Dale and Betty Bass, Edna Phillips, Linda Gordy, Gene Florence, Flo and Gene Ross, Jane Miller, Becky and Jeff Goldstein, Richard and Wilma Ross, and to all the others who have spent their time and effort in finding glass and making it available to collectors like us to be able to buy and enjoy.

To Rakow Research Library, Corning Museum of Glass, Corning, New York for its assistance in locating information on Pavel Decorating Company and Glastonbury, Incorporated.

To John Boyd, Boyd's Crystal Art Glass, Incorporated, for his help with the names of colors of souvenirs from the National Imperial Glass Collectors' Society Conventions.

Last but certainly not least, our acknowledgment and sincerest thanks to Donna Baker, our editor, who cheerfully helped us through the long process of writing this book, the book we have always wanted to write. Her cheerful personality was always present. She helped us change one book into two books—a not too easy task. She was also there for us throughout the revision of this book, always ready with help and encouragement. And to Bruce Waters, our sincere thanks for his help in sending us on our way to photograph the glass for the book. He shared professional assistance so easily and gave his compliments freely. Bruce also designed a striking cover for this revision, no easy task after the beautiful cover he provided for the first edition.

Credits for Third Edition

Keith Burkart and Paul Gould shared the news of their find of the Candlewick 400/79, (#14990) Hurricane Candleholder with originally wrapped candle in an original box. You can imagine how excited I was when they visited me and gave this to me as a gift. Never before had we known about candles wrapped in cellophane with the printed words "candles by LENOX." This was special because Lenox Incorporated owned Imperial from 1973 to 1981.

Bev and Jim Harris deserve a great deal of credit for continuing to share our glass collecting fun as we have for many years. Several times in the last five years, they have called and said, "It is time for a Road Trip." We have gone east to Ohio, north to Michigan, and west to Wyoming. Branson has been on the list more than once. Naturally, we stop at every interesting antique shop or venue. Bev and I spend hours on the telephone talking about many subjects, i.e. the decline in the prices of our favorite glass patterns as well as other collectibles. We also remember all the high prices we have paid and the bargains that we have found.

Since only one interesting fact about Candlewick had surfaced, I tried to think of other ways to add some new interest to the book. Updating prices is not the only story to add to a book. During the months of thinking about this revision, I have had a non-glass friend share thoughts with me. That friend, Bobbie Griffin, a retired journalism teacher, gave me this assistance. It helped to get feedback from a very different point of view. Together we looked at factory advertising material, and Bobbie agreed with me that all collectors would enjoy viewing actual advertising drawings. We had fun playing with different arrangements for the cover of the book. It is never fun doing all of these things alone, and she made a tedious task easier and more enjoyable.

These friends added greatly to this book, and to them I add my appreciation.

Preface

Most collectors are familiar with some patterns of glass for which the Imperial Glass Corporation was famous. However, collectors are not always aware of the amount and the many types of glass that the company produced. In 1978, we became avid collectors of Imperial Glass, particularly the Candlewick and Cape Cod patterns. We made our first trip to the factory in 1980 and wrote our first book, Imperial Cape Cod: Tradition to Treasure, in 1982. We had already met Mrs. Tommie Carroll, a former Imperial Representative (now deceased), at the Dallas Trade Mart. She was instrumental in our early research by lending us her catalogs and other printed material.

On that first trip to the factory in 1980, we met Miss Lucile Kennedy, Assistant to the President of Imperial Glass Corporation. Miss Kennedy opened her office and records to us, and thus supplied us with a wealth of data to draw upon in researching our first book. She continues to encourage us in our research.

In the period since 1980, we have missed only one year making a trip to the factory and now the factory area. In addition, we joined the National Imperial Glass Collectors' Society (NIGCS) and became acquainted with other collectors of Imperial glass. We have made strong and lasting friendships within that group, and the annual NIGCS Convention is a reunion we do not want to miss. We have made thirty-four trips to the factory area for conventions and board meetings for a total of approximately eighty-five thousand miles.

Due to financial hardships, the Imperial Company began to sell wares from its archives and basement storage area in 1983. We were fortunate enough to have made several friends among the Imperial employees, and they helped us look into and buy from special reserves. While we were searching in the basement, a friend stepped forward to help us. Helen Clark of the accounting department came down to bring us a flashlight for our hunt. That beam is still burning today as Helen continues to shed light on our many questions!

By 1991, we had found many more items of the Cape Cod pattern, and enough material and information to publish a new, revised edition of Imperial Cape Cod: Tradition to Treasure. Even as we researched the first Cape Cod book, however, our interest in milk glass began to intensify. Thus, while the updating of the Cape Cod book took precedence, we also made voluminous notes on milk glass production by Imperial, as we searched company records before the 1982 bankruptcy. In 1992, our next book, Imperial's Vintage Milk Glass, made its appearance. We believe this book was of interest to both milk glass collectors and Imperial Glass collectors, because many of the six hundred plus molds used to produce milk glass items were previously used to produce items in color and were subsequently reissued in many of the beautiful colors that Imperial created.

We had been collecting Candlewick and Cape Cod glass perfumes and colognes for a long time. Then, we started adding milk glass colognes and found that we were hunting for other Imperial boudoir items as well. We shared our finds with Helen, and discussed with her the relevant facts of each. As always, Helen came to the rescue with pertinent documentation that she had. She also spent time helping us find new items, to the point that she called us when she heard of pieces for sale. One day in 1990, Helen called about the sale of several colognes that Imperial made for Irving W. Rice. Naturally we bought them. Four hundred plus items later, we are completely hooked on that area of collecting!

During the years since the closing of Imperial, Helen has shared with us notes and records about the Irving W. Rice Company. In the fall of 1993, we went to the Rakow Library at the Corning Glass Museum to research all the Imperial Glass records. With the help of this material and the invaluable information on the Irving W. Rice card file supplied by Helen, we were able to build a substantial data bank of documented material. The publication of Imperial's Boudoir, Etcetera . . . A Comprehensive Look at Dresser Accessories for Irice and Others © 1996 allowed us to share another of Imperial's contributions to the glass world.

Through our collecting years we have been asked many questions about Candlewick at conventions, shows, meetings, and by telephone and letter. There have been numerous requests made that we write a book on Candlewick—to put our observations and answers into a book for all Candlewick collectors. Finally, we decided to follow some of the urging and coaxing of fellow collectors to write down our discoveries from our Imperial research files and from our personal observations. The result was Imperial Candlewick, Little Known Facts © 1999.

Soon we arrived at the need for an updated book on Imperial's milk glass. With our first book on this subject sold out, a few undocumented items to report on, several pieces to photograph that were not pictured previously, and a desire to include the wonderful milk glass boudoir pieces, we decided to undertake a second version of Imperial's Vintage Milk Glass. This led to the publication in 2001 of Milk Glass, Imperial Glass Corporation, Plus Opaque, Slag and More.

After the release of the second milk glass book in 2001, several friends again started asking for a Candlewick book with photos. As one so aptly put it, "if they [Schiffer Publishing, Ltd.] can make milk glass look that great, just think what they could do to Candlewick." Since our book Imperial Candlewick,

Little Known Facts © 1999, had sold out, we started thinking about following our hearts and writing a book that included many photographs showing the story of Imperial's most popular pattern, which just happened to be our wedding crystal.

We started making production charts on January 1, 2001. The following summer, we took 1800 slides for this project, a feat that took longer than we anticipated. Again, Helen Clark made factory records available to us. One little mention of a company or an object would take on an important meaning when we would find another mention in another paper. We would move from the card file, to the catalogs, to the price lists, to the memorandums and back over everything again. More help came when we received word in mid-October 2001 that the factory catalogs and papers that had belonged to Mrs. Tommie Carroll could be ours if we still wanted to buy them. We had waited fifteen years for the opportunity to buy these papers and now they could help fill in gaps with the other materials we had.

As in all of our research, we have used the company catalogs to assemble charts of each mold number, with the catalog and price lists in which it appeared for sale. In this manner, we could determine approximately in which year an item was introduced and when it was last cataloged for sale. We feel that these dates of production add a unique facet to a collector's knowledge, and aid in the building of a collection. How long a piece remained in production helps determine a value. Naturally, a piece may have been produced before it was shown in a catalog, just as a piece was usually still available for order after being dropped from the catalog. However, researchers and collectors usually think of production dates as being from the first time an item was cataloged until the last time it was cataloged.

There will always be questions regarding the research methods used in any project. We have tried to deal with catalog facts and not undocumented theories. Our dates were established by using the written material that was available. Due to fewer company catalogs and records before 1950, earlier detailed dates are impossible.

After eighteen months of working on this project, reality began to surface. In talking with our publisher and editor, it became clear that we had too much material for a single book. We were fortunate that our publisher wanted to see the total work before making a decision about the size of the book. Together we decided that with the amount of information and photographs taken, collectors would be better served if all the material were presented in two separate but obviously related books. With the help of our editor, we reorganized the material to present the total story of Candlewick in two segments. This first book contains the crystal line of Candlewick, while the second book, Candlewick: Colored and Decorated Lines, is the story of decorated Candlewick. We trust that collectors will enjoy, learn, and benefit from this in-depth and comprehensive approach.

We only hope that this book will answer questions that some may have, and that it will help collectors to know what the pieces look like that they are hunting for. Maybe it will only be a book that you will pick up from time to time to leaf through and think, "I have that one!" or maybe "Oh, would I love to have that one!"

However you use the book…seek, find, enjoy.

Electro No. 10-C

A Guide to Using This Book

The main purpose of this book is to help you identify the different pieces of Imperial's Candlewick pattern. Part I provides collectors with a brief history of the Imperial Glass Corporation as well as background information on Candlewick. Part II covers the total Crystal Line. We have attempted to show examples of every piece of the popular Candlewick pattern. In the few instances where it was impossible to do this, we have used a catalog or company photograph to illustrate those items. Part III takes a look at the few still undocumented items that have been found, as well as a brief review of Candlewick similarities and reproductions. It would require a whole book to fully cover similarities and reproductions; we leave that to some one else.

It is just as important to read what has been said about the items as well as to study the photographs. We have attempted to put pertinent information into each caption but often more is needed to tell the story. When necessary, that is presented in the text before each photograph. Keep in mind that when we give a listing of items, we will first list the mold number, then the description, then the price range. Other information will be included when useful.

Imperial used the prefix 400/ for most of the Candlewick line. The numbers to the right of the forward diagonal are numbers assigned by Imperial to specify the particular identification of the individual item. A few times Imperial changed the identification number during the production years of the piece. This is confusing to researchers and collectors, but it is something that has to be accepted.

When a set is composed of two, three, or more pieces the item number may be a combination of the individual numbers. This is not always the case and can be quite confusing. It increases the challenge of interpreting the information and understanding it—that is a vital part of any research study. The stemware lines were designated by one number for the items in that design group.

Imperial used letters after the designated item number for design information. In factory paper, there was a list of "Symbols for Shapes." Since not all letters in the list pertained to Candlewick, we have edited them to indicate the meaning they had with Candlewick.

A Round [oval]
B Bowl
C Crimped
D Flat plate
E Turned-up handles or sides

F Float or shallow bowl
H Heart or fancy crimp
J Slight outward roll at top
L Rolled over and out
N Slight inward roll at top
R Rolled over and down
S Square
TB Tid Bit
V Plate with cupped edge
X Not on the symbol's list but is on two items

A combination of letters simply means a combination of shapes, e.g., 400/40CV would represent Candlewick and candleholder, crimped with vase. (Although "V" for Vase was not on the factory symbol list, it is easy for collectors to interpret the meaning of CV as being Crimped Vase. Not all letters used as mold identifications are on the list we found.) Most double letters you just have to accept as identification numbers, but some may give you a clue to the description. In looking at the charts and working on this part, it is interesting that most of the use of letters occurred in items made in the late 1930s and early 1940s. Fewer letters seem to be used in the higher mold numbers and then only when those numbers are sets. We cannot guess what formula Imperial was using in its numbering of items.

Imperial used different words as names for items throughout the forty-nine year life of Imperial Candlewick. For example, consider comporte and compote, candlestick and candleholder, partitioned and divided, and nappy and bowl. It would be difficult to attempt to use all of the names on every item; it would also be confusing and cumbersome. Therefore, we will use the names that appeared most often in catalogs that collectors are most likely to see. In addition, although in today's usage the word "ashtray" is generally used as one word, we have used it as two words since that is the way Imperial wrote the word in all of its catalogs. We have attempted to project all information as closely as Imperial did for the sake of Imperial history.

All Candlewick collectors want the signs Imperial made to advertise the company and in particular those sign made to advertise Candlewick. Rather than group these signs in one place in the book, we chose to intersperse them throughout the book for added appeal and interest. It will be like an Easter Egg hunt when you find one! Be sure to check the index under Signs to find all page locations of these popular items.

Measurements

Measurements given by Imperial in its description of items sometimes refer to the height and sometimes refer to the width. With the lists of mold numbers and descriptions, we will give measurements as Imperial gave them. In building the charts, we have found that many of these measurements changed through the years by a half-inch, inch, and sometimes two inches. On occasion, we have mentioned these changes if it seemed important. Often we have just used a combination of the two sizes given by Imperial, such as a change from 6" to 6 1/2". Collectors must remember that Candlewick is handmade and therefore the measurements will seldom be exact; that is the part of the enjoyment of owning handmade glassware.

Collectors have often asked for measurements of all stemware to be included in books. Here we are giving those measurements. Every piece was measured by the same person, with the same ruler, and using pieces from the same collections. As we have just noted, however, handmade glass measurements will vary so we ask you to allow for that when using the measurements. We will first give the height, then the diameter of the top opening, and lastly the diameter of the foot. Please allow us the same error tolerance afforded to political analysts—3 to 4%.

Mold	Description	Height	Top Dia.	Foot Dia.
3400	9 oz. Goblet	7 1/2"	3 5/8"	3"
3400	6 oz. Saucer Champagne or Tall Sherbet	5 1/8"	4"	2 15/16"
3400	4 oz. Cocktail	4 5/8"	3 7/16"	2 1/2"
3400	4 oz. Wine	5 5/8"	2 3/4"	2 1/2"
3400	5 oz. Claret	6 5/16"	3 1/16"	2 5/8"
3400	1 oz. Cordial	4 1/2"	2 1/16"	1 3/4"
3400	5 oz. Low Sherbet	3 5/8"	4"	2 3/4"
3400	8 oz. Finger Bowl	2 7/16"	4 3/8"	2 11/16"
3400	5 oz. Juice Tumbler	4 11/16"	2 7/8"	2 3/4"
3400	9-10 oz. Footed Tumbler	5 13/16"	3 3/4"	2 3/8"
3400	12 oz. Footed Tumbler	6 3/8"	4"	2 7/8"
3400	6 oz. Parfait	6 5/16"	2 9/16"	2 1/2"
3400	4 oz. Oyster Cocktail	3 5/16"	3 1/8"	2 1/4"
3400	9 oz. Seafood Icer	4 1/8"	3 7/8"	3"
3400	4 oz. Insert for Seafood Icer	1 11/16"	4 3/8"	
3800	9-11 oz. Goblet	5 7/8"	2 7/8"	2 15/16"
3800	7 oz. Tall Sherbet	4 1/2"	3 3/4"	2 7/8"
3800	6 oz. Low Sherbet	3 7/16"	3 13/16"	2 7/8"
3800	4 oz. Cocktail	3 1/2"	2 9/16"	2 3/8"
3800	3 oz. Wine	3 11/16"	2"	2"
3800	4 oz. Claret	4 5/8"	2 3/8"	2 1/8"
3800	1-1 1/2 oz. Cordial	3 3/8"	1 11/16"	1 3/4"
3800	6 oz. Finger Bowl	2 1/8"	3 15/16"	2 1/2"
3800	5 oz. Footed Juice Tumbler	4 1/4"	2 3/8"	2 1/4"
3800	9 oz. Footed Water Tumbler	5 1/4"	3 1/16"	2 3/4"
3800	12 oz. Footed Ice Tea Tumbler	5 15/16"	3"	2 13/16"
3800	Brandy 2 oz.	4 3/16"	1 3/8"	1 1/2"
3800	4 oz. Oyster Cocktail (same as 3400)	3 5/16"	3 1/4"	2 1/4"
3800	12 oz. Seafood Icer	4 5/8"	3 7/8"	3"
3800	4 oz. Insert for Seafood Icer (same as 3400)	1 11/16"	4 3/8"	
400/15	6 oz. Tumbler	3 3/4"	3"	2 1/4"
400/15	10 oz. Tumbler	4 7/16"	3 11/16"	2 3/4"
400/15	13 oz. Tumbler	4 7/8"	3 7/8"	2 11/16"
400/18	7 oz. Old Fashioned	4"	2 13/16"	2 5/8"
400/18	Tumbler or Water 9 oz.	5 1/8"	2 13/16"	2 11/16"
400/18	Tumbler, Water or Iced Tea 12 oz.	5 3/4"	2 7/8"	2 11/16"
400/18	Sherbet 6 oz.	3 5/16"	3 9/16"	2 11/16"
400/18	Cocktail 3 1/2 oz.	3 15/16"	3 1/16"	2 9/16"
400/18	Tumbler, Juice 5 oz.	4 1/2"	2 1/16"	2 1/4"
400/18	Parfait 7 oz.	5 5/16"	2 1/8"	2 3/16"
400/19	Juice Tumbler, 5 oz.	4"	2"	2 1/4"
400/19	Sherbet or Dessert, 5 oz.	2"	3 3/4"	2 5/8"
400/19	Old Fashioned 7 oz.	3 3/8"	2 7/8"	2 3/4"
400/19	Water Tumbler, 10 oz.	4 3/4"	2 3/4"	2 1/2"
400/19	Iced Tea Tumbler, 12 oz.	5 3/8"	2 5/8"	2 5/8"
400/19	Water Tumbler, 14 oz.	6"	2 5/8"	2 5/8"
400/19	Wine 3 oz.	3"	2"	2 1/4"
400/19	Cocktail 3 1/2 oz.	2 1/2"	2 1/4"	2 1/8"
400/19	Cocktail 2 oz.	2 3/8"	1 7/8"	2 1/8"
400/19	Egg Cup, big beads	3 3/4"	2 5/8"	2 1/4"
400/19	Egg Cup, small beads	3 11/16"	2 11/16"	2 1/8"
400/142	Juice Tumbler 3 1/2 oz.	3 1/4"	2 3/8"	1 13/16"
400/190	Goblet 10 oz.	6 3/4"	3"	3 1/8"
400/190	Cocktail 4 oz.	4"	3 1/8"	2 5/8"
400/190	Saucer Champagne/ Tall Sherbet 5 oz	4 7/16"	3 7/8"	3"
400/190	Wine, 5 oz.	5 3/8"	2 9/16"	2 5/8"
400/190	Cordial, 1 oz.	4"	1 3/4"	2 1/4"
400/190	Seafood Cocktail	5"	4 3/4"	3"
400/195	Tumbler, 8 oz	[not available to measure]		
400/195	Tumbler, 12 oz.	4 1/8"	2 7/8"	2 5/8"
400/195	Tumbler, 16 oz.	4 3/8"	3"	2 5/8"
400/195	Iced Drink, 14 oz.	5 3/16"	3 1/16"	3 1/8"
400/195	Water, 11 oz.	4 7/8"	2 7/8"	3"
400/195	Old Fashioned, 9 oz	3 1/2"	2 5/8"	2 1/4"
400/195	Dessert, 6 oz.	3 9/16	3 9/16"	3"
400/195	Juice or Whiskey Sour, 6 oz.	4 13/16"	2"	2 1/8"
400/195	Cocktail, 4 oz.	4"	2 3/4"	2 1/4"
400/195	Wine, 2 oz.	3 5/8"	1 1/2"	1 7/8"
4000	Cordial 1 1/4 oz.	3 1/4"	1 3/4"	1 3/4"
4000	Cocktail 4 oz.	4 3/8"	3"	2 1/2"
4000	Wine, 5 oz.	5 1/8"	2 3/8"	2 1/2"
4000	Tall Sherbet or Champagne, 6 oz.	4 13/16"	3 1/2"	3 1/16"
4000	Goblet, 11 oz.	6"	3 1/8"	3"
4000	Iced Tea, 12 oz.	6 1/4"	2 5/8"	2 7/8"
111	Cocktail, 2 1/2 - 3 oz.	3 11/16"	3"	2 1/2"

We will attempt to explain one feature that puzzles all collectors. Items sometimes have a raised ridge on the underneath of the piece. Other examples of the same pieces will not have this but instead will have a ground and polished bottom. When the items have the extra ridge of glass that one can take hold of, it is called a marie. A marie is found on a snapped-up item (see "Finishing of Snapped-up and Stuck-up Ware" on page 14 for more detailed information on this distinction).

All price lists from 1937 to 1953 listed the 400/1D, 400/3D, 400/5D, 400/10D, 400/13D, 400/17D, 400/20D, 400/20V with ground and polished bottoms. In addition, the bowls 400/1F, 400/3F, 400/5F, 400/7F, 400/13F and 400/17F were listed with ground and polished bottoms. From 1953 on, this was no longer shown so it is believed that it was just understood that these items were ground and polished. Other items in the long list of Candlewick could have changed during the years but these were never noted on price lists. Sometimes the marie bottom was the early design; on other items the ground and polished bottom was the early version, later changing to the marie bottom. We have been told that when an item could be produced cheaper without harming the quality it would be done for economical reasons. It was less expensive to produce a snapped-up item than a ground and polished item.

The dates—when an item was introduced and when it was dropped from production—are guides to how difficult an item will be to find. The shorter the production time, the more difficult it will be to find a certain item. A brief production time will also greatly influence prices. Another factor in scarcity is whether an item would have been used in groups of six, eight, or twelve for a table setting versus items such as pitchers, large platters, or any item where only one would be necessary. Try imagining a piece that you truly desire and see if it is one of those items where only one would have been acquired by a household—it really makes a huge difference in the scarcity of a particular item. Production dates for all items can be found in the price guide.

400/77 After Dinner Cup. The example on the left has a ground and polished bottom while the cup on the right has the snap bottom with the marie on the bottom of the cup. A red hot punty rod is "stuck" to the bottom of some items to allow a finisher to put the item into a furnace for reheating; the bottom of that item then must be ground and polished. A marie refers to a distinctive ridge on the bottom. In this case, a snap rod grabs the marie so that the finisher can reheat the item in the furnace.

Lenox Computer Numbers
1974-1984

Below are the mold numbers for Candlewick items in production after 1973, when Lenox acquired Imperial Glass Corporation. At this time, Lenox began changing the mold numbers in Imperial's lines to computer numbers that Lenox used in their record system. For these Candlewick items, we are listing the Lenox computer number first, followed by the Imperial mold number. The description (Lenox Item Name) is that used by Lenox in catalogs beginning in 1974 and continuing until 1981 when Lenox sold the Imperial line to Arthur Lorch. Robert Stahl bought Imperial in 1982 and placed the company into bankruptcy in an effort to restructure it. The computer numbers continued in the catalogs until the close of the factory in 1984.

These numbers and cross reference are provided here so that if you are fortunate enough to find catalogs dated after 1973, you will know the original Candlewick mold numbers. Some of the items were still in stock when the factory closed in 1984.

Lenox	Imperial	Lenox Item Name
14200	3400	Goblet
14220	3400	Dessert/Champagne
14240	3400	Wine
14260	3400	Iced Beverage
14005	400/19	Low Dessert
14010	400/19	5 oz. Tumbler
14090	400/19	12 oz. Tumbler
14360	400/1D	6" Bread and Butter Plate
14370	400/3D	7" Dessert Plate
14372	400/23D	7" Plate with Seat
14380	400/5D	8 1/2" Luncheon/Salad Plate
14400	400/10D	10 1/2" Dinner Plate
14402	400/72D	10" 2-Handled Plate
14410	400/68D	11 1/2" Pastry Tray
14415	400/75V	12 1/2" Torte Plate
14416	400/124D	12 1/2" Oval Platter
14417	400/145D	12" 2-Handled Plate
14427	400/20V	17" Torte Plate
14430	400/35	Saucer
14435	400/35	Cup and Saucer
14437	400/37	Coffee Cup and Saucer
14438	400/37	Cup
14439	400/98	Oval Plate
14440	400/20	2 pc. Punch Set
14450	400/20	15 pc. Punch Set
14451	400/20	6 qt. Punch Bowl
14460	400/96	Salt and Pepper Set
14470	400/247	Salt and Pepper Set

14530	400/30	Sugar and Cream Set
14535	400/29/30	Sugar, Cream, and Tray
14536	400/29	7" Oblong Tray
14545	400/122	Individual Sugar and Cream Set
14555	400/42B	4 3/4" 2-Handled Nappy
14560	400/1F	5" Nappy
14565	400/84	5 1/2" Bowl
14570	400/40H	5" Handled Bon Bon
14572	400/51F	6" Round Handled Mint
14578	400/73H	9" Handled Heart
14580	400/23	2 pc. Mayonnaise Set
14585	400/289	3 pc. Marmalade Set
14590	400/54	6 1/2" Relish Tray
14592	400/55	8 1/2" 4-Part Relish Tray
14594	400/268	8" 2-Part Relish Tray
14596	400/56	10 1/2" 5-Part Relish Tray
14598	400/256	11" 2-Part Oval Relish Tray
14600	400/58	8" Oval Server
14610	400/161	1/4# Butter and Cover
14640	400/40/0	6 1/2" Handled Basket
14642	400/73/0	12" Handled Basket
14670	400/103D	11" Cake Stand
14680	400/183	6" 3-Toed Bowl
14686	400/52	6" 2-Handled Divided Server
14690	400/62B	7" 2-Handled Bowl
14692	400/69B	8 1/2" Bowl
14694	400/72B	8 1/2" 2-Handled Bowl
14696	400/145B	10" 2-Handled Bowl
14698	400/75F	10" Float Bowl
14724	400/66B	5 1/2" Low Compote
14780	400/79R	3 1/2" Candleholder
14782	400/80	4" Candleholder
14848	400/108	Table Bell
14850	400/450	3 pc. Ash Tray Set
14851	400/440	4" Ash Tray
14852	400/133	5" Ash Tray
14853	400/150	6" Ash Tray
14870	400/144	Box and Cover
14990	400/79	2 pc. Hurricane Lamp
14994	400/22	2 pc. Hurricane Lamp
14995		Hurricane Shade for 14994
14996		2 pc. Hurricane Lamp
14997	400/170	Candleholder
14998		Hurricane Shade for 14996
31150	400/416	20 oz. Pitcher
31151	400/419	40 oz. Pitcher
31152	400//424	64 oz. Pitcher
51454	400/91	Punch Ladle
51675		10" Cake Cover for 400/103D and 400/75V

Pricing

The price guide in this book is just that—a guide. It has been compiled by using prices seen on pieces for sale in antique malls, shops, shows, and similar places in various locations. The prices do not reflect those very good low prices you find in those fun to search places nor do they reflect the exaggerated high prices that are sometimes seen in auctions of any kind. The Price Guide reflects what a knowledgeable buyer will pay a knowledgeable seller for an item. To quote a friend, "Prices are in the eyes of the beholder." Besides that, we say, "Judge a price by demand, desirability, and the length of time an item was produced."

In the price guide we have used an asterisk (*) when there has not been enough activity to give an estimate of price, i.e., the piece is seldom presented for sale due to rarity. There will be two asterisks (**) beside items for which we have estimated the possible dates of production. The abbreviation "NP" indicates that the item was not priced (primarily applies to large sets). An "NI" found beside items indicates new information or information that we have provided in the past through other sources. You will want to pay special attention to these.

We would like to emphasize that it is our theory that if a collector studies and knows what is Imperial Candlewick, then what is not Imperial Candlewick will take care of itself. Every collector should have all available resources to make himself or herself as knowledgeable as possible.

A price guide is not intended to set prices. Neither the authors nor the publisher assume any responsibility for losses that might be incurred by the use of the price guide.

All collectors love to see advertising items used by the American glass manufacturers. Several examples of advertising materials are placed randomly in the book. They were found in material from the 1940s. The heading on a four-page pamphlet is "Imperial Candlewick" advertising folder. The instructions were "please route to your advertising department."

"Mats and Electros—The inside and back pages of this folder illustrate what Imperial Candlewick Crystal groups are available either in mat or electro form for use in your own newspaper or direct mail advertising. Order them now so you will have them when you need them."

On the Electros page is "Tie Up With Our National Advertising Program by Using These "Imperial Candlewick" Electros in Your Advertising Program."

On the Mat page was this information, "Illustrations on This Page Available in Mat Form Only."

Closing Thoughts for the Third Edition

Long-time collectors are going to think the prices in this edition are extremely low. They are lower than at the peak of Candlewick collecting. This is partly due to the avid collectors having large collections containing most of the items available. They are not going out and hunting more. We early collectors were very competitive and ran prices high with our drive to get those sought-after rare pieces. There are not many new collectors coming into the arena, and they are buying only when the price is low.

The downturn of the economy has affected the prices, also. These factors seem to be the reality of any collection, and maybe collecting will rebound along with the economy.

Aside from revised prices, there is only one new piece of information for this edition, and while it is very interesting, it is not about a piece of glass. Along with that new information, there are some neat illustrations of Imperial's advertising drawings that have been added at random.

Even though the value of our collection has fallen, it has served a wonderful purpose—through our 26 years of NIGCS conventions and glass shows we made many new friends. I no longer have my collecting companion; I lost him in 2006. I do, however, have many friends with whom to share glass talk and reminisce about old times.

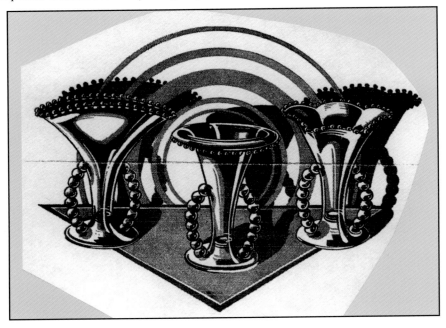

Electro No. 1-C

Part I
Historical Perspective

A Short History of The Imperial Glass Company

"Pride of workmanship, skill, and a deep devotion to quality were the prime motivators of Imperial's glassworkers."

A group of investors organized the Imperial Glass Company in 1901. After a period of "several years of construction, installing furnaces, and creating a number of initial moulds," the first Imperial glass was produced in 1904 in Bellaire, Ohio.

Imperial's earliest production was clear pressed glass. Sales were made to the five and dime stores for items such as covered butter dishes, berry bowls, and pickle dishes. These lines expanded into lamp shades, jelly glasses, pitchers, salt and pepper shakers, sugars and creamers, and other similar types of glass.

The period from 1910 to 1929 saw several new Imperial lines. First was Nuart iridescent ware. In this group were the colored and frosted electric lamp shades in an imitation "Tiffany" style. Following Nuart, Imperial introduced Nucut Crystal, which was a handpressed reproduction of English cut glass. (Collectors Crystal was a reintroduction (1950s) of the Nucut and was one of Imperial's most popular giftware lines.)

"Imperial Jewels. . .exquisite freehand iridescent 'stretch glass' items" were introduced in 1916. This was a "high point" of Imperial's production that involved many shops making pressed wares as well as blown and freehand ware.

From 1904 to 1922, the company flourished, though the market changed as machine made glassware came to the forefront. In 1922, the mass-produced glass markets caused Imperial to try new ideas, including the creation of Imperial's "Art Glass," an innovation that proved to be unsuccessful.

In 1929, the forces of the Depression, combined with further loss of major markets, forced Imperial to enter bankruptcy. The company continued operations while in receivership, and with an order from Quaker Oats Company in 1931 for a premium to be packaged in its product, Imperial was able to stay in business.

The company was reorganized and named the Imperial Glass Corporation.

The Quaker Oats premium was the forerunner of today's Cape Cod pattern, a line that survived until the demise of Imperial in 1984. Another jewel to continue until the closing in 1984 was Candlewick, a pattern that was introduced in 1936. Candlewick contained the largest number of items in any Imperial line. It eventually became more popular than the earlier favorite, Cape Cod.

A 1930s catalog pictured thirty pieces of opal glass from this time period. According to the only 1930s price list available, Imperial produced twenty-four pieces of opal glass in 1932. These are the earliest company documentations found of milk glass produced by Imperial Glass Company. The height of milk glass production of approximately six hundred items was in the 1950s, with production falling off to less than forty items made after 1970. February 1, 1951, was the introduction of the famous superimposed IG hallmark that was in use for twenty-three years. This mark is often found on Imperial milk glass items.

Imperial had many private mold customers. Companies and individuals brought their molds to Imperial for glass items to be specially made. Imperial also supplied items from

Imperial Glass Corporation on June 24, 1984, just ten days after the last run of regular production was made.

its own lines to many different distributors and private mold customers, who then added decorations and marketed these items under their company's name. A few of those companies were Sears Roebuck Inc., Butler Brothers, Lightolier [Lighting] Company, Keystone Silver, Inc., Midwest Chandelier Company, Oneida, Ltd., and Irving W. Rice, Inc.

At the beginning of World War II, changes began taking shape in imports. American companies could no longer import glass products from European countries. Irving W. Rice, New York, was a major importer of colognes and powder boxes. With the onset of the war, Irving W. Rice turned to Imperial Glass Corporation to supply the dresser items for which I. Rice was so well known. The year 1939 was the beginning of a long and strong relationship between the two companies that continued through the 1940s. Correspondence in the late 1960s suggested that the two companies were attempting to resume relations. However, in 1973 when Lenox took control of Imperial Glass Corporation, all private mold work was ceased.

Imperial began acquiring glass companies in 1940. The first purchase was Central Glass Works (1940), followed by the purchase of the molds of the Heisey Company (1958). Two lines from the Heisey Company became strong Imperial lines. Heisey Provincial and Old Williamsburg were produced by Imperial in crystal as well as colors. The purchase of Cambridge Glass Company (1960) added Rosepoint and a strong line of candelabra.

World War II and the postwar period were the boom years of Imperial's production. Not surprisingly, the peak of production of Cape Cod and Candlewick was reached and sustained during this time. Contributing to this success were the countless thousands of households being established by young families after the war, and the prosperous American economy, which followed.

In 1972, seeing the need for capital investment, Imperial stockholders arranged a stock exchange with Lenox Incorporated. This was accomplished on December 29, 1972, and in 1973, Lenox began marking Imperial glass with an "LIG" mark. In June 1981, Arthur Lorch, a private investor, bought the company from Lenox. The new mark, "ALIG", began appearing in 1982 and was used only during that year. In the fall of 1982, Lenox foreclosed on its note with Mr. Lorch.

Mr. Robert F. Stahl, Jr., a management consultant, bought the company in late 1982 and filed for Chapter 11 bankruptcy in an effort to reorganize the company. A small amount of glass produced carried the NI mark for "New Imperial." The last day of general production was June 15, 1984. Appropriately, the last item off the production line was a 4" swan with 6-15-84 in raised numbers on the inside. In August 1984, after all efforts failed, liquidation was ordered. Consolidated Liquidation Company and Lancaster Colony combined to buy the assets of Imperial Glass Corporation and went on to sell the last remnants of the bankrupt business. Liquidation was completed with the sale of the building to Mrs. Anna Maroon in March 1985.

Mrs. Maroon invested much time and money trying to find a business to occupy the defunct Imperial factory building. It was her desire to provide an economic stimulus to Bellaire, Ohio, and at the same time preserve this historical building, which had meant so much to so many people for many years. The anchor of this endeavor was the Imperial Hay Shed. Originally, the Hay Shed had been the storage place for hay used in packing glass to be shipped. During the later years, the Hay Shed was an outlet for research and development pieces and factory seconds. From 1985 to 1995, the Hay Shed was an Imperial glass consignment shop that was often the first stop for collectors attending the annual convention of the National Imperial Glass Collectors' Society.

The Bellaire Glass and Artifacts Museum played a vital part in drawing visitors to the partially renovated factory building. There were other tenants, but not enough to fulfill the dream of saving the Imperial Glass Corporation factory building, and the building was razed in June 1995. The Hay Shed outlet was moved to a building on adjacent property. On the ground where the Imperial Glass Corporation once stood, now stands a shopping center. A blacktop parking lot now covers the area where collectors once spent hours and days searching for shards and reminiscing about the greatness of Imperial Glass.

We wrote in our first book, Imperial Cape Cod: Tradition to Treasure that ". . . as collectors of Imperial Glass, we have a strong feeling that Imperial will never lose its identity as a producer of fine crystal. In a mass production world, 'Imperial continues to create only handcrafted glassware. Pride of workmanship, skill, and a deep devotion to quality are the prime motivators of Imperial's glassworkers.'" With the close of Imperial, this should be restated: "Imperial continued to create only handcrafted glassware. Pride of workmanship, skill, and a deep devotion to quality were the prime motivators of Imperial's glassworkers."

Quoted parts of this history have been condensed from A Consumer and Retail Guide to Handcrafted Glassware by Imperial Glass Corp. Remaining information was obtained through printed information from old records of the Imperial Glass Corporation.

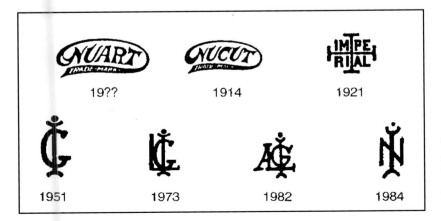

NUART 19??   NUCUT 1914   IMPERIAL 1921

IG 1951   LIG 1973   ALIG 1982   NI 1984

These are the marks used by the Imperial Glass Corporation. The dates shown are the dates when the marks were registered or are generally accepted as first used. We do not have registration records for Nuart, but it preceded Nucut.

Making Glass at Imperial

As you view the pieces of Candlewick in this book or in your own collection, you may want to learn more about how they were produced. The following information provides a "virtual tour" of what glassmaking was like at the Imperial factory. It is taken from A Consumer and Retail Guide to Handcrafted Glassware by Imperial Glass Corp. and reprinted with permission of the Lancaster Colony Corporation

Production

Although the creation of molten glass is the true first step to glassmaking, Imperial's handmade glass would not be the distinctive product it is without the molds that give the products their shapes and intricate designs.

Imperial's molds are made of a special cast iron alloy. All of the designs are worked into the molds with hammer and chisel. The same way, in fact, that a sculptor working in marble would do. The difference here is the designs must by "sculpted" into the mold material in the reverse of the design wanted on the glass. Final polishing of a mold is done with small, handmade files that enable the moldmaker to create very intricate detailing.

Raw Materials

Seventy-two percent of glass is sand. It must be exceptionally pure, because any foreign matter in the sand, such as iron particles, could cause the glass to become discolored. Glass is also composed of soda ash, potash, sodium nitrate, limestone, lead, borax, feldspar, and a number of metallic oxides used to create glass of different colors.

Mixing

Wagons full of prepared "batches"—all ingredients mixed in their proper proportions and ready to be melted into glass—are kept in the Mixing Room. Broken pieces of glass called "cullet" (cut-offs from the manufacturing process, and rejected items) are brought to the Mixing Room, crushed if necessary, and then mixed with the new raw materials. Though glass can be made using the raw materials only, cullet is used as means of economy.

All raw materials are weighed precisely, and then poured into a receiving hopper. When the batch is complete, the raw materials are mixed together in a mixing drum. After mixing, the batch is discharged onto a rubber conveyor belt and carried over a powerful electromagnet. This magnet removes any traces of iron which, if not removed before the batch is melted, might impair the color of the glass.

"Hot Metal" Department

At Imperial, three types of glass melting units are used: "day tanks," of one-ton capacity each; a "continuous tank," where 100 tons of glass are kept molten 24 hours a day, 365 days a year; and a "pot furnace." The day tank and continuous tank are open-hearth type furnaces where the melting flame is in direct contact with the glass. The pot furnace has a number of covered crucibles which protect the molten glass from the furnace flame. From these crucibles glass is drawn for making colored glass. The average melting temperature of our furnaces is 2640 degrees F. The glass itself is worked at 1800 degrees F. to 2100 degrees F. depending on the size of the article being made and the type of glass being used.

Actual production of a handcrafted glass requires the combined efforts of many skilled workers. Groups of craftsmen work together in a "shop," producing one specific item at a time. It takes years to become a skilled glass worker, and to replace employees who have retired or passed away. Imperial has an apprentice program. These apprentices, men and women, are learning the many skills necessary to become glass craftspeople.

One such skill is "gathering." A "gatherer" "winds up" or gathers molten glass on a clay ball, the size of which partially determines the amount of glass to be gathered. This is done much in the same way that honey is gathered on a spoon. The gatherer then withdraws the hot glass from the furnace and places it over a mold allowing the glass to drop into the mold.

As the glass drops into the mold, the "presser," using a pair of shears, cuts off just the right amount of hot glass to fill the mold. The presser forces the plunger into the mold to form the item. He must exert the right amount of pressure: too little and the glass will not fill the mold and take on the proper shape. Too much pressure, and the glass "crizzles" or "checks" (cracks). After forming, the plunger is withdrawn, the mold opened, and the glassware removed. This entire process is called "hand pressing."

Finishing of Snapped-up and Stuck-up Ware

To fire polish and/or change the shape of an item, it's attached to one of two types of rod-like iron tools: a "puntie" or a "snap." The face or surface of a puntie is red hot, and newly formed glass will easily attach itself to the hot iron. A snap, however, is a long rod with movable jaws on one end. The jaws on the snap open up to grip the glass item.

After being mounted on a snap or puntie, the glass item is placed into a small furnace called a "glory hole." The item heats up, becomes quite soft, and must be spun to maintain its shape. The "finisher" now shapes the item with a charred wooden tool. Oak or apple wood is used, since neither contains rosin, which could seriously mark the glass.

Fire polishing is done for two reasons: first, to give the surface of the glass a higher brilliancy; and second, to soften the glass if it requires a final shaping.

After finishing, the item is detached from either the snap or the puntie, and placed in a Lehr (annealing oven) to be tempered. Snapped-up items require no further processing after annealing, while items stuck-up must be ground and polished after annealing to remove any rough edges remaining on the foot or base of an item that has stuck to a puntie.

Iron Mold Blowing

In this process, the mold is kept very hot so the glass will not wrinkle when it touches the iron. The glass is gathered in the normal manner and the blower pre-shapes the gob of glass as usual.

The blower lowers the pre-shaped gob into the mold and inflates the glass by mouth. Then he gives the glass a puff of compressed air to create a better impression of the mold designs on the glass. This could be done by lung power only, but using compressed air lessens the work load on the blower and insures better reproduction of designs.

After being blown into shape, the item may be finished into a more refined shape or placed in the Lehr.

Plate Making

Plates are usually pressed in the form of a shallow bowl. When reheated in a glory hole they become soft enough so that the centrifugal force developed as the "snap" is twirled causes the glass to flatten out into the shape of a plate. Now the finisher need only make slight adjustments to achieve the final plate shape.

Stuck Handles

When a handle is attached to an item, the same type of glass is used, or glass of exactly the same expansion. The gatherer gathers a gob of glass on a puntie, and rolls it out to a smooth round cylinder. Then he re-heats the glass and gives it to the "handler" who attaches the handle to the item.

Annealing

All glass must be annealed (heat tempered) by passing through a "Lehr" before it can be processed further. The glass is placed on a conveyor belt at one end of the Lehr. It then moves slowly toward the opposite end. The temperature at the hot end, where the glass first enters, is 1000 degrees F., and at the other end, where the glass is removed, room temperature or a little higher. If the glass were not annealed it would burst or break upon cooling.

At the "exit" end of the Lehr, a major step in Quality Control occurs: inspection for a variety of flaws: pitting, scratches, discoloration, improper shape, and other imperfections. Items that don't pass inspection are discarded, and are one source of the cullet used in the Mixing Room. After inspection, the glassware is labeled and wrapped for final packing. Those items that require further processing are inspected and then moved to the Finishing Department or other departments for such work. After the other finishing processes are complete, there's another inspection, and then the finished pieces are ready for labeling, wrapping, and packing for shipment.

Finishing

Cracking Off

Every piece of blown ware must be shaped so that it can be inflated to completely fill the mold and assume the proper shape. After annealing it's necessary to "crack off" the unwanted cap or top portion of the glass.

The glass is scored by a carborundum wheel at the point where the glass is to be cut off. It's then placed on a rotating socket, and a sharp flame plays across the glass where the scratch was made. In a few seconds the glass will crack off along this scratch. The resulting edge is sharp and uneven and must be ground smooth and fire polished.

Some items can't be cracked off because of their complex shapes. Such pieces are sawed off by a carborundum saw. This operation is time-consuming but does eliminate the need for further grinding after the sawing is done. Polishing may or may not follow, depending upon the item involved.

Roughing

A piece of glass, which has been stuck-up for finishing, has sharp pin-points of glass on its bottom as a result of this operation. These items must be ground and polished. For this first, or rough grinding, the grinding wheels used are of steel, over which flows a water "slurry" of carborundum.

Grinding

A grinding machine is used to grind the top edges of stemware and tumblers. Though the edges are ground smooth and flat, they're still quite sharp and require fire polishing before the item is usable.

Smoothing

After stuck-up ware has been rough ground, it receives a final grinding. The grinding wheels are made of natural sandstone.

All grinding must be done with a continuous stream of water flowing over the grinding surface. This aids in the grinding process and cools the glass.

Polishing wheel

The final step in finishing stuck-up ware is polishing. The polishing wheel is cork and the polishing compound is a water slurry of pumice and "rotten stone." (Rotten stone is a type of clay used to keep pumice in suspension.)

The ground surfaces are polished so they are just as bright as the surrounding glass. Immediately after polishing, the glassware is washed so that the polishing compound does not cake and dry on the glass.

Belt Grinding

Certain items of stemware and other pieces are so shaped that machine grinding is not sufficient. These items are ground or beveled, free-hand, on a special belt. The belt is coated with carborundum grains and jets of water are directed on the belt to facilitate grinding.

Glazing

The rim of the glassware, after being properly ground and wiped clean, is glazed. A hot flame is directed down on the edges of the glass, melting the edges to make them suitable for use as drinking glasses. The glass must be of such quality that it can enter this hot fire and not crack. After glazing, the glassware is again annealed. This removes the strain caused by glazing the top edge.

Decorating

Cutting

In this process a glass article is decorated with patterns cut into its surface. The first step is to lay out and mark onto the surface of the glass an outline of the pattern to be cut. The glass is then cut into with cutting wheels until the desired design is achieved. In some cases this design is left in its original gray texture; in others the cut design is polished with cork wheels or by an acid polishing process until the whole design sparkles with the same brilliancy as the uncut surface of the glass. When a cut pattern is left in an unpolished gray frosted finish, it is called gray cut; if it is polished, it is called a rock crystal cut.

Etching

A piece of glass can be beautifully frosted by dipping it into a special chemical solution. When a design is to be etched onto the surface, the glass is coated inside and out with an acid-resisting solution, leaving uncoated only the part which is to be the eventual design pattern. The glass is then immersed in a special acid bath for a specific period of time. The glass is then removed from the acid bath and thoroughly washed in hot water. During washing the acid-resistant material is removed and the article emerges from washing with the design etched into its surface.

Sandblasting

Glass can be also frosted by sandblasting. The process consists of spraying an abrasive material, such as sand, onto the glass at high pressure and great velocity. Glass can be frosted all over by sandblasting to a silky-satin finish of a deep rough finish, depending on the time of exposure to the blast of sand and the coarseness of the sandblasting material. With this same process and with the aid of masks, very intricate patterns can be produced when either the outline of the design is carved into the glass by sandblasting or the outline of the design is left clear and the background carved away. With sandblasting, beautiful ornamentations in various depths and in various densities and shading can be created.

Gold Decorating

Gold decorating involves exacting, skill work. Decorators apply a liquid gold compound to such crystal items as barware and decanters. After decorating, the gold is fired onto the glass for lasting beauty. The result is sparkling crystal enhanced with the most traditional of precious metals—22 carat gold.

In a world dominated by mass production, Imperial continues to create only handcrafted glassware. Pride, skill and devotion to quality are the prime motivators of Imperial's glass masters. The delicate touch of a person whose life is devoted to handcraftsmanship makes the creation of fine glass more than just a skill. Rather, it is an art form reached only through a close relationship of body and mind.

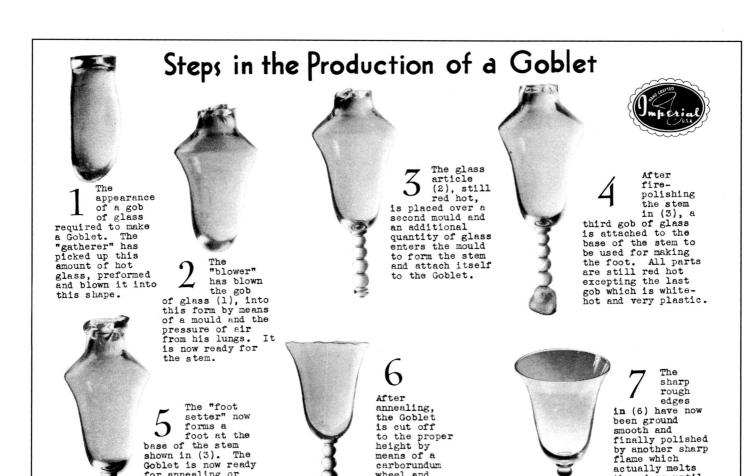

Steps in the Production of a Goblet

1 The appearance of a gob of glass required to make a Goblet. The "gatherer" has picked up this amount of hot glass, preformed and blown it into this shape.

2 The "blower" has blown the gob of glass (1), into this form by means of a mould and the pressure of air from his lungs. It is now ready for the stem.

3 The glass article (2), still red hot, is placed over a second mould and an additional quantity of glass enters the mould to form the stem and attach itself to the Goblet.

4 After fire-polishing the stem in (3), a third gob of glass is attached to the base of the stem to be used for making the foot. All parts are still red hot excepting the last gob which is white-hot and very plastic.

5 The "foot setter" now forms a foot at the base of the stem shown in (3). The Goblet is now ready for annealing or heat-treating which takes place in a large continuous furnace called a lehr.

6 After annealing, the Goblet is cut off to the proper height by means of a carborundum wheel and the application of a sharp flame.

7 The sharp rough edges in (6) have now been ground smooth and finally polished by another sharp flame which actually melts the edges until they are round. After a second annealing process which follows this, the Goblet is complete.

IMPERIAL GLASS CORPORATION · *Bellaire, Ohio*

This Imperial factory paper provides a vivid illustration of what went into the production of a Candlewick goblet. Words alone cannot do justice to this process.

Mat No. 108

A Little Candlewick Background

Earl Newton, Imperial's Chicago Sales Representative, was brought to Imperial as president in 1931. It was under his direction that Candlewick was dreamed of, designed, and born.

Imperial Glass Company introduced Candlewick in 1936. For years, collectors of Candlewick have taken this date as a fact. Some rumors have suggested that pieces were seen much earlier than that. We understand that research pieces were made as early as 1935. Because of the unattractive mold marks, however, Candlewick was left sitting on shelves until a way was found to cover the mold marks with a feature that is now described as ribs.

It has been documented that other companies had patterns similar to Candlewick that were produced before Imperial's pattern appeared, so it follows that Imperial's pattern was not entirely original. It is also thought that Candlewick may have been influenced by the needlework style called Candlewicking. The company even used this reference in early advertising material. Other theories abound about other glass patterns that may have influenced the design of Candlewick. On a handwritten note in the factory records was a mention that Mr. Newton brought to Imperial a piece of French Cannon Ball glass. Most likely, the Imperial Candlewick design is the result of many things rather than any one single event or incident.

Some time ago we found a two-piece mayonnaise set that resembled Candlewick. It was so similar that one would almost think it was a set of Imperial Candlewick. Upon close inspection, however, the etched word Tchecoslovaque was discovered. This placed the date for the item in the mid 1930s, when this was the French spelling of Czechoslovakia. Perhaps Imperial's design was influenced as well by the maker of this set. There was also a pattern named Boule that could have influenced the course of design for Imperial.

We do know that Imperial had to have experimented with Candlewick long before it was produced. It is not possible to say one day that a product is going to be made and the next day it is out on the market. Much design work must be done, molds need to be made, and everything has to be in place for production.

Early molds were made, but as noted above these joint molds were designed in a manner that left undesirable mold marks in the finished items. Later the joint molds were modified so that ribs covered the mold marks. The items involved would be the 400/67B, 400/67D, 400/74B, 400/74J, 400/74N, and 400/74SC. In 1936, Carl Uhrmann came on the scene and was credited with changing the joint mold to a block mold that eliminated the vertical lines and made it unnecessary to have the ribs in the designs. Later Mr. Uhrmann was named Plant Superintendent; eventually, he was named President of Imperial Glass Corporation.

Mr. Newton was president from 1931 until 1940, when Carl W. Gustkey took over the presidency. Mr. Gustkey died in 1967 and was followed by Carl Uhrmann, who was president until he retired in 1974. (It is exciting for us to look back to the 1983 convention when we met Mr. and Mrs. Uhrmann. They were such a gracious couple.) Each of these gentlemen played a huge part in the total life of Imperial and this story of Candlewick.

The first catalog featuring any Candlewick was published in 1937 and shows approximately fifty items. No stemware or tumblers were in this first offering. Until this time, Imperial did not have the "shops" or the craftsmen to make the blown stemware. This entailed the use of a "hokey-pokey" shop. However, it appears that about 1937 Imperial did establish a means for making the blown stemware that we have come to love.

The 3400 line of stemware was introduced in 1937 and the 3800 line followed in 1938. New collectors mistakenly think that the 3800 line is older than the 3400 line. More 3400 crystal stemware is found than the 3800 crystal because it was produced for a longer period of time. However, more ruby 3800 line is found than the ruby 3400 line. We need to remember that it may not be when an item was introduced but rather how much was produced and what the popularity factor was for the item that determines its availability today.

The following Candlewick patent information is provided in its entirety so that nothing will be lost in summarizing:

Patent Number	Date Applied	Mold Number	Description
100,577	7/28/36	400/74	3-toed Bowl
100,578	7/23/36	400/5	8" Salad Plate [400/5D]
100,579	7/28/36	400/19	Footed Ice Tea Tumbler
104,222	4/20/37	400	Lighting bowl
127,271	5/20/41	400/48	Tall Footed Compote [400/48F]
128,113	7/8/41	400/100	Twin Candleholder
128,812	8/12/41	400/68	Handled Pastry Tray [400/68D]
130,486	11/25/41	400/35	Handled Tea Cup
131,250	1/27/42	400/63	Bowl [400/63B]
133,955	9/29/42	400	Hurricane Lamp Adapter [400/152]
134,312	6/24/42	777/2	Hurricane Eagle Adapter

TO ALL SALESMEN:

It should be helpful for you to have complete information on all the Design Patents that Imperial has secured from the United States Government for protection of our ideas.

When you examine the list of "Patents" you will immediately notice that only a few items in each line have been patented. However, coverage by patent rights is fairly broad and sizes of articles are not considered. Therefore, all sizes of Candlewick plates are protected by Design Patent #100, 578; all sizes of Candlewick bowls by Design Patent #131, 250, etc.

Note that patent #100,577 is for a three-toed bowl. All bowls that have ever been shown in catalogs and photographs are four-toed. It has always been assumed that the three-toed patent design was only a design that resulted in the four-toed bowl.

Candlewick has been made in crystal, ruby, Ritz Blue, miscellaneous colors, slag, and milk glass. It has been cut, etched, and hand-painted. It has had gold, silver and cranberry stain applied. Metal and wood have been combined with it. Candlewick was so popular that other companies bought it to add their own decorative touches to it. All of these variations add to the enjoyment of collecting Imperial Candlewick.

Imperial seemed to have no set rule about the bead size on Candlewick pieces. The design appeared to be determined by the shape, size, and proportions of the item being designed. Artistic appeal might have guided the design of the graduated beads, handles, etc.

Candlewick reached its height of popularity in the late 1940s. Probably this was because there were so many young newly married couples during the war years and the post-war economy made it possible for those couples to buy nice things for the home. About three hundred items were offered for sale at the peak times for Candlewick. In Imperial's last catalog, 1982-1983, there were twenty-nine items in the line.

Counting Candlewick can be very confusing. Do you count by pieces, by items, or by sets? Do you include lids separately? Does it really make a difference? Suffice it to say, there are slightly over seven hundred pieces and sets. Keep in mind that these numbers apply only to crystal Candlewick. We do not want to try estimating the number of colored or decorated items that Imperial made in the Candlewick pattern, and there is no way to know all of the decorations other companies added to Candlewick.

It is important to know that what appears at first to be Candlewick may not be. For the present, most collectors are satisfied to know that there are similar appearing items that were imported before the advent of Candlewick, as well as items that were imported after the end of Imperial Candlewick. Collectors should also know that Imperial Candlewick molds have been sold and are being used to make reproductions. They must be knowledgeable enough to identify them.

Collectors, also, must know about American made similarities that have long confused both new collectors and inexperienced dealers. We have a very strong belief about collecting Imperial Candlewick: If a collector studies and learns all that is possible about Imperial Candlewick, he or she will know what is right and will not need to be so concerned about what is not right. One of our goals for this book is to help collectors do just that.

Collecting Candlewick is a wide-open field for collectors who want to hunt for it and enjoy it. Local clubs and national societies meet just to talk about it. When all is said and done, many long and lasting friendships have been influenced by Candlewick. The next step will be when the young of today inherit what has brought so much pleasure to their families. Take care of it!

Electro No. 5-C

Part II

Crystal Line of Candlewick

This photographic look at Candlewick will illustrate all of the items considered to be in the total crystal production. Various pieces will be included in logical categories based on the most general use of the piece. First, therefore, you will need to decide if a piece would typically be used when setting a table for dining or other food serving. If it does not fit into a table setting, use your imagination to think of the item's purpose.

We will begin by showing and discussing items used for food serving that require multiple numbers, such as place settings for four, six, eight, or more people. From there, we will progress to serving pieces for a luncheon, dinner or party. The next listing will present numerous different sets that Imperial designed for its Candlewick pattern. This group will include console sets, decanter sets, and party sets, to name but a few. The final category, the miscellaneous group, includes everything that does not fit into a general and larger group. So, let us begin the exploration of this large and beautiful pattern that attracts so many avid collectors. Remember to read captions carefully as some discuss more than one item under a photograph.

Framed photograph (3' x 4') that hung on the factory wall of the Imperial Glass Corporation from the 1950s until closing. $200-250.

Place Settings

Listed here are the stems, bowls, plates, and other items that are associated with place settings for a dinner table. We will not attempt to describe every piece because you will be getting a photographic view of Imperial's Candlewick.

Stems, Tumblers, Icers, Coasters

Considering that Imperial designed almost seven hundred pieces of Candlewick to be used either as single items or sets, what you are about to see will be a real delight. There surely could not be a single glass tabletop item that was left out of this popular design.

3400 Line of Stems: 1937-1984

There are eight lines of stems and tumblers that include seventy-one items. No wonder beginning collectors have difficulty remembering all the different names and numbers. Let us begin now and venture into this world of glass.

3400, 9 oz. Goblet, $10-16; 5 oz. Claret, $30-36; 4 oz. Cocktail, $10-14; 6 oz. Saucer Champagne or Tall Sherbet, $8-14; 4 oz. Wine, $15-18; 1 oz. Cordial, $26-30. Some of this line was in production from 1937-1984. Other pieces came in after 1937 and went out before 1984.

3400, 12 oz. Footed Tumbler, $14-18; 10 oz. Footed Tumbler, $14-16; 5 oz. Low Sherbet, $18-26; 5 oz. Footed Juice Tumbler, $18-20; 6 oz. Parfait, $35-40.

3400, 4 oz. Oyster Cocktail, $14-20; #111 Cocktail, $20-25, 1-bead pulled stem. It holds 3 1/2 oz. These are shown together for comparison of size and shape.

3400 Finger Bowl (right), $*; 3800 Finger 3800 Bowl (left); 3400 Bowl (right). The 3800 Finger Bowl is 6 oz. The 3400 Finger Bowl is 8 oz. We did not have a 3800 Finger Bowl in crystal, but this comparison is so important we are showing it in ruby.

3400, 2 pc. Seafood Cocktail (left), 9 oz., $60-65; 3800 2 pc. Seafood or Fruit Cocktail Icer (right), 12 oz., $60-75.

On an inter-company newsletter from the 1950s was the interesting information that Imperial had Bryce Glass Company make some of its 3400 stemware. Of course, Imperial took its molds to Bryce and had this done to Imperial specifications. The newsletter reiterated that all glass companies use this avenue when they cannot meet a production requirement on time. The sales force was told that no differences could be found.

The example on the left in this picture is from the Imperial Glass Factory and has the identification label still affixed. The first four items are 3400 Seafood Cocktails and each varies a little bit in the stem. These are shown to help you see the slight variations you may find in the 3400 Seafood Cocktail stem. The 3800 Seafood Cocktail on the far right is also from the Imperial Factory and is shown to help you identify that stem.

All these stems are "pulled stems" and therefore the size and shape will not be consistent and symmetrical. Pulled stems are actually formed and pulled in the soft glass as it is being formed for the stem. Unlike most of the Candlewick stems, which are formed in a mold and then attached to the bowl of the vessel, the pulled stem is not put into a mold; rather it is all free form.

The 10 oz. Footed Tumbler replaced the 9 oz. Footed Tumbler in 1948. We believe that it is actually the same item, but the catalog illustration measurement was changed because the produced items measured closer to 10 oz. than 9 oz.

3800 Line of Stems: 1937-1943

We do not have a complete group of the 3800 stems in the crystal line because we were intent on building a set of 3800 Ruby stems. (Please refer to the color section in our book on Candlewick: Colored and Decorated Lines for a comparison of all 3800 stem sizes and proportions in Ruby.)

It is very interesting that Imperial did not ever give the volume measurements for the 3800 line in its catalogs or price lists. The company did provide that information for the other lines of stems and tumblers. The measurements given for the 3800 are those from our stems and those of other collectors.

3800, 9-11 oz. Goblet, $20-28; 7 oz. Tall Sherbet or Champagne, $20-28; 6 oz. Low Sherbet, $16-20; 4 oz. Claret, $30-38; 1-1 1/2 oz. Cordial, $55-65; 2 oz. Brandy, $*; 12 oz. Seafood Cocktail, $60-75. That is not a typographic error on the 9-11 oz. for the 3800 Goblet. We have measured several and find that the goblets do indeed vary from 9 oz. to 11 oz. Again, we stress that these 3800 measurements are ours as Imperial did not list them in their catalogs or price lists.

3800, 2 1/2-3 oz. Wine (right), $30-38; 3800 1-1 1/2 oz. Cordial (left), $30-45. The 3800 Cordial is a well-discussed item. It is our strong opinion that the 3800 Cordial and the 4000 Cordial are the same item. The catalog illustrations look the same. Since Imperial did not ever publish a capacity size on the 3800, the difference cannot be established by measurement. We know from documentation that the 3800 Cordial was made in Ruby and Ritz Blue. All the crystal cordials we have found are identical in size to the Ruby and Ritz Blue 3800 Cordial. Until it is proven by official record that these two cordials are different, we will assume that they are the same.

3800, 1 oz. Cordial, $55-65, 2 oz. Brandy, $*. The 3800 Brandy is a very elusive item so please observe the shape and the comparison with the 3800 Cordial. Remember that Imperial stems do not have a safe edge, i.e., a "slightly thicker edge," around the rim. Inexpensive glass will usually have the safe edge around the bowl of the article.

3800, 6 oz. Finger Bowl, $★, also shown with the 3400 Finger Bowl in earlier photograph; 4 oz. Cocktail, $14-20; 12 oz. Tumbler, $20-28; 9 oz.-10 oz. Tumbler, $20-28; 5 oz. Tumbler, $20-28.

4000 Line of Stems: 1949-1960

4000, 11 oz. Goblet, $24-28; 6 oz. Tall Sherbet, $24-28; 5 oz. Wine, $24-28; 4 oz. Cocktail, $24-28; 12 oz. Ice Tea or Hiball, $24-28; 1 1/4 oz. Cordial, $55-65. Items with discolored labels are Imperial's identification labels and are from Imperial's Archives.

400/18 Line of Stems: 1949-1951

We found this company memorandum on the 400/18 line of stems very interesting and thought that collectors would enjoy it also. (NI)

400/18, 7 oz. Old Fashioned, $34-45; 400/18, 3 1/2 oz. Cocktail, $34-45.

January 1, 1950, "Here is another line of stemware for Candlewick. We do not wish it to deliberately replace anything we are now making for the Candlewick line, all of which is guaranteed open stock, but we do believe that this is one of the most attractive stemware lines available today. You will note in this line, as in other stemware items presented to you at this time. . .that we have made a definite attempt to hold down height, to widen items and to otherwise make them fit into current trends."

"The new line of footed pieces (400/18) for the Candlewick line, may shock some of you. You may feel that we are making a serious mistake in bringing them out in face of our competition [Anchor Hocking's Boopie]. We showed some of these finished pieces to prominent buyers in late 1948. We had some of these pieces with us in my suite at the Pittsburgh Show in January 1949. Our design application on this particular item has been pending in Washington for literally months and months. We have good reason to believe that it will be granted. Afterward, fireworks may explode in a certain spot or two in America! In the meantime, you should present this line as (1) having been under development since the fall of 1948 (2) as having been requested for quite a long while by many of our prominent outlets and (3) you may say, if you wish, that our design in these actual shapes predates our competition by over a year!"

Enough was written in the memorandum for us to know that the competition referred to was Anchor Hocking, and many collectors will certainly know what item they were talking about: "Boopie." The Boopie pattern (shown in the Similarities section on page 161) is the most frequently confused similarity to Imperial's Candlewick. It is often labeled incorrectly and bought by new Candlewick collectors. The most telltale feature of Boopie is the safe edge, a thicker rolled edge on the drinking rim. Boopie has beads close together (but not quite touching) on the circumference of the foot in addition to raised ribs that radiate from each bead to the point where the foot attaches to the bowl of the stem. In the early years of glass research it was called Boopie as a means of identification and the name has lasted until today.

We, as collectors, never really question or care which design was first. We only care that people today are confused about what is Candlewick and what is not Candlewick.

400/18, 12 oz. Ice Tea, $50-56; 9 oz. Water, $50-56; 6 oz. Sherbet, $45-50; 5 oz. Footed Juice, $85-100; 7 oz. Footed Parfait, $90-1000.

400/190 Line of Stems: 1943-1967

400/190, 10 oz. Goblet, $14-16; 5 oz. Dinner Wine, $22-26; 5 oz. Champagne or Tall Sherbet, $10-12; 3 1/2 oz.-4 oz. Cocktail, $10-14; 1 oz. Cordial, $60-65; Seafood Icer, $65-70.

400/19 Line of Tumblers: 1941-1979

Most of the 400/19 line of tumblers were introduced between 1941 and 1943. The items were dropped at various times and the last was dropped in 1979.

400/19, 14 oz. Ice Tea Tumbler, $14-18; 12 oz. Ice Tea Tumbler, $12-14; 10 oz. Water Tumbler, $10-12; 5 oz. Juice Tumbler, $10-12; 5 oz. Low Footed Sherbet, $12-14.

In the following photograph, the 2 oz. Cocktail is an undocumented item. It was specially made by Imperial for a private customer in the Bellaire area. When we bought our 2 oz. Cocktail, it was one of twelve for sale. No other specific information was available.

400/19, 7 oz. Old Fashioned, $24-30; 3 oz. Wine, $18-20; 3-3 1/2 oz. Cocktail, $25-28; 2 oz. Cocktail, $*. NI.

400/19, 6 oz. Egg Cup, large beads, 1948-1960, $40-48; 400/19, 6 oz. Egg Cup, small beads, 1941-1943, $55-65.

400/195 Stem Line: 1952

The seven drink items in the following two photos also did not make it to a catalog. These items did not even make it to a price list but were offered only in a 1952 bulletin.

400/195, 14 oz. Iced Drink, $125-150; 11 oz. Water, $125-150 (ours was a victim of a shipping accident); 6 oz. Dessert, $125-150.

400/195, 9 oz. Old Fashioned, $125-150; 6 oz Juice, $125-150; 2 oz. Wine, $125-150; 4 oz. Cocktail, $125-150.

400/195 Tumblers: 1953-1954

400/195, 16 oz. Tumbler, $125-150; 12 oz. Tumbler, $125-150. The 8 oz. Tumbler, $125-150, is missing from this photograph. The 400/195, 8 oz. Tumbler will be similar to the 400/195, 9 oz. Old Fashioned shown in the previous photograph except for the 1 oz. difference. In addition, the space between the base and the bowl of the 400/195, 8 oz. Tumbler is a little larger on the 400/195 Old Fashion.

400/15 Line of Tumblers: 1962-1963

A short life was the fate of the 400/15 Tumblers. They were never in a catalog, but they were in the 1953 Card File and dated 1962 and 1963. These tumblers were offered to customers only by memorandum.

400/15, 13 oz. Footed Tumbler, $100-125; 10 oz. Footed Tumbler, $100-125; 6 oz. Footed Tumbler, $100-125.

The 400/35 Saucer was used for both the 400/35 Tea Cup and the 400/37 Coffee Cup. In 1943, it was also called the Marmalade Saucer for the 400/89.

400/78, 4 1/2" Coaster. The 10-spoke coaster was made from 1941 to 1970, $7-8. The 5-spoke coaster was shown only in 1939 according to early factory records, $17-20.

The 400/35 Tea Cup and Saucer shown here was introduced in the 1939 Catalog. It has the handle commonly referred to as the question mark handle, $8-14.

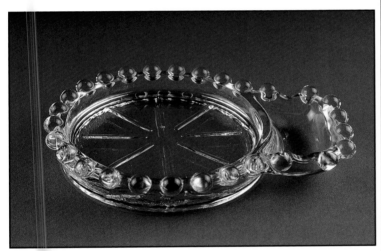

400/226 Coaster with Spoon Rest, $10-12.

400/37 Coffee Cup and Punch Cup, $5-8. The Coffee Cup uses the 400/35 Saucer, $5-8.

Candlewick Sign, $125-150. This is the most desirable advertising sign for Candlewick collectors.

400/77 After Dinner Cup and 400/77 After Dinner Saucer; another name for this is a demi cup and saucer. The size of the After Dinner Saucer is 5" with 1 3/4" center circle, $16-20.

400/35 Tea Cup, $24-30. This is the earliest tea cup made for Candlewick. Note the tiny ridge on the upper and lower part of the handle. This cup preceded the 400/35 Tea Cup with the beaded question mark handle (shown on previous page).

400/211, 5 oz. Punch Cup, $24-30. This cup is deeper and less slanted than the tea cup. The beaded handle is round and not the usual question mark handle of the tea and coffee cup. This cup has often been referred to as the early punch cup. Actually, the 400/211 cup was made from 1950 to 1955 while the 400/37 Punch Cup was introduced in 1938.

Bowls, Cream Soup, Baked Apple, Bouillon, Icer Set

400/50/23, 5 1/4" Cream Soup on 8" Plate, $42-52.

400/53X, 6" Baked Apple, $18-25.

400/126 Bouillon Cup, $35-42. This cup is made from the 400/35 Tea Cup with a second handle added to the mold. In a 1943 advertising booklet, the Bouillon Cup was offered with a 400/35 saucer.

A #530 Sherbet Liner and a #530, 5 1/2 oz. Tumbler complete the 400/53/3 Icer Set. Neither the liner nor the tumbler is Candlewick by itself. We have compared many of the 5 1/2 oz. tumblers from Fostoria and Cambridge icer sets and find them to be the same size, shape, and quality. We question in our minds if Imperial and other glass companies bought these components from the same supplier, or if Imperial did indeed make them. However, we do not have this answer.

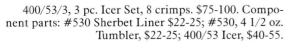

400/53/3, 3 pc. Icer Set, 8 crimps. $75-100. Component parts: #530 Sherbet Liner $22-25; #530, 4 1/2 oz. Tumbler, $22-25; 400/53 Icer, $40-55.

Plates, Strawberry Set, Crescent Salad Plate

400/34, 4 1/2" Individual Butter Plate, Coaster, or Ash Tray, $8-10; 400/1D, 6" Bread and Butter Plate, $8-10; 400/3D, 7" Salad Plate, $8-10; 400/5D, 8" Salad Plate, $8-10; 400/7D, 9" Luncheon Plate, $10-14; 400/10D, 10" Dinner Plate $25-35; 400/13D, 12" Service Plate $25-35. The 400/17D, 14" Torte Plate, $35-45 and the 400/20D, 17" Torte Plate, $50-60 are not shown, but they are this shape and have the wide center circle seat.

400/83, 2 pc. Strawberry Set, $75-80; note the raised circle seat to receive the 400/64 Sugar Dip, $14-16. There are two different 400/64 Sugar Dips—one with 16 beads and one with 18 beads. The one with 16 beads goes with the Strawberry Set. This set was also called a Seafood Set in the 1949 Catalog.

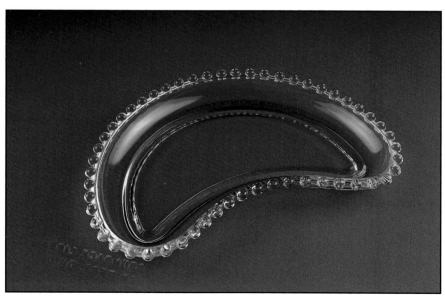

400/120, 8 1/4" Crescent Salad Plate. This is a neat plate to use for purposes other than a salad plate. The plate is attractive on the table used as a pickle or relish plate. $45-60.

Serving Pieces

Serving Bowls

400/1F, 5" Fruit Bowl, $10-12; 400/3F, 6" Fruit Bowl, $12-14; 400/5F, 7" Bowl, $21-25; 400/7F, 8" Bowl, $21-28; 400/10F, 9" Bowl, $32-42; 400/13F, 10"-10 1/2" Bowl, $32-42; 400/17F, 12" Bowl, $42-53. Note that the size of the 400/13F varies. It is not easy to build a set of the F bowls in which the bowls graduate uniformly and have the same coloring.

400/13B, 11" Centre Bowl, $55-70; component part of: 400/8613B Console Set; 400/8013B Console Set.

400/42B, 4 3/4" 2-Handled Fruit, $8-12; 400/52B, 6"-6 1/2" 2-Handled Bowl, $10-14; 400/62B, 7" 2-Handled Bowl, $12-16; 400/72B, 8 1/2" 2-Handled Bowl, $17-20. These four bowls make up the 400/4272B, 4 pc. Bowl Set. There is also a 400/145B, 10" Bowl, $30-37; and a 400/113B, 12" Bowl with the same shape and the 2-handles, $95-110.

400/53S, 5" Square Round Bowl, made for W.J. Hughes and Son, Toronto, Canada, $65-80. Not shown is the 400/92S, 12" Square Bowl made for Lipman, Sterling, Ltd., U.K., $*. We know that these two bowls were made for these two different companies. It follows that other sizes were probably made from other standard round bowl molds as well. At least collectors will have some idea of the background for the shape of the "square round" bowl. NI.

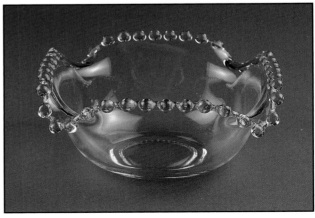

The 400/63B, 10 1/2" Bowl, 400/104B, 14" Bowl, and 400/106B, 12" Bowl are all shaped the same and vary only in their sizes. Note the graduated beads on the sides. In addition, these bowls are used in several console sets. Refer to the Console Set section for more details.

Three bowls are designed the same and differ only in size; only the 400/106B, 12" Bowl is shown here. They are the 400/63B, 10 1/2" Bowl, $37-44; 400/106B, 12" Bowl, $45-50; 400/104B, 14"-14 1/2" Bowl, $135-150. These bowls all have graduated beads on the sides. The 400/104B, 14"-14 1/2" Bowl is the more difficult to find of these three and is part of the 400/104 Chilled Fruit Set.

The 400/65 Covered Vegetable and Candy was first shown and listed in Catalog A, 1939. The catalog very clearly shows a domed lid. It is not a gradual dome, but rather the lid is raised just inside the ridge and rounded up to the underneath of the finial. In the 1939 catalog it was labeled as both a covered vegetable and covered candy and was not divided. The next catalog, Catalog B, shows the candy as 400/65 and divided. Upon close scrutiny, you can see that the lid is only slightly raised on the candy. In Catalog B, the vegetable is now 400/65/1 and the lid is still very much domed. Every time the vegetable is shown after that, the lid continues to be very much domed. We have seen several examples of the 400/65/1 Covered Vegetable with the less domed or only slightly domed lid. The domed lid would be considered rare. Perhaps very few covered vegetable bowls with domed lids have survived the years.

400/65/1, 8" Covered Vegetable, domed lid, $★. Early number was 400/65. The 400/65 Vegetable or Candy will often be found with a lid that is not domed, $140-175. The two lids are shown separately here for easy comparison. NI.

400/67B, 9" Low Footed Fruit Bowl or Compote, ribbed, $100-110 (without cut); 400/67B, 9" Low Footed Fruit Bowl or Compote, not ribbed $110-115. Early ones have ribs and a domed foot while the later ones are plain with a flat foot. The bowl of this compote flares out slightly. In the undocumented section, you will see another version from this mold that does not have the flare but rather is shaped in a more rounded upward form.

400/67C, 9" Footed Crimped Bowl or Compote, $120-140. The mold was also used for the 400/196, 2 pc. Epergne Set and the 400/196FC Flower Candle Centerpiece.

400/69B, 8 1/2" Vegetable Bowl inside, $20-28; 400/75B, 10 1/2" Bowl, $28-35. The 400/75B is also used in the 400/75B Salad Set and 400/8075B Console Set.

400/72, 8 1/2" 2-Handled Divided Bowl, $60-70; 400/52, 6"-6 1/2" 2-Handled Divided Jelly, $20-25.

400/74B, 8 1/2" Bowl, 4-toed, $55-75. This early bowl has ribs that covered the mold marks.

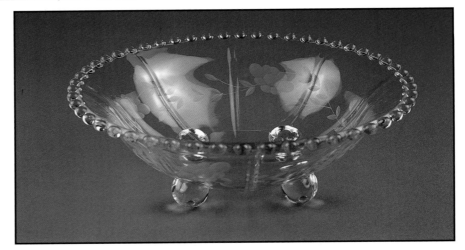

400/74SC, 9" Bowl, $50-55. This is one of the earliest bowls and has the ribs in the mold. It also has four round balls on the bottom and is called 4-toed. Shown are a pair of 400/74SC, 9" Bowls, illustrating how different artisans, at different times, turned out variations in the shaping of an item. This gives true meaning to the words "hand-crafted."

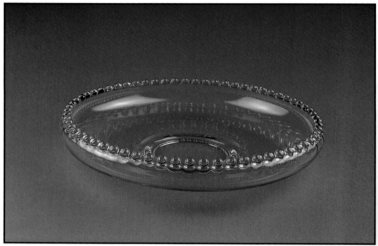

400/75F, 10"-11" Float Bowl, $25-30; component part of: 400/8075B Console Set. 400/92F, 12" Float Bowl, $32-40; component part of: 400/920F Console Set; 400/9275 Console Set; 400/9279R Console Set; 400/244 Hostess Helper Set. These two float bowls have the same shape and the only difference is in the size. Only one is shown; be sure you note which one is used in certain sets.

400/84, 6 1/2" Divided Bowl, $32-35; component part of: 400/84, 4 pc. Mayonnaise Set; 400/94 Buffet Salad Set, and 400/95 Mayonnaise Set.

400/85, 6" Cottage Cheese Bowl, $25-35; 400/85 is the 400/84 Bowl without the divider. This is an example of the multiple uses of basic molds combined with different plungers to produce an entirely different item.

400/92B, 12" Bowl, $40-54; component part of:
400/925 Salad Set. Not shown 400/75B, 10 1/2"
Bowl (same shape), $28-35.

400/92L, 13" Mushroom Centre Bowl, $42-54; component
part of: 400/127L Console Set; 400/8692L Console Set.

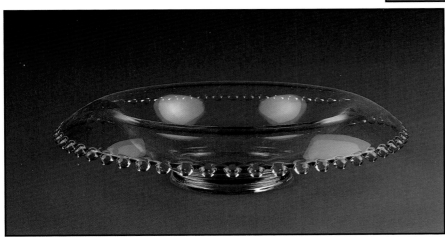

400/92R, 13" Mushroom Centre Bowl, $55-65.
This bowl is not listed but is shown in the 400/136
Console Set in a 1941 catalog. We assigned this
number according to the associated piece, 400/92L
Console Bowl, and added the R for the description
of the rolled over design.

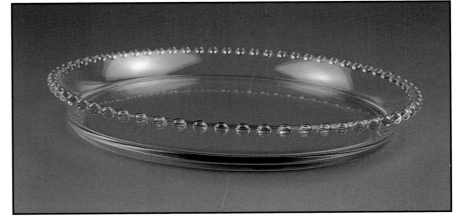

400/101, 13" Float Bowl, measures 1 1/4" deep, $150-175; component part of:
400/101/79B Console Set. The ones that we have seen have not had the clear look
of most Imperial Candlewick. They have a thick look that is not as transparent.

400/103C, 10" Footed Fruit Bowl, Crimped, $150-175. This is a tall
footed bowl with a diameter of 10". It is crimped and has three large
beads for the stem. This bowl is sometimes considered a compote.

400/103F, 10" Footed Fruit Bowl, $195-225. The 400/103F is 6 1/2" tall and the bowl is about 1" deep. It is another item made from the same mold as the 400/103C, 400/103D, and 400/103E. Also, it is sometimes thought of as a compote.

400/113B, 12" 2-Handled Bowl, $95-110; 400/145B, 10" 2-Handled Bowl, $30-37 (not shown). Shown here are the 400/113B and the 400/42B to illustrate the largest and smallest of the 2-handled bowl design. Remember, there is also a set of four graduated sizes of the two-handled bowls as shown on page 31.

400/114A, 10"-11" Partitioned 4 1/2" Deep Bowl, 2-handled and has a scalloped partition, $400-475. Not shown is the 400/113A, 10" Deep Bowl, 2-handled and 4 1/2" deep, $★. The two bowls are the same except that the 400/113A has no partition.

400/124A, 11" Oval Bowl, 2 1/4" deep. $★.

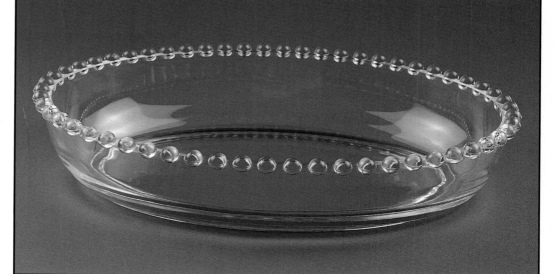

This 400/125A, 11" Partitioned Bowl is 2 1/4" deep and the partition is scalloped, $225-250. We received ours in the mail many years ago. It was a delightful surprise when we opened it, because we did not realize until then that the partition was scalloped.

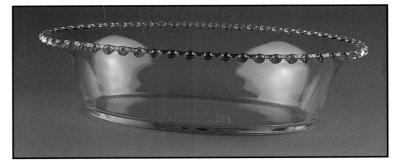

400/131B, 14" Oval Bowl, $210-225; component part of 400/1531B, 3 pc. Console Set.

400/182, 8 1/2" 3-toed Bowl, $85-95. It often is a surprise to collectors that this bowl has graduated beads on the end. It is 8 1/2" wide by 4 3/4" from the bottom of the toes to the top.

Left: 400/183, 6" 3-toed Bowl, $50-55. Center: 400/205, 10" 3-toed Bowl, $110-125. Right: 400/206, 4 1/2" 3-toed Nappy, $50-60. Note that all three bowls have the small beads. The 400/183 is 2 1/2" high; the 400/205 is 3 1/2" high; and the 400/206 is 5 1/2" high. The 400/183 is part of the 400/623 Mayonnaise Set.

400/214, 10" Dish and Cover, $420-450. This delicate, rare cover is domed with a curved beaded handle on top. The dish is 10" long (including the two tab handles) by 4 1/2" wide and has no partition.

400/216, 10" Dish and Cover, $385-450. The cover for the 400/214 is the same as the cover for this 400/216. It is domed with a curved beaded handle on top. The dish is 10" long (including two tab handles) by 4 1/2" wide and has three sections.

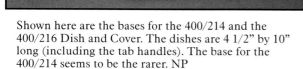

Shown here are the bases for the 400/214 and the 400/216 Dish and Cover. The dishes are 4 1/2" by 10" long (including the tab handles). The base for the 400/214 seems to be the rarer. NP

400/231, 5" Square Bowl, $60-70; 400/232, 6" Square Bowl, $70-80; 400/233, 7" Square Bowl, $70-80. These bowls nest very well. The 5" Square Bowl is 2 1/4" deep; the 6" Square Bowl is 2 1/2" deep; the 7" Square Bowl is 3" deep. These have been reproduced by Dalzell Viking and have caused some concern. Generally, the reproductions are heavier and not as clear. Dalzell Viking items should be marked with an acid etched name, but that can be easily removed. Seconds by Dalzell Viking should have DX on the bottom but we understand that does not always occur.

400/243, 5 1/2" Sauce Bowl, $28-30. Note that the sides slant slightly in toward the bottom.

Plates

A few of the serving plates will not be shown here but will be included instead with the items that complete certain sets. One example is the 400/23D, 7"-7 1/2" Plate, AKA 400/40D. This is the under plate for the 400/23 Mayonnaise Set and the 400/733 Salad Dressing or Syrup Set. Similarly, the 400/40D, 7 1/2" Plate is the under plate for the 400/50 Cream Soup in early brochures; later this was changed to number 400/23D.

The 400/36, 6" Canapé Plate with a 2" off center, raised ring is a component part of the 400/36 Canapé Set. Also included in that group will be the 400/39 Canapé Plate with the 2 1/2" off center, raised ring for the 400/91 Cocktail Set; 400/97 Cocktail Set; 400/98, 9" Oval Plate AKA 400/38 with 2" raised ring for the 400/37 Cup or the 400/172 Tumbler.

Oval Plates and Platters, including: 400/169, 8" Oval Plate for Sauce Bowl, $32-38; 400/38, 9" Oval Salad Plate, $27-34; 400/124, 12 1/2" Oval Plate, $56-63 (early plate was number 400/124D, 12 1/2"-13" Oval Platter); 400/131D, 16" Oval Platter or Tray, $150-165.

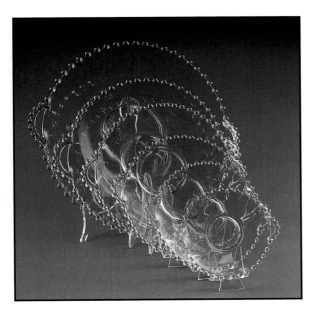

400/42D, 5 1/2" 2-Handled Plate, $8-10; 400/52D, 7"-7 1/2" 2-Handled Plate, $8-10; 400/62D, 8 1/2" 2-Handled Plate, $10-14; 400/72D, 10" 2-Handled Plate, $20-27; component parts of the 400/4272D, 4 pc. 2-Handled Plate Set, $46-60. Also shown are the 400/145D, 12" 2-Handled Plate, $20-25; 400/113D, 14" 2-Handled Plate, $45-50 . All these plates have the small center circle bottom.

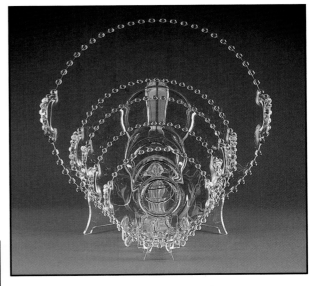

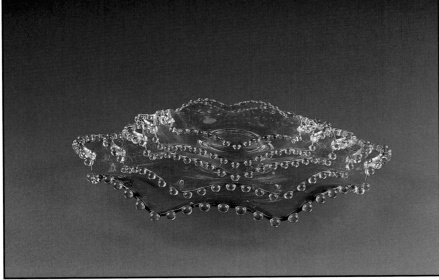

400/42E, 5 1/2" 2-Handled Plate, Tray, $10-15; 400/52E, 7"-7 1/2" 2-Handled Plate, Tray, $15-20; 400/62E, 8 1/2" 2-Handled Plate, Tray, $15-20; 400/72E, 10" 2-Handled Plate, Tray, $30-45; 400/113E, 14" 2-Handled Plate, $★. All five plates have the handles turned up. There is another size of this style plate that we believe might be overlooked. It is the 400/145E 11 1/2" Tray, $★ (see page 42). It was made only one year so be on the watch for that one.

400/52C, 6 3/4" 2-Handled Plate, $25-30; 400/62C, 8 1/2" 2-Handled Plate, $18-25; 400/72C, 10" 2-Handled Plate, $24-27; 400/145C, 11 1/2"-12" 2-Handled Plate, $25-40; 400/113C, 14" 2-Handled Plate, $115-125. All five plates are crimped.

Pictured next is the 400/52E, 7"-7 1/2" 2-Handled Plate, shown with the 400/145H Muffin Tray for size comparison. Note that these have the sides turned up. The 400/52E with the sides turned up has the same number as the plate with the handles turned up. The one with the sides turned up appeared in the 1953 to 1958 material as 7"-7 1/2" and then appeared in 1961 to 1968 material as 9". Collectors have often been confused when the 400/52E was called the "mini muffin tray." However, if a collector had a 9", we can see why it might be called a "mini muffin tray." Remember to watch for both of these.

400/145H, 11 1/2" Muffin Tray, $300-325 (shown for size comparison); 400/52E, 7"-7 1/2", 2-Handled Plate, $20-25.

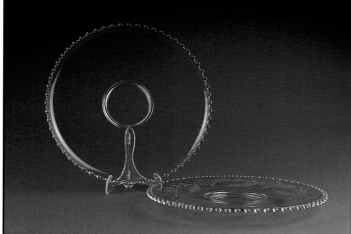

400/75V, 12 1/2"-13" Plate Cupped (left), $18-25; 400/75D, 13 1/2" Plate (right), $★. The 400/75V, 12 1/2"-13" Cupped Plate is used in the 400/7375, 4 pc. Salad Set and the 400/4975, 4 pc. Salad Set. The 400/75D Flat Plate has a proportionally small center circle. This plate is used in the 400/75B Salad Set.

400/92D, 13 1/2"-14" Plate, $46-52; component part of: 400/925 Salad Set; 400/94, 4 pc. Buffet Salad Set; 400/9266B, 2 pc. Cheese and Cracker Set. Shown are two views of the 400/92D. Not shown is the 400/92V, 13 1/2" Cupped Plate, $32-36; component part of the 400/925 Salad Set.

400/20V, 17" Torte Plate, two views, $42-56; component part of: 400/20 Punch Set.

Trays

Shown first in this section are the two trays used many times for salt and pepper sets, sugar and cream sets, and condiments.

Back: 400/29, 6 1/2"-7" Tray, $8-10. Front: 400/96T, 5" Tray, $10-12. The 400/29, 6 1/2"-7" Tray is a component part of: 400/29/6, 6 pc. Cigarette Set; 400/29/30 Sugar, Cream and Tray Set; 400/29/64/44 Cigarette Set; 400/122/29 Sugar, Cream and Tray Set; 400/701, 5 pc. Condiment Set; 400/2794 Oil and Vinegar; 400/2911 Oil and Vinegar Set; 400/2989 Twin Jam Set; 400/2990 Condiment Set; 400/5629 Mustard and Ketchup Set. The 400/96T, 5" Tray is a component part of: 400/96/3 Salt, Pepper, Tray Set; 400/2296 Sugar, Cream, Tray Set; 400/7796 Vinegar and Oil Set.

400/51M, 6" Handled Card Tray, $90-115 This tray is very flat with only the back of the plate and the handle bent upward. It is definitely round at the front with absolutely no hint of a point at the front.

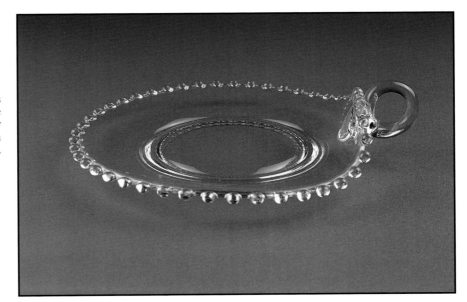

400/68D, 11 1/2"-12" Handled Pastry Tray, $20-35. At the top of the center handle, there are large beads that form the shape of a heart. There are also two large beads in the heart shape opening.

41

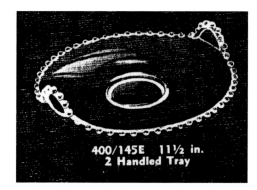

400/68F, 10 1/2" Handled Fruit Tray, $100-135. The 400/68D Pastry Tray has been cupped to make the Fruit Tray.

400/145E 11½ in. 2 Handled Tray

400/145E, 11 1/2" 2-Handled Tray, $★. Collectors have often overlooked this item because it is called a tray rather than a plate and is not usually shown with the turned-up handled plates. It was made only one year. When you are shopping for Candlewick, you had better carry a tape measure.

400/145H, 11 1/2" 2-Handled Muffin Tray, $300-325. Evidently, not many households bought the Muffin Tray as evidenced by the scarcity of the tray. The sides are turned up.

400/151, 10" Tray, $30-38. This tray has a raised circular design in the bottom and does not come with a mirror. There is a 400/151 Tray with a mirror that was made for Irice in the 1940s. Always look underneath the mirror because you might find that it is the 400/151, 10" Lazy Susan Tray. That tray has a raised circular design with a 3 1/2" circle of stippling to hide the bearings that make up the Lazy Susan Set. On the underside of the Lazy Susan Tray is a definite 3/8" channel forming a 3" circle to receive the metal bearings.

400/154, 11 1/2"-12" Deviled Egg Server, $85-100; has been reproduced by Dalzell Viking.

400/159, 9 1/4" Oval Tray, $17-20. The plain bottom tray is a utility tray. The other version of this tray has fine curved lines on the bottom to support a mirror. This version, M-152, was made for Irving W. Rice in the 1940s. The plain oval tray is used as a component in these sets: 400/1567, 5 pc. Condiment Set; 400/1574, 5 pc. Condiment Set; 400/1589 Twin Jam Set; 400/1596 Condiment Set; 400/2796, 5 pc. Condiment Set; and 400/5996 Condiment Set.

400/171, 8" Tray, $27-30; component part of: 400/1769, 4 pc. Condiment Set; 400/1786 Condiment Set; and 400/2769, 4 pc. Condiment Set.

400/221, 5 1/2" Handled Lemon Tray, Tri-Stem, $28-35. The term "tri-stem" is not an Imperial name but rather one used by collectors to identify this style. This is one of seven tri-stem items and is the easiest one to find. Some items in the group of tri-stems are at the top of the rarest list.

Cakes, Banana Stand

50th Anniversary Cake on 400/20D, 17" Plate. Small dots of icing decorate the cake to simulate Candlewick beads. This is an appropriately decorated cake for celebrating fifty years of marriage and fifty years of choosing Candlewick for the wedding pattern.

400/67D, 10" Low Cake Stand, ribbed, $40-45; 10" 1-bead cake stand. In the side view photograph, the earlier version on the right has the ribs on it with a slightly domed foot; the later version on the left has no ribs and the foot is flat. The difference in height is caused by the later version having the new feature in the design of the mold. Also note the new wafer of glass above the stem ball.

400/67D 10" Low Cake Stand, no ribs, $46-50.

400/75V (#14415), 12 1/2" Torte Plate, Cupped with Cake Cover, $78-86. This item is in the 1982-1983 catalog. The cake cover is very hard to recognize when it is separated from the Candlewick Torte Plate. The cake cover is 10" in diameter and 4 7/8" side height. It tapers upward to a total height of 7 7/8" with a 2" solid knob. The West Virginia Glass Company, Weston, West Virginia, made the cover. It was bought by Imperial and combined with Candlewick.

400/103D, 11" Tall Cake Stand, 3-bead stem, $60-65. The 400/103D (#51675) Cake Stand and Cover appeared in the 1980 catalog. 400/103D Cake Stand and Cover, $120-135. This same cover is on a Collector's Crystal tall cake stand and you might see that for sale and be able to buy it for your Candlewick collection.

400/223, 12" Cake Tray, Tri-Stem, $★; shown with the 400/221, 5 1/2" Lemon Tray for comparison of size. In factory paper, there is also shown a 400/222, 8" Bon Bon, Tri-Stem, center handled 8" plate, $★. It is the same style as the 400/223, 12" Cake Tray and the 400/221, 5 1/2" Lemon Tray. All three of these items are on the 1950 Price List but are not illustrated in any catalogs. This is one of the most exciting items in our collection. A great deal of the excitement is due to the way it became ours. A good friend found it, called us, and said, "this belongs in your collection!" It came our way during the research on this book. Please note that 400/223 is a Tri-Stem Cake Tray and not the Tri-Stem Cake Stand. NI.

400/160, 13"-14" Birthday Cake Plate, $335-400. There are 72 recessed holes for candles. If your candles are a little too large for the holes, we suggest that you sharpen the ends of the candles in an inexpensive plastic pencil sharpener.

400/??? Cake Stand, Tri-Stem, $★. This item does not have a number on it and does not match any number in the 1950 or other price lists. We are uncertain if it was made. There was a company note on one of the 1950 Tri-Stem memorandums that they were dropped because of the difficulty of producing. This is a company illustration taken from proposed new items. NI.

400/103E Banana Stand, $1540-1680; made from the 400/103D Cake Stand with the sides turned up; 3-bead stem.

46

Salt Dips, Salt And Peppers

400/19, 2 1/4" Salt Dip, $12-15. This salt dip has large beads and is very shallow.

400/61, 2" Salt Dip, $12-15; component part of 400/616 Individual Salt Set.

The production life of the 400/96 Salt and Pepper was 1938 to 1984. In March of 1998, we received a telephone call from a friend in Los Angeles, California. He had just seen the March 24, 1998, issue of The Globe featuring a special article on the movie Titanic. One part of the special article featured a menu of the last meal on the ill-fated voyage in 1912. Accompanying the recipes in the article was a photo of that last meal and, lo and behold, one of the table setting items in the photo was nothing other than Imperial's 400/96 Candlewick Salt and Pepper. Although this was a slight anachronism, they looked very elegant on the dinner table!

400/96 Salt and Pepper Set, $12-17. The nine large bead set appeared in 1941 and continued until mid-to-late 1940s. The neck threading is 7/8".

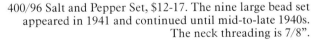

400/96 Salt and Pepper Set, $10-15. The set with the eight large bead base started in the late 1940s. In the beginning the top threading was 7/8" and later changed to 5/8". Plastic lids were used in the early 1940s and metal lids began in the mid 1940s.

400/96/3 Salt, Pepper, and Tray Set, $21-24; component parts: 400/96 Salt and Pepper Set and 400/96T Tray.

400/109 Individual Salt and Pepper Set, $10-14. Early 1940s sets had the plastic lids and the metal lids appeared in mid-to-late 1940s. The threading size is 1/2".

400/116 Footed Salt and Pepper Set, $85-100. The 400/116 is a 1-bead salt and pepper with plastic lids for 7/8" threading. This is the most difficult to find salt and pepper set.

400/167 Salt and Pepper Set, 4 1/2" height, $14-18. This set was introduced in 1948 and had metal lids for 5/8" threading.

400/190 Salt and Pepper Set, $35-42. This salt and pepper set was also introduced in 1948 and will have the metal lids for 7/8" threading. This set has the same stem as the 400/190 stemware line—hollow and flared.

400/247 Salt and Pepper Set, $18-20. The height of the 400/247 is 4" including the top of metal cap. The set has straight sides on top of a base of eight beads smaller than the 400/96 set. It has a 5/8" threading size.

Grouped together for easy comparison are the various lids found on Imperial's Candlewick Salt and Pepper Sets. Shown in the front row are the plastic lids (the 400/109, early lid for the 400/96 Salt with 9 beads, and the 8-bead 400/96); in the second row are the metal lids (400/109 and 400/96) and in the back row are examples of non-Imperial lids (a light metal and a sterling lid with an ivory inset). The two examples in the back row are lids used by companies that purchased salt and pepper sets from Imperial for "after factory" distribution. NP

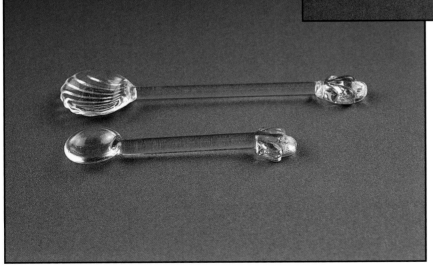

400/616 Salt Spoon (front), $15-20; 4000 Salt Spoon (back), $12-14; The 400/616 Salt Spoon is 2 5/8" long and has a plain bowl with a fleur-de-lis on the handle end. The 4000 Salt Spoon is 3 3/8" long and has a ribbed bowl with a fleur-de-lis on the handle end. These spoons present a puzzling situation. Various factory lists show the 400/616 AKA 4000 and yet we can see in Catalog E that both are illustrated. The 400/156 Ketchup Spoon is also known as the 4000. We believe that the 400/616 is the salt spoon and the 4000 is the Ketchup Spoon as they fit the proportions of the sets best. That is also the way they look in the catalog illustrations. At the end of our research for this book, a friend found a 4000, ribbed bowl spoon that is only 3 3/16" long. Do you suppose Imperial made a short version of the 4000 to be used as a salt spoon?

Sugar and Creams

400/18 Sugar and Cream Set, $140-160. This set has an applied handle that does not touch the top of the cream. The base of this set has the domed foot of the 400/18 stemware line. The sugar is the 400/18 Old Fashion. A short production time makes this set hard to find.

400/30 Sugar and Cream Set, $12-14. Early brochures show this as 6 oz. The height is 2 7/8".

400/30 Sugar and Cream Set, $12-14. The later version, not including the spout, is 3 1/4" tall. Surprisingly, it too holds 6 ounces. While the early version has only a small pouring spout pulled from the cup, the later version has an elongated spout.

400/29/30 Sugar, Cream, and Tray Set, $22-28; component parts: 400/29 Tray; 400/30 Sugar and Cream. This is the early style 400/30 on the 400/29, 6 1/2"-7" Tray.

400/29/30 Sugar, Cream, and Tray Set, $22-28; component parts: 400/29, 6 1/2" Tray and 400/30 Sugar and Cream. This later style is the taller version with larger pouring spout and on the 400/29, 6 1/2" Tray. The tray changed to 7" in 1977. 400/2930 was the first way this set was listed. Later it was listed as 400/29/30 Sugar, Cream and Tray Set. This is just one of many slight number changes through the production years.

400/111, 6 1/2" Tray, two raised seats, $65-70; component part of: 400/111 Tête-à-Tête; 400/122/111 Sugar, Cream, and Tray Set.

400/31 Sugar and Cream Set, unknown cut, $45-55 if not cut; early style had the beaded foot and plain handle.

400/31 Sugar and Cream Set, $18-25; later style had the plain foot and beaded handle.

400/122/111 Sugar, Cream and Tray Set, $85-95; component parts: 400/122 Individual Sugar and Cream; 400/111, 6 1/2" Tray with two seats. Not shown is the 400/122/29 Individual Sugar and Cream Set on the 400/29 Tray $20-25. Again, there was a style change for the 400/122 Individual Sugar and Cream with the early style being shorter and having a smaller pouring spout. The later style is taller and has a larger pouring spout. Some of the earlier 400/122 had a ground and polished bottom and the later versions had the marie on the bottom.

400/126 Sugar and Cream Set AKA 400/153, $80-90. It is only documented in the 1943 Price List and is hard to find. The cream is a 400/35 Tea Cup with a small spout pulled on it. The sugar is a 400/35 Tea Cup with a second handle added to it. The sugar is also the 400/126 Bouillon Cup.

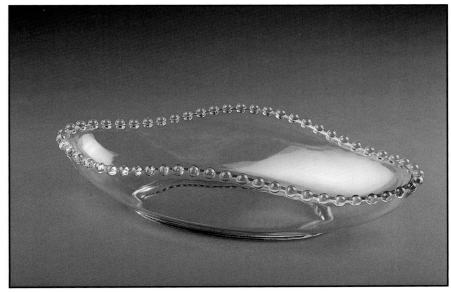

400/46, 11" Oval Celery Boat, $52-62. When discussing this piece with other collectors, we found it easy to refer to it as the "canoe" and others always understood it. Collectors need a way to make communications about Candlewick a little easier to understand! The celery boat is used as the bowl on the 400/137 Oval Compote.

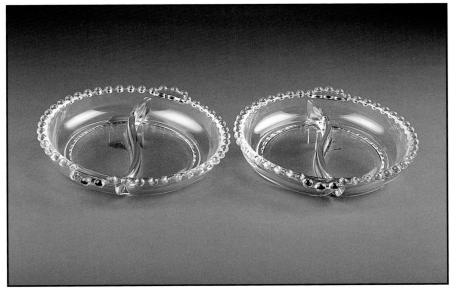

400/54, 6 1/2" Relish Tray, $10-12. Here is probably the most frequently found piece of Candlewick. Imperial sold more than 400,000 of these trays to a distributor to be repackaged and sold with their product from 1954 to 1964. The tray is round with two sections and two tab handles. An interesting variation of this item is one that can be found with the curved divider reversed in the relish. The original "S" design was seen last in the 1971R Catalog and the reversed divider was first illustrated in the 1972 Catalog. The "S" divider on the left hand tray is the early one. The later tray on the right is the 400/54 Relish Tray, reversed "S" divider, $12-14.

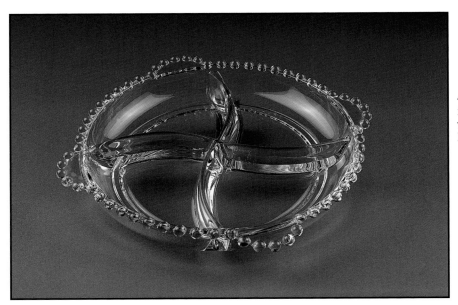

400/55, 8 1/2" Relish Tray, $18-20. This is another fairly common item. Probably many relish dishes were sold as gift items and for bridal showers. It has four tab handles and four sections.

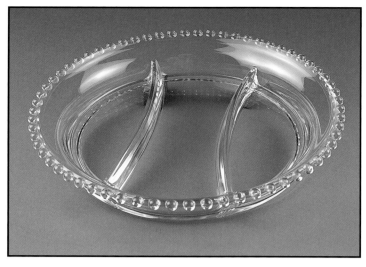

400/56, 10 1/2" Relish, $32-35. This is the early version of the 400/56 Relish. It has three long sections.

400/56, 10 1/2" Relish, $35-38. In 1949, the design of the 400/56 changed to five pinwheel sections and five tab handles.

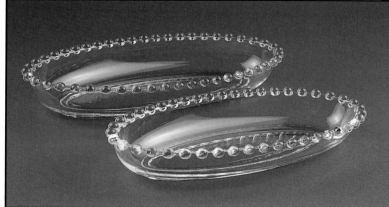

400/57, 7 1/2" Oval Pickle or Celery Tray (front), $25-32; 400/58, 8 1/2" Oval Pickle or Celery Tray (back), $14-18. Some collectors might overlook the 400/58 because when the 400/57 and 400/58 are seen separately, one does not always observe the difference in sizes.

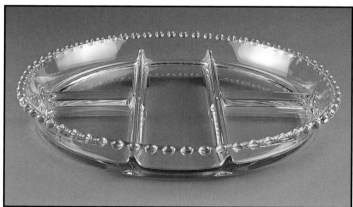

400/102, 13"-13 1/2" Relish, $60-65. It is round and has five sections; two partitioned sections on either side border the long center section.

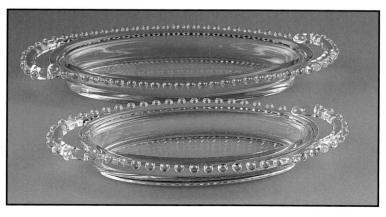

400/105, 13"-13 1/2", Celery Tray (back), $32-38; 400/217, 10"-10 1/2" Pickle Tray (front), $28-35. The open handles are included in the measurements for both trays.

Pictured here is the 400/1112, 4 piece Relish and Dressing Set using the early version of the 400/112 as the base of the set. The early version has three sections plus the center circle section. It is shown in catalogs with the long slender ladle with the 3-bead end on it. The ladle shown here is for the later version. We do not know if any of the long slender 3-bead ladles have been found.

400/1112, 4 pc. Relish and Dressing Set, $64-90; component parts: 400/89, 3 Partitioned 10 1/2" Relish; early version with three sections and no handles, long slender 3-bead spoon, $*; later version, 400/112 (shown below), has five sections and five tab handles, $28-35. Be sure you have a 400/89 Marmalade as the 400/289 does not fit this properly. Early versions 400/112, $32-38.

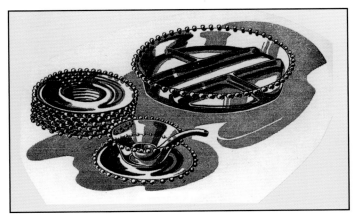

Electro No. 9-C

400/208, 10" 3 Partitioned Relish, $77-88. The 400/208 looks more like a bowl than a relish. It is 3-toed and has a height of 3 1/4".

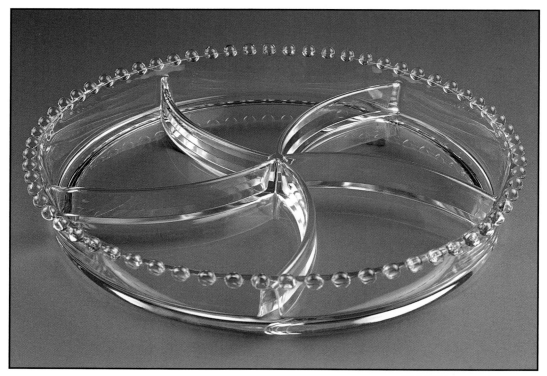

400/209, 13 1/2" Partitioned Relish, $315-385. This large relish is spectacular. It has five sections in a pinwheel design. It is very rare although it did have a three year production span. The first one we saw was on a Kromex tray, in a private collection. Finally, we had the pleasure of finding the 400/209 Relish for ourselves at an antique show.

400/215, 12" x 7" Oblong Relish Tray, Partitioned, four sections and two tab handles, $60-66; the 400/213, 10" Oblong Relish Tray is not shown, $★. The two relishes are designed the same; the sections are a long one with three small sections opposite the long one. The measurements do include the tab handles. The 400/213 and 400/215 are both illustrated in Catalog E. If both of these had not been illustrated in the same catalog, we might wonder if there are really two sizes. We have not seen the 400/213 size.

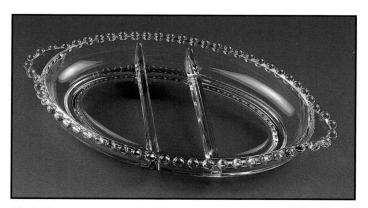

400/234, 7" Square Relish, $90-105. This is one of the few square items. It has two sections and is 1 3/8" deep.

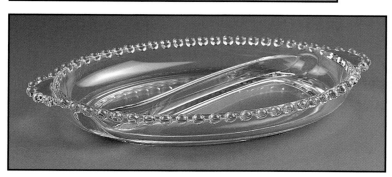

400/256, 10 1/2" Oval Relish, $28-32; 400/268, 8" 2 Partitioned Oval Relish, $18-21 (not shown). Both have two sections made with an "S" curve divider. The two tab handles are included in the measurements.

400/262, 10 1/2" 3 Partitioned Relish, $88-105. This relish, with two tab handles, is also called a butter and jam. It is oval with two dividers slanted across the center.

Saved the best to last—new identification! Finally, proof of the number and description of a piece of Candlewick that has haunted us. The 6" "Ash Tray" or "Relish," as it was often referred to, has caused collectors to ask many questions. While researching this book, we at first passed over a reference in a paper about Oneida Silver before finally realizing that we were reading about an item description we had not heard before. On a chart showing the number of pieces sold to Oneida during certain years was an entry for "400/257, 6" Cheese Dish." Suddenly I thought, "There isn't a 6" Cheese Dish." With flashing lights, I realized that the questionable "ash tray/relish" with the small beads fit this description. We had this set in an Oneida box with a Twilight butter spreader. Certainly a butter spreader would be put with a cheese dish! NI.

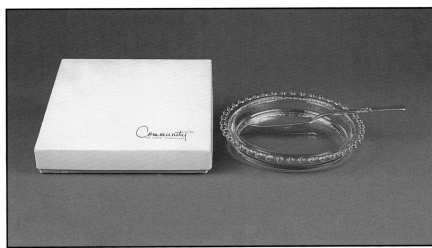

400/257, 6" Cheese Dish. This mystery dish now has an official number. It was an item made for Oneida Ltd. to be combined with one of their butter spreaders and gift boxed for an Oneida production. Dish only, $14-18. NI.

Advertising layout provided by Oneida to its customers. It is for the 400/54 Relish and South Seas Silverplate. Oneida ordered more of these relishes than any other Imperial item for the promotions. Advertisement printed by permission of Oneida, Ltd.

...TO INTRODUCE
South Seas
in
COMMUNITY
The Finest Silverplate

THE
"PARTY SET"
with RELISH DISH
(in *IMPERIAL GLASS*)
and
2 SERVING PIECES
$2.95
REGULAR
$7.00
VALUE

Jellies, Marmalades

The 400/89, 400/1989, and 400/8918 Marmalades all take the same lid, which is 3 1/2" in diameter with a slot in the lid. All the lids have beads around the lid with a 2-bead finial and a ridge for secure fitting.

Please note that all information about the marmalade ladles can be found in the special section on Ladles. Having all the ladles together will let you see a comparison of sizes.

400/33, 4" Individual Jelly or Ash Tray, $10-14. This item was also sold to lighting companies and can be found on table lamps. (For more information, see examples in the Boudoir section of our book on Candlewick: Colored and Decorated Lines.)

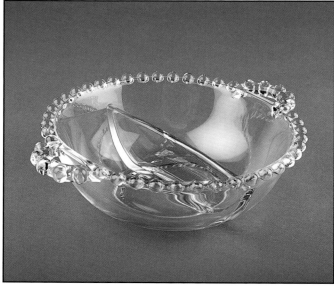

400/52, 6"-6 1/2" Handled, Divided Bowl or Jelly, $18-21.

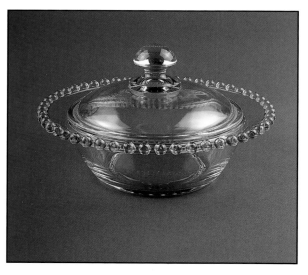

400/59, 5 1/2" Covered Jelly. This uses the 400/144 Lid with round half knob, $42-46 (not cut). This is also called a covered candy and it, too, had the round half knob. A later version with a 2-bead finial (see next photo) was called a covered candy.

When the 400/59 is found with a 2-bead lid, it is considered the 400/59 Covered Candy, $27-30. The 400/59 with half-round finial (shown here for comparison and in previous photo) is either a Covered Jelly or a Covered Candy.

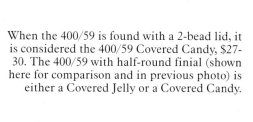

400/89, 4 pc. Marmalade Set, $34-42; component parts: 400/89 Marmalade Bowl and Cover; 400/35 Marmalade (Tea Cup) Saucer; 400/130 Marmalade Ladle, 3 beads. The 4 pc. Marmalade Set is also listed as 400/89/3 because Imperial was not always consistent in counting lids or stoppers. The bowl of the 400/89 is 2 3/4" tall, and is more delicate than the bowl of the 400/289, which is 3 1/4" tall.

400/89, 4 pc. Marmalade with long, slender, 3-bead spoon, $*. We have not heard of any collectors who have found the long slender ladle with three beads.

400/89, 4 pc. Marmalade (shown without saucer), $38-46; component parts: 400/89 Marmalade; 400/35 Marmalade Saucer; 5 1/2" long ladle with one bead on tip (not a perfect bead) and shell bowl. In an early Imperial brochure the marmalade lid has a raised bump on it.

400/157, 4 3/4" Covered Jelly or Honey, $64-74. By adding the 400/144 Cover with two beads to the 400/157 Cheese Compote, you have the 400/157 Covered Jelly; component part of: 400/92 Cheese and Cracker Set. Without the cover, the 400/157 does not look as if it belongs in the Candlewick family.

A comparison of marmalade bases, 400/89 on the left and the 400/289 on the right, showing the slight difference in size of the bottoms and height.

400/289, 3 pc. Marmalade Set, $24-30. The bowl height of this set is 3 1/4". The bottom of the bowl of the 400/289 is heavier than the 400/89 Marmalade Bowl. For this set, Imperial used a 4 5/8" plastic ladle from 1953-1968, except for 1966 when the catalog showed the 400/289 with a 400/130 Marmalade Ladle, 4 3/4", 3 beads.

400/289, 2 pc. Marmalade Set. A 5" metal ladle was combined with the 400/289 Marmalade Set from 1971 to 1981, $24-27. From 1982 to 1984, no ladle was included, $17-24. A company notation indicated that "most households have their own ladles and there is no need for Imperial to buy a metal ladle to include in the set."

400/1589 Twin Jam Set, $80-95; component parts: 400/159, 9 1/4" Oval Tray; 400/89 Marmalade Bowl and Cover; 400/130 Marmalade Ladle, 3 beads.

400/1989, 3 pc. Marmalade Set AKA 400/19/89, $42-46; component parts: 400/19 Old Fashion; 400/89 Lid; 400/130 Marmalade Ladle, 3 beads; long slender ladle with 3 beads in early version, $★.

400/2989, 3 pc. Twin Jam Set, $58-80; component parts: 400/29, 6 1/2"-7" Tray; 400/89 Marmalade Bowl and Cover; 400/130 Marmalade Ladle, 3 beads. Imperial counted the 3 pc. Marmalade as one item in this set.

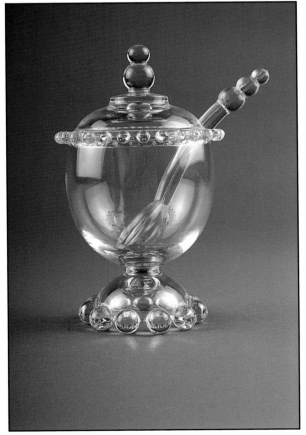

400/8918, 3 pc. Marmalade Set, $74-90; component parts: 400/18 Old Fashion; 400/130 Marmalade Ladle, 3 beads. The total height of this set is 4 1/2".

Mayonnaise, Mayonnaise Sets

400/23, 3 pc. Mayonnaise Set (later version), $24-30; component parts: 400/23B, 5 1/4" Mayonnaise Bowl; 400/23D, 7"-7 1/2" Plate; 400/165 Ladle, 5"-6", 3 beads or 400/135 Ladle, 6 1/2", 2 beads. In an early brochure, this bowl has straight sides slanted outward. Later version of the 5 1/4" Mayonnaise Bowl has a more rounded shape.

400/40, 3 pc. Mayonnaise Set, $24-27; component parts: 400/40, 5 1/2" Bowl; 400/40D, 7"-7 1/2" Plate; #615 Ladle, 4 1/2"-5", no beads.

400/40H/23D, 3 pc. Mayonnaise Set, $30-38; AKA 400/49, 3 pc. Mayonnaise Set; component parts: 400/49H, 5" Heart Shaped Fruit; 400/23D, 7"-7 1/2" Plate; 400/165 Ladle, 5"-6", 3 beads.

400/42/3, 3 pc. Mayonnaise Set, $27-30; component parts: 400/42B, 4 3/4" Bowl, 2-handled; 400/42D, 5 1/2" 2-Handled Plate; 400/130 Marmalade Ladle, 3 beads (not shown). 400/52BD, 3 pc. Mayonnaise Set, $27-34; AKA 400/52/3, 3 pc. Mayonnaise Set; component parts: 2-handled 400/52B, 6"- 6 1/2", 2-Handled Bowl; 400/52D, 7"-7 1/2" 2-Handled Plate and 400/135 Ladle, 2 beads or 400/130 Marmalade Ladle, 3 beads. The bowls and plates to these two sets are the same styles, but the 400/52/3 is larger than the 400/42/3 Mayonnaise Set.

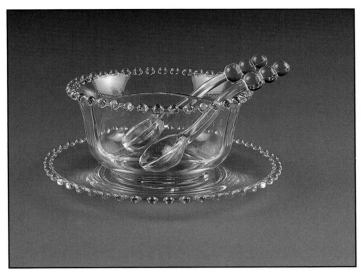

400/84, 4 pc. Mayonnaise Set (shown with different ladles), $49-66; component parts: 400/84D, 8" Plate; 400/84, 6 1/2" Divided Bowl; 400/135 Ladle, 6 1/2", 2 beads (not shown) or 400/165 Ladle, 5"-6", 3 beads or 160/165 Ladle, 5", 1 bead. 400/84 4 pc. Mayonnaise Set; component parts: 400/84D, 8" Plate; 400/84, 6 1/2" Divided Bowl; #615 Ladle, no beads.

The 400/84D Plate has a very unique feature. In the center of the plate, there is a 1/8" raised ring of glass with a 3 5/8" diameter. This ridge holds the 400/84 Mayonnaise Bowl in place on the under plate.

400/95, 4 pc. Salad Dressing Set, $60-75; component parts: 400/72D, 10" 2-Handled Plate; 400/84, 6 1/2" Divided Bowl; #615 Ladle, 4 1/2"-5", no beads or 400/165 Ladle, 5-6", 3 beads.

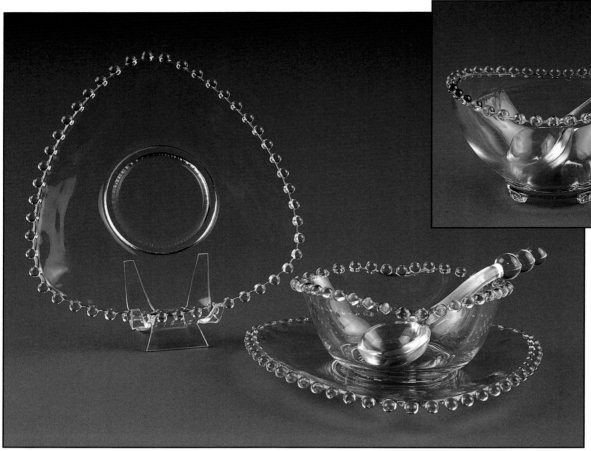

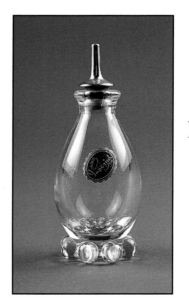

400/623 Mayonnaise Set, $70-77; component parts: 400/183, 6" 3-toed Bowl and 400/165 Ladle, 5"-6", 3 beads.

400/496, 3 pc. Mayonnaise Set, $245-270; component parts: 400/266, 7 1/2" Tri-angular Plate; 400/49/1, 5" Bowl; 400/165 Ladle, 5"-6", 3 beads. The 400/266, 7 1/2" Triangular Plate is used only in this set, $225-241. It is a round plate pulled into a triangle with rounded, slanted sides. The sides are approximately 7 1/4".

A 400/95, 3 pc. Individual Cheese and Cracker or Buffet Set, $★ was listed on the 1943 Price List, but no other information was available in the material that we have.

Cruets, Condiment Sets, Lazy Susan

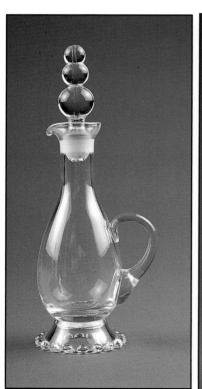

400/70, 4 oz. Cruet and Stopper, handled, $42-52; 400/71, 6 oz. Cruet and Stopper, handled, $52-66; component parts of: 400/701, 5 pc. Condiment Set; 400/70/71/29, 3 pc. Condiment Set.

400/117, 4 oz. Bitters & Metal Tube, $46-56.

400/119, 6 oz. Oil or Vinegar with Stopper, $25-28; component parts of: 400/148/2, 7 pc. Condiment Set; 400/148/5, 8 pc. Condiment Set; 400/1567, 5 pc. Condiment Set; 400/1596, 5 pc. Condiment Set; 400/1769, 4 pc. Condiment Set; 400/2911, 3 pc. Oil and Vinegar Set; 400/5996, 5 pc. Condiment Set.

400/121/O, 6 oz. Oil with Stopper, Etched Oil, $60-65; 400/121/V, 6 oz. Vinegar with Stopper, Etched Vinegar, $60-65; component parts of: 400/148/4, 7 pc. Condiment Set.

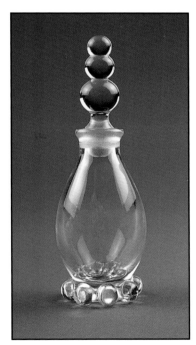

400/177, 4 oz. Oil and Stopper, $32-40.

400/164, 4 oz. Oil and Stopper, unhandled, $32-38; 400/166, 6 oz. Vinegar and Stopper, unhandled, $52-60; component parts of: 400/1574, 5 pc. Condiment Set.

400/274, 4 oz. Cruet and Stopper, $32-35; 400/275, 6 oz. Cruet and Stopper, $35-38; component parts of: 400/2794, 3 pc. Condiment Set; 400/2796, 5 pc. Condiment Set.

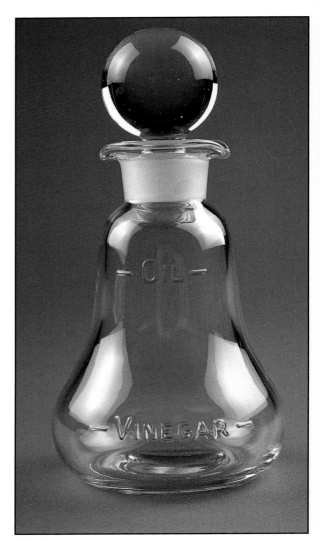

400/277 Salad Dressing Bottle and Stopper, $190-210: This is an unusual piece and one that is difficult to identify as Candlewick. It has the raised letters for the words, Oil and Vinegar. It is 6 1/2" tall and has a large 1 1/2" diameter ball stopper.

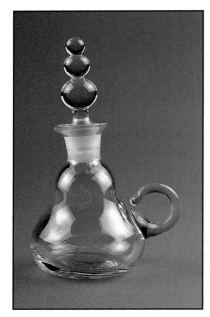

400/278, 4 oz. Handled Cruet and Stopper, $46-50; 400/279, 6 oz. Handled Cruet and Stopper, $46-50.

The shape of the 3-bead Cruet Stopper varied during the company's production years. Shown here on the left is an example of the variation with a smaller top bead. Catalog pages show the 400/119 and 400/121 in 1941 with the smaller top bead. The 1949 catalog shows these cruets with the larger top bead appearing.

As sets, the 400/148 Condiments Sets are very difficult find. We have found only two complete sets. It is strange the way that they are numbered: 400/148/2, /4, /5, and /6. We do not find any records of /1 or /3.

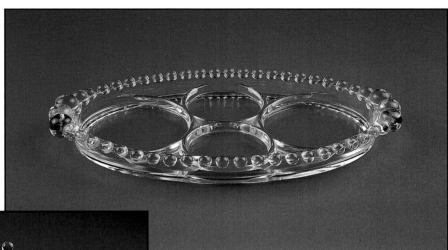

7400/148, 9 1/4" Condiment Tray, $140-175. This condiment tray with four indentations is hard to find. It is the same size and shape as the 400/159 Tray (see page 43). Component part of: 400/148/2, 7 pc. Condiment Set; 400/148/4, 7 pc. Condiment Set; 400/148/5, 8 pc. Condiment Set; and 400/148/6, 9 pc. Condiment Set.

400/148/2, 7 pc. Condiment Set, $275-335; component parts: 400/148 Condiment Tray; 400/116 Footed Salt and Pepper; (2) 400/119, 6 oz. Oil and Vinegar.

Imperial Sign, familiar oval with French edge; note the outline of the champagne in the background, $88-122.

A rubbing of the early triangle label used on Candlewick, taken from the large etched plate. This label is not often seen.

400/148/4, 7 pc. Condiment Set, $345-410; component parts: 400/148 Condiment Tray; 400/116 Footed Salt and Pepper; Etched 400/121 Oil and Vinegar and Stoppers.

No. 400-148/6
Condiment Set, Plain

or

as shown...

No. 400/148/4
Condiment Set

400/148/4 and 400/148/6; Imperial Glass Corporation photograph.

400/148/5, 8 pc. Condiment Set, $260-320; component parts: 400/148 Condiment Tray; 400/89 Marmalade Bowl and Cover; 400/130 Marmalade Ladle, 3 beads; 400/116 Footed Salt and Pepper; 400/119, 6 oz. Oil or Vinegar.

400/148/6, 9 pc. Condiment Set, $295-365; component parts: 400/148 Condiment Tray; 400/89, (2) Marmalade Bowl and Cover; 400/130 Marmalade Ladle, 3 beads; 400/116 Footed Salt and Pepper.

400/701, 5 pc. Condiment Set, $100-130; component parts: 400/70, 4 oz. Handled Cruet; 400/71, 6 oz. Handled Cruet; 400/29, 6 1/2"-7" Tray.

400/1567, 5 pc. Condiment Set, $80-95; component parts: 400/159, 9 1/4" Oval Tray; 400/167 Salt and Pepper; 400/119, 6 oz. Oil and Vinegar (2).

400/1574, 5 pc. Condiment Set, $95-110; component parts: 400/159, 9 1/4" Oval Tray; 400/167 Salt and Pepper; 400/164, 4 oz. Oil (2).

400/1596, 5 pc. Condiment Set, $74-88; component parts: 400/159, 9 1/4" Oval Tray; 400/96 Salt and Pepper Set; 100/119, 6 oz. Oil and Vinegar (2).

400/1769, 4 pc. Condiment Set, $62-80; component parts: 400/171, 8" Tray; 400/96 Salt and Pepper Set; 400/119, 6 oz. Oil and Vinegar.

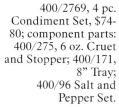

400/1786, 4 pc. Condiment Set, $62-74; component parts: 400/171, 8" Tray; 400/89/3, 3 pc. Marmalade Set; 400/96 Salt and Pepper Set.

400/2769, 4 pc. Condiment Set, $74-80; component parts: 400/275, 6 oz. Cruet and Stopper; 400/171, 8" Tray; 400/96 Salt and Pepper Set.

400/2794, 3 pc. Oil and Vinegar Set, $80-90; component parts: 400/275, 6 oz. Vinegar; 400/274, 4 oz. Oil; 400/29, 6 1/2"-7" Tray.

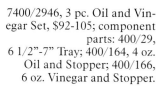

400/2796, 5 pc. Condiment Set, $95-108; component parts: 400/159, 9" Tray; 400/274, 4 oz. Oil or Vinegar; 400/275, 6 oz. Oil or Vinegar; 400/96 Salt and Pepper Set.

7400/2946, 3 pc. Oil and Vinegar Set, $92-105; component parts: 400/29, 6 1/2"-7" Tray; 400/164, 4 oz. Oil and Stopper; 400/166, 6 oz. Vinegar and Stopper.

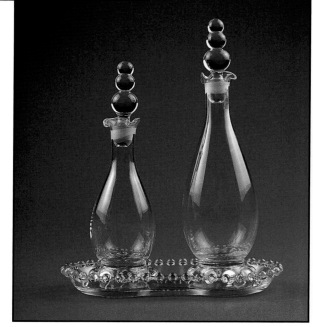

400/2911, 3 pc. Oil and Vinegar Set, $58-68; component parts: 400/29, 6 1/2"-7" Tray; 400/119, 6 oz. Oil or Vinegar (2).

400/2990, 5 pc. Condiment Set, $78-100; component parts: 400/29, 6 1/2"-7" Tray; 400/177, 4 oz. Oil and Vinegar (2); 400/109 Individual Salt and Pepper Set (remember the lids can be plastic or metal).

400/5996, 5 pc. Condiment Set, $77-95; component parts: 400/159, 9 1/4" Oval Tray; 400/119, 6 oz. Cruet; 400/89 Marmalade Bowl and Cover; 400/96 Salt and Pepper Set; 400/130 Marmalade Ladle, 3 beads.

400/7796, 3 pc. Oil and Vinegar Set, $72-90; component parts: 400/177, 4 oz. Oil and Vinegar (2); 400/96T Tray.

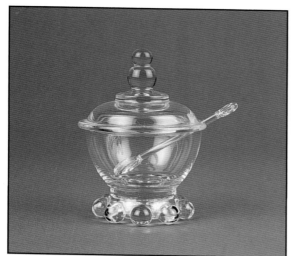

400/156 Covered Mustard with Spoon, $35-42. This item has a ground rim that was done at the factory. The 400/19, 3 oz. Cocktail was cut and ground to a height of 2 1/8" so that the top would be wider and could receive the 2 15/16" diameter lid. The lid has no beads around it and the slot is tiny to accommodate the 400/156, AKA 4000 Salt Spoon.

On the right is the 400/19, 3 1/2 oz. Cocktail. This piece, if ground down, becomes the base for the 400/156 Covered Mustard on the left. The 400/156 will have a ground top edge rather than a fire polished edge.

400/5629, 3 pc. Mustard and Ketchup Set, $90-110; component parts: 400/156 Covered Mustard with Spoon (2); 4000 Spoon AKA 400/616; 400/29, 6 1/2"-7" Tray. The catalog entry for the 4000 spoon AKA 400/616 has caused confusion. It says the spoons are the same, but from catalog illustrations it is easy to see they are not.

New collectors are sometimes puzzled about the 400/151 tray as they do not have the following information available. This item is used as a 10" round tray and has a design of wide circles on the underneath. Imperial sold this tray, E-666, with a mirror to Irving W. Rice (Irice) for use as a vanity tray. (Note that Imperial used the Irice numbering system for items Imperial made for Irice. In turn, Irice used the same numbers to advertise and sell those items.) A modified style of this tray is used for the 400/1503 Lazy Susan. A few times collectors have found the Lazy Susan tray with a mirror on it so be sure to check all mirrored trays if you are hunting for the Lazy Suzan tray.

When used as the tray for the Lazy Susan, there is an indentation on the tray's underside of a definite 3/8" channel forming a 3" diameter to receive the metal bearings. On the topside of the tray is a 3" by 1/2" circle of stippling to hide the bearings. There is a modified style of the 400/133, 5" Ash Tray that has a recessed channel to receive the ball bearings for the Lazy Susan. This is the only ash tray designed for this use.

400/1503 Lazy Susan, 3 pc., $135-165; component parts: 400/151, 10" Tray; 400/151 Ball Bearing; 400/151, 5" Base AKA 400/133 Ash Tray with a special indention on the bottom side to receive the Ball Bearings.

400/1510, 8 pc. Lazy Susan Condiment Set, $242-280; component parts: 400/151 Tray; 400/96 Salt and Pepper; 400/274, 4 oz. Cruet and Stopper; 400/275, 6 oz. Cruet and Stopper; 400/89 Marmalade Bowl and Cover; 400/151, 5" Base, 400/130 Marmalade Ladle, 3 beads or 400/165 Ladle, 5"-6", 3 beads.

Ladles, Salad Forks and Spoons, Knife, Muddler, Punch Ladles

Ladles always present a bit of puzzlement. It is difficult to remember which ladle goes in which set, etc. We have grouped all the ladles together with their measurements for quick reference. Refer to the set in question and see which ladle goes with that set. You will also note that often Imperial used various ladles in sets at different times.

400/135 Mayonnaise Ladle; 6 1/2" long, 2 beads. $8-10.
400/165 Mayonnaise Ladle; 5"-6" long, 3 beads. It is larger proportioned than the 400/130. $10-12.
400/130 Marmalade Ladle; 4 3/4" long, 3 beads. $10-14.
160/165 Mayonnaise Ladle; ladle used in the Candlewick 400/84 Mayonnaise Set; 5" long, 1 bead. It is documented for the Cape Cod sets. $10-14.
615 Ladle, $10-12; early ladle was 4 1/2"-5" with no beads. $8-10.

400/289 Ladle, $8-10; plastic ladle (front) was used from 1953-1968, metal ladle (back) was used from 1971-1980.

160/165 Mayonnaise Ladle (back); ladle used in the Candlewick 400/84 Mayonnaise Set; 5" long, 1 bead. It is documented with a number for the Cape Cod sets. $10-12.
160/130 Ladle (front); documented for Cape Cod sets; might be found in a Candlewick set; 4" long, 2 beads. $10-14.

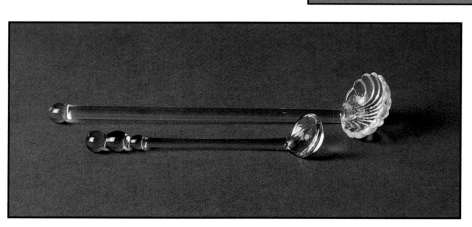

Some 400/89 Marmalades have a 6" ladle with shell bowl and single bead at the end. The bead is less than perfect and drops off slightly. Also shown here is a 4" spoon with three beads that are graduated from small to large toward the tip end. This is most likely a whimsy, but deserves a brief moment in the spotlight. It did come from a large, old collection of Candlewick. It is too short to be the sought after spoon used in the 400/89 Marmalade (see page 59).

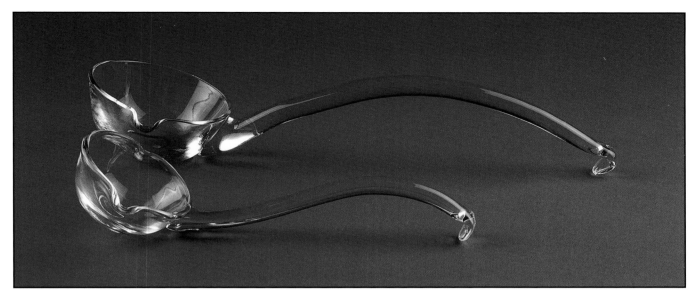

400/91 Punch Ladle (back), 13", one pouring spout, $30-40. The handle tip end of this ladle has a piece of glass that is turned down. The underneath of the bowl is smooth and does not have an extra ridge of glass on it.
400/139 Punch Ladle (front), 9"-9 1/2" two pouring spouts, $65-75; AKA 400/255 Punch Ladle. The handle tip end is also turned down.

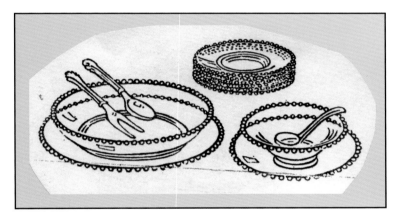

Mat No. 105

400/75 Salad Fork and Spoon (right), $25-42. This set is the true Candlewick Salad Fork and Spoon. Imperial also made this set for Irving W. Rice in the 1940s decorated with gold and platinum. #701 Salad Fork and Spoon (left), $21-25. In the early years Imperial used the #701 Reeded Fork and Spoon with Candlewick as well as several other sets. There is a vertical ribbed design on the handles. This set comes in several colors that we know about: Viennese Blue, amber (light yellow) light green, black, and frosted crystal.

4000 Knife, $275-315; 8 1/2" long with 4 half beads along the design on both sides of the flat handle.

Pitchers, Ice Tubs

The #176 Stirring Rod is 12"; documented in the Continental pattern. Our stirrer came from an Imperial representative and is only 11 1/16". The paddle on the end is a flat 1 1/2" circle with a waffle pattern on both sides of the paddle. The bead on the other end is 5/8" diameter. We have found similar stirrers in Duncan Miller Canterbury Martini Pitchers, leading us to speculate as to whether Imperial made its own stirrers or bought them from another company. Again, that does not really make any difference. Another stirrer we have came from the Imperial factory and is 12" with the 1 1/2" paddle and a small bead. We feel that both of them are correct.

Shown are the three small pitchers. First is the 400/19, 16 oz. Lilliputian Pitcher, $175-215. This little beaded foot pitcher has a quite appropriate name. Next is the 400/16, 1 Pint Pitcher, $175-206. It is the smallest of three with the beaded handle. Last is the 400/416, 20 oz. Pitcher, $70-88, the smallest of the pitchers with no beads. This is one of three pitchers from Imperial's Continental pattern that was combined with Candlewick. It has no beads on the base or handle. Imperial introduced the no bead pitchers in 1968 after the beaded pitchers were dropped.

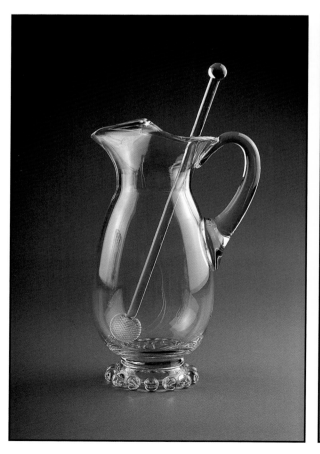

400/18, 40 oz. Manhattan Pitcher, $175-200. There are three pitchers with a plain handle and a beaded foot. Here is the middle size of the beaded foot group. Shown inside this pitcher is the #176 Stirring Rod, $32-38.

400/18, 80 oz. Pitcher, $155-190. Largest of the beaded foot pitchers, it holds 5 pints. Remember, there is a tendency for the large pitchers to crack below where the bottom of the handle is attached. It seems that the weight is too much for the body of the pitcher to withstand. It is wise to hold your hand below the base of the pitcher when using it.

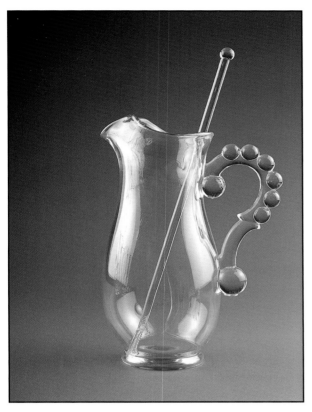

400/19, 40 oz. Juice, Cocktail, Martini, $192-225. The Martini Jug with the beaded handle was pictured in catalogs with the #176, 12" stirring rod, $32-38.

400/419, 40 oz. Pitcher, $53-70. Another pitcher from Imperial's Continental pattern, it was introduced in 1968. Imperial used the Continental line of pitchers in items that were hand-painted. (Please refer to the Hand-painted section in our book on Candlewick: Colored and Decorated Lines.)

400/24, 80 oz. Ice Pitcher, Water, $130-140. This is another pitcher that should be supported from the base to keep it from fracturing below the bottom of the beaded handle. Just a word of wisdom from one whom has experienced breakage of a wedding pitcher!

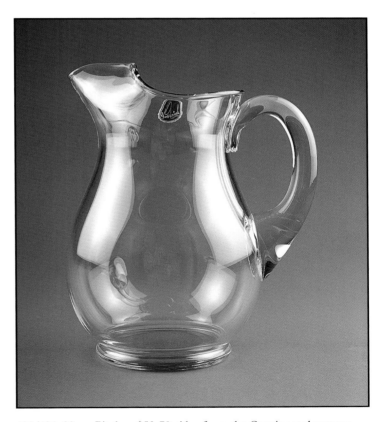

400/424, 80 oz. Pitcher, $53-70. Also from the Continental pattern and produced from 1968-1974. From 1974-1978, it was made to hold 64 oz., $★. (For decorations on this pitcher, please refer to the Hand-painted section in our book on Candlewick: Colored and Decorated Lines.)

The three bears have nothing on Imperial Candlewick Pitchers; they came in large, medium, and small. For size comparison, shown here are the 400/18, 80 oz.; 400/424, 80 oz.; and 400/24, 80 oz. The 400/424 was catalogued as 80 oz. from 1967 until 1974, when it was changed to 64 oz. It was dropped from the line in 1978.

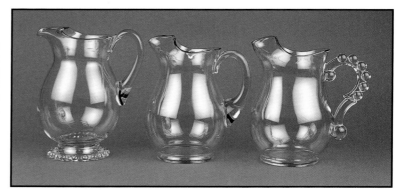

Next shown are the 40 oz. pitchers: the 400/18; 400/419; and 400/19.

Last shown are the small pitchers: the 400/19, 16 oz.; 400/16, 16 oz.; and 400/416, 20 oz.

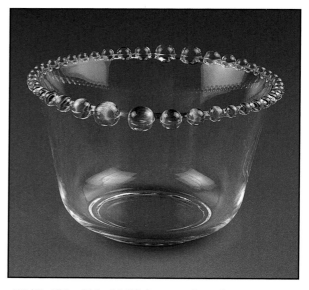

400/168, 7" 2-Handled Ice Tub; two tab handles, 5 1/2" height, $122-136.

400/63, 8" Ice Tub, 5 1/2" deep, graduated beads on sides, $63-80; component part of: 400/63/104, 19 pc. Chilled Fruit Set.

Butter, Toast Set, Sauce Set, Syrup Set

Pictured in the Plate section is the 400/34, 4 1/2" Individual Butter, Plate or Coaster as it is sometimes named.

400/144, 5 1/2" Butter Dish and Cover; two tab handles; measurement does not include tab handles, $25-28.

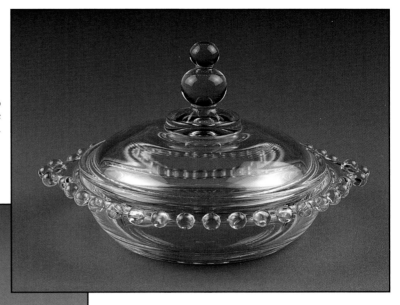

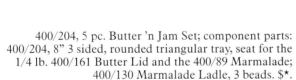

400/161, 1/4 lb. Oblong Butter and Cover, $25-28.

400/204, 5 pc. Butter 'n Jam Set; component parts: 400/204, 8" 3 sided, rounded triangular tray, seat for the 1/4 lb. 400/161 Butter Lid and the 400/89 Marmalade; 400/130 Marmalade Ladle, 3 beads. $★.

400/204, Plate, Triangular, 8"; Base for the 400/204 Butter 'n Jam Set; plate has raised seats to receive component parts: 400/161 Lid and 400/89 Marmalade. $★.

400/262, 10 1/2" Butter and Jam Set;
AKA 400/262, 10 1/2" 3 pt. Relish.
$88-105.

400/276 California Butter and Cover, no
beads on cover (back), 1950-1961, $88-105;
400/276 California Butter and Cover, beads
on cover (front), 1962-1968, $70-105.

460/161

The 460/161 Covered Butter on this Imperial factory photograph does not have the 400/ prefix
of the Candlewick line, but the lid certainly does fit the line. The bottom tray is from the Cape
Cod line, which has a prefix of 160. You can see how the combination of the two lines became the
460/161. We bought a set like this at an auction during the NIGCS 2000 Convention. Everyone
questioned us about why we bought this "marriage" of the two patterns. Our answer was to wait
until next year and you will know why. We remembered seeing this photograph in company
files and thought it would be fun to buy one that came from the factory in this combination. Of
course, anyone could put one together, but it was interesting to see one appear from a factory
employee consignment at the auction.

If the Toast Cover is separated from the Toast Plate, it is hard to identify. First, be sure to check for the hollow knob. The knob measurements are 1" height and 1 1/2" diameter. The overall measurements of the cover are 5 7/8" diameter and 4" total height. It is very thin and delicate and does not have a safe edge on the base of the cover.

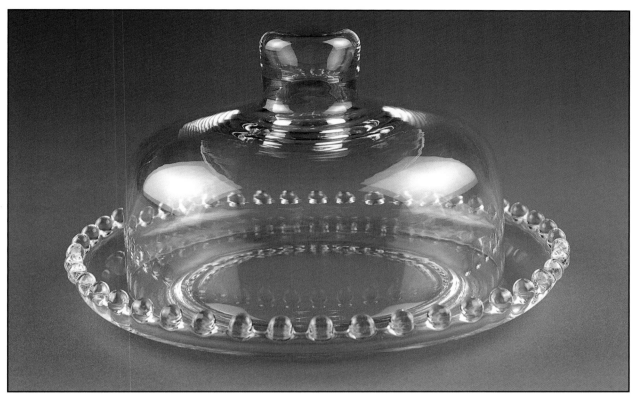

400/123, 7 1/2" Covered Toast, Cheese or Butter Set, $262-315. There is no safe edge on the rim.

This set was bought from Imperial by another company and was advertised with the suggestion that it could be monogrammed for the special person. The set consisted of the 400/13D Service Plate and Toast Cover. This Toast Cover is larger than the 400/123. The measurements are 6 1/8" diameter by 5" height. It is the same thin and delicate cover as the 400/123, 7 1/2" Covered Toast, Cheese or Butter Set. $★

The cover on the left is for the 400/123 Toast Set and is shown beside the cover for the set using the 400/13D Service Plate. The set without a number was combined by a private customer of Imperial Glass Company and is discussed in the previous photo.

400/733 Salad Dressing Set or Syrup Set, $410-435; component parts: 400/23D, 7" Plate with seat; 400/330, 14 oz. Syrup Pitcher. The Syrup Pitcher is a difficult piece to identify when it is separated from its Candlewick liner. It holds 14 oz. and has four indentions (dimples) around the bottom. The top opening is formed on a slant and is a ground and polished edge. The spout also has a ground and polished edge. This pitcher is from the Svelte line that includes three other sizes of pitchers; two are larger and one is smaller, a cream pitcher. The syrup pitcher may also be found with an etch of Trader Vic's logo. In Imperial's general line is another group of similar pitchers. That group has the openings formed straight across the top. The group has no indentations around the bottom. Those pitchers are interesting and desirable, but they did not go with the Candlewick.

400/169 Sauce Boat and Plate Set, $110-122; component parts: 400/169, 8" Oval Plate, $32-38; plate has an oval ring, slightly recessed, to receive the 400/169, 7" Sauce Boat, $74-80. The sauce boat does not have any beads on it.

Imperial Sign with the familiar blue letters and French edge plus the word "Handcrafted," $88-122.

For collectors' enjoyment, here is the company's advertising illustration for the 400/169 Sauce Boat and Plate Set.

Sets

Console Sets, Float Bowls

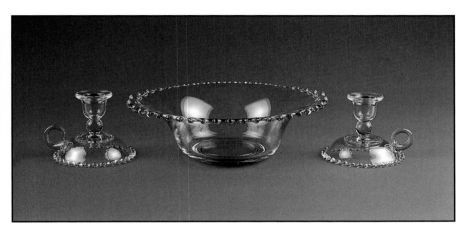

400/63B/81, 3 pc. Console Set, $110-135; component parts: 400/63B, 10 1/2" Belled Bowl; 400/81 Candleholder with handle.

400/63B/170, 3 pc. Console Set, $60-68; component parts: 400/63B, 10 1/2" Belled Bowl; 400/170 Low Candleholder, large beads.

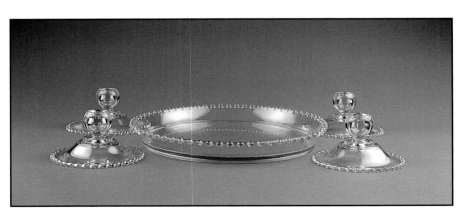

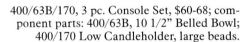

400/101/79B, 5 pc. Float Bowl Console Set, $252-270; component parts: 400/101, 13" Float Bowl; 400/79B Flat Candleholder (4).

400/127L, 4 pc. Console Set, $220-255; component parts: 400/92L, 13" Mushroom Console Bowl; 400/127B, 7 1/2" x 2 1/4" Base; 400/100 Twin Candleholder (2).

400/136, 4 pc. Console Set, $475-535; component parts: 400/92R Mushroom Float Bowl; 400/127B, 7 1/2" Base; 400/129R Urn Candleholder (2).

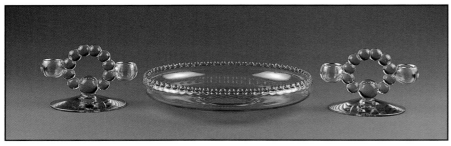

400/920F, 11 1/2"-12" Float Bowl; 400/100 Twin Candleholder (2), $95-115, $65-80.

400/6300B, 3 pc. Console Set, $104-124; component parts: 400/63B, 10 1/2" Belled Bowl; 400/100 Twin Candleholder (2). 400/1006B, 3 pc. Console Set (not shown), $77-90; component parts: 400/106B, 12"-12 1/2" Bowl; 400/100 Twin Candleholder. 400/1004B, 3 pc. Console Set (not shown), $168-190; component parts: 400/104B, 14"-14 1/2" Bowl; 400/100 Twin Candleholder. There are three sets each using a different size of bowl with graduated beads with the 400/100 Twin Candleholder.

400/1474, 3 pc. Console Set (not shown), $180-204; component parts: 400/104B, 14"-14 1/2" Bowl; 400/147 Candleholder (2). 400/1476, 3 pc. Console Set, $90-104; component parts: 400/106B, 12"-12 1/2" Bowl; 400/147 Candleholder. These two sets are the same styles but the 400/104B is a larger version of the bowl.

400/1531B, 3 pc. Console Set, $415-460; component parts: 400/131B, 14" Oval Bowl; 400/115, 3 Lite Candleholder (2).

400/7570, 4 pc. Console Set, $★; component parts: 400/75F, 10"-11" Float Bowl; 400/170 Candleholders (2); 400/150, 6" Base; AKA as 400/151; has the underneath bottom completely recessed to hold the 400/75 Bowl.

400/8013B, 3 pc. Console Set, $85-90; component parts: 400/80 Candleholder (2); 400/13B, 11" Centre Bowl. Not shown is the 400/8113B, 3 pc. Console Set; component parts: 400/81 Candleholder, Handled; 400/13B, 11" Centre Bowl, $100-115.

400/8063B, 3 pc. Console Set, $54-64; component parts: 400/80 Candleholder (2); 400/63B, 10 1/2" Belled Bowl.

400/8075B, 3 pc. Console Set, $34-47; component parts: 400/80 Candleholder (2); 400/75B, 10"-10 1/2" Bowl.

400/8613B, 3 pc. Console Set, $110-130; component parts: 400/86 Mushroom Candleholder (2); 400/13B, 11" Centre Bowl.

400/8692L, 3 pc. Console Set, $87-110; component parts: 400/86 Mushroom Candleholder (2); 400/92L, 13" Mushroom Bowl.

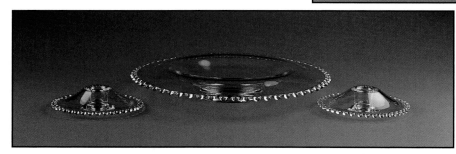

400/9275, 4 pc. Console Set, $★; component parts: 400/92F, 12" Float Bowl, 400/150 Base AKA 400/151 is the 6" Ash Tray with the underneath bottom recessed to secure the 400/92F Float, 400/175 Candleholder.

400/9279FR, 3 pc. Console Set, $75-85; component parts: In 1943, 400/92R Mushroom Bowl; 400/79R Candleholder (2). In 1948, 400/92F Float Bowl; 400/79R Candleholder (2).

400/127B, 7 1/2" x 2 1/4" Console Base AKA Belled Bowl; 7 1/4" by 2 1/4" deep, $130-135; component part of: 400/136 Console Set; 400/127L Console Set. This bowl is better known as a console base than as a bowl. It will have the 1/4" indention on the underneath side to receive the 400/92L Console Bowl.

Decanters, Decanter Sets

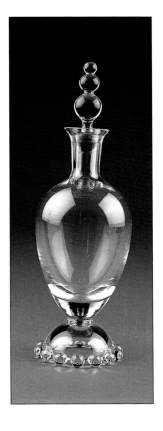

Electro No. 12-C

400/18, 18 oz. Cordial Bottle and Stopper, $*. As the mold number indicates, this has the same base design as the 400/18 stems.

400/82, 15 oz. Cordial Bottle, Handled and 3-bead Stopper, $★; 3800 Cordials complete the set. It is interesting that the handled cordial bottle is found more than the 400/82/2 Unhandled Bottle, 3-bead stopper, top edge is ground and polished at the factory.

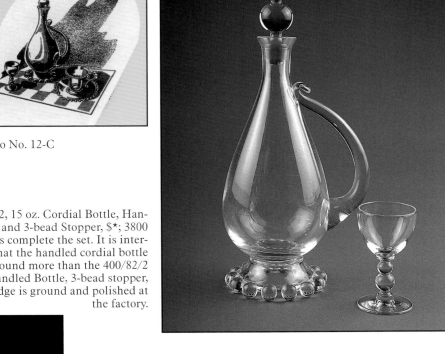

400/82/2, 15 oz. Cordial Bottle and Stopper, $★; note that the 3-bead stopper is the stopper with a large bottom bead. This is a characteristic of the stopper in the 400/121 Etched Oil or Vinegar. The bottom bead on the stopper is larger than on other cruet stoppers. In addition, the top bead is smaller than other top beads on other stoppers. This is also true of the 400/121 Etched Oil or Vinegar Stopper. This is the most difficult cordial bottle to find. If you find a 400/82 or 400/82/2 Cordial Bottle without a stopper, you might find a 400/121 Oil stopper that would fit. The neck of the 400/82 Cordial bottle is narrow and a cruet stopper would have to be ground down to fit; top edge is ground and polished at factory; component part of: 400/82, 10 pc. Cordial Set.

Company photograph showing the 400/82 Cordial Bottle and 3800 Cordials.

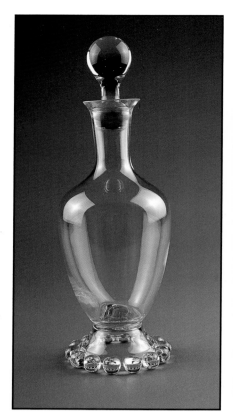

400/163, 24 oz. Decanter and Stopper, $262-315. This the easiest of the decanters to find. It has one solid, large ball stopper. It is 10 1/2" tall and the neck is not ground; top edge is ground at the factory The stopper is 3 3/8" long with a 1 5/8" diameter ball. Component part of: 400/1630 8 pc. Wine Set with 400/190 Wines; 400/1639 Wine Set with 400/19 Wines.

400/1630, 8 pc. Wine Set, $388-446 component parts: 400/163 Decanter; 400/190 Wines.

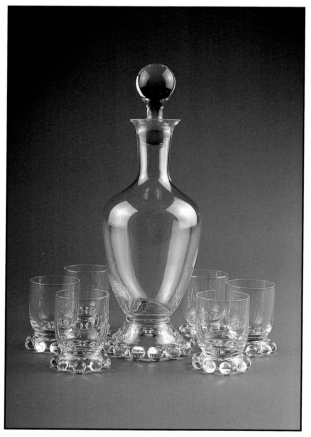

400/1639, 8 pc. Wine Set, $332-422; component parts: 400/163 Decanter; 400/19 Wines.

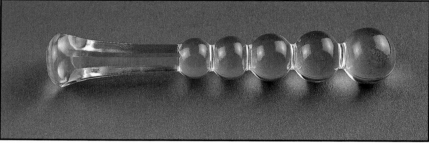

400/19 Muddler, $17-20. Through the years, we have had many smiles when glass collectors would stand and look at a Candlewick Muddler. Eventually, some would get brave enough to ask what it was. For readers who may also not know, a muddler is an instrument shaped similarly to a bat. It is used to mix or make cloudy the sugar and bitters in a drink mixed with liquor, e.g., an Old Fashion. In other words, a muddler is to a drink what a pestle is to prescription medication. Did you know that there are enough different glass-patterned muddlers that some people collect only muddlers? It is also interesting that some people mistake a muddler for a knife rest.

Candlewick Calendar with the correct 1947 calendar, $200-220.

Canapé, Party Sets, Hostess Helpers, Snack Set

400/36, 6" Plate with 2" off center seat, $12-14;
400/39, 6" Plate with 2 1/2" off center seat, $14-16.
The 400/36 Plate is a component part of the 400/36
Canapé Set. The 400/39 Plate is a component part of:
400/91 Cocktail Set with the 3400 Oyster Cocktail;
400/97 Cocktail Set with the #111 Stem.

400/36, 2 pc. Canapé Set with 2" raised ring seat,
$21-25. On this set is the #142, 3 1/2 oz. Juice Tumbler. The #142 Juice Tumbler was not listed with a
Candlewick 400 number when it was first used with
Candlewick. In 1948, it became the 400/142 Tumbler.
The 400/142 does not have the general design of
Candlewick. From the 1930s to 1950s, Imperial made
the #142 to be used with other items as well as the
Candlewick line. This little tumbler can be found in
many colors, with many different decorations, and
can comprise a collection by itself. (Check the #142
section in our book on Candlewick: Colored and
Decorated Lines for a look at the numerous variations
one can find in the 400/142 Juice Tumbler.)

400/91, 2 pc. Cocktail Set, $26-33; component
parts: 400/39, 6" Cocktail Plate with 2 1/2" Seat;
3400 Oyster Cocktail.

400/97, 2 pc. Cocktail Set, $32-36; component parts: 400/39, 6" Cocktail Plate with 2 1/2" seat; #111 Cocktail Glass, 4 oz. Cocktail. (All of ours hold only 3 1/2 oz.) It has one pulled bead on the stem and is 3 3/4" tall. This cocktail does not have an assigned regular Candlewick number. In the lists of component parts, it is simply listed as #111.

400/98, 2 pc. Party Set, $25-28; component parts: 400/37 Coffee Cup; 400/98, 9" Oval Plate with 2" seat.

400/99, 2 pc. Snack Set, $28-38; component parts: 400/98, 9" Oval Plate with 2" seat; 400/142 Juice Tumbler.

400/111 Tête-à-Tête, $★; component parts: 400/111 Oblong Tray with two raised ring seats; 400/77AD Cup; 3800 Brandy, 2 oz.

400/88, 2 pc. Cheese and Cracker Set, $40-47; component parts: 400/72D, 10" 2-Handled Plate; 400/88, 5 1/2" Compote.

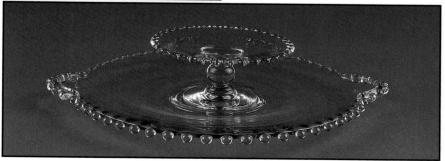

400/92, 3 pc. Cheese and Cracker Set, $110-140; component parts: 400/92D, 14" Plate; 400/157 Cheese Compote; 400/144 Cover.

400/145, 2-pc. Cheese and Cracker Set, $54-64; component parts: 400/145D, 12" Plate; 400/157 Cheese Compote.

400/9266B, 2-pc. Cheese and Cracker Set, $57-67; component parts: 400/92D, 14" Plate; 400/66B, 5 1/2" Low Compote, no beads on stem.

We found an interesting paper, dated 10/31/58, which mentions the beginning of the 400/228 Chip and Dip:

"New Buffet Pieces - Chip and Dip Plates. These involve plunger changes only. . .No. 3; 400/17D; 14 1/2" Wide Bottom Candlewick Plate. This plunger to have a 7" circle partition with a 'swung' divider. Be sure it is going to be at least 1 1/2" deep—better 2". Be certain these plain plates are in stock before changing this plunger. Crystal only."

When one digs endlessly into Candlewick records, every scrap of paper can add little dabs of information and interest. Remember that this paper said to be sure that the plain 400/17D Plates are in stock before changing the plunger. The 400/17D stayed in the line until 1967. It makes one wonder if enough plates were in stock to last from 1958 to 1967. Probably a 14" plate would not be a very productive seller.

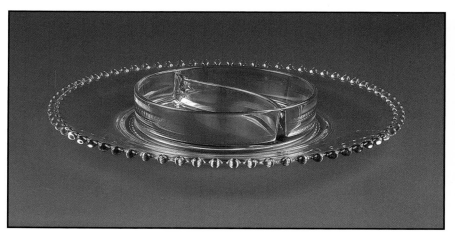

400/228, 14" Chip and Dip, $415-455. Catalog illustrations have caused collectors to think that this item is two pieces while it is only one piece. It is a great piece for serving at parties.

400/244, 5-Pc. Hostess Helper Set, $250-300; component parts: 400/243 Sauce Bowl; 400/92F Float and three metal cups that hang on the sides for toothpicks.

These two views of the metal clip for the 400/244 Hostess Helper Set will give collectors a better chance of finding the missing cups. Measurements are: cup height 1 3/4" and cup width (including hanger) 1 3/4".

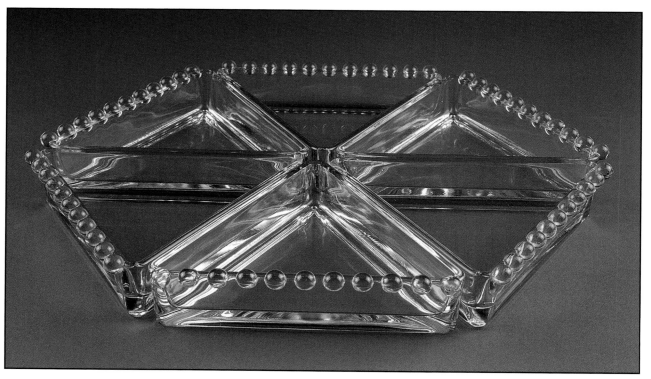

400/2696, 6-pc. Hospitality Set, $1500-1700; six pie shape wedges, 400/269, 6 1/2" with beads on one side.

400/??? Mystery still hovers over this Hospitality Set. In 1994, we were able to document it by finding it pictured in a 1957 Imperial desk calendar. That picture shows a worker with the 12" by 2 1/4" deep, flat bottom bowl on a punty rod beside a furnace. We have found no written memorandum on this item and have found no entry in the 1953 card file, catalog, or price list. Because it has the same 1/2" ledge around it as the 400/213, 400/214, 400/215, and 400/216, we have felt confident that it was an Imperial Candlewick item. In the center of the bowl is a raised ring, 2 1/2" in diameter, to secure the small bowl insert. The bowl is not a regular line piece; it has slanted sides and is similar to another bowl in an Imperial general line. This was another clue to the authenticity of the set. The bowl for the center is 4 3/4" diameter and 2 1/4" deep. $★. NI.

400/139/1 Snack Jar and Cover, ground and polished top edge. $770-910.

Punch Sets

The 400/37 Punch Cup or Coffee Cup has the well-known question mark handle. The 400/211 Punch Cup is the punch cup that has a round beaded handle. It has often been called the "early punch cup." That is not correct, however, as the 400/37 Coffee Cup or Punch Cup was earlier. The 400/37 was produced from 1938-1984 and the 400/211 Punch Cup was made from 1950-1955. These cups are shown individually in the Cup and Saucer section.

There is an important feature to remember about the 400/139 Punch Set and 400/139 Snack Jar. These items have a ground and polished rim at the opening. This was done at the factory and does not indicate repairs made in production.

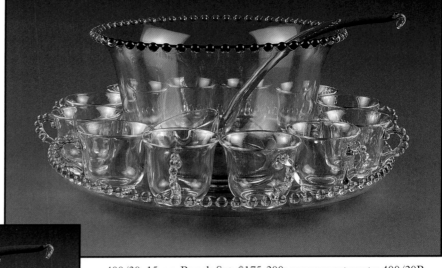

400/20, 15-pc. Punch Set, $175-200; component parts: 400/20B, 6 qt. 13" Bowl, $75-85; 400/20V, 17" Cupped Plate, $42-56; 400/91, Punch Ladle; 400/37 Punch Cup.

400/128, 15-pc. Punch Set, $300-350; component parts: 400/20B, 6 qt. Bowl, $75-85; 400/128B, Base, $75-85, 10" wide x 3" deep; 400/91 Punch Ladle; 400/37 Punch Cup.

400/210, 15-pc. Punch Set, $★; component parts: 400/210, 10 Quart Punch Bowl, $235-265; 400/210B, Base, 9" wide x 3 3/4" deep; 400/91 Punch Ladle; 400/211 Cup with round handle instead of question mark handle. Be sure to check the punch cup shapes in the Cup and Saucer section of this book.

The May 6, 1949 issue of the Wheeling Intelligence newspaper, Wheeling, West Virginia, shows a photo of Joe E. Brown with his leading lady, Marion Lorne. They and the rest of the cast of Harvey were being entertained at a local reception. In the photo, Mr. Brown is holding a Candlewick 400/37 Punch Cup and on the table are stacks of Candlewick plates. We apologize that the quality of our copy of the article would not allow for reprinting here.

Also, here is a handy tip for collectors using their punch sets: Take a small piece of plastic tubing, cut a slit in it, and place around the punch ladle at the point where the ladle touches the rim of the punch bowl. This gives the server a more secure feeling while serving punch. It might save the bowl or ladle from breakage as well.

400/210 Punch Bowl Base, 9" by 3 3/4", $*; 400/128B, Punch Bowl Base, 10" x 3"; component part of 400/128 Punch Set. The bases are also called Belled Bowls. Because these bowls are best known for their use as the bases for several sets, we are showing them in this section. When found alone in a shop, they are usually sitting upright as a bowl. If you pick one up, you may be puzzled to see that the bottom of the bowl is recessed about 1/4". Gradually you realize that you have finally found one of the "bases." When the bowl is turned upside down, the recessed bottom is used to secure the item sitting on top of the base. At the far right in this photograph is the 400/127 Console Base, 7 1/2" x 2 1/4", shown here because of the similar design of its recessed bottom.

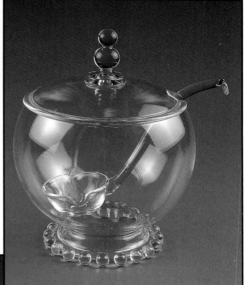

400/139/2 Covered Punch Bowl and Ladle Set, $635-770; component parts: 400/139 Covered Punch Bowl, top edge is ground and polished at the factory during production; 400/139 Small Punch Ladle with two spouts, AKA 400/255 Ladle.

400/139, 11-pc. Cocktail Set, $737-905; component parts: 400/139 Covered Punch Bowl; 400/255 Ladle; #111 Stem Cocktail with pulled bead stem. Not shown, 400/139/19 11-pc. Cocktail Set, $824-985; component parts: 400/139 Covered Punch Bowl; 400/255 Ladle; 400/19 Cocktail.

400/139/77 Family Punch Set, $715-845; component parts: 400/139 Covered Punch Bowl; 400/255 Ladle; 400/77 AD Cup.

400/1930, 11-pc. Cocktail Set, $715-870; component parts: 400/139 Covered Punch Bowl; 400/255 Ladle; 400/190 Cocktail.

Salad Sets

400/106B/75, 3-pc. Salad Set, $60-77; component parts: 400/106B, 12"-12 1/2" Bowl, $40-50; 400/75 Fork and Spoon.

400/735, 3-pc. Salad Set, Handled Heart, $124-165; component parts: 400/73H, 9"-10" Handled Heart Bowl; 400/75 Fork and Spoon.

400/925, 4-pc. Salad Set, $94-104; component parts: 400/92B, 12" Bowl; 400/92V, 13 1/2" Cupped Plate or 400/92D Flat Plate; 400/75 Fork and Spoon. Not shown 400/75B, 4-pc. Salad Set (400/75B, 400/75V, 400/75 Spoon and Fork), $60-77.

400/4975 Salad Set, $130-175; component parts: 400/49H, 9" Heart Bowl; 400/75V Cupped Plate; 400/75 Fork and Spoon Set.

400/7375 Salad Set, Handled Heart, $140-185; component parts: 400/73H, 9"-10" Handled Heart Bowl; 400/75V Cupped Plate; 400/75 Fork and Spoon Set.

Miscellaneous

Ash Trays and Accessories

The 400/33 is quite a versatile item. Not only is it an ash tray or a jelly dish; it also has another use. It can be found on lighting fixtures. So far, we have found it on two table lamps. Be sure to look up at ceiling fixtures and down at all table lamps, as it is exciting to find a piece of Candlewick adapted to a light fixture. Imperial Glass sold many glass parts to light fixture companies; these parts were subsequently utilized in table lamps, wall lights, and ceiling fixtures.

This 400/150 Ash Tray is a souvenir of the Union Savings Bank. This building is now the home of the National Imperial Glass Museum, Bellaire, Ohio. A visit to the museum is a must for all glass collectors.

400/19 Ash Tray, 2 3/4", $7-9.

400/33, 4" Ash Tray or Jelly Dish, $12-16. We are showing this one because it has a delicate etching on the underside that reads "Hand Made Imperial." $60-75.

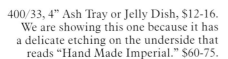

A March 24, 1941 Imperial memorandum says that the 400/44 was a 4 oz. juice. It does not show a picture for that juice. In another place, it lists the 400/44 as the 400/19 Wine. However, an illustration in Catalog B clearly shows the 400/44 as a 2 oz. small bead 2 3/8" wine. We also have a company photo with this small bead 2 3/8" wine labeled with 400/44. We do have another version of this cigarette holder. It is a small bead 4 oz. "wine," 2 15/16" tall. It is decorated with gold to match the rest of the cigarette set so we know that it was intended to be a set. The 400/19, 3 oz. Wine is also used with the 400/296 Cigarette Set. The 400/19, 7 oz. Old Fashion is used with the 400/1929. Keep in mind that there are at least six different cigarette holders mentioned as being used with the cigarette sets.

400/44 Cigarette Holder, small beads on base, $32-38.

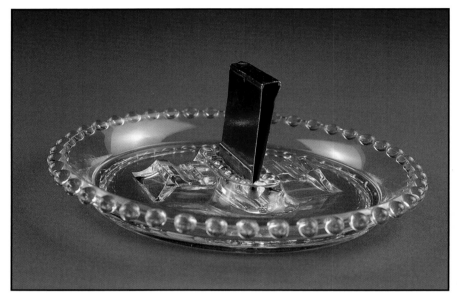

400/60, 6" Ash Tray; round with a raised glass match holder in center, $88-112.

400/64 Ash Tray or Nut Dip or Sugar Dip, 2 3/4", $14-16; component part of: 16 beads, Sugar Dip; 400/83 Strawberry Set; AKA as Seafood Set. 400/64, Ash Tray, 18 beads, $10-12.

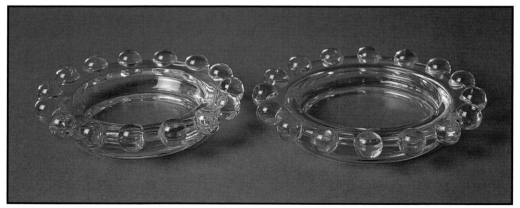

On the left in this photo is the 400/440 Ash Tray with 15 beads, $5-8. On the right is an undocumented 4 1/2" Ash Tray with 16 beads. In a January 1943 memorandum, there is a reference about a Mardi Gras tumbler (the #176 Continental tumbler) in Aquamarine, Green, Cranberry, and Topaz along with a 400/440 Crystal Coaster. It is a conclusion of the authors that the 4 1/2" 16 bead Ash Tray is the coaster that was made to go with the Mardi Gras Tumbler. NP

400/118 Ash Tray, B'tween Place, $38-46. During 1941-1943, the 400/118 Ash Tray had a protruding place for two cigarettes and a book of matches to rest. In 1950, the design was changed so the protrusion held only two resting cigarettes (without matches). Four of the later design ash trays were boxed and sold as the 400/118 Ash Tray, Bridge Set, $21-25. Single, $7-8.

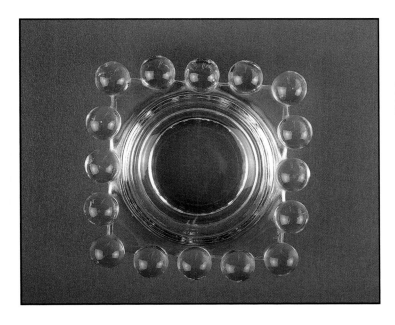

400/176 Ash Tray, $18-21. This is a 3 1/4" square ash tray with a round well in the center to receive the ashes.

The 400/150 Ash Tray has an important added feature that is little known. On the underneath side of some of the ash trays is a recessed area that covers most of the bottom. We knew about one. An astute collector shared his two different bases with us. The underneath of the base for the 400/9275 (marie bottom) measures 4 1/2" with an inner measurement of 4 1/4". The underneath of the base for the 400/7570 (ground and polished bottom) measures 4 1/4" with the inner measurement of 3 3/4". You will recognize this base immediately upon finding one.

400/450, 3-pc. Ash Tray Set, $18-24; component parts: 400/440, 4" Ash Tray (front), $5-8; 400/133, 5" Ash Tray (right), $6-8; 400/150, 6" Ash Tray (left), $6-8.

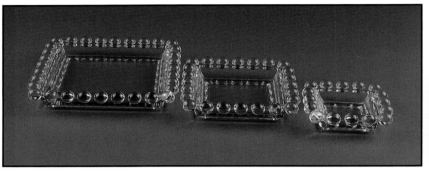

400/650, Ash Tray Set, $75-84; component parts: 400/653, 5 3/4" Square Ash Tray, $25-28; 400/652, 4 1/2" Square Ash Tray, $25-28; 400/651, 3 1/4" Square Ash Tray, $25-28.

There are two versions of this next cigarette box and the early one is seldom found. The boxes are the same shape and size; the lids are domed. On the early box, the extra raised rectangle area on the dome is 1/2" from all sides of the edge. On the later box lid, the raised rectangle area on the dome is only 1/4" from the edge.

400/134/6 Cigarette Set, $48-58; component parts: 400/134 Covered Cigarette Box, 5 1/4" by 4 1/4"; 400/134/1 Ash Tray, 3" by 4 1/2", $6-8. The later cigarette box is in this set. The box pictured alone is the early style. Note that the raised rectangle on the top is smaller than the one on the later style box. Early box, $35-38.

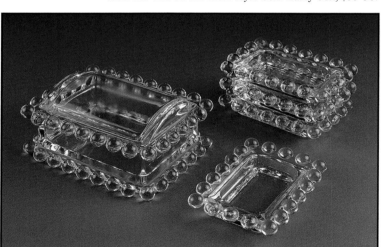

400/1929 Cigarette Set, $55-73; component parts: 400/19 Ash Tray; 400/19 Old Fashion; 400/29 Tray. Note that the 400/19 Old Fashion rather than the 400/19 Wine is correct.

400/29/6, 6-pc. Cigarette Set, $60-80; component parts: 400/29, 6 1/2"-7" Tray; 400/19, 3 oz. Wine; 400/64, 2 3/4" Ash Tray or Sugar Dip.

400/29/64/44 Cigarette Set, $74-91; component parts: 400/29, 6 1/2"-7" Tray; 400/64, 2 3/4" Sugar Dip; 400/44 Cigarette Holder. (Note: When this number was first introduced it used a 400/19 Wine under the number 400/44.)

Imperial advertising matches.

Baskets, Bells

There are three variations of the 400/40/0, 6 1/2" Basket, two of which are shown here. All three have free form applied handles, about 1/2" in diameter. The most common basket is the one with a marie bottom and the sides turned up to leave about a 4 3/4" opening between the handles. There is a bead missing on the edge at the point where the handle attaches to the side. The second version also has the marie bottom and a 1/2" diameter handle. The difference is that the sides are turned up more, making the opening distance between the handle only about 2 1/4".

The third version of the 400/40/0, 6 1/2" Basket (not shown here) is very dainty. The handle on this dainty one is about 1/4" in diameter. Rather than a marie bottom, it has a ground and polished bottom—in other words it was made "stuck up." Stuck up meant that the glass item was stuck to the iron punty rod for re-heating in the furnace—it did not have a marie for the snap rod to fasten to it. We found it very exciting to see "made stuck up" written by the 400/40/0 entry in a 1941 price list. This led us to believe that our third version of the basket was not just a whimsy made by an artisan, but was done on orders. When you hold this "stuck up" basket in your hand, you know immediately that it is different. (This basket is also cut and can be seen in the Cut Patterns section of our book, Candlewick: Colored and Decorated Lines.)

The larger basket, the 400/73/0, 11" Basket, was made in two versions. From 1939 to 1960, catalog illustrations show this basket with the sides turned up high and the handle attached about 1 1/2" down the side. On a later version, from 1977-1978, the sides are not turned up as much and the handles are attached just barely below the beaded edge. No beads are missing from the edge of either large basket. Although the early version was shown for so many years, it is seldom found in the central part of the United States. Sometimes we think that perhaps the company did not change the illustrations in the catalogs to correspond with changes made in the production shape. This is only a thought, one that we have not as yet attempted to pursue.

The first photograph below shows the early version of the 400/40/0 Basket and the 400/73/0 Basket. The second photograph shows the later version of the 400/40/0 Basket and the 400/73/0 Basket.

400/40/0, 6 1/2" Basket, $25-35; 400/73/0, 11" Basket; early version with handles fastened midway down the side of the basket, $125-150.

400/40/0, 6 1/2" Basket, $25-35; 400/73/0 11" Basket; later version, slightly turned-up sides and handles fastened near the basket edge, $125-150.

400/273, 5" Basket, Beaded Handle, $158-210. The basket with the beaded handle is just that—it has a beaded handle. It is a rather heavy, clunky basket compared to the others. It was made for only ten years and is scarcer than the others; therefore it commands a higher price. This basket was also made for Crown Silver Company. This handle was not free form, rather it was made in a mold.

Imperial Glass Corporation advertisement for its customers.

103

Factory documentation exists only for the 400/108, 5" Bell and 400/179, 4" Bell. The 400/108 Bell was made using the 3400 Wine, 4 oz. without putting the foot on it. The mouth is slightly wider than the wine and the edge is slightly belled inward. This bell shape is much prettier than the "wine" shape. We do not know if this special shaping of the bell was always done because we have not seen other bells with the "belled" look at the bottom. We see many that look exactly like the wine without the foot. When it is a factory bell, you should be able to see a tiny wire loop fastening the clapper. There should be no visible glue.

The 400/179, 4" Bell was made using the 3400 Cordial mold, also without attaching the foot. The 400/179 has been documented since the very first printing of books on Candlewick. However, it was uncertain until about 1988 that it was made by the factory from the 3400 Cordial. For proof, one that was still in the original box was brought to us to admire. What a thrill! Since that discovery, we know that some bells have been made from a 3400 Cordial.

The 400/179 is very scarce and when you find one, it may be "homemade." It is difficult to provide guidance as far as definitely identifying one of these bells. Start by looking for the tiny hook holding the clapper, which should hang almost the whole depth of the bell. Also look closely at the way the chain is fastened into the bowl of the cordial. If it has a slight yellow cast at the point of fastening it MIGHT not be the original from the factory. The factory bells have a little white material holding the chain in place. Finally, look carefully at the large bead on the end of the handle and try to determine if you think that it has had the foot cut off. At the factory, the foot was never put on.

In the following photograph the bell on the left is a bell made from a 3400 Claret but may be a "homemade" item. We do know that the 3400 Claret has been found as a bell and could have been a factory item, although it does not appear in any factory information. Ours did come with an Imperial tag and from the factory area, but is still suspect.

Here is a great description taken from an Imperial memorandum about the quality of the clapper installation in the bell: "Clapper—chain anchor in our new Candlewick bell will not Pull out, Fall out, Shake out, Unravel, Warp, Bend, Bust, or Run down at the heel." You cannot beat that description!

Remember, the 400/108, 5" Bell and the 400/179, 4" Bell can be documented. The bell made from the 3400 Claret is not documented but could have been a factory item. Do not be misled by bells made from any other 3400 stems.

Bell made from 3400 Claret (not documented as factory production), NP; 400/108, 5" Bell, $42-49; 400/179, 4" Bell, $56-65.

Candleholders, Hurricane Lamps, Candleholders With Eagles

The 400/40CV Flower Candleholder has an overall height of 5 1/4", eight crimps, and no beads. The miniature flower vase that fits inside is 4 1/2" tall and has a rounded tip at the base to insert into the candleholder. The way this fits into the candleholder is confusing and causes collectors to question if it is the correct vase; one would expect the base of the miniature vase to be shaped like the end of a candle—cylindrical and with a flat bottom. We bought our pair in 1985 from the estate sale of an Imperial representative and therefore we know that they are correct. A few years later we bought a pair exactly the same, which reinforces the correctness. There are several miniature vases and they will be discussed in the vase section.

Imperial named some of the candleholders Flower Candleholders because they advertised them with flowers placed around the candles,

400/40C, 5" Flower Candleholder, $35-50; component part of: 400/40CV Flower Candleholder, $75-100. Our pair came originally with the vase pointed at the bottom.

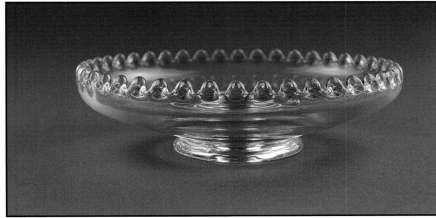

400/40F, 6" Flower Candleholder, $28-40. The 6" Flower Candleholder is round and cupped, similar to the "F" bowl series.

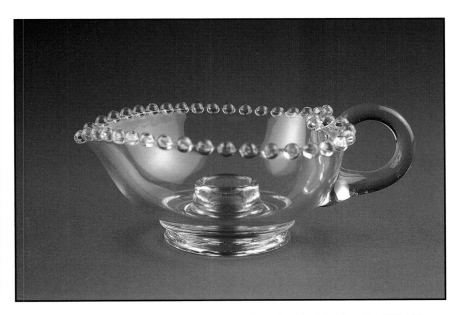

400/40HC, 5" Flower Candleholder; heart shaped and with a handle, $75-100.

Enjoy this company photograph showing the 400/40HC as a candleholder with floating flowers.

400/40S, 6 1/2" Flower Candleholder, $50-60. Here is the unusual square shape made from a round bowl. Again, this could hold flowers around the candle. Our example came with this 400/40V Miniature Vase in early 1980. We feel that it is an original set—not pieced together.

400/66C, 4 1/2" Flower Candleholder; another flower candleholder with the crimped shape, $60-65. It is 4 1/2" tall and 5 1/4" diameter with a 2-bead stem.

400/66F, 4" Flower Candleholder, $60-65. This is a more difficult to find flower candleholder. It is 4" tall and 5 1/2" diameter, shallow and cupped, with a 2-bead stem.

The 400/79B Flat Candleholder is hard to find. It is 6" wide by 3 1/4"-3 1/2" tall. The beaded edge lies flat but the base under the candle cup is domed upward. The 400/79B Candleholder comes in two versions. The later version has a rim on the candle cup while the earlier version does not have this rim on the candle cup.

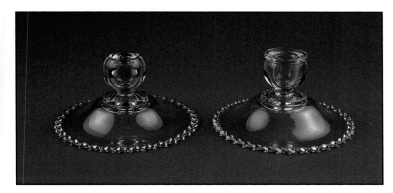

400/79B Flat Candleholder. The earlier version of the 400/79B Candleholder (left) does not have the candle cup rim, which was added in 1949. Component part of: 400/79, 2-pc. Hurricane Lamp; 400/79R/2 Candleholder with Eagle; 400/101/79B Float Bowl Console; 400/152, 3-pc. Hurricane; 400/152R, 3-pc. Hurricane Lamp; 400/9279 FR, 3-pc. Console Set. Early version $35-42; later version $32-38.

400/79R Candleholder, $12-15. It has the edge rolled up and the overall measurements are 6" wide x 3 1/2" tall. It was made with and without a candle cup rim, which will make for a little difference in height.

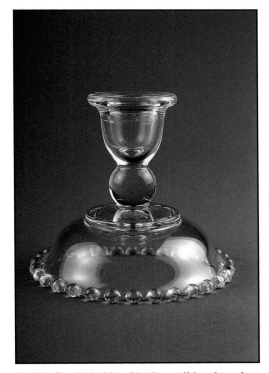

400/80 Candleholder, $8-10; small beads and a domed foot are the details of this 3 1/2" low candleholder. Component part of: 400/80/2 Eagle Candleholder; 400/8013B, 3-pc. Console Set; 4008063B, 3-pc. Console Set; 400/8075B, 3-pc. Console Set. Refer to the section on Reproductions for more information on this candleholder.

400/81, 3 1/2" Handled Candleholder, $35-42. Add a handle to the 400/80 Candleholder and you have the 400/81, 3 1/2" Handled Candleholder; component part of: 400/63B/81 Console Set; 400/76 Hurricane; 400/81/2 Eagle Candleholder.

400/86 Mushroom Candleholder, $25-32; component part of: 400/8613B, 3-pc. Console Set and 400/8692L, 3-pc. Console Set. The 400/86 Mushroom Candleholder is 5 3/4" in diameter. It is domed and fairly flat towards the outer edge. It matches the shape of the 400/92L Console Bowl.

We are using the number 400/86R with the Domed Mushroom Candleholder. This item was never in a catalog, price list, or any other paper that we have. It is 5 3/8" in diameter and completely domed in shape. It seems to match the 400/92R Console Bowl that is part of the 400/136 Console Set. This set combines the 400/92R Console Bowl with the 400/129R Urn Candleholder. The 400/86R Candleholder is very hard to find and evidently made for such a short time that it never made a catalog or price list. We believe the date of this could be c. 1941.

400/86R Domed Mushroom Candleholder, $★. This Candleholder is not shown in any catalog. Since it is a mushroom shape as is the 400/86, one would assume that it could be a 400/86 with a letter after it to distinguish the shape. It matches the shape of the 400/92R so it seems logical that it could be numbered 400/86R. It probably predates the 400/129R.

400/90, 5" Candleholder, Handled, $38-46; 5" wide with beaded handle. The height of this one is 3 3/4". It rolls up more than the 400/79R.

It is unknown if this 400/90 is one of a kind, or if there was a regular production line of this candleholder that is turned up considerably more than the documented one

400/100 Twin Candleholder, $18-21; component part of: 400/100/2-2 Twin Eagle Candleholder; 400/127L, 4-pc. Console Set; 400/920F, 3-pc. Console Set; 400/1004B, 3-pc. Console Set; 400/1006B, 3-pc. Console Set; 400/6300B, 3-pc. Console Set. Some of these candleholders are more domed at the base. This causes about 1/4" variance in height. The early ones were domed and about 4 1/2" tall.

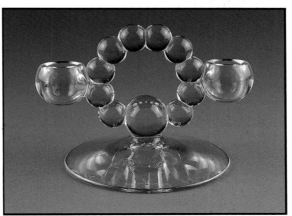

400/115, 3 Light Candleholder, $100-115; component part of: 400/115/1, 3-lite Eagle Candleholder; 400/1531B, 3-pc. Console Set. This is 9 1/2" long with three candle cups.

The 400/129R Urn Candleholder is listed as 6" in a 1941 Catalog and 4 1/2" in a 1943 price list. We have never seen a 6" Urn Candleholder. The 400/138B Vase may be from the same mold. If so, the 6" vase would be rolled downward to form the 4 1/2" candleholder. It seems impossible to make a 6" candleholder out of this 6" vase. Maybe someone inadvertently picked up the 6" vase size for the finished candleholder. We have seen this candleholder vary in size by approximately 1/4". If any collector has the 6" Urn Candleholder, please let us know.

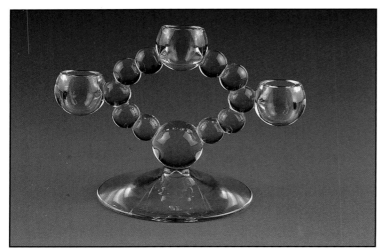

400/129R Urn Candleholder, 4 1/2" tall, $140-158. One catalog showed this candleholder as 6" in height so you might want to watch for it—in case it does exist.

400/147 Candleholder, $25-28; component part of: 400/1474, 3-pc. Console Set. This is similar to the 400/100 Candleholder. It has three candle cups rather than two. Again, the earlier versions have a more domed base rather than the fairly flat base of the later versions.

400/170, 3 1/2" Candleholder, large beads, $12-14; component part of: 400/63B/170 Console Set; 400/7570, 4-pc. Console Set. This candleholder was still in stock when Imperial closed in 1984.

400/175, 6 1/2" Candleholder, $100-115; component part of the 400/9275. The stem of this candleholder is the same stem as on the 400/103C Footed Fruit Bowl, 400/103D Cake Stand, 400/103E Banana Stand, and 400/103F Footed Fruit Bowl.

The only catalog picture of the 400/178 Candleholder is shown as the 400/178 Hurricane. Three versions of the base have been found. All three versions are shallow bowls with beads on the outer edge. One has a 3 1/2" circle of small beads on the inside to support the shade. Instead of the circle of small beads, another version has six raised ribs in a 3 1/2" diameter circling the candle cup to hold the shade in place. The third version (shown here) is plain on the inside and is the candleholder.

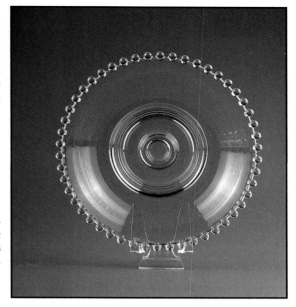

400/178 Candleholder, $*. This candleholder is often called the saucer candleholder. As a candleholder, it will be plain on the inside and will not have the circle of beads or the six raised ribs as does the hurricane base. Only in the last few years have collectors discovered that there are three saucer bases. NI.

400/196FC, 9" Flower Candle Centerpiece, $55-65. Catalogs list this piece as 9", however, the ones that we have measured have been 8". It is 5" tall. This candleholder is the base to the 400/196, 2-pc. Epergne Set. Also, the 400/67C Footed Fruit Bowl is the candleholder without the candle cup.

400/207, 4 1/2", 3-toed Candleholder, $70-80. This is the 400/206, 3-toed Nappy with a candle cup in it and small beads on the edge.

Flowers add a nice touch when placed in the 400/196FC Flower Candle Centerpiece, as shown in this company photograph.

The next candleholder has the tri-stem and is one of the most difficult candleholders to find. Watch closely for any fractures in the glass where the three arches of beads come together for the stem. This is a weak point and may be why not many were produced or survived. Of the items with the tri-stem, the lemon tray and compote are the easiest to find.

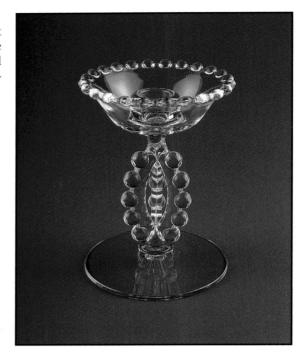

400/224, 5 1/2" Candleholder, Tri-Stem, $135-158. This candleholder is not the base to the 400/264 Hurricane Lamp, as has sometimes been assumed. Careful attention to detail reveals a major difference in the two. The candleholder has a smooth surface surrounding the candle cup while the 400/264 Hurricane base has a ledge inside the cup that holds the shade (see page 118). This ledge extends about 5/8" from the beaded edge. NI.

400/280, 3 1/2" Single Candleholder, $210-215. Besides being difficult to identify, this piece is unusually hard to find. We say that even though a friend has found three pairs. Most collectors, however, have trouble finding a single example of this candleholder. Because of the lack of small beads on it, one might not find it displayed with Candlewick.

400/1752 Prism Candleholder, 7 1/2", $190-205. A collector might be fortunate enough to be able to piece this candleholder together. Watch carefully for the 400/152 Adapter with tiny holes for the wires to fasten to the prisms (see next photo). Component parts: 400/175, 6 1/2" Tall Candleholder; 400/152 Lamp Adapter.

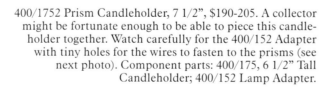

400/152 Adapter with holes for attaching prisms to complete the 400/1752 Prism Candleholder and the 400/1753 Hurricane (see page 119), $50-60. Replacement prisms can be found today at antique malls, glass shows, and other similar sources. (For this photograph, we chose not to remove the prisms as they were originally attached.)

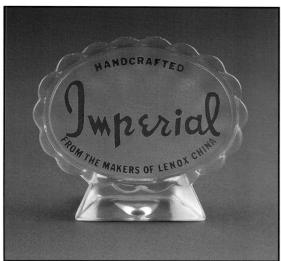

Imperial Sign, frosted oval with French edge. $88-105.

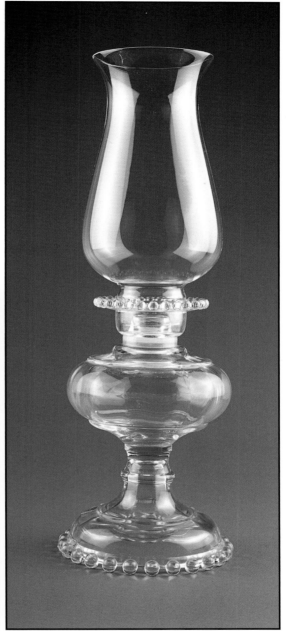

400/26, 3-pc. Hurricane Lamp, $1050-1260; component parts: 400/26 Base; 400/26 Crimped Shade; 400/152 Lamp Adapter. This hurricane is among the most coveted of the hurricane lamps. The adapter for the 400/26 has the peg cut off so that it is not visible through the bowl of the lamp. The peg is cut off so close to the base of the adapter that it leaves a hole through it. Some collectors think that the adapter had been adapted to take an electrical cord. However, in all the factory papers we have seen, we have found no hints that the company sold the 400/26 to be adapted for an oil burner or for an electrical fitting. This Hurricane was only shown one time and then it was on a supplemental catalog sheet. It was shown with the crimped shade but most have been found with the straight shade.

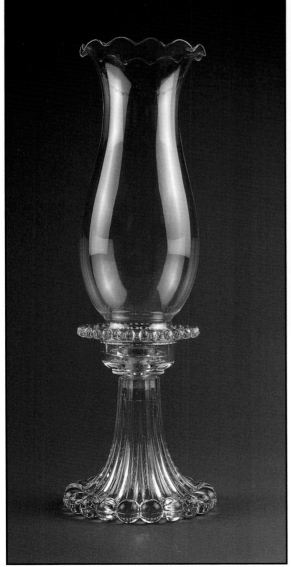

400/32 16" Hurricane Lamp (AKA 400/155), $300-350; component parts: 400/155 Base, $215-235; 400/152 Lamp Adapter; 400/152 Chimney, Crimped Shade. This base is what collectors generally refer to as the "Lightolier" part. The name was coined because Imperial made this part for the Lightolier [Lighting] Company as well as for Imperial's general line. Be sure to watch for ceiling fixtures and table lamps using the 400/155 Base. It is 4 3/4" tall, 5" base diameter with a neck diameter of 1 1/4". At the top edge, there is a 1/16" recessed ridge. When this part is used to hold an Eagle Ornament or Adapter, the top recessed 1/16" ridge is not on the base. The Lightolier number is G-790.

The 400/76 Hurricane Candle Lamp is a total of 9 1/2" tall. The shade is 2 1/4" diameter at the base. Imperial has another shade similar to this one and that is the one that goes on the 1604 Hurricane Lamp in the Cape Cod line. On the Candlewick shade, the shade starts to bulge out 2" from the bottom. On the Cape Cod shade, the shade starts to bulge out only 1/2" from the bottom. Production years for the Cape Cod Hurricane Lamp precede those for Candlewick by only a year. This shade might just vary because it is hand-made. In addition, the hurricane could have left the factory with either shade on it. We have seen a shade that looks exactly like these but fits too tightly on the candleholder. It might have been correct, but be very cautious when buying this lamp.

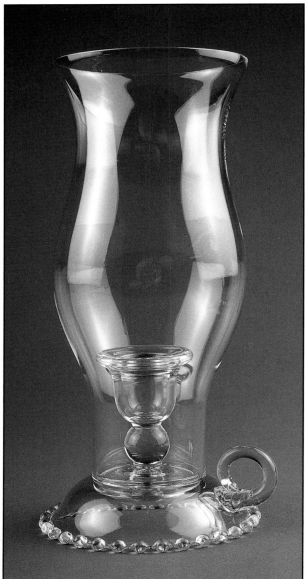

400/76, 2-pc. Hurricane Candle Lamp, $315-385; component parts: 400/76 Shade; 400/81, 3 1/2" Candleholder. The second photograph shows two size shades that we have on our 400/76. We have two slightly different measurements for our shades: 8 1/4" and 7 1/2".

On the left is the 400/152 Shade as it is before the cap is cut off to form the top of the shade. On the right is the finished 400/152 Shade.

114

The easiest of the hurricane lamps to find is the 400/79. The shade for this is what we call a generic shade. Imperial did not make the shade—they bought it from West Virginia Glass, Weston, West Virginia. Most of the glass companies bought some glass from other companies. This happened if it was more economical or if the factory did not have the time to make an item to fill all the orders that were placed.

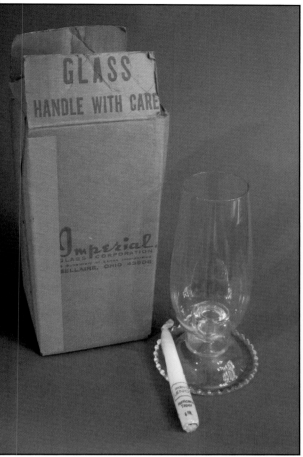

400/79, 2-pc. Hurricane Lamp, 10 1/2", $64-84, found in original box. Component parts: 400/79R Candleholder; 400/79 Shade. This item carried over into the Lenox era and was #14990. There are two possible sizes for the shades with this hurricane; the overall catalog measurement illustrations, however, do not reflect that difference. One shade is 9" tall and the slender bottom neck is 1 1/4" long. The other shade is 8 1/4" tall and the slender bottom neck is 1/2" long. We do feel that both are correct. The West Virginia Glass Company, Weston, West Virginia, made the shades for Imperial. We do not know which shade would be the earlier version.

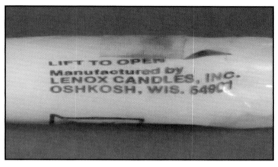

The box also contained the candle still wrapped in cellophane with the Lenox wording intact. The box with the Lenox Mould number and the Lenox name on wrapper indicate that this was produced between 1977 and 1979.

400/142K/HL, 15" 3-pc. Hurricane Lamp, $*; component parts: 400/142K, 7" Rose Bowl; 400/152 Shade, Straight Top; 400/152 Adapter. Now you are looking at one of several very hard to find lamps. Adapters usually have pegs on them to insert into the candleholders. The adapter without the peg goes with the 400/142K/HL. Not having the peg improves the appearance of this lamp.

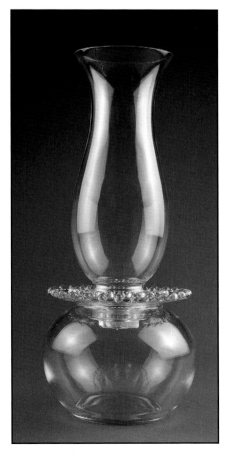

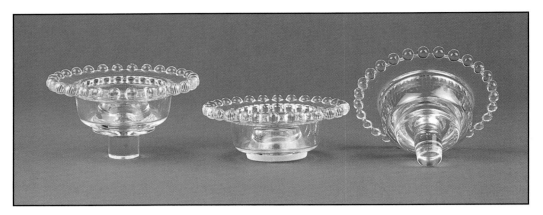

400/152 Adapter, $35-42; component part of: 400/32, 400/152R, 400/152, 400/1753, 400/155, 400/26 and 400/142K/HL Hurricane Lamps. The adapter on the left has a peg on the bottom to insert into a candleholder to allow the candleholder to hold a shade and make a hurricane lamp. The circle edge of the adapter has beads on it. In the center is the adapter that has had the peg removed from it. The small edge left after the peg is cut off is ground to help the adapter stay in the base of the 400/26. Even with this, the adapter is not very secure. This was done at the factory to be used in the 400/26 and 400/142K/HL. The adapter on the left and the right is shown in two positions for better view of the shape.

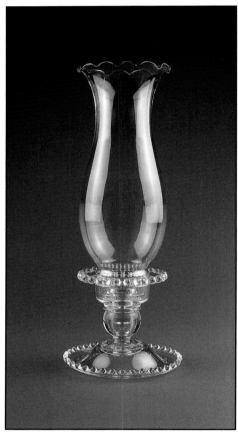

400/152 Hurricane Lamp, $158-190; component parts: 400/79R Candleholder; 400/152 Adapter; 400/152 Crimped Shade.

400/152R Hurricane Lamp, $158-190; component parts: 400/79R Candleholder; 400/152 Adapter; 400/152 Straight Top Shade.

The shade for the 400/178 is 10 1/2" tall. Ours is one of a pair that came with original shades long before collectors or dealers knew what shade could be combined with the 400/178 Candleholder to make a Hurricane. Imperial records did not give an overall height to the 400/178. This shade can also be found on the 160/79 Cape Cod Hurricane. The early version of the 160/79 is a total of 9" in height (shade 7 1/2") and a later version is 12" in height. There might be a shorter version of the 400/178. We say this only because there are two versions cataloged for the Cape Cod 160/79 Hurricane. We are giving this information simply because of the similarities between pieces of Candlewick and Cape Cod.

In addition, the 10 1/2" shade is used on Hurricane #51522 from the general line of Imperial. That item had a base of Blue Satin, Pink Satin, and Crystal Satin in 1980. The shade on these different hurricanes was not made by Imperial Glass Company but rather by West Virginia Glass Company.

400/178, 2-pc. Hurricane Lamp, $*; this candleholder base has six raised ribs in a 3 1/2" diameter circling the candle cup to support the shade. A second version of the hurricane base is one with a 3 1/2" circle of small beads in the bottom. A third version of this base is plain on the inside, and it is the candleholder without a shade. NI.

400/264 Hurricane Lamp, $★. The 400/264 Hurricane on the Tri-Stem has a feature that needs to be discussed. It has long been assumed that the 400/224 Candleholder was the base for the 400/264 Hurricane. However, there is a major difference in the two. The 400/264 Hurricane base has a ledge inside the cup that holds the shade. It is a ledge extending about 5/8" inward from the beaded edge. Also, the shade for this hurricane is not just a straight-sided shade. The bottom of the 9" shade tapers inward and down about 3/4". NI.

400/264 Chimney, $★; the 9" shade flares out just a little at the top and tapers inward and down about 3/4" at the bottom. At left is the 400/264 Hurricane Base; note the ridge in the candle area to support the shade. (Compare this to the 400/224, 5 1/2" Candleholder, Tri-Stem, shown on page 112).

The only part of this 400/680 Twin Hurricane Lamp that is Candlewick is the 400/152 Adapter. The base of the #680 Twin Hurricane Lamp can be found with other adapters made by Imperial. Study the twin arms carefully and you just might find them all alone on a sale table with the seller not knowing they are part of the Candlewick family. (That is the description of a dream!)

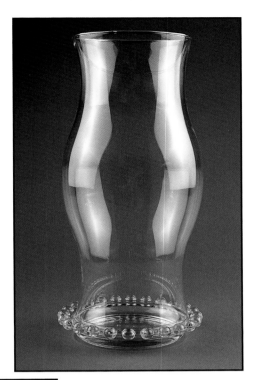

400/680 Twin Hurricane Lamp, $1050-1250; component parts: 400/680 Twin Arms for Hurricane Lamp; 400/152 Adapter; 400/152 straight top shades.

#14994, 12" Hurricane Lamp, $34-40; component parts: 400/150, 6" Ash Tray; #14995 Shade. This hurricane is one of three that carried over into the Lenox era. The shade is a generic shade made by West Virginia Glass Specialty Company.

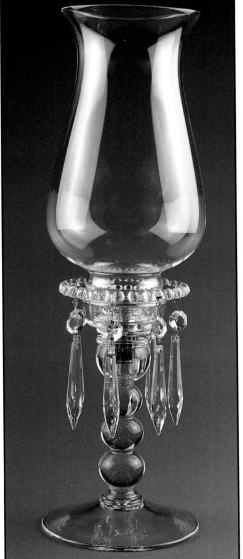

400/1753 Hurricane Lamp, $435-455; component parts: 3-pc. 400/175 Candleholder with Prisms; 400/152 Adapter; 400/26 Shade. The rare 400/26 shade with the straight top goes on this lamp. Both shades, crimped and straight, are rare, but the crimped one seems to be more elusive than the straight. The height is 16 1/2". Note that the 400/26 and 400/152 Shades with the straight tops have been reproduced. Both are marked on the neck with a logo of the 400/90 Candleholder.

#14996, 14" Hurricane Lamp, $34-60; Component parts: 400/170, 3 1/2" Candleholder, domed foot with Lenox #14997. Here is another of the three hurricanes that were in the Lenox era. Again, this shade is a generic shade made by West Virginia Glass Specialty Company.

From the notes of an Imperial sales representative, comes this information:

On November 10, 1942, Imperial Glass Corporation was granted a patent on a glass eagle candleholder with a wing spread of four inches and a height of 4 1/2 inches with patent number 134,312.

This eagle was mounted on eight [Imperial] candleholders of various heights that made for some attractive ornamental combinations. All of this passed out about the year of 1950.

All the Eagles in the documented Candlewick line are crystal. Imperial also used the Eagle Candleholders and Eagle Ornaments in several of its different candleholders, such as Cape Cod and Simplicity. The same eagles were made in black, milk glass, satin, and all over gold. We do not know how the black glass eagles were used, but we do know that the milk glass eagle was used in a black bookend. The gold eagle was also used in black bookends as well as in black and gold bookends. Two gold eagles were found in a 400/100 Candleholder with gold trim.

The next several photographs show the elegant Eagle Candleholder and the Eagle Ornament. Note that the Eagle with a candle cup behind the eagle is the #2 Adapter, and the eagle without the candle cup is the #1 Ornament.

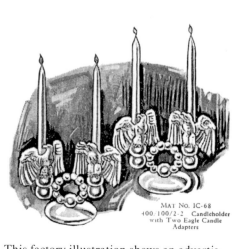

400/79R/2 Eagle Candleholder, $165-195; component parts: 400/79R Candleholder no rim; 777/2 Eagle Adapter.

400/81/2 Eagle Candleholder, $180-210; component parts: 400/81, 3 1/2" Candleholder; 777/2 Eagle Adapter.

400/80/2 Eagle Candleholder, $165-195; component parts: 400/80 Candleholder; 777/2 Eagle Adapter.

MAT No. IC-68
400/100/2-2 Candleholder with Two Eagle Candle Adapters

This factory illustration shows an advertising mat for the eagle candleholders that was made available to retail customers.

400/100/2-2 Eagle Candleholder, $345-355; component parts: 400/100 Twin Candleholder; 777/2 Eagle Adapter (2).

400/115/1 Eagle Candleholder, 9 1/2" wide, $295-310; component parts: 400/115, 3 Light Candleholder; 777/1 Eagle Ornament (2). The Eagle Ornament should be more difficult to find as Imperial did not use the Ornament as often as it used the Eagle Candleholder. Remember that the #1 Ornament does not hold a candle.

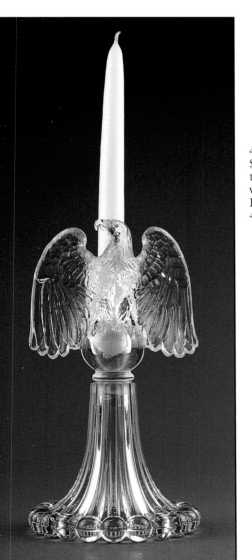

400/155 Eagle Candleholder, 9 1/2" high, $310-320; combinations of the Eagle and the 400/155 Hurricane Base can be found with both the Eagle Ornaments and the Eagle Candleholder. Component parts: 400/155 Lamp Base; 777/2 Eagle Adapter.

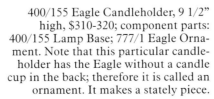

400/155 Eagle Candleholder, 9 1/2" high, $310-320; component parts: 400/155 Lamp Base; 777/1 Eagle Ornament. Note that this particular candleholder has the Eagle without a candle cup in the back; therefore it is called an ornament. It makes a stately piece.

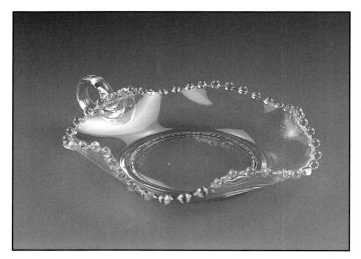

400/51C, 6" Handled Crimped Candy, $40-50; fairly difficult to find. It can be documented in only 1943. Since it was a small candy, most likely many were made then.

9400/51F, 6" Handled Candy (round), AKA 400/51, $14-17. Here is an example of Imperial's applied handle. It is simply a free form handle that is not in the mold. This item was also called a Handled Mint. It was in production until 1979 under the Lenox ownership.

400/59, 5 1/2" Covered Candy Box, $42-46. The early lid with a half round knob was on the Covered Candy and Covered Jelly and was produced from 1937-1951.

400/59, 5 1/2" Covered Candy Box, 2-bead finial $28-30; the 400/144 Lid with a 2-bead finial was produced from 1953-1967.

400/65/2 Candy, partitioned, curved lid, $140-170. The 400/65 Covered Candy was listed during 1939; it was not partitioned and had a domed lid. $★. After that it was listed as the 400/65/2 and was partitioned, as shown here. Be sure to study the information listed with the 400/65/1 Covered Vegetable (see page 32). On the divided candy, the candy lid should be only slightly domed.

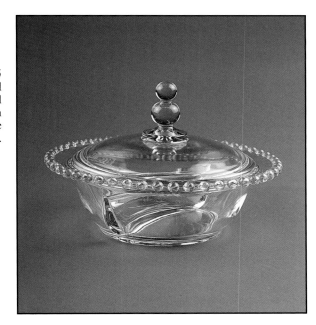

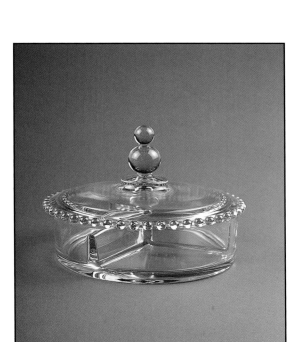

400/110, 7" Partitioned Candy Box and Cover, three sections, $60-65; divisions are straight and begin about 1/2" below top edge of candy bottom.

According to catalog illustrations, the 400/140 Candy, beaded foot, should have a domed lid just as the 400/65 Candy had. However, we have only seen it with the flatter lid. That makes us think they came out of the factory that way. It remains a mystery to us why more of the domed lids on the 400/140 Candy, the 400/139 Snack Jar, and the 400/65/1 Covered Vegetable have not been found. In twenty-five years, we have only found one of these domed lids. NI.

The 400/140 Candy with the beaded foot also has a molded bowl similar to the 400/65/1 Vegetable Bowl. We have seen and held in our hands two versions of the 400/140 Candy with the beaded foot, and they had different "bowls" on them. On one version, the bowl bottom is perfectly flat and the stem for the item is the 400/79B Candleholder with the candle cup that has the ridge on top of it. The other version is the one with the underneath of the bowl bottom recessed for the entire bottom except a 1/4" rim around the outer edge. The candle cup does not have a ridge on the top of it. These details are not important to some collectors, but there are many that want to know every variation. NI.

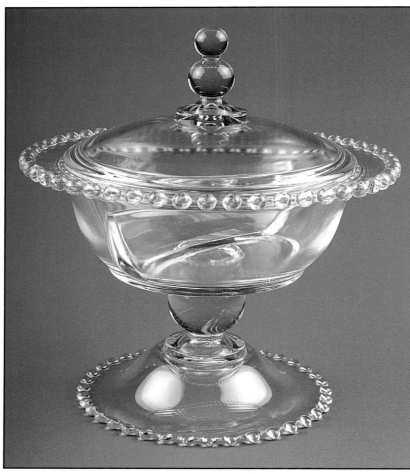

400/140 Footed Candy Jar and Cover, beaded foot, $980-1120. This is the older of the two 400/140 Candy Jars and was made from 1941-1943. It is divided and has a beaded foot. The candy jar has a flange or a collar around the top of the bowl that protrudes about 3/4". The lid has a two-bead finial. The lid should be domed like the 400/65/1 Covered Vegetable. This one has the flatter lid, as do all of the 400/140 Footed Candy Jars, beaded foot, that we have seen.

400/140 Footed Candy Jar and Cover, $190-210. The Candy Jar with the plain foot is the later style of the 400/140 Footed Candy Jar and Cover. It is not divided. Even this later candy has two versions. The earlier of the two has a more domed foot while the later one is almost flat. It is a noticeable difference. The lid has a 2-bead finial. One can see in a catalog the changes of the foot from slightly domed to flat foot.

400/149F, 7 1/2" Handled Bon Bon, made only in 1943 (left), $88-105. It is the cupped version of the 400/149D Handled Mint Tray. It has a center handle with beads in the shape of an outlined heart. 400/149D, 9" Handled Mint Tray (right), $25-30. Catalogs show the size of this handled mint tray as 9" but those that we have measured have been 8". The center handle has beads at the top in the shape of an outlined heart. These trays do not have the two large beads inside the outlined heart shape at the top of the handle that is a feature of the 400/67D Pastry Tray.

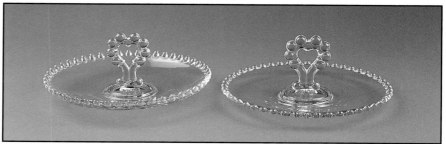

The next candy, 400/158, is the most difficult to find. It has no beads except for the two on the lid. The bottom of the 400/158 is from an old line of Imperial's covered candy dishes. A lid with a 2-bead finial was added and it was placed in the Candlewick group. Collectors have sometimes found the base and matched it with a 400/260 Candy Box lid. However, the 400/260 lid is just a little too small. The 400/158 was made in 1943 while the 400/260 did not appear until 1953, so that lid was not available when the 400/158 was made. Also note that the 400/260 lid does not have the extra edge of glass around the edge that the official 400/158 Lid has. NI.

400/158, 7" Candy Box and Cover, $280-315. None of the usual small beads are present on this candy box. The lid does have the 2-bead final. The correct lid for the 400/158 has a 1/2" ridge or thick edge around the outer edge of the lid. If you look carefully at catalog illustrations or this photograph, you can see the extra line or ridge around the lid. The thickness is felt from the underside of the lid and it fits snuggly. Some collectors have put the 400/260 Candy Lid on the 400/158, but it is not the correct lid and fits too loosely. NI.

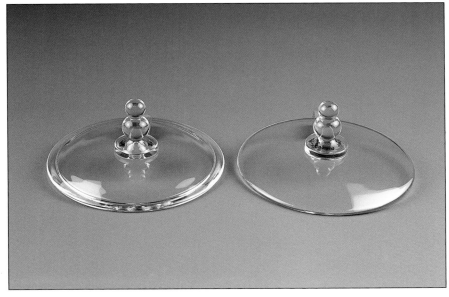

Shown here for comparison are the 400/260 Lid (left) and the 400/158 Lid (right); note the edge of the 400/158 Lid with the extra thickness. NP.

400/245, 6 1/2" Candy Box and Cover, $290-315.
The 400/245 is a very different kind of candy box.
It is a round bowl with a square flange collar and
round lid. Not too many of these are around.

400/259, 7" Candy Box and Cover, $75-85.
This is a shallow bowl and has a 2-bead finial.

400/260, 7" Candy Box and Cover, $175-190. This is a
fun item. When you lift the lid, you expect the small
beads to come up with the lid. However, the beads
are around the bowl, not on the lid. Actually, most of
the boxes have beads around the box but since this
was an early find of ours, we were surprised when the
beads were not on the lid. That was twenty years and
thousands of pieces of Candlewick ago.

The 400/655, 3 Section Jar Tower was made from 1960-1965 and the 400/656 Candy Box and Cover was offered only in 1964. It will be a surprise to many collectors that Imperial did not make the sections—they were made by the West Virginia Glass Specialty Company. The lid to the Jar Tower and Candy Box is 3" in diameter and has a 2-bead finial on it. The Tower itself is 10 3/4" tall and 6" wide. The 400/656 Candy Box and Cover is simply one section of the Jar Tower, with the same lid used on both. It is 5 1/4" tall and 6" wide. We do not have the answer as to whether Imperial made the lid for the Jar Tower, but we think that they must have because we find no records indicating they did not. (Be sure to look at another Jar Tower in the Cranberry Stained section of our book, Candlewick: Colored and Decorated Lines.)

400/655, 3 Section Jar Tower, $490-525.

The #820 Peanut Pouring Jar has caused a great deal of speculation. We first documented this in 1984. Contrary to some rumors, the lid does not have beads around it. The mug is 4 3/4" tall and has a free form handle that does not attach at the top of the handle. The lid is 3 1/2" diameter. It is NOT the lid to the 400/655 Jar Tower. The #820 Handled Covered Nut Mug is in the 1963, 1965, and 1967 general price lists. The startling information is that the Mug of the Peanut Pouring Jar was made by the West Virginia Specialty Glass Company (which was located in Weston, West Virginia) and is in their 1963 catalog. (We assume that Imperial did make the lid for the Peanut Pouring Jar, since we did not find any information indicating that they ordered the lid from another company.) Now, this information should not lessen the desirability of the Peanut Pouring Jar. Most glass companies bought some items from other companies. At times, other companies even made glass from Imperial molds for Imperial. This was a business practice used when a company could not meet a demand for a particular item or wanted to have a certain item without having to make a mold for it. NI.

#820 Peanut Pouring Jar, $★. The other side of the label is shown in the inset.

The Peanut Pouring Jar is 4 3/4" tall. Do not be misled by a shorter version of a mug, right, also made by West Virginia Specialty Glass Company.

127

The most appropriate place for providing the measurements of the various Candlewick lids is here in the Candy section, where the lids are used the most. Some will be used in other categories as well. Listed below are the diameters of the lids along with notations as to whether they have an outer ridge (individual lids will not be priced):

400/59   Covered Candy or Jelly, 4 3/4", half knob, has ridge

The next three lids are the same and interchangeable:

400/59   Covered Candy, 4 3/4", 2-bead, finial, has ridge
400/144   Butter Dish, 2-handled, 4 3/4", 2-bead finial, has ridge
400/157   Covered Jelly or Honey, 4 3/4", 2-bead finial, has ridge

400/245   Candy Box, 5 3/4", 2-bead finial, with ridge on edge
400/259   Candy Box, 5 3/4", 2-bead finial, no ridge, outer edge 3/8" thicker
400/158   Candy Box, 6 1/2", no beads except 2-bead finial, no ridge, outer edge 1/2" thicker, visible from the top
400/260   Candy Box, 6 1/2", beads are on box, 2-bead finial, smooth edge
400/65   Candy Box, 6 3/8", beads are on box, 2-bead finial; top of lid has 1/4" edge on it; AKA 400/65/2
400/65   Covered Vegetable, 6 3/8", very domed; 2-bead finial with wafer; AKA 400/65/1

400/139   Snack Jar, 6 3/8", 2-bead finial, has ridge; lid is domed
400/139   Family Punch, 6 3/8", with slot, 2-bead finial, has ridge; not domed
400/140   Footed Candy, Beaded Foot, 6 3/8", 2-bead finial, has ridge and is domed
400/140   Footed Candy, Flat Foot, 6 3/8", 2-bead finial, has ridge; not domed
400/110   Covered Candy, 7 1/2", 2-bead finial, has ridge

400/655   Candy Tower, 3", 2-bead finial, no other beads, has ridge
#820   Peanut Pouring Jar, 3 1/2", 2-bead finial, no other beads, has ridge

400/48F, 8" Compote; 4-bead stem, later version and the one most readily found, $55-65. Note that the 8" measurement is the width of the bowl. Imperial catalog items were sometimes listed by height and other times by width.

Compotes

There are two styles of the 400/45 Compote. The early one has a cupped shape to the bowl, similar to the shape of the bowl on the 400/48F. This cupped version of the 400/45 is scarce. It is illustrated in the 1939 catalog. The later style is more of a shallow slanted bowl. The 400/45 Compote has a 4-bead stem.

400/45, 5 1/2" Compote. Left, early version that is cupped, $42-52; right, later version with the more tapered sides, $15-25.

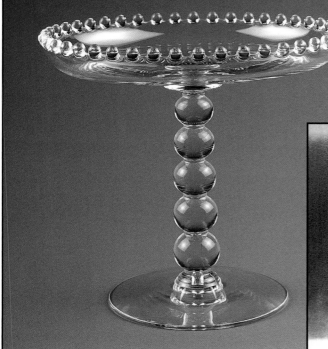

400/48F, 8" Compote, 5-bead stem, $175-245. The five-bead stem did not appear in any catalog. This Imperial photograph is the only company proof that we found to prove the validity of the 400/48F Compote with the five-bead stem. It is also on the design patent application #127,271. It is considered rare, but several, including the one shown here, have been found.

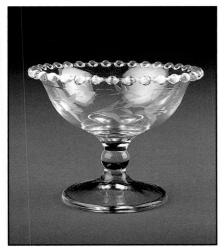

400/63B, 4 1/2" Compote, $25-30; has only a bulge on the stem where you would expect to see a perfect ball. Do not let that confuse you. Our crystal example is cut and has a smaller bowl than does our Viennese Blue one. The Viennese Blue one is more shallow and flared out.

400/66B, 5 1/2" Low Compote, no beads on stem, $18-20.

400/66B, 5 1/2" Low Compote, $14-18. On the later version of the 400/66B, there are two large beads on the stem.

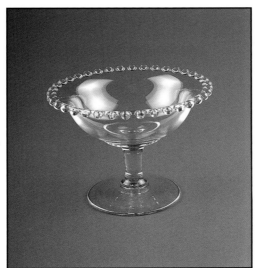

400/88, 5 1/2" Compote, early version bulge on stem, $32-38. Not shown is the 400/88, 5 1/2" Compote, later version, large bead on stem. $20-27.

400/137 Footed Oval Compote, $1050-1190. The Footed Oval Compote is 5 3/4" tall x 11" wide. Notice that this is a 400/46 Oval Celery Boat on a 400/79B Flat Candleholder. For communication purposes, we often refer to this as a canoe on a candlestick. It has worked, too. A few have been found with a horseshoe shape fracture in the bottom of the bowl. Perhaps this was caused when the two pieces were joined together during production. That might be why it had a short production period, and we do not see many of these.

400/157, 4 3/4" Cheese Compote, $35-40; component part of: 400/145 Cheese and Cracker Set. Add a lid to the 400/157 and you have a component part of: 400/92 Cheese and Cracker; 400/157 Covered Jelly or Honey.

400/220, 5" Compote, Tri-Stem, $80-90. This, along with the 400/221 Lemon Tray, is one of two tri-stem items that is easier to find. Be sure that you check carefully for fractures at the joint of the three arches of beads.

Hearts

400/40H, 5" Handled Heart Bon Bon, $18-25. It was in production from the late 1930s until the closing of Imperial. In 1941, it was made for Crown Silver ($25-32). The company records had a notation on this item, that it was to be "made Snapped" that year. "Snapped" meant that it had a marie for an iron rod to snap onto and hold during the heating process. The marie is the small ridge of glass at the bottom of an item. Now we know why some of the 5" hearts have a marie and some have a ground and polished bottom. NI.

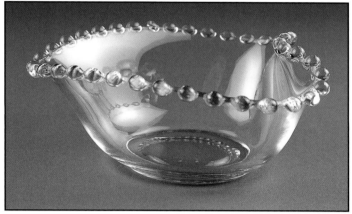

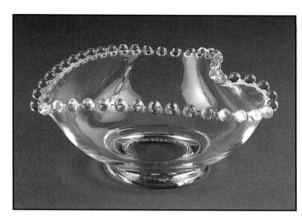

400/49H, 5" Heart, Unhandled, $10-17. The 5" heart can be found with the marie bottom (left) and with the ground and polished bottom (above). AKA 400/53H; 400/49/1.

400/49H, 9" Heart, Unhandled, $88-120.

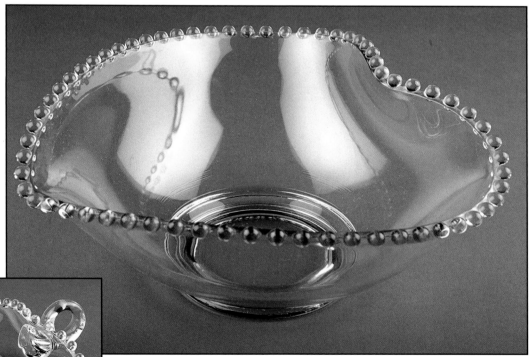

400/51H, 6"-6 1/2" Heart Shape Handled Bon Bon, $17-24. Sometimes this item is so flat that collectors might think they have found a 400/51M Card Tray. It is a shallow heart with a slight tip at the end.

400/51T, 6" Center Handled Wafer Tray, $18-20. The handle attaches from center of the bottom to the back of heart shaped dish.

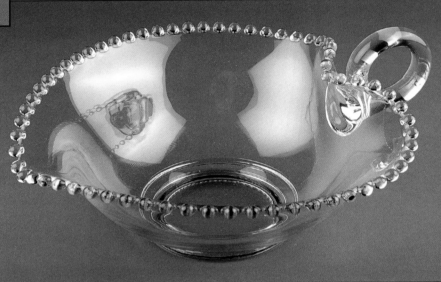

400/73H, 9"-10" Handled Heart, $105-140. This 9" Handled Heart is for flowers or fruit. Of course, it can be used for many other things.

400/172, 4 1/2" Mint Heart/Ash Tray, $10-12; 400/173, 5 1/2" Nut, Ash Tray, $12-14; 400/174, 6 1/2" Bon Bon Heart, Ash Tray, $17-20; component parts of: 400/750, 3-pc. Tid Bit Set Heart Shape, $36-42.

400/201 Handled Heart, 4 1/2", $38-46; 400/202 Handled Heart, 5 1/2" $46-52; 400/203 Handled Heart, 6 1/2", $38-46. Component parts of: 400/200, 3-pc. Handled Heart Set, $122-144.

Tid Bit Trays

There are several different ways that metal has been brought together with Candlewick. These include metal bases permanently attached to the base of a Candlewick item, handles that are removable, bases that screw on, and trays and lids that simply hold and cover the glass.

Most of the added handles we know of are on the tier tid bit trays and were added at the factory by Imperial. Longtime collectors are familiar with the large circle, small circle, oval, and triangular finger holds at the top. However, there are other handles on tier tid bits, both metal and wood, that will be thoroughly discussed. We are grouping both Imperial's factory tid bits and possible after factory tid bits in this section for easy comparison.

The 400/17TB, 2 Deck Bon Bon Set has two cupped plates with the maple handles. The bowls are the 400/1F and 400/5F with a special raised ring of glass 1 1/2" inches in diameter around the hole for the handle. The bottom bowl measures 7 1/2". (Our series of F bowls, 400/1F to 17F, do not measure true to the catalogs. We have 5", 6", 7 1/2", 8 1/2", 9", 11", 12", and 14".)

Now let us shift over to the 400/18TB, 3 High Snack Rack. This set also comes with the maple handle. However, we have found two with brass handles, one from our area and one from several states away. Both have been assembled with a slender, sleek brass handle. The bowls are the 400/1F, 400/3F, and 400/5F with the special raised glass around the hole. Recently another 2 tier tid bit with brass handles was bought by a friend in Michigan.

The flat plate tid bits seem to be very elusive. However, we have been fortunate enough to find four with different handles, all of which we feel are correct. We believe strongly that if two of the same item appear in different parts of the United States, it is not likely that they are homemade. This is the conclusion that we drew on the 400/73B, 2 Deck Tid Bit Set with a dark wooden spindle handle. One was found in the Michigan area; later one surfaced at the NIGCS Convention and it came from a southern state. The next of the flat plate tid bits we found has a metal handle with a 2" ring at the top. We have this same handle on a Washington pattern 2 Tier Tid Bit. We knew the Washington tid bit with the 2" ring at the top was combined by Imperial because it was shown in early Imperial catalogs.

From a 1943 company bulletin page, we know that the 400/73TB also came with a wooden handle with a knob at the top. Upon examination, it was determined that the wood is maple, a popular wood of that time. It has been our pleasure to find three of these with the maple handle.

There is a fourth version of the 400/73TB that just has to be an Imperial product. It has the metal handle that we are so familiar with on the 400/2701, 2 Tier Tid Bit Set; however instead of the oval at the top of the handle it has a 1 7/8" circle. It also has exactly the same lines of detail on the spindle as are found on the 400/2701.

These four flat plate tid bit trays have been found since 1994. Keep looking and do not give up.

All flat plates used on tid bits have a raised ridge of glass around the hole. Cupped plates have a recessed area close to the center hole on the underside of the plates. If the raised ridge and the recessed areas are missing from the tid bit sets, then you should suspect that they are homemade items—some people have drilled holes in plates and shallow bowls and created tid bit sets.

400/17TB, 2-Deck Bon Bon Set, $225-245. Component parts: 400/1F 5" Bowl; 400/5F, 7 1/2" Bowl; Maple Handle assembled by Imperial. We found an interesting note on the wooden handle tid bits in 1943—"no metal." It made us realize that with the war in progress, metal was not available for non-essential things. This is most likely the reason Imperial designed the wooden handle; after all, wood does not seem a likely choice to combine with crystal but do not all of us covet these sets now?

400/17TB, 2-Deck Bon Bon Set, $155-175. Component parts: 400/1F, 5" Bowl; 400/5F, 7 1/2" Bowl. We do not know if Imperial combined these or if they were an after factory item. We know of three sets that have been found with the brass handles shown here.

400/73TB, 2-Deck Tid Bit Set, $140-155; component parts: 400/40D, 8" Plate; 400/73D, 12" Plate. The ring at the top of the metal handle is 2" in diameter. The handle on our set matches exactly the one on a 2-Deck Tid Bit Set in the Washington pattern. The Washington Set AKA Mt. Vernon is pictured in a 1930s catalog.

400/18TB, 3 Hi Snack Rack, $★; Component parts: 400/1F, 5" Bowl; 400/3F, 6" Bowl; 400/5F, 7 1/2" Bowl; Sets with the maple handle as shown in a previous photograph were assembled by Imperial. Shown here is the set with the brass handles, $175-210.

400/73TB, 2-Deck Tid Bit Set, $140-155; component parts: 400/40D, 8" Plate; 400/73D, 12" Plate. The handle on this set is very dark wood. Two of these identical sets have been found, each in a different part of the country. We feel that these sets are after factory sets by a distributor and are not handcrafted.

400/73TB, 2-Deck Tid Bit Set, $★; component parts: 400/40D, 8" Plate; 400/73D, 12" Plate; Maple Handle assembled by Imperial, flat plates. During this research we determined that the bottom plate for the 2-Deck Tid Bit is a 400/73D, 12" Plate. We did not find it as a separate listing for the general line, but this plate was recorded as being made later for Crown Silver Company. NI.

This may be a rather moot point, but we do not believe that the 400/270 and 400/271 were ever offered separately to Imperial's customers; that is, they were never offered as single tid bit plates in the general list of all production items. Instead, these two plates had the 400/270 and 400/271 numbers for identification only in the component parts list. The exception to this would be items sold through the company outlet, the Hay Shed, or during the company's liquidation. In addition, Imperial might have sold the single plates to another company for their use as an after factory product.

The oval top is the most common of the metal top handles. A large circle top was shown in the 1966 catalog, while the metal triangular top handle first appeared in the 1977 catalog and was the latest issue. All of these metal handles are slender. We have seen a few tid bits with ornate handles and believe they are replacement handles.

400/73TB, 2-Deck Tid Bit Set, $140-160; component parts: 400/40D, 8" Plate; 400/73D, 12" Plate. The ring at the top of the metal handle is 1 7/8" diameter. The design of this one and the 400/2701 handle with the oval ring at the top are the same. Both have all the same line detail around the handle and on the spindle. Most likely, the company supplying the handle to Imperial changed the top of the handle sometime during the years.

400/2701, 2-Tier Tid Bit, $60-65. The 400/270, 7 1/2" Tid Bit Plate with hole is the top plate and the 400/271, 10 1/2" Tid Bit Plate with hole is the bottom plate in the 400/2701. This is the set that most collectors are familiar with.

Vases

Vases comprise the largest category of items in the Candlewick pattern; there are thirty-eight vases dating from 1937 to 1969. Only twelve of these were made after 1950. You might find it interesting to know that some bases on vases, tumblers, decanters, and other items are made from the molds used for ash trays, salts, and other bases.

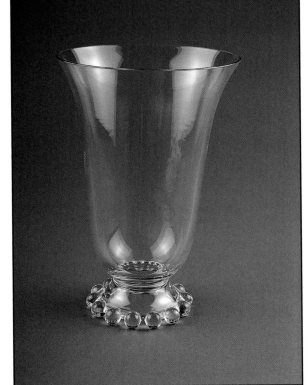

400/21, 8 1/2" Footed Vase, $140-175.

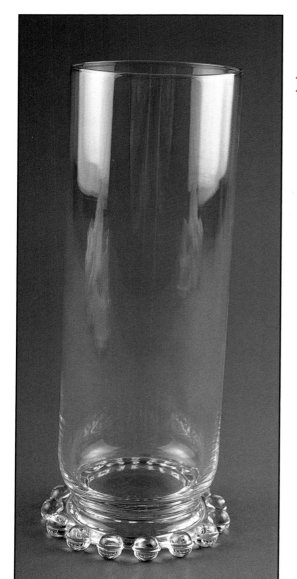

400/22, 10" Vase; vase resembles a giant
400/19 Tumbler, $175-210.

400/25, 3 3/4"-4" Footed Bud Ball Vase, $35-40; from 1948-1950 this vase was listed as the 400/25C. The neck is 3/4" wide. The Vase on the right has the 1 1/4" wide neck and matches the sketch for the Irving W. Rice article under number A-103.

Electro No. 8-C

400/27, 8 1/2" Footed Bud Vase; top edge is ground and polished at factory, Crystal, $245-280.

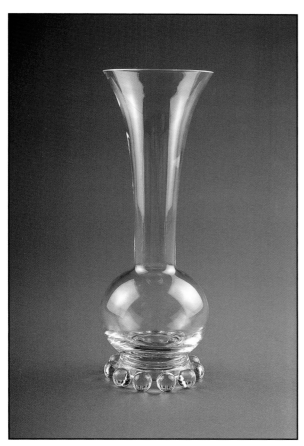

400/28, 8 1/2" Vase. The early version is the straight top. It is difficult to find, $105-140.

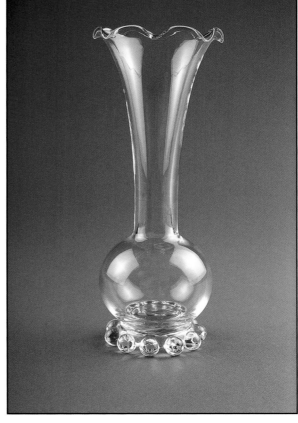

400/28C, 8 1/2" Vase; The crimped top is the later of the two 400/28 vases, $50-75.

400/74J, 7" Lily Bowl, $125-155. This Lily Bowl is 4-toed with ribs and was made from 1937-1941. The ribs were put into a mold to cover the original mold marks.

Be sure to look at the 400/74N, 6 1/2" Lily Bowl in the Undocumented section. It is the only 400/74N Bowl in crystal we have seen, and it is interesting that it does not have the rib marks. This bowl was not listed as being made in crystal for the general line, however it is the shape of the Lily Bowl Imperial produced in black for Butler Brothers. Those bowls did have the rib marks in them. Since the crystal 400/74N has no ribs, it should be dated about 1941. NI.

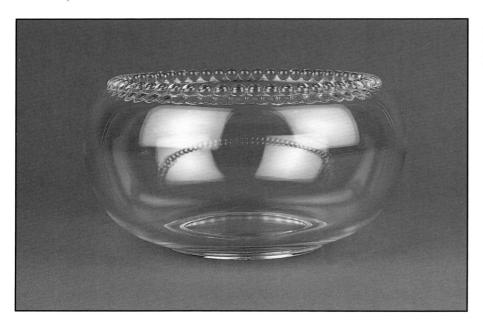

400/75N, 7 1/2" Lily Bowl, $330-385; it has no feet and is a flat bottom. In the few 400/75V Lily Bowls that we have seen, the glass has not been as clear as in other Candlewick pieces.

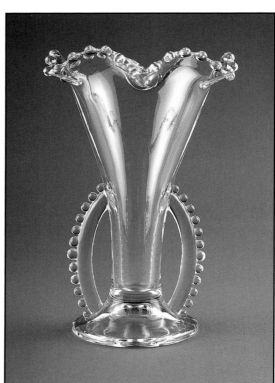

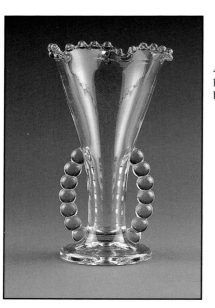

400/87C, 8" Vase, $25-35. There are beads are on the rim and the large bead side handle is curved outward.

400/87C, 8" Vase, $50-60; crimped, beads on rim with small beads outward. This vase does not appear in any catalogs and we could have put it in the Undocumented section. However, we decided to include it here so it can be compared with other versions of the 400/87C. The 400/87R and 400/87F (shown later) with the little beads curved outward are shown only in the 1937 catalog. In the 1939 catalog, the three versions of crimped, fan, and rolled have the large beads. It can therefore be assumed that this 400/87C was made in 1937 or 1938.

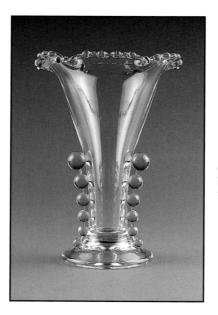

400/87C, 8" Vase, $25-30. There are beads on the rim and the large beads on the side are inward.

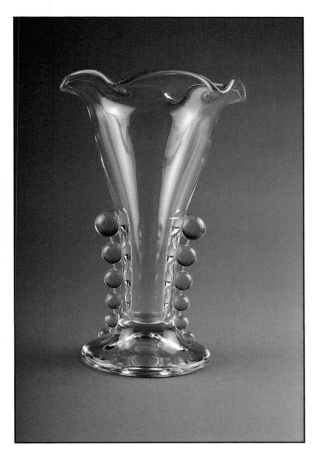

400/87C, 8" Vase, $30-35. There are no beads on the rim and the large beads on the side are inward.

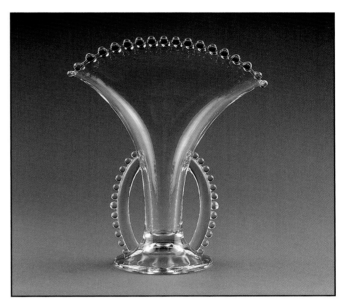

400/87F, 8" Vase, $40-45. This is a fan vase with small beads on a solid handle of glass curved outward.

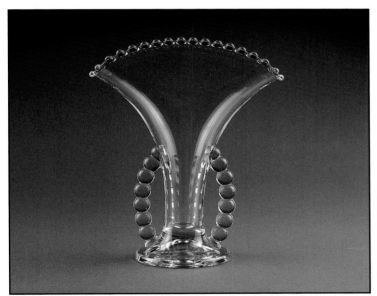

400/87F, 8" Vase, $24-30. Another of the fan vases with large beads outward.

400/87F, 8 1/2" Vase, $24-30. This fan vase has the large beads on the side inward.

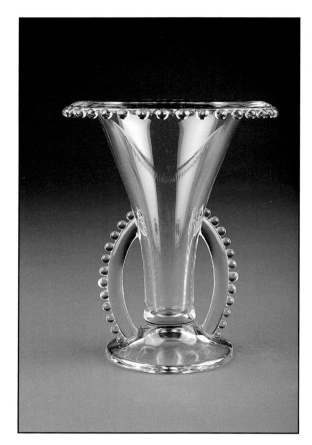

400/87R, 7" Vase, $35-45. Round vase with top rolled over and the small beads outward.

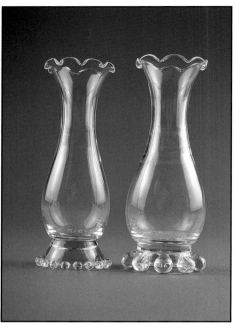

400/107, 5 3/4" Miniature Bud Vase; early version on left with small beads on slightly domed base, $52-60. 400/107, 5 3/4" Miniature Bud Vase; later version on right with large beads on base, $45-50.

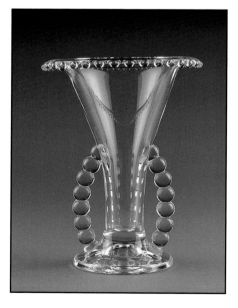

400/87R, 7" Vase, $25-35. Round vase with top rolled over and large beads outward.

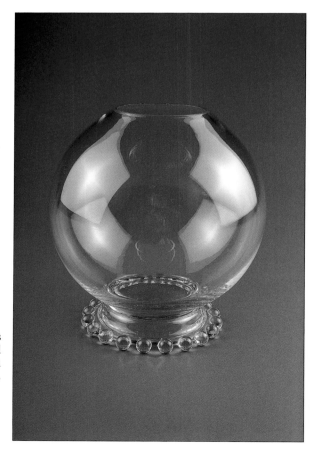

400/132, 7 1/2" Footed Rose Bowl; large beads on the base, $315-335. The top edge was ground and polished during production and is not an indication that it has been repaired.

400/132C, 7 1/4" Footed Rose Bowl, $★; catalog illustration only. The top is a crimped collar with no beads.

400/138B, 6" Footed Vase, $100-115. This vase was made for the Irving W. Rice Company as well as Imperial's general line.

400/143A, 8" Flip Vase; it has a beaded top and is not crimped, $240-260.

400/142K, 7" Rose Bowl, beaded collar, $★; component part of: 400/142K/HL Hurricane.

400/143C, 8" Flip Vase; crimped top, $60-85. Both the 400/143A and 400/143C are in the 1943 Price List.

We could not find any information on the 400/162, 10" Vase except that it is listed in the 1943 Price List. Remembering that Imperial often used its molds for more than one item, we think that we will be on the lookout for a 400/163 Decanter without a stopper. We have heard of collectors finding this decanter without a stopper and now wonder if they were really finding the 400/162 Vase. After all, it is only one number away in the number sequence. No illustration. $★.

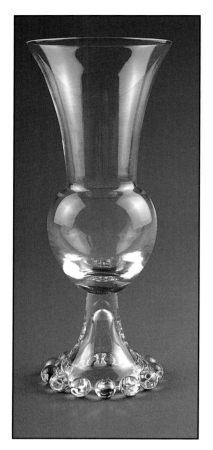

400/185C, 7" Footed Bud Vase, crimped; foot is the same as a 400/18 stem, $185-215. A straight top is shown in the catalogs. However, while several have been found with the crimped top, we are not aware of any with the plain top being found. We have an Imperial factory paper dated June 20, 1948 with sketches of eight vases, and the only 400/185 sketched on that page has a crimped edge. 400/185, 7" Footed Bud Vase (not shown), $★. NI.

400/187, 7" Footed Bud Vase; foot is the same as a 400/18 stem, $175-190.

400/189, 9" Footed Bud Vase, $★. Keep in mind that this one has the 400/190 stem foot. That is a way to help you remember the one you are hunting.

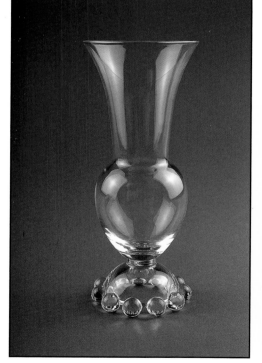

400/186, 7" Footed Bud Vase; straight top, foot is the same as a 400/18 stem, $175-185.

400/188, 7" Footed Ivy Bowl or Brandy, $120-135.

The next three vases are large versions of vases with the 400/18 foot. Of the 400/192, 400/193 and 400/194, the 400/192 seems to be the most difficult to find—though all are difficult to locate. These vases appear larger than they actually measure.

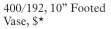

400/192, 10" Footed Vase, $★

400/193, 10" Footed Vase, $★.

400/194, 10" Footed Vase, $★. This is the most available of the three—400/192, 400/193, 400/194. When communicating with fellow collectors, we call these three the ones with the double bulges.

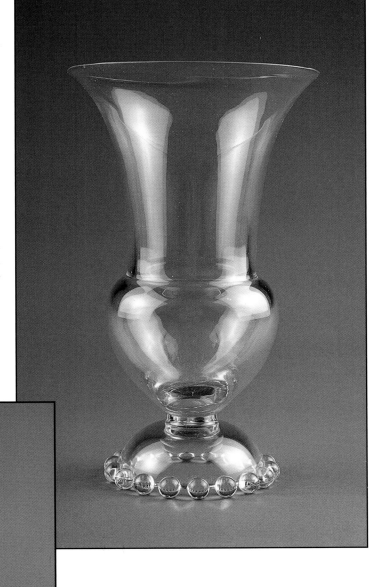

400/196, 2-pc. Epergne Set, $200-225. In catalog illustrations, it looks as if the flower vase has two beads. Some of the large vase inserts have been found with one bead. (All mini vases will be shown in a group with sizes provided.)

400/198, 6" Vase, $325-350; 400/242, 6" Rose Bowl with flower holder insert, $★. The measurements of the flower frog insert are 3 7/8" at the outer edge and 3" at the inner edge. Some inserts found have had eleven and fifteen holes for the flowers. A good way to take the insert out is to turn the vase upside down with the insert in it and then lift up the vase.

400/227, 8 1/2" Handled Vase, $420-475. This is a very difficult one to find. Possibly, the handles did not survive. The top is cut off at a slant and the top edge is fire-polished. We have not found one at any show; ours came to us from a very special collector friend.

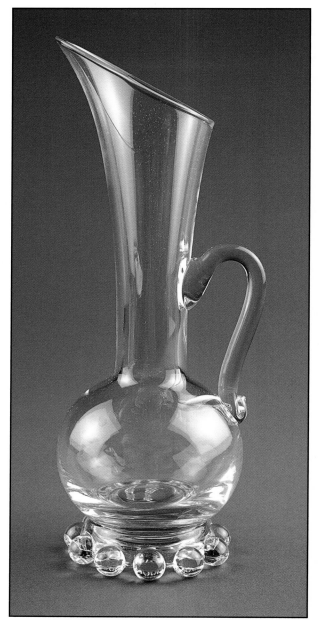

400/287C, 6" Crimped Vase, $45-50.

400/287F, 6" Fan Vase, $45-50.

The number for the 400/40 Miniature Vase covers several different designs of small vases to insert into candleholder cups. Company documentation does not define which size and design the number designates; catalog pictures provide the only clues for collectors. Sometimes when a piece is found with a 400/40 Miniature Vase, the collector or researcher can rely on the source of the item to prove whether or not it is an original combination.

There are two vases to fit the 400/196, 2-pc. Epergne. One is 7 7/8" tall and has two beads above the peg. The other is 7 1/4" tall and has only one bead above the peg. We do not think that the two vases for the 400/196 are referred to as the 400/40 Vase. In the price lists, there is only one number for the set and that is 400/196. We have not found a company description of these vases.

Four different vases can be considered the 400/40 Miniature Vase. The first two are miniature vases with beaded tops and peg bottoms; one is 5 7/8" tall and the other is 4 3/4" tall. The 5 7/8" vase came in our 400/40S and the 4 3/4" one came in our 400/40F. The miniature vases could be found in any of the candleholders.

The 4 3/4" miniature vase with a raised ridge above the peg for extra support when placed into the candleholder has six crimps and no beads on top rim. Our 4 3/4" miniature vase is cut to match the 400/86 Candleholder so there is no question that it is an Imperial miniature vase for the candleholders.

The 4 1/2" miniature vase has eight crimps, a rounded point at the bottom, and no beads on the top rim.

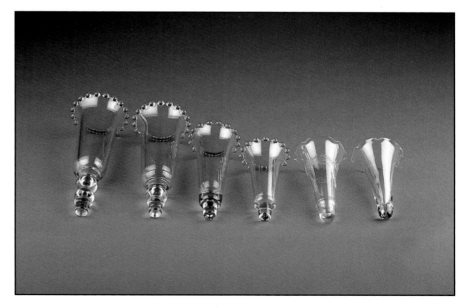

Miniature Vases (left to right): 400/196 Vase, 2-bead, 7 7/8"; 400/196 Vase, 1-bead, 7 1/4"; 400/40V flower candleholder vases with beaded tops, 5 7/8" and 4 3/4"; plain top with a ridge above peg, 4 3/4"; plain top with a round tip, 4 1/2". Price range: $35-60.

Dessert Set, Luncheon Set, Breakfast Set, Junior Place Set

Although all of the Candlewick sets will not be illustrated, they will be listed below to give collectors an idea of what pieces Imperial did combine to be sold as a set. Candlewick was considered an open stock pattern that one could add to as a need arose. A few of these sets were illustrated in catalogs and others were simply listed as sets on price sheets. However, Imperial did package these sets. The first four of the following photographs were illustrated in catalogs.

400/63/104 Chilled Fruit Set, $275-310; component parts: 400/104B, 14" Bowl; 400/63, 8" Ice Tub; 400/139 Ladle AKA 400/255; 400/19 Footed Fruit (8); 400/1D, 6" Plate (8).

400/114A/2, 3-pc. Dessert Set, $545-575; component parts: 400/114A Bowl; 400/255 Ladles AKA 400/139 (2).

400/311, 11-pc. Breakfast Tray Set; component parts: 400/5D, 8" Plate; 400/23B, 5 1/4" Bowl; 400/23D Plate; 400/35 Tea Cup and Saucer; 400/19, 5 oz. Juice; 400/1D Bread and Butter; 400/122 Individual Sugar and Cream; 400/19 Egg Cup. 400/313 Breakfast Set is same as 400/311 with the 400/109 Salt and Pepper added. NP.

400/316, 16-pc. Luncheon Set; component parts: 400/5D, 8" Plates; 400/29/30 Sugar and Cream with Tray; 400/35 Tea Cup and Saucer; 400/68D, 11 1/2" Handled Pastry Tray. NP

Junior Place Setting, original box, $550-650. "Proudly created by Fathers and Mothers who produce fine handmade Crystal at Imperial Glass Corporation." This set was never in a catalog or price list but was offered by company memorandum. Component parts of the set are: 400/3D, 7" Salad Plate; 400/42B, 4 3/4" Bowl, 2-handled; 400/77 Cup and Saucer; 400/190, 5 oz. Wine.

The following sets were listed in Imperial's price lists. We will not show photographs nor give prices but will include contents of the sets because some collectors are interested in what pieces Imperial included in their original sets. The luncheon sets began in 1937 and the breakfast set began in 1943. The breakfast set and several different size luncheon sets stayed in the line through 1951. There were some slight variations in numbers that we are not going to list. The 400/13 Luncheon set in 1937 was the same as the 400/135 15-pc. Luncheon Set.

400/135, 15-pc.; 21-pc.; 27-pc.; Luncheon Set for four, six, and eight: 400/5D, 8" Plate; 400/13D, 12" Plate; 400/35 Cup and Saucer; 400/31 Sugar and Cream. NP.

400/177, 15-pc.; 21-pc.; 27-pc.; Luncheon Set for four, six, and eight: 400/7D, 9" Plate; 400/17D, 14" Plate; 400/35 Cup and Saucer; 400/31 Sugar and Cream. NP.

400/322, 22-pc. Luncheon Set for six: 400/30 Sugar and Cream; 400/29 Tray; 400/68D Handled Pastry Tray; 400/35 Cup and Saucer; 400/5D, 8" Plate. NP.

400/328, 28-pc. Luncheon Set for eight: 400/2930 Sugar, Cream, Tray Set; 400/68D Handled Pastry Tray; 400/35 Tea Cup and Saucer; 400/5D, 8" Salad Plate. NP.

400/51340 (15348), 13-pc. Salad Set: 400/5D, 8" Salad Plate; 400/13F, 10" Bowl; 400/13D, 12" Plate; 400/40 Mayonnaise Bowl and Plate; 615 Ladle. NP.

Part III

Undocumented, Reproductions, Similarities, and Rarities

Undocumented

This section brings to mind stories about items that have been credited to workers who made them without permission and took them home. Former employees, however, have noted that making such "lunch box" items was not a common practice. Certainly any item as large as some of those shown here could not have been carried out in a lunch box. We have also been told by employees that certain Imperial workers had permission to make or decorate special items. Often the individuals in authority would ask for an item or a decoration to be done differently for a special purpose.

We would like to help dispel the idea that workers made a practice of creating items and taking them home without permission. Some whimsies that we have seen surely were made when a production item failed to meet required standards and so the item was changed into something else. One such item was in the Cape Cod line. It was a piece that was originally designed to be a basket. However, when something went wrong, the worker (probably on a whim) bent the handle over backwards to form a mug handle. We know of two of these items. Perhaps they were made deliberately, but that does not mean that they were "lunch box" items.

It is difficult to know if some of the items here were research and development pieces or if they were indeed just whimsies. We believe that some were definitely intended as production items but were never put into a catalog or were made only for a special order. The undocumented items will not be priced because there is no activity on them.

400/19, 3-3 1/2 oz. Cocktail on left; 400/19, 2 oz. Cocktail on right, $★. The 400/19, 2 oz. Cocktail has been undocumented for several years. Just recently, we found this 2 oz. Cocktail on an undated catalog page. Other items on the page place the 2 oz. Cocktail in the mid-to-late 1950s. It is shown here with the 400/19, 3-3 1/2 oz. Cocktail for size comparison. NI.

400/107 Vase. This vase without the usual crimped top does not appear in any catalog, but it is on a sketch sheet with other documented vases. The paper, labeled "New Vases," was dated June 1948. Perhaps this sheet of sketches showing new vases accounts for this rare find with the straight top and large beads on the base.

Would you have thought that a Candlewick Knife, Fork, and Spoon were actually sketched as possible production items? This sketch was in factory records but was not on the "new" list that accompanied the sketches. The factory note read: "Glass Handled Silverware. Two Handle sizes will fit all Shapes: Large—Soup Spoon, Knife, and Fork: Small—Tea Spoon, Salad Fork." Do you suppose the company decided that a glass knife and fork would not be acceptable eating utensils? We thought every collector would enjoy seeing this sketch, although we suggest you do not waste your time dreaming about finding any. (Sketch has been enhanced.)

400/19 Handled Mug, $★. Several of these mugs have been bought by collectors. Ours is a 400/19 Tumbler with an applied handle and is one of six that were auctioned at a former employee's estate sale in 1991. It is our understanding that these were feasibility items. A feasibility item is one designed and made by a company to test the potential reception of the product. Sometimes the company would give these items to employees to see what they thought about them; other times the items might be given to friends to gauge their reaction. This particular item did not make it to the general line offered to the public.

400/?? Relish or Candy, $★. This undocumented item was bought in the factory area. It is designed to support a lid but if a lid were placed on it, there would be little room to allow for storage of candy or relish. This item definitely fits the idea of a research and development item. NI.

400/74N, 6 1/2" Lily Bowl, $★. This number is not in Imperial's catalogs nor in the price lists of crystal items. However, this shape is on the list of black decorated items made for Butler Brothers in 1937. Those early black bowls had ribs while this one does not, so we believe it would have to have been made later, maybe about 1941. The 400/75N was in the 1941 Catalog and had no ribs so that may be the approximate date for this 400/74N, also. NI.

400/???, 8 1/2" 3-toed Graduated Bead Bowl, $★. Note the "unique" divider in the bottom. Without the divider in this bowl the number would be 400/182. Speculation has run the gamut of possibilities on the purpose of this item but no one can figure out a plausible use. We know of two other of these items so at least it is not one of a kind.

400/67B, 9" Fruit Bowl, $★; The shape of this bowl is more round than the usual shape, which is flared outward at the top.

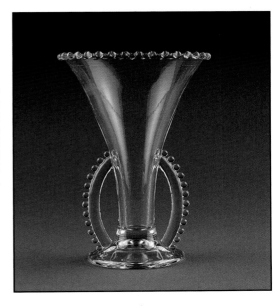

400/87, 8" Vase, $56-63. This vase is not in any catalog, but we do know of others. We are putting the date at approximately 1937. It is either the earliest example or else it came out of the mold in this shape and was not finished with either the crimped edge, the fan shape, or the rolled edge. We have other Imperial items about which a worker told us: "they came out of the mold in this shape and were not bloomed out." Although undocumented, several of these vases have been found so it is fair to suggest a price based on what collectors have paid.

400/67E Banana Stand (right), shown with the 400/103E Banana Stand for comparison. We gave this piece a number based on the mold number of the original item and added the E to indicate turned up sides. This item has been referred to as a 1-bead banana stand and would have been made from a 400/67D Cake Stand mold. It may be a whimsey. We have not heard of other 1-bead banana stands. It has more graceful lines than the general line 400/103E Banana Stand. $★.

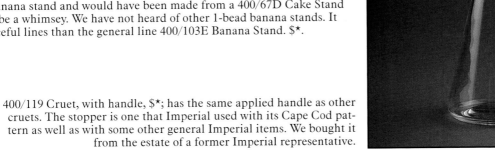

400/119 Cruet, with handle, $★; has the same applied handle as other cruets. The stopper is one that Imperial used with its Cape Cod pattern as well as with some other general Imperial items. We bought it from the estate of a former Imperial representative.

400/119 Cruet, $★. This pair of cruets is also combined with the Imperial stopper used in the Cape Cod pattern and with some other Imperial items, but does not have handles. Another pair of the same cruets has also been found. Whether they were ever intended for the general Candlewick line is unknown, but they are of interest to collectors; decorator unknown.

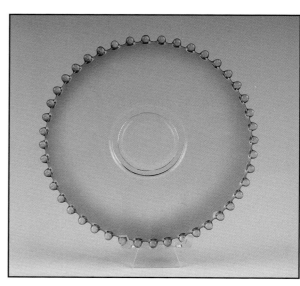

400/23D, 7"-7 1/2" Plate with seat, blue sprayed edge, $★. We found no paper information on this item, but we have been told that Candlewick blanks were sold to a New York decorating company for this type of decoration; decorator unknown.

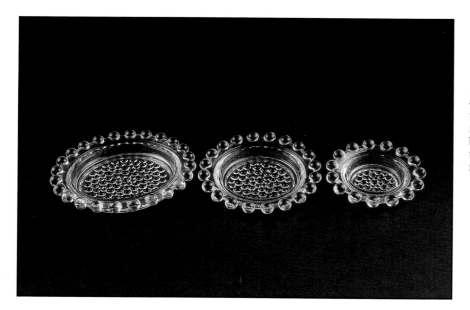

400/450 Ash Tray Set, $★. Here is a set of ash trays that collectors readily accept as Candlewick but so far the set with the bubbles in the bottom has not been documented by Imperial records. Perhaps they were made for a private customer or maybe for the restaurant trade.

400/150, 6" Ash Tray, $★. This was an R and D (research and development) item. Imperial was trying to design a treatment for an ash tray that would tie in with the Russell Wright tumblers Imperial was also producing. The treatment is not very appealing and is even less appealing in this item, which has imperfections in the forming of the ash tray. We describe it as a waffle in which the batter did not get to the edges. It was given to us by an Imperial employee who had it under the sink as a soap dish.

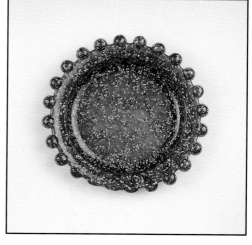

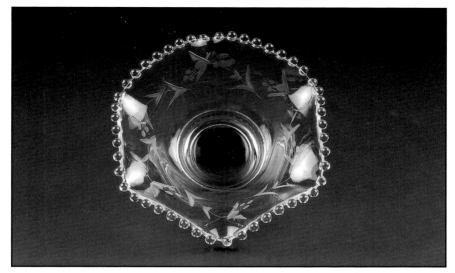

Crimped Bowl, 6", $★. This is the bowl to a mayonnaise set on a 400/23 Plate (with a marie). Both have the "Fuchsia" cut. Since it has a marie and came with a plate that also had a marie, we know this places it in an early period (plate not shown). Also, this could be the blank for the 400/40C, 6" Bowl for Crown Silver Company. This cut is on some of the 400/74SC and others in that early group.

This might not truly be an undocumented item, but it is interesting so it will be included here. This set was found during the liquidation of Imperial. The glass bowls were wrapped in tissue and in a box without the wooden handle. (The handle was handcrafted by the owner.) It is speculated that the set was drilled to become a large tid bit, perhaps for a window or similar display. The bowls are the 400/13F, 10" Float Bowl; 400/75F, 11" Float Bowl; and the 400/92F Float Bowl. The smaller bowl has a large circle bottom and the middle and largest bowls each have the small circle bottom. The standard three tier tid bit sets all have the large circle bottoms. $★.

400/133, 5" Ash Tray and 400/150, 6" Ash Tray combined to form a small 2-Tier Tid Bit. This item is not listed in any of Imperial's price lists. It may be an "after factory item" made from glass parts sold to a private customer. Several of these have been found, which seems to indicate that they were sold by a distributor. Besides the metal handle as shown here, some have had a glass rod for the handle topped with a glass marble.

Here are two very special items of Candlewick in milk glass. Both items are made from Candlewick molds. These items are not documented and were not production items. Remember, if slag is considered Candlewick, then certainly these items are Candlewick.

400/109 Individual Salt and Pepper, $★. This set of milk glass Candlewick was bought at the National Imperial Glass Collectors' Society Auction. We believe that any color of Candlewick that Imperial made from a Candlewick mold should be considered as Candlewick. As we have stated previously, if slag is accepted as Candlewick then milk glass should be accepted also. The 400/109 Individual Salt and Pepper and the 400/240F, 6" Peg Nappy in the next picture first appeared in our book Milk Glass, Imperial Glass Corporation (Schiffer Publishing, 2001).

400/240F, 6" Peg Nappy, $★. This special Milk Glass Candlewick item was bought at the factory during liquidation of the Imperial Glass Corporation. Other items made in milk glass are the 400/74SC, 4-toed Bowl and the 400/67D Low Cake Stand.

400/??? This tri-stem goblet is another item that needs to be mentioned. We have not found a number for this item and have not found it listed in the 1950 price list, where some of the other tri-stem items were found. The illustration shown here is from the Imperial files. We do have a photograph of five of these stems that we took at the 1983 NIGCS Convention. However, this drawing is of more interest than our photograph. The owner of those five goblets was one of the management group who was brought to the factory during the final stages of trying to keep Imperial in business. We were shown the goblets and the owner suggested that we take one to the 1983 NIGCS Candlewick Seminar. A few of these stems are known to exist. $★.

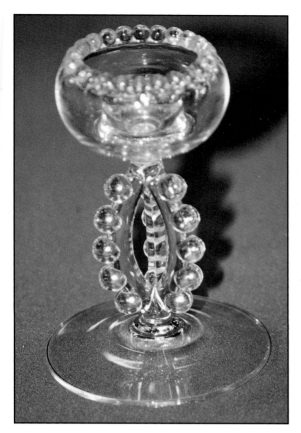

The drawing shown here is from the Imperial files and is one of several designs suggested to be made with the tri-stem for addition to the regular line. We believe that the production line 400/224 Candleholder is the result of this drawing. In 1995, we were offered one of a pair of these candleholders, but at that time we declined the offer. However, we were given permission to photograph the tri-stem candleholder as well as the 400/178 Candleholder base with the circle of beads to support the shade (see page 117). As you can see, the difference between the sketch and the actual item is that in the actual item there is a small glass bowl surrounding the candle cup. On the cataloged 400/224, that small bowl is flattened around the candle cup. It is possible that the finisher just cupped the glass up and around the candle cup on the one in the photograph here. However, we believe that this is the way this item was formed in the mold and that no hand finishing was done to the candleholder. Therefore, this might be better labeled as a whimsey. $★.

In the late 1980s, we bought a 12" plate with a marie and turned up sides. On first glance, it resembled the muffin tray but had no handles. Could it be the banana stand with no stand? No, the banana stand does not have a 4" center circle and a marie. This is one of the things you buy and try to figure out later. A few minutes after purchase we decided it must be the 400/73/0 Basket without a handle. . . it was inexpensive and it was interesting. It can be used for muffins without the fear of breaking an expensive muffin tray! We love it.

We purchased this 12" plate with a marie and turned up sides in the late 1980s. It is the 400/73/0 Basket without a handle, $★.

Reproductions

By way of definition, reproductions are copies or duplicates that are produced by a new owner using the same molds that were used to make the originals. In other words, if a company uses molds from another company to produce items, they are reproducing that item. If a company uses its own molds to issue new items at a later date (in the original or different colors), the items are reissues. The ongoing production of molds over the years is not a reissue.

We can expect to see many Candlewick reproductions as the years pass by. Several hundred of Imperial's Candlewick molds are owned by other glass companies and private parties. For example, Mirror Images owns a large number of Candlewick molds. They were reproduced by Dalzell Viking Glass Company from 1987 until it went out of business in 1998. During this period, Dalzell made a great deal of Candlewick. It was made in crystal as was that made by the Imperial Glass Corporation. Dalzell also made Candlewick in many other colors and treatments, which included cobalt, black, evergreen, ruby, cranberry, frosted pastel colors, gold beads, silver beads, confetti, and numerous other colors. Dalzell marked some of its glass with an acid etched Dalzell or DX for the seconds. Not all items are marked and the mark can be easily removed, however.

During the late 1980s and the 1990s, Dalzell Viking reproduced between twenty and thirty different items from the Imperial Candlewick molds. The reproduction measurements are not always the same as the Imperial measurements, so the corresponding Candlewick mold numbers may not always have the same measurements. Use this list only as a guide. The following items were made in crystal by Dalzell Viking:

400/1D, 6" Plate
400/5D, 8" Plate
400/5F, 6 1/2" Bowl
400/7F, 8 1/2" Bowl
400/10D, 10" Plate
400/13D, 12" Charger Plate
400/35, Tea Cup and Saucer
400/42B, 5" Two-Handled Bowl
400/42D, 5" Two-Handled Plate
400/52B, 6" Two-handled Bowl
400/62D, 8" Two-Handled Plate
400/75B, 10 1/2" Bowl
400/75D, 12" Torte Plate
400/112, 10" 5-Part Relish
400/80, Candleholder with flat base. (This item is marked with MI and shown on page 157.)

In addition to the previous crystal items, the square bowls, pastry tray, deviled egg tray, vases, quarter pound butter, small compote and perhaps others were made in colors and treatments listed in the earlier text. Generally, these reproductions are often heavier than their Imperial Candlewick counterparts. In addition, the glass often tends to have an oily feel.

Mosser Glass Company, of Cambridge, Ohio, also produces glass from Imperial Candlewick molds. Those items are made for Rosso Wholesale Glass Company. Rosso is a private glass distributor who sells to independent retailers. With the exception of cobalt blue, these items are not made in original Imperial Candlewick colors, which makes them easier to recognize. The items made by Mosser are not marked.

Boyd Art Glass Company, also of Cambridge, Ohio, owns several Imperial molds, including sixteen Candlewick molds. They have produced items from these molds in colors that were never used by Imperial. Also, Boyd marks the items they make so this should present no problems to collectors.

Some collectors may erroneously think a candle bowl made by Boyd from the top part of the 400/224 Candleholder is a similarity, rather than a reproduction from an Imperial mold. The reason for this error is that some collectors simply do not recognize the shape of the 400/224 candle cup as it looks when taken out of the mold and without any hand shaping.

The following is a list of Candlewick molds owned by Boyd Crystal Art Glass, Cambridge, Ohio:

400/19	Ash Tray, 2 3/4"	400/134/1	Ash Tray
400/33	Jelly	400/170	Candleholder
400/42B	4 1/2" 2-Handled	400/172	Heart Nut, 4 1/2"
Bowl		400/173	Heart, 5 1/2"
400/64	Nut or Sugar Dip	400/174	Heart, 6 1/2"
400/78	Coaster	400/176	Square Ash Tray
400/96T	Tray, 5"	400/224	Candle Bowl
400/118	Ash Tray	400/287C	Bud Vase, 6"
400/134	Cigarette Box		

It would take another book to thoroughly research, list, and show the items made by these companies and the colors that are possible—we leave that to someone else to write. We have aimed this research project at Imperial Candlewick so we will touch only briefly on reproductions and similarities. Throughout our twenty-five years of collecting, we have bought a few reproductions in order to have material for programs we have presented. It is important for collectors to study all information possible and learn about these reproductions, but we feel that it is far more important to learn everything possible about Imperial Candlewick. Remember—if you know what is correct, then what is not correct will pose little problem.

400/77AD After Dinner Cup and Saucer in Alexanderite by Dalzell Viking.

400/40/0, 6" Basket in Alexanderite by Dalzell Viking.

400/63B, 4 1/2" Compote by Imperial (left), for comparison with the 400/63B, 4 1/2" compote in Azure Satin by Dalzell Viking (right).

400/35 Tea Cup. Imperial Cup on the left; Dalzell Viking cup on the right.

400/80 Candleholder. Shown on the right is the Imperial candleholder with the domed foot. The candleholder on the left has a flat foot and is marked with an MI, the mark for Mirror Images.

400/33 Jelly in pink with black lettering, made by Boyd Art Glass in 1999 as souvenir for the Michiana Association of Candlewick Collectors (MACC).

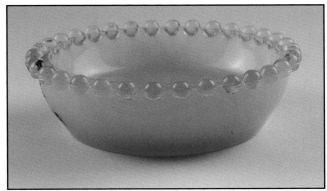

400/170 Candleholder; Boyd Art Glass.

400/176 Brown Slag Ash Tray; 400/19, 2 1/4"
Ash Tray; Boyd Art Glass Company.

400/64 Nut Cup, souvenirs for the National Imperial Glass Collectors' Society;
Boyd's Crystal Art Glass. All collectors will be grateful to John Boyd for supply-
ing this list of color names for the 400/64 Nut Cup souvenirs from the NIGCS
Conventions:

1992	Cardinal Red (unfired)
1993	Waterloo
1994	Vanilla Coral
1995	Sunkiste Carnival
1996	Capri Blue
1997	Cobalt Carnival
1998	Moss Green
1999	Nutmeg Carnival
2000	Millennium Surprise
2001	Dark Purple Fizz
2002	Milk White

Boyd Crystal Art Glass logo. This mark is on
all of Boyd's glass. It will have marks at the
points that designate the date of production.
The diamond shape logo shown represents the
years 1978-1983. For every five years after that
a mark is added at one point of the diamond.
The fourth mark around the diamond started
with 1998.

Similarities

We are using the term similarity to mean an item that resembles something else in appearance and may have characteristics very much like the item with which it is being compared. It seems that almost any glass item with beads or small balls decorating it is considered a Candlewick similarity.

During our years of collecting, we have bought some interesting similarities to use with program presentations. However, we have always urged collectors to study books and learn what can be found with regard to Imperial Candlewick. It has never been our intention to acquire so many similarities that they could become a collection unto themselves.

One especially interesting similarity is a sugar that is so much like Candlewick that we have been trying to determine if it is an Imperial product, even though it is not Candlewick. It is the same size and shape as the 400/31 Sugar. There are two differences: neither the handle nor the foot is beaded, and there is one bead on the stem instead of the usual concave stem with vertical ridges as on the 400/31 Sugar. We feel strongly that this could be an Imperial Sugar and perhaps a forerunner to the Candlewick pattern. It seems to us that this goes with the 400/116 Salt and Pepper with the 1-bead stem.

In trying to identify this sugar, we looked to an Imperial punch set that does not have the usual Candlewick beads on the edge and on the cup handles. That punch set, #85, is the size and shape of the Candlewick 400/20 Punch Set. We have tried—unsuccessfully, however—to learn if the sugar could be from that #85 line and if the 400/116 Salt and Pepper could have come from the same line. We are showing the sugar here so that you will be aware of it and know that it was not in the Candlewick line.

The makers of most of the items in the following three photographs are unknown to most of us. The important thing to know is that these items are not Imperial Candlewick.

This is not Candlewick, but we think it might be Imperial. The sugar is the exact size and shape of the 400/31 Candlewick Sugar.

Here is a replication of the 400/150 Ash Tray. The imposter on the right is 6" in diameter, but the depth of the ash tray is less than that of the authentic one. The tell tale difference is a tiny indented ridge around the outside edge of the inside bottom of the ash tray. As the owner said, "What is this indention for—ashes would only fall into it." The poor quality is also a tell tale sign—it is not a Candlewick item by Imperial Glass.

This clock with its double row of beads often causes concern for Candlewick collectors. Again, we do not know the company that produced this clock, but it is not Candlewick and not made by Imperial Glass Corporation.

Here are two more small glasses whose origin is unknown, but they are not Imperial Candlewick.

1950/196, 2-pc. Epergne Set, with ridges on outside and leaf design on inside. It has no beads on flower vase. 1950/196, 2-pc. Epergne Set without outside ridges and without a leaf design on inside. There are beads on flower vase. The epergne in the back has the Doeskin finish. $80-100.

The following group of photographs show pieces of Imperial Milk Glass that have the same kind of beads so often described as Candlewick. Imperial did not refer to these pieces as Candlewick, but we and other collectors do like to add them to our Candlewick collection.

1950/170 Low Candleholder, $20-25; 1950/75D, 11" Buffet Plate, $65-75; 1950/75C, 11" Crimped Fruit Bowl, $75-95; design inside the bowl and plate and on top of the candleholder.

1950/75H, 9" Heart, $100-150; 1950/75F, 11" Coupe Apple Bowl, $75-95; leaf design inside both items.

1950/103, 10" Footed Fruit Bowl (back), $60-75; 1950/45 Jelly Compote (left), ribs on outside bowl and leaf design inside, $35-40; 1950/45 Jelly Compote (right), no ribs on outside and no design inside, $35-40.

1950/103, 10" Footed Fruit Bowl, Forget-Me-Not Blue (front), $75-85;
1950/103, 10" Footed Fruit Bowl, Midwest Custard (back), $70-80.

Sooner or later, nearly every Candlewick collector hears about a Boopie stem. Boopie was made by Anchor Hocking and preceded Imperial's 400/18 line. There are several different sizes of Boopie stems. All have the safe edge feature that is found on an inexpensive glass—it is a thicker rounded edge at the top edge of the glass. Boopie has beads around the base of the foot, close together but not touching. There is a raised rounded ridge radiating from the beads to the center of the foot to the point that the foot attaches to the stem. Make yourself aware of this item that confuses so many new Candlewick collectors.

Imported similarities. On the left is a 4 1/2" bowl, labeled Bohemia; it was bought in 1991 in a store in Paris and still has the label on it. On the right is a 6" bowl from Munich. It has a ground and polished ridge on the bottom. It too was bought in a shop in 1991. Knowing of our interest in Candlewick, a friend saw these on a trip to Europe and brought them to us for study.

Mayonnaise Set with an acid mark: Tchecoslovaque. We were told this was the French spelling of Czechoslovakia. It consists of a 5 1/4" bowl and 7" plate, similar to the 400/23. The set has a seamless form to it. It is gently rounded rather than having a bottom edge.

Flat Tray, beads touch, 8 1/2"; unknown origin.

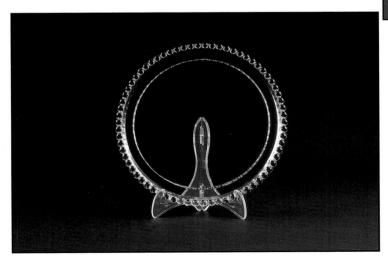

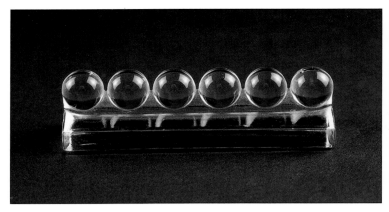

Knife rest. We bought this because it is the closest thing to Imperial Candlewick that we have ever seen. We saw our first one in the early 1980s in the Midwest. In 1990, we saw a set of eight that were part of a European Knife Rest collection. We bought one to have for future reference. We still have not learned anything about this item. It must belong in the European similarities.

These two small tumblers have caused new collectors some concern. They are not Candlewick and are of unknown origin. In the tumbler on the left, note that the beads are tucked under the bottom more than with Candlewick. In the tumbler on the right, note that the beads are larger than the beads on similar Candlewick items.

Left to right: 3-toed, 6 1/4" bowl, unknown origin; coaster with raised flowers, marked German Democratic Republic; square 5 1/2" bowl; unknown origin.

Frosted Tray, 8" with large beads. This item was made in China and was for sale in a large retail store for $3.95 in 1999.

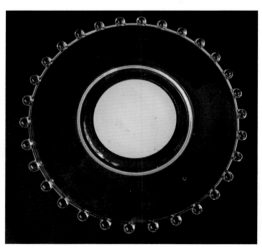

Above and right: At last we have labels to give us information on these two items that have been mysteries for so long.

162

Bell and Wine; these two items could be Imperial. They were in a large Candlewick collection and the owner bought these glasses at the same time as she bought her Candlewick. She was told at the store that they were Candlewick. The quality is the same and the shape of the bowl is the same shape as the 400/190 stems. At a recent NIGCS employee program a former worker told of an incident when, during production, the wrong stem was put onto the wrong bowl. Could this be a production mistake?

782   5¼ in. Oval
Twin Candleholder

The Imperial #782 Candleholder was first produced without the beads on the outside edge (#169) in the late 1930s. We do not have a documented date for the re-designed candleholder with the beads, but it was in the early 1940s. This date was established by study of the other items on the loose catalog page where the #782 with beads was shown. We could never find the #782 listed as Candlewick in any of our factory papers.

Clear Cake Stand; unknown origin. In addition to the crystal cake stand, we have seen a light green; we think it might be a recent production.

10" Plate on inexpensive shiny metal. This plate has the wavy edge that is the characteristic of imported items. We feel just a little hesitant to put this in the 100% similarities section but feel this is the most appropriate place.

Milk Glass does not usually cause concern, but we are including these items just in case the question arises. These pieces are from the Con-Cora line made by Consolidated Lamp and Glass Company in the 1950s and can be found with and without the decoration. The cake stand is two pieces plus the bearing. The bearing is similar in design to the Candlewick 400/1503 Lazy Susan bearing, but the Candlewick bearing is smaller than the Consolidated one and they are not interchangeable.

Rarities

Collectors, particularly new collectors, like to know what pieces are considered hard to find, rare, and very rare. As you review the lists below, remember that these are all relative words—relative to what you are comparing them with. To beginning collectors, all items might be considered rare. To advanced collectors, just the items not in their collections might be considered rare. So just keep in mind that much depends on the person who is designating the category.

Very Rare

400/15	All Tumblers
400/18TB	3 Tier Tid Bit, Cupped, Wooden Handle
400/26	Crimped Shade
400/32	Lightolier Hurricane
400/48F	8" Compote, 5-Bead Stem
400/73C	10" Crimped Bowl
400/73DC	12" Crimped Plate
400/74N	6"-6 1/2" Lily Bowl
400/82	Bottle with Handle
400/82/2	Cordial Bottle, No Handle
400/113A	10" 2-Handled Bowl
400/129	6" Urn Candleholder
400/132C	Rose Bowl Crimped
400/133	5" Ash Tray, Milk Glass, Shield
400/137	Oval Footed Compote
400/145E	11 1/2" Tray, Handles Up
400/158	7" Partitioned Candy
400/178	8 1/2" Candleholder
400/178	Hurricane
400/185	7" Vase, Straight Top
400/187	7" Vase
400/192	10" Vase
400/193	10" Vase
400/195	All Glasses
400/204	Butter 'n Jam Set
400/209	Relish
400/210	Punch Base
400/213	10" 4 Part. Relish
400/222	8" Handled Bon Bon, Tri-Stem
400/223	12" Handled Cake Tray, Tri-Stem
400/225	Goblet, Tri-Stem
400/22?	Cake Stand, Tall, Tri-Stem (if ever made)
400/227	8 1/2" Handled Vase
400/264	Hurricane, Tri-Stem
400/496	Mayo Set
400/680	Twin Hurricane
400/1753	3 pc. Hurricane
400/2696	Hospitality Set
3800	Brandy
400/??	Slender, Long 3-Bead Spoon

Rare

400/17TB	2 Tier Tid Bit, Cupped, Wooden Handle
400/18	Decanter
400/19	Egg Cup

400/38	Oval Salad Plate
400/73TB	2 Tier Tid Bit, Flat, Wooden Handles
400/75N	7 1/2" Lily Bowl
400/76	Hurricane
400/92B	12" Bowl
400/103E	Banana Stand
400/104B	14" Bowl
400/113E	14" Crimped Plate
400/114A	10" Divided Bowl
400/127B	7 1/2" Console Base
400/139	Covered Snack Jar
400/140	Beaded Foot Candy
400/142K/HL	Hurricane
400/145H	Muffin Tray
400/148	Condiment Tray, Indents
400/150	Ash Tray, Ritz Blue, Eagle/Stars
400/155	Lightolier Part with Eagle
400/189	9" Vase
400/194	10" Vase
400/201	Handled Heart
400/214	Covered Dish
400/216	Covered Dish, Partitioned
400/277	Salad Dressing Bottle
400/280	Candleholders, 1-Bead
400/330	Syrup Pitcher
400/655	Candy Tower, Charcoal
400/656	Candy Box, Charcoal
400/1752	Prism Hurricane

Hard to Find

400/18	Parfait
400/18	Juice
400/26	Hurricane
400/40	Miniature Vases
400/51M	Card Tray
400/68F	Fruit Tray
400/111	Tête-à-Tête Tray
400/124A	11" Oval Bowl
400/125A	11" Partitioned Oval Bowl
400/126	Bouillon Cup
400/149F	8" Cupped Mint Tray
400/179	Bell
400/139/2	Family Punch Bowl
400/175	6 1/2" Candle Holder, Tall 3-Bead
400/186	7" Vase
400/207	3-toed Candleholder
400/243	Sauce Bowl
400/244	5 pc. Hostess Helper
400/245	Square Candy
400/255	Small Ladle
400/260	Candy
400/440	4" Ash Tray, Ruby, V
3400	Finger Bowl
3800	Finger Bowl
4000	Knife

Closing Thoughts

This work is the culmination of twenty-five years of collecting and researching Candlewick. Candlewick was the true beginning of our glass collecting. Many of you know that we first wrote on Imperial Cape Cod but that was only because we knew that others were already working on Candlewick research. While we did not begin collecting Candlewick until 1978, our love of Candlewick began in 1948 when it became our wedding pattern.

We recognize and recommend the books on Candlewick written by earlier authors: Virginia Scott and Mary Wetzel-Tomalka. Occasionally our dates, measurements, or descriptions may not be the same as theirs but this would be due to each of us having different records to interpret and bring to you in our own written form. Our facts are not to say "these are right" or "those are wrong," but rather that this is what we have composed from our interpretation of the records that we have.

The words are ours unless noted otherwise and the facts are from Imperial Glass Corporation. All information compiled is from factory paper and photographs, personal collections, pictures and observations—none is based on hearsay. We appreciate the permission granted from Lancaster Colony, the last owner of the assets of Imperial, for the use and publication of photographs and documents. With permission from Oneida, we are pleased to be able to share an Oneida advertisement showing the combination of a product of that company and Imperial Glass Corporation.

On a totally personal note, I would like to acknowledge that this project would never have reached this conclusion without the constant help of my husband. He assumed many tasks apart from the book project that allowed me to focus on details that only one person could accomplish. Without hesitation he juggled the equipment for the massive number of photographs necessary for this book, helped build charts, organized slides, hunted through factory papers, and followed up on "go get." He has checked and re-checked the position of the slides. More than all of that, he has been patient, listened to all ideas, and offered suggestions. Some have wondered how two people could author a book, but there is much more than just the words on paper.

According to Samuel Johnson, "What is written without effort is generally read without pleasure." We can say with all sincerity that this book was written with very much effort! It took a little reorganizing to present the total story of Candlewick in two books, but here it is. We hope that you learn from and enjoy the outcome.

Closing Thoughts for Revised Second Edition

It is with a sense of gratitude that we thank the collectors of Imperial Candlewick for making necessary a second edition of Candlewick: The Crystal Line. Without your enthusiastic acceptance of our book, this update would not have been needed.

G/777/3 Black Suede Bookend Base, Gold Trimmed, with burnished gold eagle, 1943; Imperial Glass Corporation.

We have added some new photos to this edition, as well as measurements for use in comparison of items that collectors often inquire about. Imperial advertising and original company photographs always add interest, especially when they show much admired pieces of Candlewick. No newly documented pieces have been found since the first edition was printed, but we are sure collectors will enjoy the sketch showing a Candlewick knife, fork, and spoon. Can you imagine those even being considered as possibilities?

New collectors often think Candlewick prices are unreasonably high, while seasoned collectors worry that prices are lower today. Remember that often we hear only about the unusually high price or incredibly low price. Adjustments to the prices in this book were made in accord with information that was shared with us. Be armed with knowledge and enjoy what you collect.

If you find a mistake in a book, as you very well may, remember that mistakes are evidence of someone trying to accomplish something...so just enjoy the fruits of their labor. (Do let us know, however, if there's something in this volume that should be corrected in the next edition!)

It has been great to share our interest in Candlewick with others. Knowing that collectors have enjoyed, used, and benefited from Candlewick: The Crystal Line has been a wonderful reward for our efforts.

Bibliography

A Consumer and Retail Guide to Handcrafted Glassware, Imperial booklet, Imperial Glass Corp., Bellaire, Ohio 43906.

Garrison, Myrna and Bob. Imperial Candlewick, Little Known Facts. Self published, 1999.

Imperial Factory Papers, Catalogs, Price Guides, and Photographs. 1904-1984.

Wetzel-Tomalka, Mary. Candlewick The Jewel of Imperial. Marceline, Missouri: Walsworth Publishing Company. 1995.

Scott, Virginia R. The Collector's Guide to Imperial Candlewick. Athens, Georgia, 1980.

Resources

National Imperial Glass Collectors' Society
P.O. Box 534
Bellaire, OH 43906
www@imperialglass.org

National Imperial Glass Museum
3200 Belmont Street
Bellaire, OH 43906

Michiana Association of Candlewick Collectors
(MACC—membership, $12 per year)
17370 Battles Road
South Bend, IN 46614
www.macc-candlewick.org

Advertisement from House Beautiful, December 1948. "Christmas Loot for Connoisseurs of Crystal."

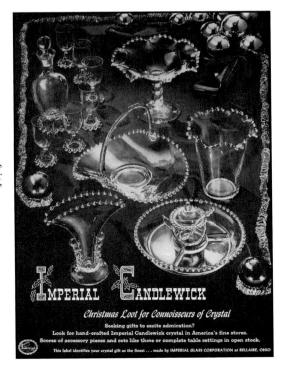

Price Guide

Sets are not always priced as the sum of the parts; sometimes the sets are higher and at other times, lower.

Measurements are given as they appear in different catalogs.

NI = New Information
NP = Not Priced
★ = Not Enough Activity to Price
★★ = Estimated Date

Mold	Description	Dates	Price
400/1D	6" Plate, Bread and Butter	1937-77	$8-10
400/1F	5" Fruit Bowl	1937-84	$10-12
400/3D	7" Plate, Salad or Dessert	1937-84	$8-10
400/3F	6" Fruit Bowl	1937-67	$12-14
400/5D	8"-8 1/2" Plate, Salad	1937-84	$8-10
400/5F	7" Bowl	1937-63	$21-25
400/7D	9" Plate, Luncheon	1937-67	$10-14
400/7F	8" Bowl	1937-43, 1954-63	$21-28
400/10D	10"-10 1/2" Dinner Plate	1938-84	$25-35
400/10F	9" Bowl	1938-43, 1953-63	$32-42
400/13	Luncheon Set 15 pc.	1938-43	NP
400/13B	11" Centre Bowl	1937-43	$55-70
400/13D	12" Service Plate	1937-61	$25-35
400/13F	4-pc. Salad Set (400/13F, 400/13D, long slender spoon/fork)	1938-38	$★
400/13F	10"-10 1/2" Bowl	1937-43, 1954-60	$42-53
400/13FD	2-pc. Salad Set (400/13F, 400/13D)	1937-38	$67-88
400/15	6 oz. Tumbler	1962-63	$100-125
400/15	10 oz. Tumbler	1962-63	$100-125
400/15	13 oz. Tumbler	1962-63	$100-125
400/16	1 Pint Pitcher (beaded handle)	1953-67	$175-200
400/17	4-pc. Salad Set (400/17F, 400/17D, #701)	1938-38	$88-113
400/17D	14" Torte Plate	1937-67	$35-45
400/17F	12" Bowl	1937-42	$42-53
400/17TB	Bon Bon Set, 2 Deck, Maple Handle	1943-43	$225-245
400/18	12 oz. Footed Ice Tea Tumbler	1950-51	$50-56
400/18	9 oz. Footed Water Tumbler or Goblet	1950-51	$50-56
400/18	6 oz. Footed Sherbet	1950-51	$45-55
400/18	7 oz. Footed Old Fashion Cocktail	1950-51	$34-45
400/18	3 1/2 oz. Footed Cocktail	1950-51	$34-45
400/18	5 oz. Footed Juice Tumbler	1950-51	$85-100
400/18	7 oz. Footed Parfait	1950-51	$90-100
400/18	18 oz. Cordial Bottle and Stopper	1950-51	$★
400/18	Sugar and Cream Set	1953-55	$140-160
400/18	40 oz. Manhattan Pitcher	1950-55	$175-200
400/18	80 oz. Pitcher (5 pint, beaded foot)	1950-55	$155-190
400/18TB	3 Hi Snack Rack	1943-43	$★
400/19	5 oz. Footed Juice Tumbler	1941-75	$10-12
400/19	10 oz. Footed Water Tumbler	1941-73	$10-12
400/19	12 oz. Footed Ice Tea Tumbler	1941-79	$12-14
400/19	14 oz. Footed Ice Tea Tumbler	1949-73	$14-18
400/19	3-3 1/2 oz. Footed Cocktail	1943-61	$25-28
400/19	2 oz. Footed Cocktail, 1 15/16" dia., 2 3/8" tall *(NI)*	19??	$★
400/19	3 oz. Footed Wine	1943-62	$18-20
400/19	5 oz. Low Footed Sherbet, Fruit or Dessert	1941-79	$12-14
400/19	Egg Cup (large beads, 6 oz.)	1948-60	$40-48
400/19	Egg Cup (small beads, 6 oz.)	1941-43	$55-65
400/19	7 oz. Footed Old Fashion Cocktail	1941-68	$24-30
400/19	2 1/4" Salt Dip	1948-63	$12-15
400/19	2 3/4" Ash Tray	1948-61	$7-9
400/19	4 1/2" Muddler (5 beads)	1946-55	$17-20
400/19	16 oz. Lilliputian Pitcher (beaded foot)	1948-51	$175-215
400/19	40 oz. Juice, Cocktail, Martini Pitcher (beaded handle)	1943-67	$192-225
400/19/89	3-pc. Marmalade Set (400/19 O. F., 400/89, 400/130) (AKA 400/1989)	1941-43	$42-46
400/20	15-pc. Punch Set (400/20B,400/20V, 400/91, 400/37)	1939-79	$175-200
400/20B	13" Punch Bowl (6 quart)	1939-79	$75-85
400/20/DE	15-pc. Punch Set, Gold Decorated	1943-43	$4200-5600
400/20D	17" Torte Plate (flat edge)	1939-73	$50-60
400/20V	17" Plate (cupped edge)	1941-79	$42-56
400/21	8 1/2" Vase (footed)	1939-51	$140-175
400/22	10" Vase (footed)	1939-50	$175-210
400/23	2-pc. Mayonnaise Set (400/23B, 400/23D)	1971-78	$20-28
400/23	3-pc. Mayonnaise Set (400/23B, 400/23D, 400/165 or 400/135)	1939-69	$24-30
400/23B	5 1/4" Fruit or Mayonnaise Bowl	1939-78	$10-14
400/23B	3-pc. Juice Set (#841, 4 oz. Juice Tumbler, 400/23B, 400/23D)	1943-43	$28-32
400/23D	7"-7 1/2" Plate (under plate for mayonnaise set)	1941-78	$10-14
400/24	80 oz. Lipped Ice Water Pitcher (5 pint, beaded handle)	1941-67	$130-140
400/24/19	7-pc. Drink Set (400/24, 400/19, 12 oz. Tumbler)	1943-43	$196-230
400/25	3 3/4"-4" Bud Ball Vase (footed) (AKA 400/25C)	1939-60	$35-42
400/26	3-pc. Hurricane Lamp (400/26 Base/Shade)	1943-43	$1050-1260
400/26	Shade, 9 3/4", Straight Top Edge	1941-41	$300-325
400/26	Shade, 9 3/4", Crimped Top Edge	1950-53	$300-325
400/27	8 1/2" Vase	1939-43	$245-280
400/28	8 1/2" Vase (straight top)	1939-41	$100-140
400/28C	8 1/2" Footed Bud Vase (crimped)	1943-65	$50-75
400/29	6 1/2"-7" Tray	1941-84	$8-10
400/29/6	6-pc. Cigarette Set (400/19, 400/29, 400/64)	1943-55	$60-80
400/29/30	Sugar, Cream and Tray Set (400/29, 400/30)	1941-84	$22-28

Item	Description	Years	Price
400/29/64/44	Cigarette Set (400/29, 400/64, 400/44)	1941-41	$74-91
400/30	Sugar and Cream Set (early or later)	1941-84	$12-14
400/31	Sugar and Cream Set (beaded foot)	1938-41	$45-55
400/31	Sugar and Cream Set (beaded handle)	1939-67	$18-25
400/32	16" Hurricane Lamp (400/155, 400/152 Adapter, 400/152 Shade)	1943-43	$300-350
400/33	4" Individual Jelly or Ash Tray	1937-43	$8-10
400/34	4 1/2" Plate, Ind. Butter or Coaster	1937-55	$8-10
400/35	Early Tea Cup and Saucer (no beads, small ridge top and bottom of handle)	1937-38	$24-30
400/35	Saucer (also called Marmalade Saucer in 1943)	1937-75	$5-8
400/35	Tea Cup and Saucer (beaded question mark handle)	1939-75	$8-14
400/35	Tea Cup, 6 oz. (beaded question mark handle)	1939-75	$5-8
400/36	2-pc. Canapé Set (400/36, 400/142)	1937-50	$21-25
400/36	6" Canapé Plate (2" Seat)	1937-50	$12-14
400/37	Punch Cup or Coffee Cup (7 oz.)	1938-84	$5-7
400/37	Coffee Cup and Saucer (saucer is the 400/35, 5 3/4", 1 7/8" seat)	1938-84	$10-16
400/38	9" Oval Salad Plate	1939-41	$32-38
400/38D	9" Oval Salad Plate (AKA 400/38)	1943-43	$32-38
400/39	6" Cocktail Plate (2 1/2" large seat)	1941-43	$14-16
400/40	3-pc. Mayonnaise Set	1937-41	$24-27
400/40/0	6 1/2" Handled Basket (made stuck up) (NI)	1941	$25-35
400/40/0	6 1/2" Handled Basket (for Crown Silver) (NI)	1953-84	$25-35
400/40B	5 1/2" Mayo Bowl (called finger bowl, 1937-38)	1937-41	$10-14
400/40B	5 1/2" Bowl (for Crown Silver) (NI)	1953-53	$10-14
400/40C	6" Bowl, Crimped (for Crown Silver) (NI)	1953-53	$35-50
400/40C	5" Flower Candleholder (crimped)	1950-67	$35-50
400/40CV	2-pc. Flower Candleholder (400/40C, 400/40V)	1950-55	$75-100
400/40D	7 1/2" Plate (early number for 400/50 Cream Soup under plate)	1938-38	$8-10
400/40D	6 1/2" Plate (for Crown Silver) (NI)	1953-53	$24-30
400/40F	6" Flower Candleholder	1950-60	$28-40
400/40F	6" Bowl (for Crown Silver) (NI)	1953-53	$28-40
400/40H	5" Handled Heart	1939-84	$18-25
400/40H	5" Handled Heart (snapped-up) (for Crown Silver) (NI)	1941-41	$25-32
400/40HC	5" Flower Candle Holder (heart shape)	1950-51	$75-100
400/40S	6 1/2" Candleholder (square shape)	1950-51	$50-60
400/40H/23D	3-pc. Mayonnaise Set (same as 400/49)	1941-41	$24-27
400/40V	6" Bowl (for Crown Silver) (NI)	1953-53	$28-40
400/40V	Miniature Vase	1950-55	$35-60
400/40V	Miniature Vase (Globe Silver, may be plain, 6 crimps) (NI)	1959-59**	$*
400/42/3	3-pc. Mayonnaise Set (400/42B, 400/42D, 400/130)	1948-70	$27-30
400/42B	4 3/4" 2-Handled Fruit	1937-78	$10-14
400/42D	5 1/2" 2-Handled Plate	1937-73	$8-10
400/42E	5 1/2" 2-Handled Tray (handles turned-up)	1937-43	$10-15
400/44	3" Cigarette Holder	1941-43	$32-38
400/45	5 1/2" Tall Compote (4 bead stem, cupped style)	1939-40	$42-52
400/45	5 1/2" Tall Compote (4 bead stem, new style)	1941-67	$15-25
400/46	11" Oval Celery Boat	1939-43	$52-62
400/48F	8" Tall Compote (5 large bead stem)	1937-37	$175-245
400/48F	8" Tall Compote (4 large bead stem)	1939-55	$55-65
400/49	3-pc. Mayonnaise Set (400/49H, 400/23D, 400/165)	1948-67	$24-27
400/49/1	5" Heart Shaped Fruit	1953-67	$10-17
400/49H	5" Heart Fruit (unhandled)	1939-53	$10-17
400/49H	9" Heart Shape Fruit Bowl (unhandled)	1939-55	$88-120
400/50	8" Plate, Soup (AKA 400/40D)	1953-55	$8-10
400/50	5"- 5 1/4" 2-Handled Cream Soup	1938-55	$32-38
400/50/23	Cream Soup on Plate	1943-55	$42-52
400/51	6" Mint Dish, Nappy (handled, round)	1937-41	$14-17
400/51C	6" Handled, Crimped Candy	1943-43	$40-50
400/51F	6" Handled Mint (round) (AKA 400/51)	1943-79	$14-17
400/51H	6"-6 1/2" Handled Heart Shaped Bon Bon	1943-68	$17-24
400/51M	6" Handled Card Tray	1943-43	$90-115
400/51T	6" Center Handled Wafer Tray	1944-73	$18-20
400/52	6"-6 1/2" 2-Handled, Divided Bowl or Jelly	1941-76	$18-21
400/52	Mayonnaise Ladle (Ladle #615)	1938-41	$8-10
400/52B	6"-6 1/2" 2-Handled Bowl	1937-73	$12-16
400/52BD	3-pc. Mayonnaise Set (AKA 400/52/3)	1939-44	$27-34
400/52C	6 3/4" Handled Plate, crimped	1953-68	$25-30
400/52D	7"-7 1/2" 2-Handled Plate	1937-68	$8-10
400/52E	7"-7 1/2" Plate, Tray (handles turned up)	1937-41	$15-20
400/52E	7"-7 1/2" 2-Handled Plate (sides turned up)	1953-58	$20-25
400/52E	9" 2-Handled Plate (sides turned-up)	1961-68	$*
400/52/3	3-pc. Mayonnaise Set (400/52B, 400/52D, 400/135 or 400/165) (AKA 400/52BD)	1943-68	$27-34
400/53	5 1/2" Crimped Bowl, 8 crimps	1953-55**	$40-55
400/53/3	3-pc. Icer Set (#530 liner and 5 1/2 oz. glass)	1953-55	$75-100
400/53C	5 1/2" Crimped Bowl Icer (3 glass wedges to secure tumbler)	1953-55	$40-55
400/53H	5 1/2" Heart Bowl	1955-55	$18-22
400/53S	5" Square Round Bowl (for W. J. Hughes)	1954-54	$65-80
400/53X	6" Baked Apple	1937-60	$18-25
400/54	6 1/2" Relish Tray (2 sections)	1937-71	$10-12
400/54	6 1/2" Relish Tray (2 sections, divider reversed)	1972-84	$12-14
400/55	8 1/2" Relish Tray (4 handles, 4 sections)	1937-84	$18-20
400/56	10 1/2" Relish (3 sections)	1938-48	$32-35
400/56	10 1/2" Relish Tray (5 handles, 5 sections)	1949-79	$35-38
400/57	7 1/2" Oval Pickle or Celery Tray	1937-43	$25-32
400/58	8"-8 1/2" Oval Pickle or Celery Tray	1937-76	$14-18
400/59	5 1/2" Covered Jelly (400/144 Lid with round half knob)	1937-51	$42-46
400/59	5 1/2" Covered Candy Box (400/144 Lid, 2 bead finial)	1953-67	$28-30
400/60	6" Ash Tray (match book center)	1938-41	$88-112
400/61	2" Individual Salt Dip	1941-67	$12-15
400/62B	7" 2-Handled Bowl	1937-84	$18-22
400/62C	8 1/2" 2-Handled Plate (crimped)	1950-68	$18-25
400/62D	8 1/2" 2-Handled Plate	1937-68	$10-14
400/62E	8 1/2" 2-Handled Tray	1937-43	$15-20
400/63	8" Ice Tub (5 1/2" deep)	1941-49	$63-80
400/63B	4 1/2" Compote, (bulge on stem)	1937-41	$25-30
400/63B	10 1/2" Belled Bowl (graduated beads)	1939-70	$37-44
400/63B/81	3-pc. Console Set (400/63B, 400/81)	1939-41	$110-135
400/63B/170	3-pc. Console Set (400/63B, 400/170)	1948-48	$60-68
400/63/104	19-pc. Chilled Fruit Set (400/104B, 400/63B, 400/139, 400/19 Footed Fruit, 400/1D)	1943-43	$275-310
400/64	2 3/4" Sugar Dip for Strawberry Plate (16 beads)	1941-49	$14-16
400/64	2 3/4" Ash Tray, Nut Dish, Sugar Dip (18 beads)	1941-67	$10-12

Item	Description	Years	Price
400/65	8" Covered Candy Dish (not partitioned—domed lid) (NI)	1939-39	$*
400/65	8" Covered Vegetable (not partitioned—domed lid) (NI)	1939-39	$*
400/65/1	8" Covered Vegetable Bowl (not partitioned—domed lid) (NI)	1941-51	$*
400/65/2	8" Covered Candy Box (partitioned)	1941-43	$140-175
400/66B	5 1/2" Low Compote (no beads)	1937-38	$18-20
400/66B	5 1/2" Low Compote (2 bead stem)	1939-80	$14-18
400/66C	4 1/2" Flower Candleholder (crimped)	1950-55	$60-65
400/66F	4" Flower Candleholder	1950-50	$60-65
400/67B	9" Low Footed Fruit Bowl (ribs)	1937-39	$100-110
400/67B	9" Low Footed Fruit Bowl (no ribs)	1949-60	$110-115
400/67C	9" Footed Crimped Bowl or Compote	1953-55	$120-140
400/67D	10" Low Cake Stand (domed ribbed foot, ribbed top)	1937-41	$40-45
400/67D	10" Low Cake Stand (no ribs)	1941-67	$46-50
400/67E	10" Low Banana Stand	????-??	$*
400/68D	11 1/2"-12" Handled Pastry Tray	1939-77	$20-35
400/68F	10 1/2" Handled Fruit Tray	1939-43	$100-135
400/69B	8 1/2" Vegetable Bowl	1951-72, 1975-84	$20-28
400/70	4 oz. Cruet and Stopper (handled)	1941-41	$42-52
400/70/71/29	3-pc. Condiment Set (400/70, 400/71, 400/29)	1941-41	$148-185
400/71	6 oz. Cruet and Stopper (handled)	1941-41	$52-66
400/72	8 1/2" Handled Divided Bowl	1953-63	$60-70
40072B	8 1/2" 2-Handled Bowl	1937-76	$25-30
400/72C	10" 2-Handled Plate (crimped)	1949-73	$24-27
400/72D	10" 2-Handled Plate	1937-76	$20-27
400/72E	10" Handled Tray (turned up)	1937-43	$30-45
400/73B	10" Bowl (for Crown Silver) (NI)	1953-53	$*
400/73C	10" Bowl, Crimped (for Crown Silver) (NI)	1953-53	$*
400/73D	12" Plate (for Crown Silver) (NI)	1953-53	$*
400/73DC	12" Plate (crimped) (for Crown Silver) (NI)	1953-53	$*
400/73/H	9"-10" Handled Heart	1939-55, 1977-78	$105-140
400/73/0	11"-12" Handled Basket	1939-60, 1977-78	$125-150
400/73TB	2 Deck Wooden Handle Tid Bit (flat plates, maple handle)	1943-43	$*
400/74B	8 1/2" Bowl (4-toed)	1937-41	$55-75
400/74J	7" Lily Bowl (4-toed)	1937-41	$125-155
400/74N	7 1/2" Bowl (4-toed with no ribs) (NI)	????-??	$*
400/74SC	9" Bowl (4-toed square, crimped)	1937-46	$50-55
400/75	Fork and Spoon Set	1939-67	$25-42
400/75B	10 1/2" Bowl	1939-67	$28-35
400/75B	4-pc. Salad Set (400/75B, 400/75V, 400/75)	1941-67	$60-77
400/75D	13 1/2" Plate (flat)	1943-43	$*
400/75F	10"-11" Float Bowl	1939-75	$25-30
400/75F/150	12" Bowl, Salad Set (400/150, 6" Base)	1948-48	$*
400/75N	7 1/2" Lily Bowl	1941-41	$330-385
400/75V	12 1/2"-13" Plate (cupped edge)	1939-84	$18-21
400/76	2-pc. Hurricane Candle Lamp (400/76, 400/81)	1939-41	$315-385
400/76	Shade		$400-485
400/77	A.D. Cup (4 oz.) and Saucer (5", 1 3/4" seat)	1939-55	$16-20
400/78	4" Coaster (10 rays)	1941-70	$7-8
400/78	4" Coaster (5 rays)	1939-39	$17-20
400/79	2-pc. Hurricane Lamp	1939-61, 1977-79	$64-84
400/79	Shade		$50-60
400/79B	Flat Candleholder 3 1/4" (without rim on candle cup)	1939-41	$35-42
400/79B	Flat Candleholder 3 1/4" (with rim on candle cup)	1939-41	$32-38
400/79R	Rolled Edge Candleholder 3 1/2" (with/without rim on candle cup)	1939-79	$12-15
400/79R/2	3 1/2" Candleholder (1 Eagle Candle Adapter)	1943-43	$165-195
400/80	3 1/2" Low Candleholder	1937-76	$8-10
400/80/2	3 1/2" Candleholder (1 Eagle Candle Adapter)	1943-43	$165-195
400/81	3 1/2" Candleholder (handled)	1937-43	$35-42
400/81/2	3 1/2" Handled Candleholder (1 Eagle Candle Adapter)	1943-43	$180-210
400/82	15 oz. Handled Cordial Bottle	1941-43	$*
400/82/1	10-pc. Cordial Handled Bottle, 8 Cordial, 3800	1941-43	$*
400/82/2	15 oz. Unhandled Cordial Bottle/Stopper	1943-43	$*
400/82/2	10-pc. Cordial Set (no handle) (400/82/1, 400/3800 Cocktail)	1943-43	$*
400/83	2-pc. Strawberry or Seafood Set (400/83D, 400/64)	1941-49	$75-80
400/83D	7" Plate with seat	1941-49	$90-100
400/84	4-pc. Mayonnaise Set (400/84D, 400/84, 400/135, 400/165 or #615)	1938-60	$49-66
400/84	6 1/2" Divided Bowl	1938-60	$32-45
400/84D	8" Plate With Seat for Mayonnaise	1938-60	$20-30
400/85	6" Cottage Cheese Bowl	1951-73, 1977-84	$25-35
400/86	Mushroom Candleholder	1937-43	$25-32
400/86R	Mushroom Candleholder	1941**	$*
400/87	8" Vase (flared at rim/small beads out/not in catalog) (NI)	1937-??**	$*
400/87C	8" Vase, Crimped (beads on rim/small beads out/not in catalog)	1937**	$50-60
400/87C	8" Vase, Crimped (beads on rim, large beads out)	1939-46	$25-35
400/87C	8" Vase, Crimped (no beads on rim, large beads in)	1949-51	$30-35
400/87C	8" Vase, Crimped (beads on rim, large beads in)	1951-63	$25-30
400/87F	8" Fan Vase (small beads out)	1938-38	$40-45
400/87F	8" Fan Vase (large beads out)	1939-41	$24-30
400/87F	8 1/2" Fan Vase (large beads in)	1949-63	$24-30
400/87R	7" Vase, Rolled (small beads out)	1938-43	$35-45
400/87R	7" Vase, Rolled (large beads out)	1939-41	$25-35
400/88	2-pc. Cheese and Cracker Set (400/72D 400/88)	1937-67	$40-47
400/88	5 1/2" Flat Compote, Bulge	1937-38	$32-38
400/88	5 1/2" Flat Compote (1 large bead)	1949-67	$20-27
400/88D	2-Handled Plate (AKA 400/72D)	1938-41	$30-40
400/89	Marmalade Bowl and Cover	1937-67	$24-30
400/89	Marmalade Bowl and Cover (raised bump on cover, early brochure)	1939**	$38-46
400/89	4-pc. Marmalade Set (400/89, 400/35 Saucer, long slender ladle)	1937-43	$*
400/89/3	3-pc. Marmalade Set (400/89, 400/35 Saucer, 400/130)	1961-67	$32-40
400/90	5" Handled Candleholder	1951-61	$38-46
400/91	2-pc. Cocktail Set (400/39, 3400 Oyster Cocktail)	1939-43, 1953-65	$26-33
400/91	Punch Ladle (13", no beads, 1 spout)	1939-82	$30-40
400/92	3-pc. Cheese and Cracker Set (400/92D, 400/157, 400/144 cover)	1943-50	$110-140
400/92B	12" Bowl (for Lipman Sterling) (NI)	1952-52	$*
400/92B	12" Bowl	1948-51	$40-54
400/92D	14" Plate (small center circle)	1938-67	$46-52
400/92F	12" Float Bowl	1943-67	$32-40
400/92L	13" Mushroom Centre Bowl	1938-43	$60-75
400/92R	13" Float Bowl (shown in 400/136 Set)	1943-43	$55-65
400/92S	12" Bowl, Square (for Lipman Sterling) (NI)	1952-52	$*

Cat. No.	Description	Years	Price
400/92V	13 1/2" Plate (cupped edge)	1939-67	$32-36
400/93	6 1/2" Divided Mayo Bowl (changed to 400/84)	1938-38	$45-50
400/94	4-pc. Buffet Salad Set (400/84, 400/92D, 400/135 [AKA 400/615])	1938-61	$110-125
400/95	3-pc. Ind. Cheese/Cracker or Buffet Set (1943 PL no other information)	1943-43	$★
400/95	4-pc. Salad Dressing Set (400/72D, 400/84, 400/615)	1939-43	$60-75
400/96	10-pc. Salad Set (400/92D, 400/84, 400/5D, 400/615)	1940-40	NP
400/96	Salt and Pepper Set (9 beads)	1938-43	$12-17
400/96	Salt and Pepper Set (8 beads)	1944-84	$10-15
400/96T	5" Tray	1948-68	$10-12
400/96/3	3-pc. Salt, Pepper and Tray Set	1948-67	$21-24
400/97	2-pc. Cocktail Set (400/39 2 1/2" seat, #111)	1940-43	$32-36
400/98	9" Oval Plate (with seat)	1939-61, 1977-78	$25-28
400/98	2-pc. Party Set (400/37, 400/98)	1939-61, 1977-78	$35-40
400/99	2-pc. Snack Set (400/98, 400/142)	1939-43	$28-38
400/100	Twin Candleholder	1939-68	$18-21
400/100/2	Twin Candleholder (2 eagle candle adapters)	1943-43	$345-355
400/101	13" Float Bowl (1 1/4" deep)	1939-43	$150-175
400/101/79B	5-pc. Float Bowl Console Set (400/101, 400/79B)	1939-43	$252-270
400/102	13"-13 1/2" Relish (5 sections)	1939-60	$60-65
400/103C	10" Footed Fruit Bowl (crimped, 3 large bead stem)	1943-55	$150-175
400/103D	11" Footed Cake Stand (3 large bead stem)	1939-81	60-65
400/103E	10" Banana Stand (3 large bead stem)	1943-43	$1540-1680
400/103F	10" Footed Fruit Bowl (shallow)	1939-43	$195-225
400/104B	14" Bowl (graduated beads)	1939-43	$135-150
400/105	13 1/2" Celery Tray (oval with open handles)	1939-67	$32-38
400/106B	12" Bowl (graduated beads)	1939-61	$45-50
400/106B/75	3-pc. Salad Set (400/106B, 400/75)	1939-49	$60-77
400/107	5 3/4" Bud Vase (small beads on base)	1939-49	$52-66
400/107	5 3/4" Bud Vase (large beads on base)	1950-67	$45-50
400/108	5" Table Bell	1939-81	$42-49
400/109	Salt and Pepper Set (individual)	1941-73	$10-14
400/110	7" Partitioned Candy Box and Cover (3 sections)	1941-63	$60-65
400/111	Tête-à-Tête Set (400/111, 400/77, 3800 Brandy)	1940-49	$★
400/111	6 1/2" Tray with two seats	1941-49	$65-70
400/112	10 1/2" Relish (5 sections)	1949-63	$28-35
400/112	10 1/2 Relish (4 sections)	1941-46	$32-38
400/113A	10" Bowl (2-handled, 4 1/4" deep)	1941-41	$★
400/113B	12" Bowl (2-handled)	1941-55	$95-110
400/113C	14" 2-Handled Plate (crimped)	1949-53	$115-125
400/113D	14" 2-Handled Plate	1941-67	$45-50
400/113E	14" 2-Handled Buffet Tray (turned-up handles)	1941-43	$★
400/114A	10"-11" Partitioned Bowl (4 1/4" deep, scalloped partition)	1941-43	$400-475
400/114A/2	Dessert Set (400/114A, 400/139 Ladle)	1943-43	$545-575
400/115	3 Light Candleholder	1941-43	$100-115
400/115/1	Eagle 777/1 (2 Eagle Ornament)	1943-43	$295-310
400/115/1-2	Eagle 777/1 (2 Eagle Ornament)	1943-43	$645-665
400/115/2-1	Eagle 777/2 (1 Eagle Adapter)	1943-43	$395-415
400/116	Footed Salt and Pepper Set (1 bead)	1941-43	$85-125
400/117	4 oz. Bitters and Metal Tube	1948-54	$46-56
400/118	5 1/2" B'tween Place Ash Tray (w/match)	1941-43	$38-46
400/118	5 1/2" B'tween Place Ash Tray	1950-70	$7-8
400/118	4-pc. Bridge Ash Tray Set	1950-70	$21-25
400/119	6 oz. Oil or Vinegar and Stopper	1941-50	$25-28
400/120	8 1/4" Crescent Salad Plate	1941-50	$45-60
400/121/O	"Oil" and Stopper (etched)	1941-50	$60-65
400/121/V	"Vinegar" and Stopper (etched)	1941-50	$60-65
400/122	Sugar and Cream Set (ground 1941-48) (marie 1949-80)	1949-80	$15-20
400/122/29	Cream, Sugar and Tray Set	1944-73	$20-25
400/122/111	Sugar, Cream and Tray Set (2 seats)	1943-43	$85-95
400/123	7 1/2" Covered Toast Server, Cheese or Butter	1941-51	$262-315
400/124	12 1/2" Oval Platter	1948-67, 1976-78	$80-90
400/124A	11" Oval Bowl (2 1/4" deep)	1941-43	$★
400/124D	12 1/2"-13" Oval Plate (changed to 400/124)	1941-48	$80-90
400/125A	11" 2 Section Bowl (2 1/4" deep)	1941-43	$225-250
400/126	2-Handled Bouillon Cup	1941-43	$35-42
400/126	Sugar and Creamer Set (AKA 400/153)	1943-43	$80-90
400/127B	7 1/2" Belled Bowl (base for console sets)	1941-43	$★
400/127L	4-pc. Console Set (400/92L, 400/127B, 400/100)	1941-43	$220-255
400/128	15-pc. Punch Set (with base) (400128, 400/20B, 400/37, 400/91)	1941-60	$300-350
400/128DE	15-pc. Punch Set (etched and gold decorated)	1941-53	$6000-8000
400/128B	10" Belled Bowl (400/128B Punch Bowl Base)	1941-60	$★
400/129R	6" Urn Candleholder	1941	$★
400/129R	4 1/2" Urn Candleholder	1943	$140-158
400/130	Marmalade Ladle (3 bead, 4 3/4")	1943-70	$10-14
400/131B	14" Oval Centre Bowl	1941-51	$210-225
400/131D	16" Oval Platter or Tray	1941-55	$215-235
400/132	7 1/2" Footed Rose Bowl	1943-50	$315-335
400/132C	7 1/4" Footed Rose Bowl (crimped)	1941-41	$★
400/133	5" Ash Tray	1941-67, 1977-79	$6-8
400/133	5" Ash Tray (yellow or amber)	1944-60	$14-16
400/133	Liberty 5" Ash Tray (topaz w/ shield)	1943-43	$65-75
400/133	Liberty 5" Ash Tray (milk glass w/shield)	1943-43**	$★
400/134	5 1/4" Covered Cigarette Box	1941-63	$35-38
400/134/1	4 1/2" Oblong Ash Tray	1943-63	$6-8
400/134/6	6-pc. Cigarette Set (400/134, 400/134/1)	1948-63	$48-58
400/135	Luncheon Sets (15 pc., 21 pc., 27-pc. Sets)	1937-39	NP
400/135	Mayonnaise Ladle (2 bead, 6 1/2")	1943-51	$8-10
400/136	4-pc. Console Set (400/127, 400/92R, 400/129R)	1941-43	$475-535
400/137	Footed Oval Compote (10 3/4" x 6 3/4")	1941-43	$1050-1190
400/138B	6" Footed Vase	1941-43	$100-115
400/139	Ladle (AKA 400/255 Ladle) (9"-9 1/2", 2 spouts)	1941-50	$65-75
400/139	11-pc. Cocktail Set (400/139, 400/255, #111 Stem Cocktail)	1943-50	$770-909
400/139/1	Covered Snack Set	1941-50	$770-910
400/139/2	Covered Punch Bowl & 400/255 Ladle	1943-50	$635-770
400/139/19	11-pc. Cocktail Set (400/139, 400/255, 400/19 Cocktail)	1943-43	$824-985
400/139/77	11-pc. Family Punch Set (400/139, 400/255, 400/77 AD Cups)	1943-50	$715-845
400/140	Footed Candy Jar and Cover (beaded base)	1941-43	$980-1120
400/140	Footed Candy Jar and Cover (plain foot)	1948-60	$190-210
400/142K	7" Rose Bowl (beaded collar)	1941-43	$★
400/142K/HL	15" 3-pc. Hurricane Lamp (400/142K, 400/152, 400/152)	1950-50	$★
400/143A	8" Flip Vase (not crimped)	1943-43	$240-260

400/143C	8" Flip Vase (crimped)	1943-55	$60-85
400/144	5"-5 1/2" Covered Butter (tab handles)	1943-67, 1976-80	$25-28
400/145	2-pc. Cheese and Cracker Set (400/145 and 400/157 Compote)	1943-43	$54-64
400/145B	10" 2-Handled Bowl	1943-84	$30-37
400/145C	11 1/2"-12" 2-Handled Plate (crimped)	1949-68	$25-40
400/145D	12" 2-Handled Plate or Tray	1943-84	$20-25
400/145E	11 1/2" Tray (2-handles turned up)	1943-43	$*
400/145H	11 1/2" 2-Handled Muffin Tray (turned-up sides)	1943-43	$300-325
400/147	3 Light Candleholder	1943-65	$25-28
400/147/2	3 Light with Eagle (400/147, 1 777/2 Eagle Candle Adapter)	1943-43	$200-215
400/148	9 1/4" Condiment Tray (4 indentations)	1943-43	$140-175
400/148/2	7-pc. Condiment Set (400/148, 400/116, 400/119)	1943-43	$275-335
400/148/4	7-pc. Condiment Set (400/148, 400/116, Etched 400/121)	1943-43	$345-410
400/148/5	8-pc. Condiment Set (400/148, 400/89, 400/116, 400/119)	1943-43	$260-320
400/148/6	9-pc. Condiment Set (400/148, 400/89, 400/116)	1943-43	$295-365
400/149D	8"-9" Handled Mint Tray (center heart handle)	1943-67	$25-30
400/149F	7 1/2" Handled Bon Bon (center handled, cupped)	1943-43	$88-105
400/150	6" Console Base (AKA 400/151)	1948-50	$*
400/150	6" Ash Tray	1943-68, 1977-79	$5-7
400/150	6" Ash Tray (cranberry, pink)	1944-60	$10-17
400/150	Liberty 6" Ash Tray (cranberry w/ eagle)	1943-43	$30-44
400/150	Liberty 6" Ash Tray (Ritz Blue w/eagle)	1943-43**	$*
400/151	10" Tray (raised circular design)	1943-49	$30-38
400/151	Bearings for Lazy Susan	1950-53	$65-75
400/151	5" Ash Tray for Lazy Susan (recessed channel)	1950-53	$75-85
400/151	10" Lazy Susan Tray	1950-53	$38-75
400/152	3-pc. Hurricane Lamp (crimped shade, 400/79R)	1943-60	$158-190
400/152	Adapter	1943-60	$50-60
400/152	Chimney (crimped, 10")	1943-60	$90-100
400/152	Chimney (plain top, 10")	1943-46	$100-125
400/152R	14" 3-pc. Hurricane Lamp Straight Top Shade	1943-46	$155-190
400/153	Cream and Sugar Set (AKA 400/126)	1943-43	$80-90
400/154	11 1/2" -12" Deviled Egg Server	1943-63	$85-100
400/155	9 1/2" Base, Eagle Candle Adapter/ Ornament	1943-44	$310-320
400/155	Base (part also made for Lightolier Lighting Co.)	1941-43	$140-160
400/155	3-pc. Hurricane Lamp	1941-43	$310-320
400/156	Mustard Spoon (4000 Salt Spoon)	1943-67	$12-14
400/156	Covered Mustard With Spoon (4000 Salt Spoon)	1943-67	$35-42
400/157	4 3/4" Cheese Compote	1948-49	$35-42
400/157	4 3/4" Covered Jelly or Honey (400/144 Cover)	1943-55	$65-75
400/158	7" Candy Box and Cover (3 sections) (NI)	1943-43	$280-315
400/159	9 1/4" Oval Tray (plain bottom)	1943-67	$17-20
400/160	13"-14" Birthday Cake Plate, 72 recessed holes	1943-51	$335-400
400/161	1/4 lb. Butter and Cover (oblong)	1943-84	$25-28
400/162	10 1/2" Footed Vase (only in 1943 Price List, no information)	1943-43	$*
400/163	24 oz. Decanter and Stopper	1943-50	$262-315
400/164	4 oz. Oil and Stopper	1948-51	$32-38
400/165	Mayonnaise Ladle (5"-6", 3 beads, larger than 400/130)	1944-70	$10-12
400/166	6 oz. Vinegar and Stopper	1948-51	$52-60
400/167	Salt and Pepper Set (4 1/2")	1948-70	$14-18
400/168	7" 2-Handled Ice Tub	1948-54	$122-136
400/169	8" Oval Plate	1948-67	$32-38
400/169	Sauce Boat (no beads, dimples at bottom)	1948-67	$74-80
400/169	Sauce Boat and Plate Set	1948-67	$110-122
400/170	3 1/2" Low Candleholder	1948-63, 1978-84	$12-14
400/171	8" Tray	1948-60	$27-30
400/172	4 1/2" Mint Heart	1948-63	$10-12
400/173	5 1/2" Nut Heart	1948-63	$12-14
400/174	6 1/2" Bon Bon Heart	1948-63	$14-16
400/175	6 1/2" Tall Candleholder (3 beads)	1948-55	$100-115
400/176	3 1/4" Square Ash Tray	1948-61	$18-21
400/177	Luncheon Sets (15, 21, and 27 pc.)	1937-39	NP
400/177	4 oz. Oil or Vinegar Cruet and Stopper	1948-55	$32-40
400/178	Saucer Candleholder (1 3/4" by 7 1/2") (NI)	1948-50	$*
400/178	2-pc. Hurricane Lamp (11 1/2" tall) (NI)	1948-50	$*
400/179	4" Table Bell (3400 Cordial)	1949-51	$56-65
400/182	8 1/2" 3-toed Bowl (graduated beads)	1960-68	$85-95
400/183	6" 3-toed Bowl (small beads)	1960-75	$50-55
400/185	7" Footed Bud Vase (straight top)	1948-50	$*
400/185C	7" Footed Bud Vase (crimped top) (NI)		$185-215
400/186	7" Footed Bud Vase (straight top, 400/18 foot)	1948-55	$175-185
400/187	7" Footed Bud Vase (straight top, 400/18 foot)	1948-50	$175-190
400/188	7" Footed Ivy Bowl or Brandy	1948-61	$120-135
400/189	9" Footed Bud Vase (400/190 foot)	1948-50	$*
400/190	10 oz. Goblet	1943-67	$14-16
400/190	5 oz. Tall Sherbet	1943-67	$10-12
400/190	3 1/2-4 oz. Cocktail	1943-67	$10-14
400/190	5 oz. Dinner Wine	1943-67	$22-26
400/190	1 oz. Cordial	1948-67	$60-65
400/190	Footed Seafood Cocktail, Coupette	1943-60	$65-70
400/190	Footed Salt and Pepper Set	1948-67	$35-42
400/192	10" Footed Vase (large version of 400/18 foot)	1948-50	$*
400/193	10" Footed Vase (large version of 400/18 foot)	1948-50	$*
400/194	10" Footed Vase (large version of 400/18 foot)	1948-51	$*
400/195	2 oz. Wine	1952-52	$125-150
400/195	4 oz. Cocktail	1952-52	$125-150
400/195	6 oz. Juice	1952-52	$125-150
400/195	6 oz. Dessert	1952-52	$125-150
400/195	9 oz. Old Fashion	1952-52	$125-150
400/195	11 oz. Water	1952-52	$125-150
400/195	14 oz. Iced Drink	1952-52	$125-150
400/195	8 oz. Tumbler	1953-54	$125-150
400/195	12 oz. Tumbler	1953-54	$125-150
400/195	16 oz. Tumbler	1953-54	$125-150
400/196	2-pc. Epergne Set	1949-60	$200-225
400/196FC	9" Flower Candle Centerpiece (1 or 2 bead stem vase)	1949-55	$55-65
400/198	6" Vase (400/242 without the flower insert)	1953-54	$*
400/200	3-pc. Handled Heart Set	1955-60	$122-144
400/201	4 1/2" Handled Heart	1955-60	$38-46
400/202	5 1/2" Handled Heart	1955-60	$45-52
400/203	6 1/2" Handled Heart	1955-60	$38-46
400/204	8" Triangular Plate for the Butter 'n Jam Set	1960-63	$*
400/204	5-pc. Butter 'n Jam Set, 8" rounded triangular tray, two ridges	1960-63	$*

No.	Description	Years	Price
400/205	10" 3-toed Bowl (small beads)	1960-67	$110-125
400/206	4 1/2" 3-toed Nappy (small beads)	1960-67	$50-60
400/207	4 1/2" 3-toed Candleholder (small beads)	1960-67	$70-80
400/208	10" 3 Partitioned Relish (3-toed)	1960-70	$77-88
400/209	13 1/2" Partitioned Relish (5 sections)	1959-61	$315-385
400/210	Punch Bowl (10 quart)	1949-55	$235-265
400/210	Base (8 7/8" x 3 3/4")	1949-55	$*
400/210	15-pc. Punch Set (400/211 Cup, rounded bead handle)	1949-55	$*
400/211	5 oz. Punch Cup (rounded bead handle)	1949-55	$24-30
400/213	10" Oblong Relish Tray (partitioned, 4 sections)	1949-61	$*
400/214	10" Dish and Cover (oblong, no partition)	1953-54	$420-450
400/215	12" Oblong Relish (partitioned, 4 sections)	1949-61	$60-66
400/216	10" Dish and Cover (partitioned 3 sections)	1953-54	$385-450
400/217	10" Pickle Tray (4 1/2" x 10 1/2" with open handles)	1950-67	$28-35
400/220	5" Compote (Tri-Stem)	1950-67	$110-125
400/221	5 1/2" Handle Lemon Tray (Tri-Stem)	1950-67	$28-35
400/222	8" Handled Bon Bon (Tri-Stem)	1950-50	$*
400/223	12" Handled Cake Tray (Tri-Stem) (NI)	1950-50	$*
400/224	5 1/2" Candleholder (Tri-Stem)	1950-55	$135-158
400/???	Cake Stand (Tri-Stem) (not on any price list or catalog) (NI)		$*
400/???	Goblet (Tri-Stem) (not on any price list or catalog)		$*
400/226	Coaster with Spoon Rest	1953-67	$10-12
400/227	8 1/2" Handled Vase	1959-61	$420-425
400/228	14" Chip and Dip (one piece)	1959-61	$415-455
400/231	5" Square Bowl (2 1/4" deep)	1957-63	$60-70
400/232	6" Square Bowl (2 1/2" deep)	1957-63	$70-80
400/233	7" Square Bowl (3" deep)	1957-63	$70-80
400/234	7" Square Relish (2 sections, 1 3/8" deep)	1957-63	$90-105
400/239	Peg Nappy with Candle Cup 6" (for Crown Silver) (NI)	????-??	$*
400/240B	Peg Nappy, 5 3/4" Bowl (for Crown Silver) (NI)	1953-53	$21-25
400/240D	Peg Nappy, 7" Plate (for Crown Silver) (NI)	1953-53	$18-25
400/240F	Peg Nappy, 6" Nappy (for Crown Silver) (NI)	1953-53	$21-25
400/241	Peg Nappy, Partitioned Bowl 6" (for Crown Silver) (NI)	1953-53	$28-32
400/242	6" Rose Bowl (flower holder insert)	1953-54	$*
400/243	5 1/2" Sauce Bowl	1959-63	$28-30
400/244	Hostess Helper (400/243, 400/92F, Metal Cups)	1959-63	$250-300
400/244	Metal Cup	1939-63	$35-50
400/245	6 1/2" Candy Box and Cover	1957-63	$290-315
400/247	Salt and Pepper	1949-84	$18-20
400/251B	9 1/2"-10" Peg Nappy Bowl (Monmouth Silver Co.)	1950s	$56-62
400/251D	12" Peg Nappy Plate (Monmouth Silver Co.)	1950s	$63-70
400/251F	10 1/2" Peg Nappy Float Bowl (Monmouth Silver Co.)	1950s	$63-70
400/255	Small Punch Ladle (9"- 9 1/2", AKA 400/139)	1943-50	$65-75
400/256	10 1/2" Oval Relish (2 sections)	1954-84	$28-32
400/257	6" Round Cheese Dish (small beads) (NI)	1955-55	$14-18
400/259	7" Candy Box and Cover	1949-70	$75-85
400/260	7" Candy Box and Cover	1953-60	$175-190
400/262	10 1/2" 3 Section Butter and Jam	1959-68	$88-105
400/262	10 1/2" Oval 3 Section Relish, (AKA Butter and Jam)	1969-71	$88-105
400/264	Hurricane Lamp, 13 5/8" (Tri-Stem) (NI)	1953-55	$*
400/265	Chimney (for Tri-Stem)	1953-55	$*
400/266	7 1/2" Triangular Plate (part of 400/496 Set)	1960-61	$225-241
400/268	8" 2 Part Oval Relish	1963-84	$18-21
400/269	6 1/2" Individual Server or Tray (pie shape wedge)	1961-63	$250-265
400/270	7 1/2" Tid Bit Plate With Hole (part of 400/2701)	1950-67, 1977-78	$40-45
400/271	10 1/2" Tid Bit Plate With Hole (part of 400/2701)	1950-67, 1977-78	$40-45
400/273	5" Handled Basket (beaded handle)	1953-63	$158-210
400/273	5" Handled Basket (beaded handle, for Crown Silver) (NI)	1953-53	$*
400/274	4 oz. Cruet and Stopper	1950-60	$32-35
400/275	6 oz. Cruet and Stopper	1950-60	$35-38
400/276	California Butter and Cover (no beads on cover)	1950-61	$88-105
400/276	California Butter and Cover (beads on cover)	1962-68	$70-105
400/277	Salad Dressing Bottle (stopper one large ball)	1951-60	$190-210
400/278	4 oz. Handled Cruet and Stopper	1953-67	$46-50
400/279	6 oz. Handled Cruet and Stopper	1953-67	$46-50
400/280	3 1/2" Candleholder	1953-55	$210-215
400/287C	6" Crimped Vase	1953-63	$45-50
400/287F	6" Fan Vase	1953-63	$45-50
400/289	3-pc. Marmalade (400/130 or 4 5/8" plastic ladle)	1953-74	$24-30
400/289	3-pc. Marmalade Set (5" metal ladle)	1975-81	$24-27
400/289	2-pc. Marmalade Set ("no need to buy ladle to put with it")	1982-84	$17-24
400/289	Marmalade Ladles, Plastic (1953-74) & Metal (1975-81)	1953-80	$8-10
400/311	11-pc. Breakfast Set	1943-43	NP
400/313	13-pc. Breakfast Tray Set (400/311 set plus 400/109)	1943-51	NP
400/316	16-pc. Luncheon Set, 400/5D, 400/35, 400/68, 400/29/30	1943-51	NP
400/322	22-pc. Luncheon Set (400/5D, 400/35, 400/68, 400/29/30)	1943-44	NP
400/328	28-pc. Luncheon Set (400/5D, 400/35, 400/68, 400/29/30)	1943-44	NP
400/330	14 oz. Pitcher (no beads, 4 dimples in sides)	1953-54	$280-300
400/416	20 oz. Pitcher (no beads)	1968-75	$70-88
400/419	40 oz. Pitcher (no beads)	1968-78	$53-70
400/424	80 oz. Pitcher (no beads)	1968-74	$53-70
400/424	64 oz. Pitcher (no beads)	1974-78	$*
400/440	4" Ash Tray	1943-68, 1977-79	$5-8
400/440	4" Ash Tray (Aquamarine, Blue)	1944-60	$8-10
400/440	Liberty 4" Ash Tray (Aquamarine with V for Victory)	1943-43	$55-65
400/440	Liberty 4" Ash Tray (Ruby with V for Victory)	1943-43**	$*
400/450	3-pc. Nested Ash Tray Set (crystal)	1943-68, 1977-79	$15-24
400/496	3-pc. Mayonnaise Set (400/266, 400/49/1, 400/165)	1960-61	$245-270
400/550	3-pc. Ash Tray Set Colors (blue, amber, pink)	1943-60	$28-35
400/550	3-pc. Liberty Ash Tray Set (aquamarine, topaz, cranberry)	1943-43	$175-200

400/550	3-pc. Liberty Ash Tray Set (Ruby, Milk Glass, Ritz Blue)	1943-43★★	$★
400/615	Mayonnaise Ladle (plain and no beads)	1938-41	$8-10
400/616	Salt Spoon (2 5/8" plain bowl) (AKA 4000)	1943-67	$15-20
400/616	16-pc. Individual Salt Set (400/61, 400/616 [AKA 4000])	1951-51	NP
400/616	Individual Salt Set (400/61, 400/616 [AKA 4000])	1943-67	$25-30
400/623	2-pc. Mayonnaise Set (400/183, 400/165)	1960-66	$70-77
400/650	3-pc. Square Ash Tray Set	1957-67	$75-84
400/651	3 1/4" Square Ash Tray	1957-67	$25-28
400/652	4 1/2" Square Ash Tray	1957-67	$25-28
400/653	5 3/4" Square Ash Tray	1957-67	$25-28
400/655	3 Section Jar Tower (crystal, Verde, charcoal)	1960-65	$490-525
400/656	Candy Box and Cover (1 section of candy tower)	1964-64	$190-225
400/680	Twin Hurricane Lamp (400/680, 400/152 adapter and shade)	1938-43	$1050-1250
400/701	5-pc. Condiment Set (400/70, 400/71, 400/29)	1941-41	$100-130
400/733	2-pc. Salad Dressing Set (400/330, 400/23D)	1953-54	$288-305
400/735	3-pc. Salad Set (400/73H Handled Heart, 400/75)	1950-55	$124-165
400/750	3-pc. Tid Bit Set (heart shape)	1948-63	$36-42
400/820	Peanut Pouring Jar	1963-67	$★
400/920F	3-pc. Console Set (12" Bowl, 400/92F, 400/100)	1948-51	$65-80
400/925	4-pc. Salad Set (400/92B, 400/92V, 400/75)	1948-51	$94-104
400/1004B	3-pc. Console Set (400/104B, 400/100)	1939-43	$168-190
400/1006B	3-pc. Console Set, 12" Bowl (400/106B, 400/100)	1939-51	$77-90
400/1112	4-pc. Relish Dressing Set (400/112, 400/89, 400/130)	1941-63	$65-90
400/1474	3-pc. Console Set (104B and 400/147)	1943-43	$180-204
400/1476	3-pc. Console Set (400/106B and 400/147)	1943-51	$90-104
400/1503	3-pc. Lazy Susan	1950-51	$135-165
400/1510	8-pc. Lazy Susan Condiment Set	1950-51	$242-280
400/1531B	3-pc. Console Set	1941-43	$415-460
400/1567	5-pc. Condiment Set (400/159, 400/167, 400/119)	1948-50	$80-95
400/1574	5-pc. Condiment Set (400/159, 400/167, 400/164)	1948-51	$95-110
400/1589	3-pc. Twin Jam Set (400/159, 400/89)	1946-60	$80-95
400/1596	5-pc. Condiment Set (400/159, 400/96, 400/119)	1948-50	$74-88
400/1630	8-pc. Wine Set (400/163, 400/190 Wines)	1943-51	$388-446
400/1639	8-pc. Wine/Liquor Set (400/163, 400/19 Liquors)	1943-50	$332-422
400/1752	Prism Candleholder (400/175, 400/152)	1948-55	$190-205
400/1753	3-pc. Hurricane Lamp With Prisms (400/175, 400/152, 400/26)	1948-55	$435-455
400/1769	4-pc. Condiment Set (400/171, 400/96, 400/119)	1948-55	$62-80
400/1786	4-pc. Condiment Set (400/171, 400/89, 400/96)	1948-60	$62-74
400/1929	6-pc. Cigarette Set (400/19 Ash Tray, 400/19 Old Fashion, 400/29)	1948-51	$55-73
400/1930	11-pc. Cocktail Set (400/139, 400/255, 400/190)	1948-50	$715-870
400/1989	Marmalade Set (long slender 3 bead spoon)	1941-48	$★

400/1989	3-pc. Marmalade Set (400/19 Old Fashion, 400/89 Lid, 400/130 3 Bead Ladle)	1949-68	$42-46
400/2296	Sugar, Cream, Tray Set (400/122, 400/96T)	1948-50	$75-85
400/2696	6-pc. Hospitality Set (pie shape wedge)	1961-63	$1500-1700
400/2701	2 -tier Tid Bit (400/270, 400/271)	1950-67, 1977-78	$60-65
400/2702	2 -tier Tid Bit (Evergreen)	1950-50	$400-435
400/2769	4-pc. Condiment Set (400/275, 400/171, 400/96)	1951-60	$74-80
400/2794	3-pc. Oil and Vinegar Set (400/275, 400/274, 400/29)	1951-60	$80-90
400/2796	5-pc. Oil and Vinegar Set (400/275, 400/274, 400/96, 400/159)	1951-60	$95-108
400/2911	3-pc. Oil. and Vinegar Set (400/29, 400/119)	1946-50	$56-68
400/2930	3-pc. Sugar and Cream Set (400/29, 400/30)	1941-41	$22-28
400/2946	3-pc. Oil and Vinegar Set (400/29, 400/164, 400/166)	1948-50	$92-105
400/2989	3-pc. Twin Jam Set (400/29, 400/89)	1948-50	$58-80
400/2990	5-pc. Condiment Set (400/29, 400/177, 400/109)	1948-50	$75-100
400/4272B	4-pc. 2-Handled Bowl Set (400/42B, 400/52B, 400/62B, 400//72B)	1948-65	$52-60
400/4272D	4-pc. 2-Handled Plate Set(400/42D, 400/52D, 400/62D, 400/72D)	1948-65	$46-60
400/4975	4-pc. Salad Set (9" 400/49H Heart Bowl, 400/75V, 400/75)	1946-50	$130-175
400/5629	3-pc. Mustard and Ketchup Set (400/156, 400/29)	1948-50	$90-110
400/5996	5-pc. Condiment Set (400/159, 400/119, 400/89, 400/96)	1948-50	$77-95
400/6300B	5-pc. Console Set (400/63B, 400/100)	1941-50	$104-124
400/7375	4-pc. Salad Set (400/73H, 400/75V, 400/75)	1948-50	$140-185
400/7570	4-pc. Console Set (400/75F, 6" Base 400/150, 400/170)	1948-50	$★
400/7796	3-pc. Oil and Vinegar Set (400/177, 400/96)	1948-55	$72-90
400/8013B	3-pc. Console Set (400/80, 400/13B)	1937-41	$85-90
400/8063B	3-pc. Console Set (400/80, 400/63B)	1941-50	$54-64
400/8075B	3-pc. Console Set (400/80, 400/75B)	1939-41	$34-47
400/8113B	3-pc. Console Set (400/81, 400/13B)	1937-41	$100-115
400/8613B	3-pc. Console Set (400/86, 400/13B)	1937-38	$110-130
400/8692L	3-pc. Console Set (400/86, 400/92L)	1938-43	$87-110
400/8918	3-pc. Marmalade Set (400/89, 400/130, 400/18)	1949-63	$74-90
400/9266B	2-pc. Cheese and Cracker or Buffet Set (400/92D, 400/66B)	1939-50	$54-67
400/9275	4-pc. Console Set (400/92F, 400/150 6" Base, 400/175)	1948-51	$★
400/9279FR	3-pc. Console Set (400/92F, 400/79R)	1941-51	$75-85
400/9615	5-pc. Condiment Set (400/96, 400/119, 400/159)	1946-46	$74-85
400/51340	13-pc. Salad Set (400/5D, 400/13FD, 400/40)	1937-37	NP
3400	9 oz. Goblet (4 bead)	1937-84	$10-16
3400	6 oz. Tall Sherbet, Saucer Champagne (4 bead)	1937-84	$10-14
3400	4 oz. Cocktail (4 bead)	1937-67	$10-14
3400	5 oz. Low Sherbet (1 bead)	1937-73	$18-26
3400	4 oz. Wine (4 bead)	1937-84	$15-18
3400	5 oz. Claret (4 bead)	1937-67	$30-36
3400	1 oz. Cordial (4 bead)	1937-60	$26-30
3400	5 oz. Footed Juice Tumbler (1 bead)	1937-60	$18-20
3400	9 oz. Tumbler (1 bead)	1937-47	$14-16

3400	10 oz. Water Footed Tumbler (1 bead)	1948-73	$14-16
3400	12 oz. Footed Tumbler (1 bead)	1937-84	$14-18
3400	4 oz. Oyster Cocktail	1940-63	$14-20
3400	8 oz. Footed Finger Bowl (4 1/4" d., 2 3/8" h., 2 13/16" ft. d)	1937-67	$*
3400	2-pc. Seafood Cocktail (9 oz.)	1939-67	$60-65
3400	Insert Only	1939-60	$15-20
3400	6 oz. Parfait	1949-73	$35-40
3800	9 oz.-11 oz. Goblet (2 bead)	1937-43	$20-28
3800	7 oz. Tall Sherbet, Sauce Champagne (2 bead)	1937-43	$20-28
3800	6 oz. Low Sherbet (1 bead, 3 3/4" d., 3 1/2" h., 2 7/8" ft. d.)	1937-43	$*
3800	4 oz. Claret (2 bead)	1937-43	$30-32
3800	3 oz. Cocktail (2 bead)	1937-43	$30-45
3800	2 1/2-3 oz. Wine (2 bead)	1937-43	$30-45
3800	1-1 1/2 oz. Cordial (2 bead)	1937-43	$55-65
3800	4 oz. Oyster Cocktail (3400)	1940-43	$14-20
3800	12 oz. Tumbler (1 bead)	1937-43	$20-28
3800	9 oz.-10 oz. Tumbler (1 bead)	1937-43	$20-28
3800	5 oz. Tumbler (1 bead)	1937-43	$20-28
3800	6 oz. Finger Bowl (3 3/4" d., 2" h., 2 5/8" ft. d.)	1937-43	$*
3800	2 oz. Brandy (2 beads)	1941-43	$*
3800	2-pc. Icer, Seafood or Fruit Cocktail (12 oz.)	1941-43	$60-65
4000	11 oz. Goblet (3 bead)	1949-60	$24-28
4000	6 oz. Tall Sherbet (3 beads)	1949-60	$24-28
4000	5 oz. Wine (3 beads)	1949-60	$24-28
4000	4 oz. Cocktail (3 beads)	1949-60	$24-28
4000	12 oz. Ice Tea or Hiball (1 bead)	1949-60	$24-28
4000	1 1/4 oz. Cordial (2 beads)	1950-60	$55-65
4000	Salt Spoon (AKA 616, 3 3/8" with ribbed bowl)	1943-67	$12-14
4000	Knife	1939-41	$275-315
14415	Cake Cover on 400/75V Plate	1977-79	$78-86
14490	Candleholder (400/79R)	1977-79	$12-15
14992	Shade (for 400/79R) (generic shade)	1977-79	$35-42
14994	12" 2-pc. Hurricane Lamp (400/150)	1977-84	$30-40
14995	12" Shade (for 400/150) (generic shade, if boxed)	1975-84	$34-60
14996	14" 2-pc. Hurricane Lamp (400/170)	1975-84	$34-60
14997	3 1/2" Candleholder (400/170)	1975-84	$12-14
14998	14" Shade for 14996 (400/170) (generic shade, if boxed)	1975-84	$22-40
51675	Cake Cover (10" d., 4 7/8" side h., tapers upward to 7 7/8" h.)	1977-84	$120-135
400/	Ring Holder (400/78 Coaster, ring post in center) Mark LIG	1980	$225-250
400/	Junior Place Setting (in box) (NI)	1951	$*
400/	Hospitality Set with Insert Bowl (NI)	1957**	$*
400/	Clock (5 1/2" diameter) (NI)		$*
111	Cocktail used with (400/139 Cocktail Sets)	1940-50	$20-25
139	Small Ladle (with 400/63/104, 400/114A/2, 400/139 Sets)	1941-50	$65-75
142	3 1/2 oz. Cocktail Tumbler	1937-50	$8-10
176	Stirrer (12" with 400/19 Martini Pitcher, round bead tip)	1943	$32-38
530	Liner for Icer 400/53	1953-55	$40-55
530	5 1/2 oz. Tumbler(for icer 400/53)	1953-55	$12-25
615	Ladle with Plain Handle (4 1/2"-5")	1932-46	$8-10
701	Reeded Fork and Spoon Set (ribbed handle)	1932-68	$21-25
754	5" Vase Insert (6 Crimps, ridge 1" from bottom)	1937-41**	$30-40
820	Peanut Pouring Jar (NI)	1962-68	$*
160/130	4" Ladle 2 Bead (Documented with Cape Cod)	1947-70	$10-14
160/165	5" Ladle 1 Bead (Documented with Cape Cod)	1948-70	$10-12
Sign	Oval, French Edge Frosted, with Champagne Glass		$88-122
Sign	Oval, French Edge Frosted, Handcrafted, Imperial in Blue		$88-122
Sign	Oval, French Edge Frosted, Handcrafted, Imperial in Blue, Lenox		$85-105
Sign	Paper Weight Ball, Blue Background, White Imperial		$60-70
Sign	Black Bent Glass Sign		$140-210
Sign	Black Plastic Sign, Imperial, Lenox		$30-40
Sign	Cardboard Sign, Blue, with Imperial		$25-30
Sign	Tin, Imperial Hand Painted Sign		$30-50
Sign	Candlewick Sign (Calendar Shape)		$125-150
Sign	Candlewick Calendar (1947 Calendar)		$200-220
Sign	400/33 Individual Jelly with etch "Hand Made Imperial"		$60-75

Index